Lecture Notes in Computer Science   **11750**

More information about this series at http://www.springer.com/series/7407

Étienne André · Mariëlle Stoelinga (Eds.)

Formal Modeling and Analysis of Timed Systems

17th International Conference, FORMATS 2019
Amsterdam, The Netherlands, August 27–29, 2019
Proceedings

 Springer

Editors
Étienne André 🆔
Université Paris 13
Villetaneuse, France

Mariëlle Stoelinga 🆔
University of Twente
Enschede, The Netherlands

Radboud University
Nijmegen, The Netherlands

ISSN 0302-9743   ISSN 1611-3349   (electronic)
Lecture Notes in Computer Science
ISBN 978-3-030-29661-2   ISBN 978-3-030-29662-9   (eBook)
https://doi.org/10.1007/978-3-030-29662-9

LNCS Sublibrary: SL1 – Theoretical Computer Science and General Issues

This Springer imprint is published by the registered company Springer Nature Switzerland AG
The registered company address is: Gewerbestrasse 11, 6330 Cham, Switzerland

Preface

A famous quote by Albert Einstein says,

"The only reason for time is so that everything doesn't happen at once."

Indeed, making sure that actions happen at the right time, and in the right order is a very nontrivial task. Real-time behavior lies at the core of today's modern systems, for instance to achieve coherence in data centers, coordination in robots and MRI scanners, response times for hardware, etc. As a community we have developed many formalisms, techniques, and tools to reason about time. These inventions form the core of the International Conference on FORmal Modeling and Analysis of Timed Systems—FORMATS for short.

This volume contains the proceedings of the 17th International Conference on Formal Modeling and Analysis of Timed Systems (FORMATS 2019), which was held during August 27–29, 2019, in Amsterdam, the Netherlands. FORMATS 2019 was colocated with CONCUR 2019, FMICS 2019, and several workshops.

Control and analysis of the timing of computations is crucial to many domains of system engineering, be it, e.g., for ensuring timely response to stimuli originating in an uncooperative environment, or for synchronizing components in VLSI. Reflecting this broad scope, timing aspects of systems from a variety of domains have been treated independently by different communities in computer science and control. Researchers interested in semantics, verification, and performance analysis study models such as timed automata and timed Petri nets, the digital design community focuses on propagation and switching delays, while designers of embedded controllers have to take account of the time taken by controllers to compute their responses after sampling the environment, as well as of the dynamics of the controlled process during this span.

Timing-related questions in these separate disciplines do have their particularities. However, there is a growing awareness that there are basic problems (of both scientific and engineering level) that are common to all of them. In particular, all these sub-disciplines treat systems whose behavior depends upon combinations of logical and temporal constraints; namely, constraints on the temporal distances between occurrences of successive events. Often, these constraints cannot be separated, as the intrinsic dynamics of processes couples them, necessitating models, methods, and tools facilitating their combined analysis. Reflecting this, FORMATS 2019 also accepted submissions on hybrid discrete-continuous systems and held a session on linear and non-linear dynamical systems.

FORMATS 2019 benefited from several novelties. First, in order to emphasize the practical side of the research on timed and real-time systems, we were happy to introduce tool papers into our program. Second, we organized two special sessions:

1. A special session on data-driven and stochastic approaches to real-time, organized by Martin Fränzle; and
2. A special session on timed systems and probabilities, organized by Nathalie Bertrand.

Third, following the tradition initiated in 2018, FORMATS 2019 was happy to award the best paper of the conference with the Oded Maler Award in timed systems. This prize, named after one of the founding fathers of FORMATS, commemorates the pioneering work of Oded Maler, whose untimely death in 2018 was a big loss to the community.

This year, we received a higher number of submissions than in past years, resulting in a lower acceptance rate. We received 36 long papers (of which 5 in the probabilities special session and 4 in the data special session) and 6 tool papers. After discussion, the Program Committee (PC) decided to accept 15 long papers (of which 3 in each special session) and 2 tool papers. This resulted in an overall acceptance rate of 40%. 29 PC members helped to provide at least 3 reviews for each of the 42 submitted contributions.

FORMATS 2019 is a three-day event, featuring 3 invited talks and 17 paper presentations. A highlight of FORMATS 2019 was an invited talk by Nathalie Bertrand, as well as two further invited talks jointly organized with CONCUR 2019, by Marta Kwiatkowska and Kim Larsen.

Further details on FORMATS 2019 are featured on the website: https://lipn.univ-paris13.fr/formats2019/.

Finally, a few words of acknowledgment are due. Thanks to Jos Baeten for helping with the local organization and the relationship with CONCUR. Thanks to Springer for publishing the FORMATS proceedings in the series *Lecture Notes in Computer Science*, and to EasyChair for providing a convenient platform for coordinating the paper submission and evaluation. Thanks to the Steering Committee, and notably to Martin Fränzle, for their support, to all the PC members and additional reviewers for their work (128 reviews in total) in ensuring the quality of the contributions to FORMATS 2019, and to all the authors and participants for contributing to this event.

As PC chairs, we hope that these papers in this volume will provide readers with novel insights and ideas.

July 2019   Étienne André
                                                                    Mariëlle Stoelinga

Organization

Program Committee

Alessandro Abate	University of Oxford, UK
S. Akshay	Indian Institute of Technology Bombay, India
Étienne André	Université Paris 13, France
Enrico Bini	University of Turin, Italy
Sergiy Bogomolov	The Australian National University, Australia
Franck Cassez	Macquarie University, Australia
Jyotirmoy Deshmukh	University of Southern California, USA
Martin Fränzle	Carl von Ossietzky Universität Oldenburg, Germany
Tingting Han	University of London, UK
Ichiro Hasuo	National Institute of Informatics, Japan
David N. Jansen	Chinese Academy of Sciences, China
Jan Křetínský	Technical University of Munich, Germany
Didier Lime	École Centrale Nantes, France
Brian Nielsen	Aalborg University, Denmark
Peter Ölveczky	University of Oslo, Norway
Pavithra Prabhakar	Kansas State University, USA
Karin Quaas	Leipzig University, Germany
Pierre-Alain Reynier	Aix-Marseille University, France
César Sánchez	IMDEA Software Institute, Spain
Ocan Sankur	Univ Rennes, Inria, CNRS, IRISA, Rennes, France
Ana Sokolova	University of Salzburg, Austria
Oleg Sokolsky	University of Pennsylvania, USA
Jiří Srba	Aalborg University, Denmark
Mariëlle Stoelinga	University of Twente, The Netherlands
Jun Sun	Singapore Management University, Singapore
Lothar Thiele	ETH Zürich, Switzerland
Enrico Vicario	University of Florence, Italy
James Worrell	University of Oxford, UK
Wang Yi	Uppsala University, Sweden

General Chair

Jos Baeten	CWI, The Netherlands

Steering Committee

Rajeev Alur	University of Pennsylvania, USA
Eugene Asarin	Université de Paris, France
Martin Fränzle	Carl von Ossietzky Universität Oldenburg, Germany

Thomas A. Henzinger   IST Austria, Austria
Joost-Pieter Katoen   RWTH Aachen University, Germany
Kim G. Larsen   Aalborg University, Denmark
Oded Maler *(1957–2018)*   VERIMAG, CNRS, France
Mariëlle Stoelinga   University of Twente, The Netherlands
Lothar Thiele   ETH Zürich, Switzerland
Wang Yi   Uppsala University, Sweden

Additional Reviewers

Ashok, Pranav
Bacci, Giorgio
Bacci, Giovanni
Bae, Kyungmin
Bresolin, Davide
Busatto-Gaston, Damien
Carnevali, Laura
Cervin, Anton
Ehmen, Günter
Ernst, Gidon
Gangadharan, Deepak
Genest, Blaise
Jezequel, Loïg

Kristjansen, Martin
Lal, Ratan
Lorber, Florian
Lukina, Anna
Monmege, Benjamin
Muniz, Marco
Nickovic, Dejan
Nutz, Alexander
Peruffo, Andrea
Potomkin, Kostiantyn
Rahimi Afzal, Zahra
Ray, Rajarshi
Ruchkin, Ivan

Ruijters, Enno
Šafránek, David
Sallinger, Sarah
Schilling, Christian
Schou, Morten Konggaard
Shirmohammadi, Mahsa
Sproston, Jeremy
Srivathsan, B.
Stierand, Ingo
Weininger, Maximilian
Yao, Haodong

Short Papers

When Are Dense-Time Stochastic Systems Tameable?

Nathalie Bertrand

Univ Rennes, Inria, CNRS, IRISA, France

Abstract. Many applications, such as communication protocols, require models which integrate both real-time constraints, and randomization. The verification of such models is a challenging task since they combine dense-time and probabilities. To verify stochastic real-time systems, we propose a framework to perform the analysis of general stochastic transition systems (STSs). This methodology relies on two pillars: a *decisiveness* and *abstraction*.

Decisiveness was introduced for denumerable Markov chains [1], and roughly speaking, it allows one to lift most analysis techniques from finite Markov chains to denumerable ones, and therefore to adapt existing verification algorithms to infinite-state models. We explain how to generalize this central notion to dense-time stochastic models.

In order to exploit decisiveness, we define a notion of abstraction, and we give general transfer properties from the abstract model to the concrete one. These are central to come up with qualitative and quantitative verification algorithms for STS.

Our methodology applies for instance to stochastic timed automata (STA) and generalized semi-Markov processes (GSMP), two existing models combining dense-time and probabilities. This allows us on the one hand to recover existing results from the literature on these two models –with less effort and a unified view– and on the other hand to derive new approximation algorithms for STA and GSMP.

The interested reader can refer to a joint article with Patricia Bouyer, Thomas Brihaye and Pierre Carlier for further details [2].

Short biography Nathalie Bertrand obtained her PhD from ENS Cachan in 2006, supervised by Philippe Schnoebelen. She spent a year at TU Dresden working with Christel Baier, and was in 2007 hired junior research scientist at Inria Rennes. Her expertise is in model checking specifically for probabilistic systems.

References

1. Abdulla, P.A., Ben Henda, N., Mayr, R.: Decisive markov chains. Log. Methods. Comput. Sci. **3**(4) (2007). https://doi.org/10.2168/LMCS-3(4:7)2007
2. Bertrand, N., Bouyer, P., Brihaye, T., Carlier, P.: When are stochastic transition systems tameable? J. Log. Algebraic Program. **99**, 41–96 (2018). https://doi.org/10.1016/j.jlamp.2018.03.004

Safety Verification for Deep Neural Networks with Provable Guarantees

Marta Kwiatkowska

University of Oxford, Oxford, UK

Abstract. Computing systems are becoming ever more complex, with decisions increasingly often based on deep learning components. A wide variety of applications are being developed, many of them safety-critical, such as self-driving cars and medical diagnosis. Since deep learning is unstable with respect to adversarial perturbations, there is a need for rigorous software development methodologies that encompass machine learning components. This lecture will describe progress with developing automated verification techniques for deep neural networks to ensure safety and robustness of their decisions with respect to input perturbations. The techniques exploit Lipschitz continuity of the networks and aim to approximate, for a given set of inputs, the reachable set of network outputs in terms of lower and upper bounds, in anytime manner, with provable guarantees. We develop novel algorithms based on feature-guided search, games, global optimisation and Bayesian methods, and evaluate them on state-of-the-art networks. The lecture will conclude with an overview of the challenges in this field.

Short biography Marta Kwiatkowska is Professor of Computing Systems and Fellow of Trinity College, University of Oxford. She is known for fundamental contributions to the theory and practice of model checking for probabilistic systems, focusing on automated techniques for verification and synthesis from quantitative specifications. She led the development of the PRISM model checker (www.prismmodelchecker.org), the leading software tool in the area and winner of the HVC Award 2016. Probabilistic model checking has been adopted in diverse fields, including distributed computing, wireless networks, security, robotics, healthcare, systems biology, DNA computing and nanotechnology, with genuine flaws found and corrected in real-world protocols. Kwiatkowska is the first female winner of the Royal Society Milner Award and was awarded an honorary doctorate from KTH Royal Institute of Technology in Stockholm. She won two ERC Advanced Grants, VERIWARE and FUN2MODEL, and is a coinvestigator of the EPSRC Programme Grant on Mobile Autonomy. Kwiatkowska is a Fellow of the Royal Society, Fellow of ACM and Member of Academia Europea.

Synthesis of Safe, Optimal and Compact Strategies for Stochastic Hybrid Games

Kim G. Larsen

Department of Computer Science, Aalborg University, Denmark

Abstract. UPPAAL-STRATEGO is a recent branch of the verification tool Uppaal allowing for synthesis of safe and optimal strategies for stochastic timed (hybrid) games. We describe newly developed learning methods, allowing for synthesis of significantly better strategies and with much improved convergence behaviour. Also, we describe novel use of decision trees for learning orders-of-magnitude more compact strategy representation. In both cases, the seek for optimality does not compromise safety.

Short biography Kim G. Larsen is professor in the Department of Computer Science at Aalborg University within the Distributed and Embedded Systems Unit and director of the ICT-competence center CISS, Center for Embedded Software Systems. In 2015 he won an ERC Advanced Grant with the project LASSO for learning, analysis, synthesis and optimization of cyber-physical systems. He is director of the Sino-Danish Basic Research Center IDEA4CPS, the Danish Innovation Network InfinIT, as well as the innovation research center DiCyPS: Data Intensive Cyber Physical Systems. His research interests include modeling, verification, performance analysis of real-time and embedded systems with applications to concurrency theory and model checking. In particular he is prime investigator of the real-time verification UPPAAL as well as the various new branches of the tool targeted towards planning, optimization, testing, synthesis and compositional analysis.

Contents

Special Session on Data-Driven and Stochastic Approaches to Real-Time, Including Monitoring and Big Data

Online Quantitative Timed Pattern Matching with Semiring-Valued Weighted Automata

Masaki Waga[1,2,3]([✉]) (iD)

[1] National Institute of Informatics, Tokyo, Japan
mwaga@nii.ac.jp
[2] SOKENDAI (The Graduate University for Advanced Studies), Tokyo, Japan
[3] JSPS Research Fellow, Tokyo, Japan

Abstract. *Monitoring* of a signal plays an essential role in the runtime verification of cyber-physical systems. *Qualitative timed pattern matching* is one of the mathematical formulations of monitoring, which gives a Boolean verdict for each sub-signal according to the satisfaction of the given specification. There are two orthogonal directions of extension of the qualitative timed pattern matching. One direction on the result is *quantitative*: what engineers want is often not a qualitative verdict but the *quantitative measurement* of the satisfaction of the specification. The other direction on the algorithm is *online* checking: the monitor returns some verdicts before obtaining the entire signal, which enables to monitor a running system. It is desired from application viewpoints. In this paper, we conduct these two extensions, taking an automata-based approach. This is the first *quantitative* and *online* timed pattern matching algorithm to the best of our knowledge. More specifically, we employ what we call *timed symbolic weighted automata* to specify quantitative specifications to be monitored, and we obtain an online algorithm using the *shortest distance* of a weighted variant of the zone graph and *dynamic programming*. Moreover, our problem setting is *semiring-based* and therefore, general. Our experimental results confirm the scalability of our algorithm for specifications with a time-bound.

Keywords: Quantitative monitoring · Timed automata · Weighted automata · Signals · Zones · Dynamic programming · Semirings

1 Introduction

Background Monitoring a system behavior plays an essential role in the runtime verification or falsification of *cyber-physical systems (CPSs)*, where various formalisms such as temporal logic formulas or automata are used for *specification*. Usually, a CPS is a *real-time* system, and real-time constraints must be included

Thanks are due to Ichiro Hasuo for a lot of useful comments and Sasinee Pruekprasert for a feedback. This work is partially supported by JST ERATO HASUO Metamathematics for Systems Design Project (No. JPMJER1603) and by JSPS Grants-in-Aid No. 15KT0012 & 18J22498.

© Springer Nature Switzerland AG 2019
E. André and M. Stoelinga (Eds.): FORMATS 2019, LNCS 11750, pp. 3–22, 2019.
https://doi.org/10.1007/978-3-030-29662-9_1

Table 1. Comparison of the problem settings with related studies

	Quantitative?	Online?	Dense time?	Result of which part?
[8]	No	Yes	Yes	All sub-signals (pattern matching)
[7]	Yes	No	Yes	All sub-signals (pattern matching)
[21]	Yes	Yes	No	The whole signal
[14]	Yes	Yes	Yes	The whole signal
This Paper	**Yes**	**Yes**	**Yes**	**All sub-signals (pattern matching)**

in the specification. An example of such a specification is that the velocity of a self-driving car should be more than 70 km/h within 3 s after the car enters an empty highway. *Timed automata* [3] is a formalism that captures real-time constraints. They are equipped with clock variables and timing constraints on the transitions. Applications of monitoring of real-time properties include data classification [11] and Web services [26] as well as CPSs (e.g., automotive systems [22] and medical systems [13]).

The behavior of a CPS is usually described as a *real-valued signal* that is mathematically a function σ mapping a time t to the condition $\sigma(t) \in \mathbb{R}^n$ of the system at time t. Usual automata notions (e.g., NFA and timed automata) handle only finite alphabets, and in order to monitor signals over $\mathbb{R}^n$, automata must be extended to handle infinite alphabets. *Symbolic automata* [30] handle large or even infinite alphabets, including real vectors. In a symbolic automaton over a real vector space $\mathbb{R}^n$, each location (or transition) is labeled with a *constraint* over $\mathbb{R}^n$ instead of one vector $v \in \mathbb{R}^n$; therefore, one location (or transition) corresponds to infinitely many vectors.

Monitoring can be formulated in various ways. They are classified according to the following criteria. Table 1 shows a comparison of various formulations of monitoring problems.

Qualitative vs. quantitative semantics. When an alphabet admits subtraction and comparisons, in addition to the qualitative semantics (i.e., true or false), one can define a *quantitative* semantics (e.g., robustness) of a signal with respect to the specification [2,7,17,19]. *Robust semantics* shows how robustly a signal satisfies (or violates) the given specification. For instance, the specification $v > 70$ is satisfied more robustly by $v = 170$ than by $v = 70.0001$. In the context of CPSs, *robust semantics* for signal temporal logic is used in robustness-guided falsification [5,16]. *Weighted automata* [18,27] are employed for expressing such a quantitative semantics [20,21].

Offline vs. online. Consider monitoring of a signal $\sigma = \sigma_1 \cdot \sigma_2$ over a specification $\mathcal{W}$. In offline monitoring, the monitor returns the result $\mathcal{M}(\sigma, \mathcal{W})$ after obtaining the entire signal σ. In contrast, in online monitoring, the monitor starts returning the result before obtaining the entire signal σ. For example, the monitor may return a partial result $\mathcal{M}(\sigma_1, \mathcal{W})$ for the first part σ_1 before obtaining the second part σ_2.

Discrete vs. dense time. In a discrete time setting, timestamps are natural numbers while, in a dense time setting, timestamps are positive (or nonnegative) real numbers.

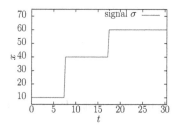 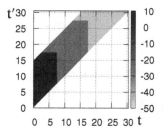

Fig. 1. Piecewise-constant signal σ (left) and an illustration of the quantitative matching function $(\mathcal{M}(\sigma, \mathcal{W}))(t, t')$ for $[t, t') \subseteq [0, 30.5)$ (right). In the right figure, the score in the white areas is $-\infty$. The specification $\mathcal{W}$ is outlined in Example 1. In the right figure, the value at $(3, 15)$ is 5. It shows that the score $(\mathcal{M}(\sigma, \mathcal{W}))(3, 15)$, for the restriction $\sigma([3, 15))$ of σ to the interval $[3, 15)$, is 5.

Result of which part? Given a signal σ, we may be interested in the properties of different sets of sub-signals of σ. The simplest setting is where we are interested only in the whole signal σ (e. g.,[14,21]). Another more comprehensive setting is where we are interested in the property of *each* sub-signal of σ; problems in this setting are called *timed pattern matching* [7,28,32].

Our Problem. Among the various problem settings of monitoring, we focus on an *online* algorithm for *quantitative timed pattern matching* [7] in a *dense* time setting. See Table 1. Given a piecewise-constant signal σ and a specification $\mathcal{W}$ expressed by what we call a *timed symbolic weighted automaton*, our algorithm returns the *quantitative matching function* $\mathcal{M}(\sigma, \mathcal{W})$ that maps each interval $[t, t') \subseteq [0, |\sigma|)$ to the (quantitative) semantics $(\mathcal{M}(\sigma, \mathcal{W}))(t, t')$, with respect to $\mathcal{W}$, for the restriction $\sigma([t, t'))$ of σ to the interval $[t, t')$, where $|\sigma|$ is the duration of the signal. An illustration of $\mathcal{M}(\sigma, \mathcal{W})$ is in Fig. 1. In [7], quantitative timed pattern matching was solved by an offline algorithm using a syntax tree of *signal regular expressions*. In this paper, we propose an *online* algorithm for quantitative timed pattern matching with automata. To the best of our knowledge, this is the first online algorithm for quantitative timed pattern matching. Moreover, our (quantitative) semantics is parameterized by a *semiring* and what we call a *cost function*. This algebraic formulation makes our problem setting general.

Example 1. Let σ be the piecewise-constant signal in the left of Fig. 1 and $\mathcal{W}$ be the specification meaning the following.

- At first, the value of x stays less than 15, and then the value of x becomes and remains greater than 5 within 5 s.
- We are only interested in the behavior within 10 s after the value of x becomes greater than 5.
- We want the score showing how robustly the above conditions are satisfied.

The right of Fig. 1 illustrates the result of quantitative timed pattern matching. Quantitative timed pattern matching computes the semantics $(\mathcal{M}(\sigma, \mathcal{W}))(t, t')$,

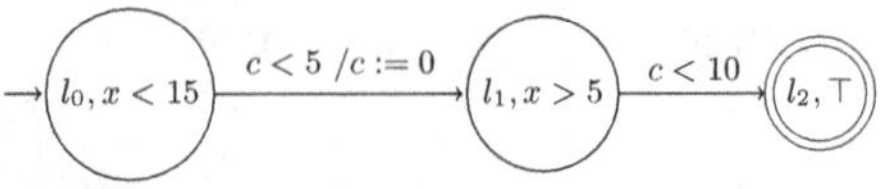

$$\kappa_r\big(u,(a_1 a_2 \ldots a_m)\big) = \inf_{i\in\{1,2,\ldots,n\}} \kappa_r\big(u,(a_i)\big)$$

$$\kappa_r\Big(\bigwedge_{i=1}^{n}(x_i \bowtie_i d_i),(a)\Big) = \inf_{i\in\{1,2,\ldots,n\}} \kappa_r\big(x_i \bowtie_i d_i,(a)\big) \text{ where } \bowtie_i \in \{>,\geq,\leq,<\}$$

$$\kappa_r(x \succ d,(a)) = a(x) - d \quad \text{where } \succ \in \{\geq,>\}$$

$$\kappa_r(x \prec d,(a)) = d - a(x) \quad \text{where } \prec \in \{\leq,<\}$$

Fig. 2. Example of a TSWA $\mathcal{W} = (\mathcal{A}, \kappa_r)$ which is the pair of the TSA $\mathcal{A}$ (upper) and the cost function κ_r (lower). See Definition 5 for the precise definition.

with respect to $\mathcal{W}$, for each sub-signal $\sigma([t,t'))$ of σ. The current semantics shows how robustly the conditions are satisfied. The semantics $(\mathcal{M}(\sigma,\mathcal{W}))(3,15)$ for the sub-signal $\sigma([3,15))$ is 5, which is the value at $(3,15)$ in the right of Fig. 1. This is because the distance between the first constraint $x < 15$ and the first valuation $x = 10$ of the sub-signal $\sigma([3,15))$ is 5, and the distance between the second constraint $x > 5$ and the valuations $x = 10$, $x = 40$, and $x = 60$ of the sub-signal $\sigma([3,15))$ is not smaller than 5. The semantics $(\mathcal{M}(\sigma,\mathcal{W}))(10,15)$ for the sub-signal $\sigma([10,15))$ is -25, which is the value at $(10,15)$ in the right of Fig. 1. Thus, the sub-signal $\sigma([3,15))$ satisfies the condition specified in $\mathcal{W}$ more robustly than the sub-signal $\sigma([10,15))$.

Our algorithm is *online* and it starts returning the result before obtaining the entire signal σ. For example, after obtaining the sub-signal $\sigma([0,7.5))$ of the initial 7.5 s, our algorithm returns that for any $[t,t') \subseteq [0,7.5)$, the score $(\mathcal{M}(\sigma,\mathcal{W}))(t,t')$ is 5.

Our Solution. We formulate quantitative timed pattern matching using the *shortest distance* [25] of semiring-valued (potentially *infinite*) weighted graphs. We reduce it to the shortest distance of *finite* weighed graphs. This is in contrast with the qualitative setting: the semantics is defined by the *reachability* in a (potentially *infinite*) graph and it is reduced to the reachability in a *finite* graph. The following is an overview.

Problem formulation. We introduce *timed symbolic weighted automata (TSWAs)* and define the (quantitative) semantics $\alpha(\sigma,\mathcal{W})$ of a signal σ with respect to a TSWA $\mathcal{W}$. Moreover, we define *quantitative timed pattern matching* for a signal and a TSWA. A TSWA $\mathcal{W}$ is a pair $(\mathcal{A},\kappa)$ of a *timed symbolic automaton (TSA)* $\mathcal{A}$—that we also introduce in this paper — and a cost function κ. The cost function κ returns a semiring value at each transition of $\mathcal{A}$, and the semiring operations specify how to accumulate such values over time. This algebraic definition makes our problem general. Figure 2 shows an example of a TSWA.

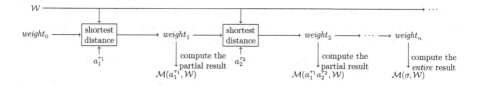

Fig. 3. Illustration of our online algorithm for quantitative timed pattern matching of a signal $\sigma = a_1^{\tau_1} a_2^{\tau_2} \cdots a_n^{\tau_n}$ meaning "the signal value is a_1 for τ_1, the signal value is a_2 for the next τ_2, ..." and a TSWA $\mathcal{W}$. The intermediate data $weight_i$ for the weight computation is represented by zones. The precise definition of the $weight_i$ is introduced later in Definition 16.

Algorithm by zones. We give an algorithm for computing our semantics $\alpha(\sigma, \mathcal{W})$ of a signal σ by the shortest distance of a *finite* weighted graph. The constructed weighted graph is much like the *zone graph* [10] for reachability analysis of timed automata. Our algorithm is general and works for any semantics defined on an idempotent and complete semiring. (See Example 4 later for examples of such semirings.)

Incremental and online algorithms. We present an incremental algorithm for computing the semantics $\alpha(\sigma, \mathcal{W})$ of a signal σ with respect to the TSWA $\mathcal{W}$. Based on this incremental algorithm for computing $\alpha(\sigma, \mathcal{W})$, we present an online algorithm for quantitative timed pattern matching. To the best of our knowledge, this is the first online algorithm for quantitative timed pattern matching. Our online algorithm for quantitative timed pattern matching works incrementally, much like in *dynamic programming*. Figure 3 shows an illustration.

Contribution. We summarize our contributions as follows.

- We formulate the semantics of a signal with respect to a TSWA by a shortest distance of a potentially *infinite* weighted graph.
- We reduce the above graph to a *finite* weighted graph.
- We give an online algorithm for quantitative timed pattern matching.

Related Work. Table 1 shows a comparison of the present study with some related studies. Since the formulation of *qualitative* timed pattern matching [28], many algorithms have been presented [8,28,29,32,35], including the online algorithms [8,35] using timed automata. *Quantitative* timed pattern matching was formulated and solved by an offline algorithm in [7]. This offline algorithm is based on the syntax trees of signal regular expressions, and it is difficult to extend for online monitoring. Weighted automata are used for quantitative monitoring in [12,20,21], but the time model was discrete.

The online quantitative monitoring for signal temporal logic [14] is one of the closest work. Since we use the clock variables of TSAs to represent the intervals of timed pattern matching, it seems hard to use the algorithm in [14] for quantitative timed pattern matching.

Parametric timed pattern matching [4,33] is another orthogonal extension of timed pattern matching, where timing constraints are parameterized. Symbolic monitoring [34] is a further generalization to handle infinite domain data. These problems answer feasible parameter valuations and different from our problem.

Organization of the Paper. Section 2 introduces preliminaries on signals and semirings. Section 3 defines timed symbolic weighted automata (TSWAs), and our quantitative semantics of signals over a TSWA. Section 4 defines the quantitative timed pattern matching problem. Sections 5 and 6 describe our algorithms for computing the quantitative semantics and the quantitative timed pattern matching problem, respectively. Section 7 presents our experimental results for the sup-inf and tropical semirings, which confirm the scalability of our algorithm under some reasonable assumptions. Section 8 presents conclusions and some future perspectives.

Most proofs are deferred to the appendix in [31] due to lack of space.

2   Preliminary

For a set X, its powerset is denoted by $\mathcal{P}(X)$. We use ε to represent the empty sequence. All the signals in this paper are piecewise-constant, which is one of the most common interpolation methods of sampled signals.

Definition 2 (signal).   *Let X be a finite set of variables defined over a data domain $\mathbb{D}$. A (piecewise-constant) signal σ is a sequence $\sigma = a_1^{\tau_1} a_2^{\tau_2} \cdots a_n^{\tau_n}$, where for each $i \in \{1, 2, \ldots, n\}$, $a_i \in \mathbb{D}^X$ and $\tau_i \in \mathbb{R}_{>0}$. The set of signals over $\mathbb{D}^X$ is denoted by $\mathcal{T}(\mathbb{D}^X)$. The duration $\sum_{i=1}^n \tau_i$ of a signal σ is denoted by $|\sigma|$. The sequence $a_1 \circ a_2 \circ \cdots \circ a_n$ of the values of a signal σ is denoted by $Values(\sigma)$, where $a \circ a'$ is $a \circ a' = aa'$ if $a \neq a'$ and $a \circ a' = a$ if $a = a'$. We denote the set $\{a_1 \circ a_2 \circ \ldots \circ a_n \mid n \in \mathbb{Z}_{\geq 0}, a_1, a_2, \ldots, a_n \in \mathbb{D}^X\}$ by $(\mathbb{D}^X)^\circledast$. For $t \in [0, |\sigma|)$, we define $\sigma(t) = a_k$, where k is such that $\sum_{i=1}^{k-1} \tau_i \leq t < \sum_{i=1}^k \tau_i$. For an interval $[t, t') \subseteq [0, |\sigma|)$, we define $\sigma([t, t')) = a_k^{\sum_{i=1}^k \tau_i - t} a_{k+1}^{\tau_{k+1}} \ldots a_{l-1}^{\tau_{l-1}} \ldots a_l^{t' - \sum_{i=1}^{l-1} \tau_i}$, where k and l are such that $\sum_{i=1}^{k-1} \tau_i \leq t < \sum_{i=1}^k \tau_i$ and $\sum_{i=1}^{l-1} \tau_i < t' \leq \sum_{i=1}^l \tau_i$.*

Definition 3 (semiring).   *A system $\mathbb{S} = (S, \oplus, \otimes, e_\oplus, e_\otimes)$ is a semiring if we have the following.*

- *$(S, \oplus, e_\oplus)$ is a commutative monoid with identity element $e_\oplus$.*
- *$(S, \otimes, e_\otimes)$ is a monoid with identity element $e_\otimes$.*
- *For any $s, s', s'' \in S$, we have $(s \oplus s') \otimes s'' = (s \otimes s'') \oplus (s' \otimes s'')$ and $s \otimes (s' \oplus s'') = (s \otimes s') \oplus (s \otimes s'')$.*
- *For any $s \in S$, we have $e_\oplus \otimes s = s \otimes e_\oplus = e_\oplus$.*

A semiring $(S, \oplus, \otimes, e_\oplus, e_\otimes)$ is *complete* if for any $S' \subseteq S$, $\bigoplus_{s \in S'} s$ is an element of S such that: if $S' = \emptyset$, $\bigoplus_{s \in S'} s = e_\oplus$; if $S' = \{s\}$, $\bigoplus_{s \in S'} s = s$; for any partition $S' = \coprod_{i \in I} S'_i$, we have $\bigoplus_{s \in S'} s = \bigoplus_{i \in I} (\bigoplus_{s \in S'_i} s)$; for any $s \in S$, we have $s \otimes (\bigoplus_{s' \in S'} s') = \bigoplus_{s' \in S'} (s \otimes s')$; and for any $s \in S$, we have

$\left(\bigoplus_{s\in S'} s\right) \otimes s' = \bigoplus_{s\in S'}(s \otimes s')$. A semiring $\mathbb{S} = (S, \oplus, \otimes, e_\oplus, e_\otimes)$ is *idempotent* if for any $s \in S$, $s \oplus s = s$ holds. For a semiring $(S, \oplus, \otimes, e_\oplus, e_\otimes)$ and $s_1, s_2, \ldots, s_n \in S$, we denote $\bigoplus_{i=1}^{n} s_i = s_1 \oplus s_2 \oplus \cdots \oplus s_n$ and $\bigotimes_{i=1}^{n} s_i = s_1 \otimes s_2 \otimes \cdots \otimes s_n$.

Example 4. The *Boolean* semiring $(\{\top, \bot\}, \vee, \wedge, \bot, \top)$, the *sup-inf* semiring $(\mathbb{R} \amalg \{\pm\infty\}, \sup, \inf, -\infty, +\infty)$, and the *tropical* semiring $(\mathbb{R} \amalg \{+\infty\}, \inf, +, +\infty, 0)$ are complete and idempotent.

Let $\mathbb{S} = (S, \oplus, \otimes, e_\oplus, e_\otimes)$ be a semiring and $G = (V, E, W)$ be a weighted graph over $\mathbb{S}$, i.e., V is the finite set of vertices, $E \subseteq V \times V$ is the finite set of edges, and $W \colon V \times V \to \mathbb{S}$ is the weight function. For $V_{\text{from}}, V_{\text{to}} \subseteq V$, the *shortest distance* from V_{from} to V_{to} is $\text{Dist}(V_{\text{from}}, V_{\text{to}}, V, E, W) = \bigoplus_{v\in V_{\text{from}}, v'\in V_{\text{to}}} \bigoplus_{v=v_1v_2\ldots v_n=v'\in Paths(G)} \bigotimes_{i=1}^{n-1} W(v_i, v_{i+1})$, where $Paths(G)$ is the set of the paths in G, i.e., $Paths(G) = \{v_1v_2\ldots v_n \mid \forall i \in \{1,2,\ldots,n-1\}., (v_i, v_{i+1}) \in E\}$. For any complete semiring, the shortest distance problem can be solved by a generalization of the Floyd-Warshall algorithm [25]. Under some conditions, the shortest distance problem can be solved more efficiently by a generalization of the Bellman-Ford algorithm [25].

3 Timed Symbolic Weighted Automata

We propose timed symbolic automata (TSAs), timed symbolic weighted automata (TSWAs), and the (quantitative) semantics of TSWAs. TSAs are an adaptation of timed automata [3] for handling signals over $\mathbb{D}$ rather than signals over a finite alphabet. In the remainder of this paper, we assume that the data domain $\mathbb{D}$ is equipped with a partial order $\leq$. A typical example of $\mathbb{D}$ is the reals $\mathbb{R}$ with the usual order. We note that TSAs are much like the state-based variant of timed automata [6,8] rather than the original, event-based definition [3].

For a finite set X of variables and a poset $(\mathbb{D}, \leq)$, we denote by $\Phi(X, \mathbb{D})$ the set of constraints defined by a finite conjunction of inequalities $x \bowtie d$, where $x \in X$, $d \in \mathbb{D}$, and $\bowtie \in \{>, \geq, <, \leq\}$. We denote $\bigwedge \emptyset \in \Phi(X, \mathbb{D})$ by $\top$. For a finite set C of clock variables, a *clock valuation* is a function $\nu \in (\mathbb{R}_{\geq 0})^C$. For a clock valuation $\nu \in (\mathbb{R}_{\geq 0})^C$ over C and $C' \subseteq C$, we let $\nu\!\downarrow_{C'} \in (\mathbb{R}_{\geq 0})^{C'}$ be the clock valuation over C' satisfying $\nu\!\downarrow_{C'}(c) = \nu(c)$ for any $c \in C'$. For a finite set C of clock variables, let $\mathbf{0}_C$ be the clock valuation $\mathbf{0}_C \in (\mathbb{R}_{\geq 0})^C$ satisfying $\mathbf{0}_C(c) = 0$ for any $c \in C$. For a clock valuation ν over C and $\tau \in \mathbb{R}_{\geq 0}$, we denote by $\nu + \tau$ the valuation satisfying $(\nu + \tau)(c) = \nu(c) + \tau$ for any $c \in C$. For $\nu \in (\mathbb{R}_{\geq 0})^C$ and $\rho \subseteq C$, we denote by $\nu[\rho := 0]$ the valuation such that $(\nu[\rho := 0])(x) = 0$ for $c \in \rho$ and $(\nu[\rho := 0])(c) = \nu(c)$ for $c \notin \rho$.

The definitions of TSAs and TSWAs are as follows. As shown in Fig. 2, TSAs are similar to the timed automata in [6,8], but the locations are labeled with a constraint on the signal values $\mathbb{D}^X$ instead of a character in a finite alphabet.

Definition 5 (timed symbolic, timed symbolic weighted automata).
For a poset $(\mathbb{D}, \leq)$, a timed symbolic automaton (TSA) over $\mathbb{D}$ is a 7-tuple $\mathcal{A} = (X, L, L_0, L_F, C, \Delta, \Lambda)$, where:

- X is a finite set of variables over $\mathbb{D}$;
- L is the finite set of locations;
- $L_0 \subseteq L$ is the set of initial locations;
- $L_F \subseteq L$ is the set of accepting locations;
- C is the finite set of clock variables;
- $\Delta \subseteq L \times \Phi(C, \mathbb{Z}_{\geq 0}) \times \mathcal{P}(C) \times L$ is the set of transitions; and
- Λ is the labeling function $\Lambda : L \to \Phi(X, \mathbb{D})$.

For a poset $(\mathbb{D}, \leq)$ and a complete semiring $\mathbb{S} = (S, \oplus, \otimes, e_\oplus, e_\otimes)$, a timed symbolic weighted automaton (TSWA) over $\mathbb{D}$ and $\mathbb{S}$ is a pair $\mathcal{W} = (\mathcal{A}, \kappa)$ of a TSA $\mathcal{A}$ over $\mathbb{D}$ and a cost function $\kappa \colon \Phi(X, \mathbb{D}) \times (\mathbb{D}^X)^\circledast \to S$ over $\mathbb{S}$.

The semantics of a TSWA $\mathcal{W} = (\mathcal{A}, \kappa)$ on a signal σ is defined by the trace value $\alpha(\mathcal{S})$ of the weighted timed transition systems (WTTS) $\mathcal{S}$ of σ and $\mathcal{W}$. The trace value $\alpha(\mathcal{S})$ depends on the cost function κ and implicitly on its range semiring $\mathbb{S}$ as well as the signal σ and the TSA $\mathcal{A}$. As shown below, the state space of a WTTS $\mathcal{S}$ is $Q = L \times (\mathbb{R}_{\geq 0})^C \times [0, |\sigma|] \times (\mathbb{D}^X)^\circledast$. Intuitively, a state $(l, \nu, t, \overline{a}) \in Q$ of $\mathcal{S}$ consists of: the current location l; the current clock valuation ν; the current absolute time t; and the observed signal value $\overline{a}$ after the latest transition. The transition $\to$ of $\mathcal{S}$ is for a transition of $\mathcal{A}$ or time elapse.

Definition 6 (weighted timed transition systems). For a signal $\sigma \in \mathcal{T}(\mathbb{D}^X)$ and a TSWA $\mathcal{W} = (\mathcal{A}, \kappa)$ over the data domain $\mathbb{D}$ and semiring $\mathbb{S}$, the weighted timed transition system (WTTS) $\mathcal{S} = (Q, Q_0, Q_F, \to, W)$ is as follows, where $\mathcal{A} = (X, L, L_0, L_F, C, \Delta, \Lambda)$ is a TSA over $\mathbb{D}$ and κ is a cost function over $\mathbb{S}$.

- $Q = L \times (\mathbb{R}_{\geq 0})^C \times [0, |\sigma|] \times (\mathbb{D}^X)^\circledast$
- $Q_0 = \{(l_0, \mathbf{0}_C, 0, \varepsilon) \mid l_0 \in L_0\}$
- $Q_F = \{(l_F, \nu, |\sigma|, \varepsilon) \mid l_F \in L_F, \nu \in (\mathbb{R}_{\geq 0})^C\}$
- $\to \subseteq Q \times Q$ is the relation such that $\big((l, \nu, t, \overline{a}), (l', \nu', t', \overline{a'})\big) \in \to$ if and only if either of the following holds.
  - **(transition of $\mathcal{A}$)** $\exists (l, g, \rho, l') \in \Delta$ satisfying $\nu \models g$, $\nu' = \nu[\rho := 0]$, $t' = t$, $\overline{a'} = \varepsilon$, and $\overline{a} \neq \varepsilon$
  - **(time elapse)** $\exists \tau \in \mathbb{R}_{>0}$ satisfying $l = l'$, $\nu' = \nu + \tau$, $t' = t + \tau$, and $\overline{a'} = \overline{a} \circ Values(\sigma([t, t + \tau)))$
- $W\big((l, \nu, t, \overline{a}), (l', \nu', t', \overline{a'})\big)$ is $\kappa(\Lambda(l), \overline{a})$ if $\overline{a'} = \varepsilon$; and $e_\otimes$ if $\overline{a'} \neq \varepsilon$

Definition 7 (trace value). For a WTTS $\mathcal{S} = (Q, Q_0, Q_F, \to, W)$, the trace value $\alpha(\mathcal{S})$ is the shortest distance $\mathrm{Dist}(Q_0, Q_F, Q, \to, W)$ from Q_0 to Q_F.

For a signal σ and a TSWA $\mathcal{W}$, by $\alpha(\sigma, \mathcal{W})$, we denote the trace value $\alpha(\mathcal{S})$ of the WTTS $\mathcal{S}$ of σ and $\mathcal{W}$.

Example 8. By changing the semiring $\mathbb{S}$ and the cost function κ, various semantics can be defined by the trace value. Let $\mathbb{D} = \mathbb{R}$. For the Boolean semiring $(\{\top, \bot\}, \vee, \wedge, \bot, \top)$ in Example 4, the following function κ_b is a prototypical example of a cost function, where $u \in \Phi(X, \mathbb{D})$ and $(a_1 a_2 \dots a_m) \in (\mathbb{D}^X)^\circledast$.

$$\kappa_b\big(u, (a_1 a_2 \ldots a_m)\big) = \bigwedge_{i=1}^{m} \kappa_b(u, (a_i))$$

$$\kappa_b\big(\bigwedge_{i=1}^{n}(x_i \bowtie_i d_i), (a)\big) = \bigwedge_{i=1}^{n} \kappa_b\big(x_i \bowtie_i d_i, (a)\big) \quad \text{where } \bowtie_i \in \{>, \geq, \leq, <\}$$

$$\kappa_b(x \bowtie d, (a)) = \begin{cases} \top & \text{if } a \models x \bowtie d \\ \bot & \text{if } a \not\models x \bowtie d \end{cases}$$

For the sup-inf semiring $(\mathbb{R} \amalg \{\pm\infty\}, \sup, \inf, -\infty, +\infty)$ in Example 4, the trace value defined by the cost function κ_r in Fig. 2 captures the essence of the so-called space robustness [7,19]. For the tropical semiring $(\mathbb{R} \amalg \{+\infty\}, \inf, +, +\infty, 0)$ in Example 4, an example cost function κ_t is as follows.

$$\kappa_t\big(u, (a_1 a_2 \ldots a_m)\big) = \sum_{i=1}^{n} \kappa_r(u, (a_i))$$

$$\kappa_t\big(\bigwedge_{i=1}^{n}(x_i \bowtie_i d_i), (a)\big) = \sum_{i=1}^{n} \kappa_t(x_i \bowtie_i d_i, (a)) \quad \text{where } \bowtie_i \in \{>, \geq, \leq, <\}$$

$$\kappa_t(x \succ d, (a)) = a(x) - d \quad \text{where } \succ \in \{\geq, >\}$$

$$\kappa_t(x \prec d, (a)) = d - a(x) \quad \text{where } \prec \in \{\leq, <\}$$

Example 9. Let $\mathcal{W} = (\mathcal{A}, \kappa)$ be a TSWA over $\mathbb{R}$ and $\mathbb{S}$, where $\mathcal{A}$ is the TSA over $\mathbb{R}$ in Fig. 2, σ be the signal $\sigma = \{x = 10\}^{2.5}\{x = 40\}^{1.0}\{x = 60\}^{3.0}$. When $\mathbb{S} = (\mathbb{R} \amalg \{\pm\infty\}, \sup, \inf, -\infty, +\infty)$ and κ is the cost function κ_r in Example 8, we have $\alpha(\sigma, \mathcal{W}) = 5$. When $\mathbb{S} = (\mathbb{R} \amalg \{+\infty\}, \inf, +, +\infty, 0)$ and κ is the cost function κ_t in Example 8, we have $\alpha(\sigma, \mathcal{W}) = 35$.

4   Quantitative Timed Pattern Matching

Using TSWAs, we formulate quantitative timed pattern matching as follows.

Definition 10 (quantitative timed pattern matching). *For a TSWA $\mathcal{W}$ over the data domain $\mathbb{D}$ and complete semiring $\mathbb{S}$, and a signal $\sigma \in \mathcal{T}(\mathbb{D}^X)$, the quantitative matching function $\mathcal{M}(\sigma, \mathcal{W})\colon dom(\sigma) \to S$ is $(\mathcal{M}(\sigma, \mathcal{W}))(t, t') = \alpha\big(\sigma([t, t)), \mathcal{W}\big)$, where $dom(\sigma) = \{(t, t') \mid 0 \leq t < t' \leq |\sigma|\}$ and S is the underlying set of $\mathbb{S}$. Given a signal $\sigma \in \mathcal{T}(\mathbb{D}^X)$ and a TSWA $\mathcal{W}$ over the data domain $\mathbb{D}$ and complete semiring $\mathbb{S}$, the quantitative timed pattern matching problem asks for $\mathcal{M}(\sigma, \mathcal{W})$.*

Example 11. Let $\mathcal{W}$ be the TSWA shown in Fig. 2, which is defined over the reals $\mathbb{R}$ and the sup-inf semiring $(\mathbb{R} \amalg \{\pm\infty\}, \sup, \inf, -\infty, +\infty)$, and σ be the signal $\sigma = \{x = 10\}^{7.5}\{x = 40\}^{10.0}\{x = 60\}^{13.0}$. The quantitative matching function $\mathcal{M}(\sigma, \mathcal{W})$ is as follows. Figure 1 shows an illustration.

$$\big(\mathcal{M}(\sigma,\mathcal{W})\big)(t,t') = \begin{cases} 5 & \text{when} & \begin{aligned} & t \in [0,7.5), t' \in (0,17.5], t'-t < 10 \text{ or} \\ & t \in [0,7.5), t' \in (10,17.5], t'-t \in [10,15) \end{aligned} \\[1em] -25 & \text{when} & \begin{aligned} & t \in [7.5,17.5), t' \in (7.5,27.5], t'-t < 10 \text{ or} \\ & t \in [2.5,17.5), t' \in (17.5,27.5], t'-t \in [10,15) \end{aligned} \\[1em] -45 & \text{when} & \begin{aligned} & t \in [17.5,30.5), t' \in (17.5,30.5], t'-t < 10 \text{ or} \\ & t \in [12.5,30.5), t' \in (27.5,30.5], t'-t \in [10,15) \end{aligned} \end{cases}$$

Although the domain $\{(t,t') \mid 0 \le t < t' \le |\sigma|\}$ of the quantitative matching function $\mathcal{M}(\sigma,\mathcal{W})$ is an infinite set, $\mathcal{M}(\sigma,\mathcal{W})$ is a piecewise-constant function with finitely many pieces. Moreover, each piece of $\mathcal{M}(\sigma,\mathcal{W})$ can be represented by a special form of convex polyhedra called *zones* [15].

Definition 12 (zone). *For a finite set of clock variables C, a zone is a $|C|$-dimensional convex polyhedron defined by a finite conjunction of the constraints of the form $c \bowtie d$ or $c - c' \bowtie d$, where $c, c' \in C$, $\bowtie \in \{>, \ge, \le, <\}$, and $d \in \mathbb{R}$. The set of zones over C is denoted by $\mathcal{Z}(C)$. By a zone $Z \in \mathcal{Z}(C)$, we also represent the set $\{\nu \mid \nu \models Z\} \subseteq (\mathbb{R}_{\ge 0})^C$ of clock valuations.*

Theorem 13. *For any TSWA $\mathcal{W}$ over $\mathbb{D}$ and $\mathbb{S}$ and for any signal $\sigma \in \mathcal{T}(\mathbb{D}^X)$, there is a finite set $\{(Z_1, s_1), (Z_2, s_2), \ldots, (Z_n, s_n)\} \subseteq \mathcal{Z}(\{c_{\text{begin}}, c_{\text{end}}\}) \times S$ such that $Z_1, Z_2, \ldots, Z_n$ is a partition of the domain $\{(t,t') \mid 0 \le t < t' \le |\sigma|\}$, and for any $[t,t'] \subseteq \mathbb{R}_{\ge 0}$ satisfying $0 \le t < t' \le |\sigma|$, there exists $i \in \{1, 2, \ldots, n\}$ and $\nu \in Z_i$ satisfying $\nu(c_{\text{begin}}) = t$, $\nu(c_{\text{end}}) = t'$, and $(\mathcal{M}(\sigma,\mathcal{W}))(t,t') = s_i$.* □

5   Trace Value Computation by Shortest Distance

We present an algorithm to compute the trace values $\alpha(\mathcal{S})$. Since a WTTS possibly has infinitely many states and transitions (see Definition 6), we need a finite abstraction of it. We use zone-based abstraction for what we call *weighted symbolic timed transition systems (WSTTSs)*. In addition to the clock variables in the TSA, we introduce a fresh clock variable T to represent the absolute time.

Definition 14 (weighted symbolic timed transition system). *For a TSWA $\mathcal{W} = (\mathcal{A}, \kappa)$ over $\mathbb{D}$ and $\mathbb{S}$, and a signal $\sigma = a_1^{\tau_1} a_2^{\tau_2} \cdots a_n^{\tau_n} \in \mathcal{T}(\mathbb{D}^X)$, where $\mathcal{A} = (X, L, L_0, L_F, C, \Delta, \Lambda)$, the weighted symbolic timed transition system (WSTTS) is $\mathcal{S}^{\text{sym}} = (Q^{\text{sym}}, Q_0^{\text{sym}}, Q_F^{\text{sym}}, \rightarrow^{\text{sym}}, W^{\text{sym}})$ defined as follows.*

- $Q^{\text{sym}} = \{(l, Z, \overline{a}) \in L \times \mathcal{Z}(C \amalg \{T\}) \times (\mathbb{D}^X)^{\circledast} \mid Z \ne \emptyset, \forall \nu \in Z. \nu(T) \le |\sigma|, \overline{a} = \varepsilon \text{ or } \overline{a} \circ \sigma(\nu(T)) = \overline{a}\}$
- $Q_0^{\text{sym}} = \{(l_0, \{\mathbf{0}_{C \amalg \{T\}}\}, \varepsilon) \mid l_0 \in L_0\}$
- $Q_F^{\text{sym}} = \{(l_F, Z, \varepsilon) \mid l_F \in L_F, \exists \nu \in Z. \nu(T) = |\sigma|\}$
- $\rightarrow^{\text{sym}} \subseteq Q^{\text{sym}} \times Q^{\text{sym}}$ *is the relation such that $((l, Z, \overline{a}), (l', Z', \overline{a'})) \in \rightarrow^{\text{sym}}$ if and only if one of the following holds.*
  (transition of $\mathcal{A}$) *there exists $(l, g, \rho, l') \in \Delta$, satisfying $Z' = \{\nu[\rho := 0] \mid \nu \in Z, \nu \models g\}$, $\overline{a} \ne \varepsilon$, and $\overline{a'} = \varepsilon$.*

(**punctual time elapse**) $l = l'$, $\overline{a'} = \overline{a} \circ Values(\sigma([\tilde{\nu}(T), \tilde{\nu}'(T)]))$, and there is $i \in \{1, 2, \ldots, n\}$ satisfying $Z' = \{\nu + \tau \mid \nu \in Z, \tau \in \mathbb{R}_{>0}\} \cap M_{i,=}$, where $\tilde{\nu} \in Z$, $\tilde{\nu}' \in Z'^1$, $M_{i,=} = \{\nu \mid \nu(T) = \sum_{j=0}^{i} \tau_j\}$.

(**non-punctual time elapse**) $l = l'$, $\overline{a'} = \overline{a} \circ Values(\sigma([\tilde{\nu}(T), \tilde{\nu}'(T)]))$, and there is $i \in \{1, 2, \ldots, n\}$ satisfying $Z' = \{\nu + \tau \mid \nu \in Z, \tau \in \mathbb{R}_{>0}\} \cap M_i$, where $\tilde{\nu} \in Z$, $\tilde{\nu}' \in Z'$, and $M_i = \{\nu \mid \sum_{j=0}^{i-1} \tau_j < \nu(T) < \sum_{j=0}^{i} \tau_j\}$.

- $W^{\text{sym}}((l, Z, \overline{a}), (l', Z', \overline{a'}))$ is $\kappa(\Lambda(l), \overline{a})$ if $\overline{a'} = \varepsilon$; and $e_{\otimes}$ if $\overline{a'} \neq \varepsilon$

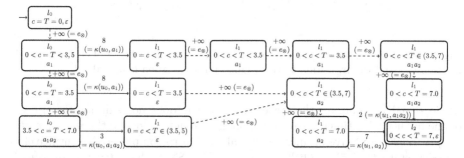

Fig. 4. WSTTS $\mathcal{S}^{\text{sym}}$ of the TSWA $\mathcal{W}$ in Fig. 2 and the signal $\sigma = a_1^{3.5} a_2^{3.5}$, where $u_0 = x < 15$, $u_1 = x > 5$, $a_1 = \{x = 7\}$, and $a_2 = \{x = 12\}$. The states unreachable from the initial state or unreachable to the accepting state are omitted. The transition for time elapse which can be represented by the composition of other transitions are also omitted. A dashed transition is for the time elapse and a solid transition is for a transition of $\mathcal{A}$.

Although the state space Q^{sym} of the WSTTS $\mathcal{S}^{\text{sym}}$ may be infinite, there are only finitely many states reachable from Q_0^{sym} and therefore, we can construct the reachable part of $\mathcal{S}^{\text{sym}}$. See the appendix of [31] for the proof. An example of a WSTTS is shown in Fig. 4. For a WSTTS $\mathcal{S}^{\text{sym}}$, we define the *symbolic trace value* $\alpha^{\text{sym}}(\mathcal{S}^{\text{sym}})$ as the shortest distance $\text{Dist}(Q_0^{\text{sym}}, Q_F^{\text{sym}}, Q^{\text{sym}}, \rightarrow^{\text{sym}}, W^{\text{sym}})$ from Q_0^{sym} to Q_F^{sym}.

Theorem 15. *Let $\mathcal{W}$ be a TSWA over $\mathbb{D}$ and $\mathbb{S}$, and $\sigma \in T(\mathbb{D}^X)$ be a signal. Let $\mathcal{S}$ and $\mathcal{S}^{\text{sym}}$ be the WTTS (in Definition 6) and WSTTS of $\mathcal{W}$ and σ, respectively. If $\mathbb{S}$ is idempotent, we have $\alpha(\mathcal{S}) = \alpha^{\text{sym}}(\mathcal{S}^{\text{sym}})$.* $\square$

Because of Theorem 15, we can compute $\alpha(\mathcal{S})$ by (i) constructing the reachable part of $\mathcal{S}^{\text{sym}}$; and (ii) computing the symbolic trace value $\alpha^{\text{sym}}(\mathcal{S}^{\text{sym}})$ using an algorithm for the shortest distance problem. For example, the symbolic trace value of the WSTTS in Fig. 4 is $\alpha^{\text{sym}}(\mathcal{S}^{\text{sym}}) = \max\{\min\{8, 2\}, \min\{8, 7\}, \min\{3, 7\}\} = 7$. However, this method requires the

---

[1] The choice of $\tilde{\nu}$ and $\tilde{\nu}'$ does not change $\sigma(\tilde{\nu}(T))$ and $\sigma(\tilde{\nu}'(T))$ due to the definition of Q^{sym}.

Algorithm 1. Incremental algorithm for trace value computation

---

Require: A WSTTS $\mathcal{S}^{\text{sym}} = (Q^{\text{sym}}, Q_0^{\text{sym}}, Q_F^{\text{sym}}, \to^{\text{sym}}, W^{\text{sym}})$ of $\sigma = a_1^{\tau_1} a_2^{\tau_2} \cdots a_n^{\tau_n}$ and $\mathcal{W}$
Ensure: R is the symbolic trace value $\alpha^{\text{sym}}(\mathcal{S}^{\text{sym}})$
1: $weight \leftarrow \{(l_0, \{\mathbf{0}_{C \amalg \{T\}}\}, \varepsilon, e_\otimes) \mid l_0 \in L_0\}; R \leftarrow e_\oplus$ ▷ initialize
2: **for** $i \in \{1, 2, \ldots, n\}$ **do**
3:   | $weight \leftarrow incr(a_i, T_i)$, where $T_i = \sum_{k=1}^{i} \tau_k$ ▷ We have $weight = weight_i$.
4: **for** $(l, Z, \bar{a}, s) \in weight$ **do**
5:   | **if** $(l, Z, \bar{a}) \in Q_F^{\text{sym}}$ **then**
6:   | | $R \leftarrow R \oplus s$

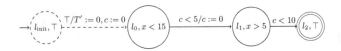

Fig. 5. Matching automaton $\mathcal{A}_{\text{match}}$ for the TSA $\mathcal{A}$ shown in Fig. 2. The fresh initial location l_{init} and the transition to the original initial location l_0 are added.

whole signal to compute the trace value, and it does not suit for the use in online quantitative timed pattern matching. Instead, we define the *intermediate weight* $weight_i$ and give an incremental algorithm to compute $\alpha(\mathcal{S})$. Intuitively, for each state $(l, Z, \bar{a}) \in Q^{\text{sym}}$ of the WSTTS $\mathcal{S}^{\text{sym}}$, the *intermediate weight* $weight_i$ assign the shortest distance to reach $(l, Z, \bar{a})$ by reading the sub-signal $a_1^{\tau_1} a_2^{\tau_2} \cdots a_i^{\tau_i}$ of $\sigma = a_1^{\tau_1} a_2^{\tau_2} \cdots a_n^{\tau_n}$.

Definition 16 (*incr*, *weight$_i$*). *For a TSWA* $\mathcal{W} = (\mathcal{A}, \kappa)$ *over the data domain* $\mathbb{D}$ *and complete semiring* $\mathbb{S}$, $a \in \mathbb{D}^X$, *and* $t \in \mathbb{R}_{>0}$, *the* increment function

$$incr(a, t): \mathcal{P}(L \times \mathcal{Z}(C \amalg \{T\}) \times (\mathbb{D}^X)^\circledast \times S) \to \mathcal{P}(L \times \mathcal{Z}(C \amalg \{T\}) \times (\mathbb{D}^X)^\circledast \times S)$$

is as follows, where $\mathcal{A} = (X, L, L_0, L_F, C, \Delta, \Lambda)$ *and* $(Q_{a,t}^{\text{sym}}, Q_{a,t,0}^{\text{sym}}, Q_{a,t,F}^{\text{sym}}, \to_{a,t}^{\text{sym}}, W_{a,t}^{\text{sym}})$ *is the WSTTS of* a^t *and* $\mathcal{W}$.

$$incr(a, t)(w) = \{(l', Z', \overline{a'}, s') \in L \times \mathcal{Z}(C \amalg \{T\}) \times (\mathbb{D}^X)^\circledast \times S \mid \forall \nu' \in Z'. \nu'(T) = t,$$
$$s' = \bigoplus_{(l,Z,\bar{a},s) \in w} s \otimes \text{Dist}(\{(l, Z, \bar{a})\}, \{(l', Z', \overline{a'})\}, Q_{a,t}^{\text{sym}}, \to_{a,t}^{\text{sym}}, W_{a,t}^{\text{sym}})\}$$

For a TSWA $\mathcal{W}$ *over* $\mathbb{D}$ *and* $\mathbb{S}$, *a signal* $\sigma = a_1^{\tau_1} a_2^{\tau_2} \cdots a_n^{\tau_n}$, *and* $i \in \{1, 2, \ldots, n\}$, *the* intermediate weight *weight$_i$ is defined as follows, where* $T_j = \sum_{k=1}^{j} \tau_k$. $weight_i = (incr(a_i, T_i) \circ \cdots \circ incr(a_1, T_1))(\{(l_0, \{\mathbf{0}_{C \amalg \{T\}}\}, \varepsilon, e_\otimes) \mid l_0 \in L_0\})$

Because of the following, we can incrementally compute the symbolic trace value $\alpha^{\text{sym}}(\mathcal{S}^{\text{sym}})$, which is equal to the trace value $\alpha(\sigma, \mathcal{W})$, by Algorithm 1.

Theorem 17. *For any WSTTS* $\mathcal{S}^{\text{sym}}$ *of a signal* $\sigma = a_1^{\tau_1} a_2^{\tau_2} \cdots a_n^{\tau_n}$ *and a TSWA* $\mathcal{W}$, *we have the following, where* Q_F^{sym} *is the accepting states of* $\mathcal{S}^{\text{sym}}$.

$$\alpha^{\text{sym}}(\mathcal{S}^{\text{sym}}) = \bigoplus_{(l,Z,\bar{a}) \in Q_F^{\text{sym}}} \bigoplus_{(l,Z,\bar{a},s) \in weight_n} s$$

□

6 Online Algorithm for Quantitative Timed Pattern Matching

In quantitative timed pattern matching, we compute the trace value $\alpha(\sigma([t, t')), \mathcal{W})$ for each sub-signal $\sigma([t, t'))$. In order to try matching for each sub-signal $\sigma([t, t'))$, we construct the *matching automaton* [8] $\mathcal{A}_{\text{match}}$ from the TSA $\mathcal{A}$. The matching automaton $\mathcal{A}_{\text{match}}$ is constructed by adding a new clock variable T' and a new initial state l_{init} to the TSA $\mathcal{A}$. The new clock variable T' represents the duration from the beginning t of the sub-signal $\sigma([t, t'))$. The new state l_{init} is used to start the sub-signal in the middle of the signal. We add transitions from l_{init} to each initial state l_0 of $\mathcal{A}$, resetting all of the clock variables. Figure 5 shows an example of $\mathcal{A}_{\text{match}}$. We also define the auxiliary $incr_<$ for our online algorithm for quantitative timed pattern matching.

Definition 18 (matching automaton [8] $\mathcal{A}_{\text{match}}$). *For a TSA $\mathcal{A} = (X, L, L_0, L_F, C, \Delta, \Lambda)$ over $\mathbb{D}$, the matching automaton is the TSA $\mathcal{A}_{\text{match}} = (X, L \amalg \{l_{init}\}, \{l_{init}\}, L_F, C \amalg \{T'\}, \Delta', \Lambda')$ over $\mathbb{D}$, where $\Delta' = \Delta \amalg \{(l_{init}, \top, C \amalg \{T'\}, l_0) \mid l_0 \in L_0\}$, $\Lambda'(l_{init}) = \top$, and $\Lambda'(l) = \Lambda(l)$ for $l \in L$.*

Algorithm 2. Online algorithm for quantitative timed pattern matching

---

Require: A signal $\sigma = a_1^{\tau_1} a_2^{\tau_2} \cdots a_n^{\tau_n}$ and a TSWA $\mathcal{W} = (\mathcal{A}, \kappa)$
Ensure: M is the quantitative matching function $\mathcal{M}(\sigma, \mathcal{W})$.
1: $\mathcal{A}_{\text{match}} \leftarrow$ the matching automaton of $\mathcal{A}$
2: $weight \leftarrow \{(l_0, \{\mathbf{0}_{C \amalg \{T, T'\}}\}, \varepsilon, e_{\otimes}) \mid l_0 \in L_0\}$; for each $[t, t') \subseteq [0, |\sigma|)$, $M(t, t') \leftarrow e_{\oplus}$
3: **for** $i \in \{1, 2, \ldots, n\}$ **do**
4: $\quad weight \leftarrow (incr_<(a_i, T_i))(weight)$, where $T_i = \sum_{k=1}^{i} \tau_k$
5: $\quad$ **for** $(l, Z, \varepsilon, s) \in weight, \nu \in Z$ **do**
6: $\quad \quad$ **if** $l \in L_F$ **then**
7: $\quad \quad \quad M(\nu(T') - \nu(T), \nu(T')) \leftarrow M(\nu(T') - \nu(T), \nu(T')) \oplus s$.
8: $\quad weight \leftarrow (incr(a_i, T_i))(weight)$, where $T_i = \sum_{k=1}^{i} \tau_k$

Definition 19 ($incr_<$). *For a TSWA $\mathcal{W} = (\mathcal{A}, \kappa)$ over the data domain $\mathbb{D}$ and complete semiring $\mathbb{S}$, $a \in \mathbb{D}^X$, and $t \in \mathbb{R}_{>0}$, the partial increment function*

$$incr_<(a, t) \colon \mathcal{P}(L \times \mathcal{Z}(C \amalg \{T\}) \times (\mathbb{D}^X)^{\circledast} \times S) \to \mathcal{P}(L \times \mathcal{Z}(C \amalg \{T\}) \times (\mathbb{D}^X)^{\circledast} \times S)$$

is as follows, where $\mathcal{A} = (X, L, L_0, L_F, C, \Delta, \Lambda)$ and $(Q_{a,t}^{\text{sym}}, Q_{a,t,0}^{\text{sym}}, Q_{a,t,F}^{\text{sym}}, \to_{a,t}^{\text{sym}}, W_{a,t}^{\text{sym}})$ is the WSTTS of the TSWA $\mathcal{W}$ and the constant signal a^t.

$$incr_<(a, t)(w) = \{(l', Z', \overline{a'}, s') \in L \times \mathcal{Z}(C \amalg \{T\}) \times (\mathbb{D}^X)^{\circledast} \times S \mid \forall \nu' \in Z'. \nu'(T) < t,$$

$$s' = \bigoplus_{(l, Z, \overline{a}, s) \in w} s \otimes \text{Dist}(\{(l, Z, \overline{a})\}, \{(l', Z', \overline{a'})\}, Q_{a,t}^{\text{sym}}, \to_{a,t}^{\text{sym}}, W_{a,t}^{\text{sym}})\}$$

Algorithm 2 shows our online algorithm for quantitative timed pattern matching. We construct the matching automaton $\mathcal{A}_{\text{match}}$ from the TSA $\mathcal{A}$ (line 1), and we try matching by reading each constant sub-signal $a_i^{\tau_i}$ of the signal $\sigma = a_1^{\tau_1} a_2^{\tau_2} \cdots a_n^{\tau_n}$ much like the illustration in Fig. 3. For each i, first, we consume a prefix $a_i^{\tau_i'}$ of $a_i^{\tau_i} = a_i^{\tau_i'} a_i^{\tau_i''}$ and update *weight* (line 4). Then, we update the result M for each $(l, Z, \varepsilon, s) \in weight$ if $l \in L_F$ (line 7). Finally, we consume the remaining part $a_i^{\tau_i''}$ and update *weight* (line 8).

Complexity Discussion. In general, the time and space complexities of Algorithm 2 are polynomial to the length n of the signal $\sigma = a_1^{\tau_1} a_2^{\tau_2} \cdots a_n^{\tau_n}$ due to the bound of the size of the reachability part of the WSTTS. On the other hand, if the TSWA has a time-bound and the sampling frequency of the signal is also bounded (such as in Figs. 6 and 7), time and space complexities are linear and constant to the length n of the signal, respectively.

7 Experiments

We implemented our online algorithm for quantitative timed pattern matching in C++ and conducted experiments to answer the following research questions. We suppose that the input piecewise-constant signals are interpolations of the actual signals by sampling.

RQ1. Is the practical performance of Algorithm 2 realistic?

RQ2. Is Algorithm 2 online capable, i.e., does it perform in linear time and constant space, with respect to the number of the entries in the signal?

RQ3. Can Algorithm 2 handle denser logs, i.e., what is the performance with respect to the sampling frequency of the signal?

Our implementation is in https://github.com/MasWag/qtpm. We conducted the experiments on an Amazon EC2 c4.large instance (2 vCPUs and 3.75 GiB RAM) running Ubuntu 18.04 LTS (64 bit). We compiled the implementation by GCC-4.9.3. For the measurement of the execution time and memory usage, we used GNU time and took an average of 20 executions. We could not compare with [7] because their implementation is not publicly available.

As the complete semiring $\mathbb{S}$, we used the sup-inf semiring $(\mathbb{R} \amalg \{\pm\infty\}, \sup, \inf, -\infty, +\infty)$ and the tropical semiring $(\mathbb{R} \amalg \{+\infty\}, \inf, +, +\infty, 0)$ in Example 4. We used the cost functions κ_r in Example 8 for the sup-inf semiring, and κ_t in Example 8 for the tropical semiring. We used the automotive benchmark problems shown in Figs. 6, 7 and 8. A summary of quantitative timed pattern matching is on the right of each figure. The specified behaviors in the TSWAs are taken from ST-Lib [23] and known to be useful for automotive control applications.

Fig. 6. OVERSHOOT: The set of input signals is generated by the cruise control model [1]. The TSA is for the settling when the reference value of the velocity is changed from $v_{ref} < 35$ to $v_{ref} > 35$. The left and right maps are for the sup-inf and tropical semirings, respectively.

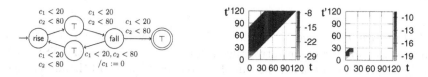

Fig. 7. RINGING: The set of input signals is generated by the same model [1] as that in OVERSHOOT. The TSA is for the frequent rise and fall of the signal in 80 s. The constraints rise and fall are rise $= v(t) - v(t-10) > 10$ and fall $= v(t) - v(t-10) < -10$. The left and right maps are for the sup-inf and tropical semirings, respectively.

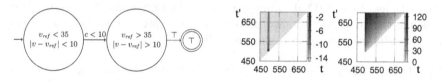

Fig. 8. OVERSHOOT (UNBOUNDED): The set of input signals is generated by the same model [1] as that in OVERSHOOT. The TSA is almost the same as that in OVERSHOOT, but the time-bound ($c < 150$) is removed. The left and right maps are for the sup-inf and tropical semirings, respectively.

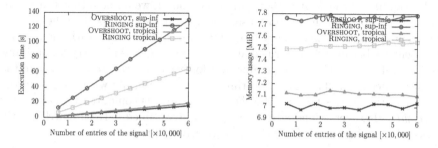

Fig. 9. Change in execution time (left) and memory usage (right) for OVERSHOOT and RINGING with the number of the entries of the signals

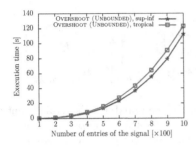 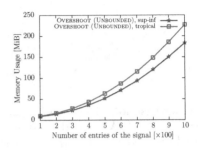

Fig. 10. Change in execution time (left) and memory usage (right) for OVERSHOOT (UNBOUNDED) with the number of the entries of the signals

RQ1: Practical Performance. Figures 9 and 10 show the execution time and memory usage of our quantitative timed pattern matching for the TSWAs $\mathcal{W}$ and signals σ. Here, we fixed the sampling frequency to be 0.1 Hz and changed the duration $|\sigma|$ of the signal from 60,000 s to 600,000 s in OVERSHOOT and RINGING, and from 1,000 s to 10,000 s in OVERSHOOT (UNBOUNDED).

In Fig. 9, we observe that Algorithm 2 handles the log with 60,000 entries in less than 20 s with less than 7.1 MiB of memory usage for OVERSHOOT, and in about 1 or 2 min with less than 7.8 MiB of memory usage for RINGING. In Fig. 10, we observe that Algorithm 2 handles the log with 10,000 entries in less than 120 s with less than 250 MiB of memory usage for OVERSHOOT (UNBOUNDED). Although the quantitative timed pattern matching problem is complex, we conclude that its practical performance is realistic.

RQ2: Change in Speed and Memory Usage with Signal Size. Figures 9 and 10 show the execution time and memory usage of our quantitative timed pattern matching. See RQ1 for the detail of our experimental setting.

In Fig. 9, for the TSAs with time-bound, we observe that the execution time is linear with respect to the duration $|\sigma|$ of the input signals and the memory usage is more or less constant with respect to the duration $|\sigma|$ of the input signals. This performance is essential for a monitor to keep monitoring a running system.

In Fig. 10, for the TSA without any time-bound, we observe that the execution time is cubic and the memory usage is quadratic with respect to the number of the entries in $|\sigma|$. The memory usage increases quadratically with the number of the entries because the intermediate weight $weight_j$ has an entry for each initial interval $[\tau_i, \tau_{i+1})$ of the trimming and for each interval $[\tau_k, \tau_{k+1})$ where the transition occurred. The execution time increases cubically with respect to the number of the entries because the shortest distance is computed for each entry of $weight_j$. However, we note that our quantitative timed pattern matching still works when the number of the entries is relatively small.

RQ3: Change in Speed and Memory Usage with Sampling Frequency. Figure 11 shows the execution time and memory usage for each TSWA $\mathcal{W}$ and signal σ of OVERSHOOT and RINGING. Here, we fixed the number of the entries to be 6,000 and changed the sampling frequency from 0.1 Hz to 1.0 Hz.

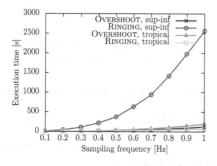 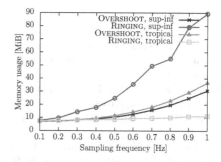

Fig. 11. Change in execution time (left) and memory usage (right) for OVERSHOOT and RINGING with the sampling frequency

In Fig. 11, we observe that the execution time is cubic, and the memory usage is more or less quadratic with respect to the sampling frequency of the signals. This is because the number of the entries in a certain duration is linear to the sampling frequency, which increases the number of the reachability states of the WSTTSs quadratically. Despite the steep curve of the execution time, we also observe that the execution time is smaller than the duration of the signal. Therefore, our algorithm is online capable at least for these sampling frequencies.

Performance Comparison Between the Benchmarks. In Fig. 9, we observe that the execution time and memory usage of RINGING are higher than those of OVERSHOOT. This is because the TSA of RINGING of is more complex than that of OVERSHOOT: it has more states and clock variables, and it contains a loop. We also observe that for RINGING, the execution time for the tropical semiring is shorter. This is because staying at the locations with $\top$ minimizes the weight for tropical semiring, and we need less exploration.

8   Conclusions and Future Work

Using an automata-based approach, we proposed an online algorithm for quantitative timed pattern matching. The key idea of this approach is the reduction to the shortest distance of a weighted graph using zones.

Comparison of the expressiveness of TSWAs with other formalisms e. g., *signal temporal logic* [24] or *signal regular expressions* [7] is future work. Another future work is the comparison with the quantitative semantics based on the distance between traces presented in [21].

References

1. tprasadtp/cruise-control-simulink: Simulink model for Cruise control system of a car with dynamic road conditions. https://github.com/tprasadtp/cruise-control-simulink
2. Akazaki, T., Hasuo, I.: Time robustness in MTL and expressivity in hybrid system falsification. In: Kroening, D., Păsăreanu, C.S. (eds.) CAV 2015. LNCS, vol. 9207, pp. 356–374. Springer, Cham (2015). https://doi.org/10.1007/978-3-319-21668-3_21
3. Alur, R., Dill, D.L.: A theory of timed automata. Theor. Comput. Sci. **126**(2), 183–235 (1994). https://doi.org/10.1016/0304-3975(94)90010-8
4. André, É., Hasuo, I., Waga, M.: Offline timed pattern matching under uncertainty. In: 23rd International Conference on Engineering of Complex Computer Systems, ICECCS 2018, Melbourne, Australia, December 12–14, 2018, pp. 10–20. IEEE Computer Society (2018). https://doi.org/10.1109/ICECCS2018.2018.00010
5. Annpureddy, Y., Liu, C., Fainekos, G., Sankaranarayanan, S.: S-TaLiRo: a tool for temporal logic falsification for hybrid systems. In: Abdulla, P.A., Leino, K.R.M. (eds.) TACAS 2011. LNCS, vol. 6605, pp. 254–257. Springer, Heidelberg (2011). https://doi.org/10.1007/978-3-642-19835-9_21
6. Asarin, E., Caspi, P., Maler, O.: A Kleene theorem for timed automata. In: Proceedings of the 12th Annual IEEE Symposium on Logic in Computer Science, Warsaw, Poland, June 29 - July 2, 1997, pp. 160–171. IEEE Computer Society (1997). https://doi.org/10.1109/LICS.1997.614944
7. Bakhirkin, A., Ferrère, T., Maler, O., Ulus, D.: On the quantitative semantics of regular expressions over real-valued signals. In: Abate, A., Geeraerts, G. (eds.) FORMATS 2017. LNCS, vol. 10419, pp. 189–206. Springer, Cham (2017). https://doi.org/10.1007/978-3-319-65765-3_11
8. Bakhirkin, A., Ferrère, T., Nickovic, D., Maler, O., Asarin, E.: Online timed pattern matching using automata. In: Jansen, D.N., Prabhakar, P. (eds.) FORMATS 2018. LNCS, vol. 11022, pp. 215–232. Springer, Cham (2018). https://doi.org/10.1007/978-3-030-00151-3_13
9. Bartocci, E., Majumdar, R. (eds.): RV 2015. LNCS, vol. 9333. Springer, Cham (2015). https://doi.org/10.1007/978-3-319-23820-3
10. Bengtsson, J., Yi, W.: Timed automata: semantics, algorithms and tools. In: Desel, J., Reisig, W., Rozenberg, G. (eds.) ACPN 2003. LNCS, vol. 3098, pp. 87–124. Springer, Heidelberg (2004). https://doi.org/10.1007/978-3-540-27755-2_3
11. Bombara, G., Vasile, C.I., Penedo, F., Yasuoka, H., Belta, C.: A decision tree approach to data classification using signal temporal logic. In: Abate, A., Fainekos, G.E. (eds.) Proceedings of the 19th International Conference on Hybrid Systems: Computation and Control, HSCC 2016, Vienna, Austria, April 12–14, 2016, pp. 1–10. ACM (2016). https://doi.org/10.1145/2883817.2883843
12. Chatterjee, K., Henzinger, T.A., Otop, J.: Quantitative monitor automata. In: Rival, X. (ed.) SAS 2016. LNCS, vol. 9837, pp. 23–38. Springer, Heidelberg (2016). https://doi.org/10.1007/978-3-662-53413-7_2
13. Chen, S., Sokolsky, O., Weimer, J., Lee, I.: Data-driven adaptive safety monitoring using virtual subjects in medical cyber-physical systems: a glucose control case study. JCSE **10**(3) (2016). https://doi.org/10.5626/JCSE.2016.10.3.75
14. Deshmukh, J.V., Donzé, A., Ghosh, S., Jin, X., Juniwal, G., Seshia, S.A.: Robust online monitoring of signal temporal logic. In: Bartocci and Majumdar [9], pp. 55–70. https://doi.org/10.1007/978-3-319-23820-3_4

15. Dill, D.L.: Timing assumptions and verification of finite-state concurrent systems. In: Sifakis, J. (ed.) CAV 1989. LNCS, vol. 407, pp. 197–212. Springer, Heidelberg (1990). https://doi.org/10.1007/3-540-52148-8_17

16. Donzé, A.: Breach, a toolbox for verification and parameter synthesis of hybrid systems. In: Touili, T., Cook, B., Jackson, P. (eds.) CAV 2010. LNCS, vol. 6174, pp. 167–170. Springer, Heidelberg (2010). https://doi.org/10.1007/978-3-642-14295-6_17

17. Donzé, A., Maler, O.: Robust satisfaction of temporal logic over real-valued signals. In: Chatterjee, K., Henzinger, T.A. (eds.) FORMATS 2010. LNCS, vol. 6246, pp. 92–106. Springer, Heidelberg (2010). https://doi.org/10.1007/978-3-642-15297-9_9

18. Droste, M., Kuich, W., Vogler, H.: Handbook of Weighted Automata, 1st edn. Springer, Heidelberg (2009). https://doi.org/10.1007/978-3-642-01492-5

19. Fainekos, G.E., Pappas, G.J.: Robustness of temporal logic specifications for continuous-time signals. Theor. Comput. Sci. 410(42), 4262–4291 (2009). https://doi.org/10.1016/j.tcs.2009.06.021

20. Jaksic, S., Bartocci, E., Grosu, R., Nguyen, T., Nickovic, D.: Quantitative monitoring of STL with edit distance. Formal Meth. Syst. Des. 53(1), 83–112 (2018). https://doi.org/10.1007/s10703-018-0319-x

21. Jaksic, S., Bartocci, E., Grosu, R., Nickovic, D.: An algebraic framework for runtime verification. IEEE Trans. CAD Integr. Circ. Syst. 37(11), 2233–2243 (2018). https://doi.org/10.1109/TCAD.2018.2858460

22. Kane, A., Chowdhury, O., Datta, A., Koopman, P.: A case study on runtime monitoring of an autonomous research vehicle (ARV) system. In: Bartocci and Majumdar [9], pp. 102–117. https://doi.org/10.1007/978-3-319-23820-3_7

23. Kapinski, J., et al.: St-lib: a library for specifying and classifying model behaviors. Technical report, SAE Technical Paper (2016)

24. Maler, O., Nickovic, D.: Monitoring temporal properties of continuous signals. In: Lakhnech, Y., Yovine, S. (eds.) FORMATS/FTRTFT -2004. LNCS, vol. 3253, pp. 152–166. Springer, Heidelberg (2004). https://doi.org/10.1007/978-3-540-30206-3_12

25. Mohri, M.: Weighted Automata Algorithms. In: Droste, M., Kuich, W., Vogler, H. (eds.) Handbook of Weighted Automata, pp. 213–254. Springer, Heidelberg (2009). https://doi.org/10.1007/978-3-642-01492-5_6

26. Raimondi, F., Skene, J., Emmerich, W.: Efficient online monitoring of web-service slas. In: Harrold, M.J., Murphy, G.C. (eds.) Proceedings of the 16th ACM SIGSOFT International Symposium on Foundations of Software Engineering, 2008, Atlanta, Georgia, USA, November 9–14, 2008, pp. 170–180. ACM (2008). https://doi.org/10.1145/1453101.1453125

27. Schützenberger, M.P.: On the definition of a family of automata. Inf. Control 4(2–3), 245–270 (1961). https://doi.org/10.1016/S0019-9958(61)80020-X

28. Ulus, D., Ferrère, T., Asarin, E., Maler, O.: Timed pattern matching. In: Legay, A., Bozga, M. (eds.) FORMATS 2014. LNCS, vol. 8711, pp. 222–236. Springer, Cham (2014). https://doi.org/10.1007/978-3-319-10512-3_16

29. Ulus, D., Ferrère, T., Asarin, E., Maler, O.: Online timed pattern matching using derivatives. In: Chechik, M., Raskin, J.-F. (eds.) TACAS 2016. LNCS, vol. 9636, pp. 736–751. Springer, Heidelberg (2016). https://doi.org/10.1007/978-3-662-49674-9_47

30. Veanes, M., Hooimeijer, P., Livshits, B., Molnar, D., Bjørner, N.: Symbolic finite state transducers: algorithms and applications. In: Field, J., Hicks, M. (eds.) Proceedings of the 39th ACM SIGPLAN-SIGACT Symposium on Principles of Programming Languages, POPL 2012, Philadelphia, Pennsylvania, USA, January 22–28, 2012, pp. 137–150. ACM (2012). https://doi.org/10.1145/2103656.2103674
31. Waga, M.: Online quantitative timed pattern matching with semiring-valued weighted automata. CoRR abs/1906.12133 (2019). http://arxiv.org/abs/1906.12133
32. Waga, M., Akazaki, T., Hasuo, I.: A boyer-moore type algorithm for timed pattern matching. In: Fränzle, M., Markey, N. (eds.) FORMATS 2016. LNCS, vol. 9884, pp. 121–139. Springer, Cham (2016). https://doi.org/10.1007/978-3-319-44878-7_8
33. Waga, M., André, É.: Online parametric timed pattern matching with automata-based skipping. CoRR abs/1903.07328 (2019). http://arxiv.org/abs/1903.07328
34. Waga, M., André, É., Hasuo, I.: Symbolic monitoring against specifications parametric in time and data. In: To appear in Proceedings of the CAV 2019
35. Waga, M., Hasuo, I., Suenaga, K.: Efficient online timed pattern matching by automata-based skipping. In: Abate, A., Geeraerts, G. (eds.) FORMATS 2017. LNCS, vol. 10419, pp. 224–243. Springer, Cham (2017). https://doi.org/10.1007/978-3-319-65765-3_13

Assessing the Robustness of Arrival Curves Models for Real-Time Systems

Mahmoud Salem[1]([✉])([iD]), Gonzalo Carvajal[2]([iD]), Tong Liu[1],
and Sebastian Fischmeister[1]

[1] University of Waterloo, Waterloo, ON, Canada
{m4salem,t49liu,sfischme}@uwaterloo.ca
[2] Universidad Técnica Federico Santa María, Valparaíso, Chile
gonzalo.carvajalb@usm.cl

Abstract. Design of real-time systems is prone to uncertainty due to software and hardware changes throughout their deployment. In this context, both industry and academia have shown interest in new trace mining approaches for diagnosis and prognosis of complex embedded systems. Trace mining techniques construct empirical models that mainly target achieving high accuracy in detecting anomalies. However, when applied to safety-critical systems, such models lack in providing theoretical bounds on the system resilience to variations from these anomalies.

This paper presents the first work that derives robustness criteria on a trace mining approach that constructs arrival-curves models from dataset of traces collected from real-time systems. Through abstracting arrival-curves models to the demand-bound functions of a sporadic task under an EDF scheduler, the analysis presented in the paper enables designers to quantify the permissible change to the parameters of a given task model by relating to the variation expressed within the empirical model. The result is a methodology to evaluate a system to dynamically changing workloads. We evaluate the proposed approach on an industrial cyber-physical system that generates traces of timestamped QNX events.

Keywords: Arrival curves · Demand-bound functions · Trace mining

1 Introduction

Modern real-time systems are becoming increasingly complex, and their runtime behavior is subject to uncertainties arising from dynamic workloads and changes in their underlying software and hardware. For example, a platform executing a real-time application may suffer a degradation in processor performance if maliciously switched to a low-power mode, or it may sporadically increase its processor demand when handling an anomalous execution scenario. To model and analyze those systems, designers usually apply traditional formal methods that use worst-case analysis to bound any possible workload that can occur at runtime.

© Springer Nature Switzerland AG 2019
É. André and M. Stoelinga (Eds.): FORMATS 2019, LNCS 11750, pp. 23–40, 2019.
https://doi.org/10.1007/978-3-030-29662-9_2

Although traditional formal methods are relatively mature and have become a standard practice in the industry, they tend to be overly pessimistic and have limited applicability for modern practical systems with dynamic properties.

With the rise of Industry 4.0 and digital twin concepts [8,23], researchers have started using runtime traces collected from non-invasive tracing tools to improve diagnostics and prognostics. Event traces provide valuable information for performing data-driven analysis when formal methods become complicated or infeasible [1]. For example, formal methods become inadequate when analyzing complex system-level timing requirements of interacting processes. Alternatively, trace mining is proving useful for characterizing real-time systems, as they construct models using traces from different processes, in addition to component-level trace events representing core switching and resource allocations [7].

One relevant open question associated to empirical models constructed from traces is how to evaluate their effectiveness. For example, surveys [4,16,26] highlight that the primary evaluation method of empirical models used for anomaly detection is by their ability to classify normal versus anomalous behavior. However, the current research work shows a lack in the methods that derive robustness bounds on the acceptable behavior of a given system using margins provided by the empirical models. In this context, authors in [9] acknowledge that, unlike traditional formal methods, empirical models for anomaly detection are generally tuned in an ad-hoc manner without guidance by well-found theoretical framework or analysis. As a result, authors claim that there are no guarantees on the effectiveness of the empirical models after deployment.

Authors in [22] show the feasibility of a trace mining approach in modeling the behavior of a real-time system using arrival curves [13] constructed from event traces. The proposed framework computes empirical arrival curves by traversing the trace with a sliding window, capturing the maximum and minimum observation counts of different system events for windows of different length. In a typical classification setting, a normal profile for the system corresponds to a model that aggregates arrival curves computed over a set of representative traces that characterize the normal system behavior. Finally, a classifier uses the model to label unseen traces with a specified accuracy for anomaly detection purposes.

This paper presents an analysis to assess the robustness of arrival-curves models used to characterize the ranges of tolerable behavioral variations of a real-time system such as hardware degradation, external attacks, etc. The presented analysis is based on the assumption that an arrival curve can be analogous to a demand bound function. We state the problem as follows: *Given an empirical arrival curve for a system that can be represented by a sporadic task-set scheduled using an EDF scheduler, and associated upper and lower bounds on allowed variations in the demand of the task set, obtain a range of allowed variations in the task parameters (period, execution time) such that the system stays operational within the allowed variations in the expected overall demand.*

The rest of the paper is organized as follows: We present the background and assumptions for the system models in Sect. 2. We derive the bounds on the task parameters that correspond to the deviation in the dbf of the task model in

Sect. 3, and we perform an asymptotic analysis to these variation bounds of the task parameters corresponding to the change of the demand deviation in Sect. 4. In Sect. 5, we evaluate the robustness assessment framework of empirical arrival-curves models of an actual real-time system. Section 6 discusses the validity of our assumptions, Sect. 7 reviews the related work, and finally Sect. 8 concludes the paper.

2   Arrival Curves and Demand Bound Functions

This section reviews some basic definitions of arrival curves and establishes a relationship between these curves and demand bound functions for a given task model $T(p, e, d)$ with period p, execution time e, and deadline d. The relationship between arrival curves and dbf provides the basis for the theoretical analysis presented in the paper since our work attempts to fill the gap between the empirically constructed arrival curves and the theoretical models of demand-bound functions that are typically used for formal analysis of a given system. We evaluate and validate the assumptions presented in this section using data from a real-world application in Sect. 5.

2.1   Overview of Arrival Curves

Arrival curves are widely used abstractions for modeling temporal workloads in real-time systems. Multiple frameworks based on Network Calculus [13] rely on arrival curves to model worst-case workloads and perform exhaustive analysis of real-time systems at design-time, obtaining guaranteed performance metrics before system deployment [28]. More recently, multiple authors have shown that analyzing the properties of arrival curves constructed from execution traces collected while the system is operating opens new avenues in applications such as resource management [12,18] and anomaly detection [22]. The ever-increasing accessibility of system-specific traces from embedded systems and the availability of tools to accelerate the construction of accurate empirical arrival curves [5] facilitate the development of new data-driven methods to complement traditional formal methods in the analysis of modern real-time systems.

Arrival curves are functions of interval time domain that provide upper and lower limits to the number of events that can occur in a system within any time interval of length Δt. Starting from a timestamped trace of events, it is possible to obtain an empirical arrival curve by sliding a window of varying length Δt, and registering the maximum and the minimum number of events enclosed within the window while traversing the trace. The resulting curves bound the lower and upper event counts versus the corresponding time interval lengths.

An empirical arrival curve representing a maximum count of events for different interval lengths is a non-decreasing function that starts at the origin [22], and it can be approximated by a line passing through the origin. In the rest of this section, we present the dbf of a sporadic task model under EDF scheduler, which can also be approximated through a line passing through the origin.

This assumption allows us to relate the arrival curves with the dbf of a given task-set, enabling us to perform a mathematical analysis for the resilience of systems to the dynamically changing workloads.

2.2   Assumed Task Model and Demand Bound Functions

Definition 1. *A task $T(p, e, d)$ is a dispatchable entity in the system where the period p is the number of time units between successive dispatches, e is the execution time (in time units) required to complete the work, and the deadline d is the maximum time available to complete the work after dispatching.*

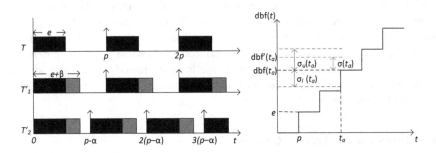

Fig. 1. Graphical representation of variations in task parameters and dbf.

A demand-bound function (dbf) models the maximum processor demand by a task over any interval of length t [2]. The dbf of a given sporadic task under EDF assumption is defined as:

$$\text{dbf}(t) = \left\lfloor \frac{t + p - d}{p} \right\rfloor e \tag{1}$$

We will consider that the sporadic task has an implicit deadline $(d = p)$ and there are no overloads, restricting the possible values of e to $]0, p]$, with $p \in \mathbb{R}$.

Due to the empirical nature of the target arrival-curves model, the purpose of the chosen task model is to provide a reasonable approximation to the arrival curve that describes an increasing events count versus an increasing sliding window interval [22]. Hence, we choose the specified sporadic task model with an implicit deadline under EDF scheduler, which yields an increasing function that steps e units every p time units. The function can be approximated by a straight line with slope $\frac{e}{p}$. We evaluate the choice of this task model and the empirical model approximation in Sect. 5.

Variations in the nominal task parameters can either increase or decrease the task demand. In practical settings, changes in the task parameters may arise from changing operational conditions. We formalize the range of possible values of the altered task parameters as follows:

Definition 2. *Decreasing the period of a task.* α *is defined as the reduction of the task period p in time units, therefore $\alpha \in (-\infty, p\,[$.*

Definition 3. *Increasing the execution time of a task.* β *is defined as the increase of the task execution time e in time units, therefore $\beta \in\,]-e, (p - \alpha) - e\,[$.*

We define α as a decrement and β as an increment for mathematical convenience. But to generalize our analysis, we highlight that both Definitions 2 and 3 allow negative values for α and β.

We now introduce the general model for an altered task $T'(p - \alpha, e + \beta)$, which incorporates the variations in period and execution time while maintaining the condition of implicit deadlines but for the altered period in this case, i.e., $(d - \alpha = p - \alpha)$. We can obtain a corresponding altered dbf as follows:

$$\mathrm{dbf}'(t) = \left\lfloor \frac{t}{p - \alpha} \right\rfloor (e + \beta) \tag{2}$$

Let us now consider that for each interval length t, we define arbitrary bounds on allowed variations in the nominal dbf from Eq. 1 (with $\alpha = \beta = 0$), restricting the valid values of dbf′ for a given application.

Definition 4. *Variation Bound on Task Demand. We denote the allowed variations of the dbf at time interval t as $\sigma(t) = dbf'(t) - dbf(t)$, where $\sigma(t) \in [\sigma_l(t), \sigma_u(t)]$, and $\sigma_l(t), \sigma_u(t) \in \mathbb{R}$.*

The restriction in the allowed values of $\sigma(t)$ can be either set by the system designer according to some specific operational accuracy requirement or can represent some uncertainty in the specifications. Note that Definition 4 permits describing deviations above and below the nominal demand. This is a key difference of our analysis with respect to related work on sensitivity analysis from the scheduling domain [20,27,29–31], which focuses on verifying that the demand stays below a certain limit such that the system remains schedulable. We contrast our work with sensitivity analysis in Sect. 7.

Figure 1 illustrates the previous definitions for the variations in the nominal task parameters and the corresponding dbf. The diagram on the left shows the timeline for the execution of a task T with period p and execution time e, and also the execution of tasks T'_1 and T'_2 that include variations in the nominal parameters. In specific, T'_1 increments the nominal execution time by β time units (represented in the shaded green box), and T'_2 aggregates a reduction in the period. Both T'_1 and T'_2 generate a demand above the nominal value. The diagram to the right shows the step-wise nominal dbf together with the terms defined earlier for allowed variations at a certain point t_a. In this case, the demand of the altered task dbf′(t_a) is above the nominal value, but within the specified boundaries of allowed variations $\sigma_l(t_a)$ and $\sigma_u(t_a)$.

Considering the previous definitions, we can tackle the problem introduced in Sect. 1 by finding the region of allowed values of α and β, such that the value of $\sigma(t)$, representing the deviation in the demand of the altered task $\mathrm{dbf}'(t)$ with respect to the nominal demand $\mathrm{dbf}(t)$, stays within the predefined range $[\sigma_l(t), \sigma_u(t)]$. Traditionally for the assumed task model, a utilization-based approach is the solution to evaluate timing properties of a given real-time system; however, this work uses demand-bound functions since we hypothesize their feasible abstraction to empirical arrival curves as we demonstrate in Sect. 5.

3   Computing Bounds on Task-Model Alteration

In this section, we relate the demand deviation bound to a feasibility region for the parameters α and β of the altered task model T'. The mathematical foundations assume a specified demand variation bound for a given task. However, the analysis presented in this section can be directly extended to specified demand variation bounds for multiple independent tasks, i.e., a task T_i has a specified demand variation bound σ_i where $\sum_i \sigma_i = \sigma$. Such problem breaks down into multiple sub-problems that can be solved by finding the feasible region for each α_i and β_i for each task T_i separately.

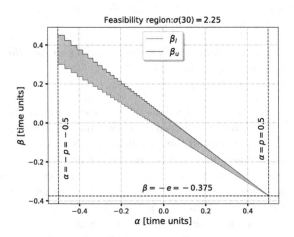

Fig. 2. Permissible task parameter alteration in Example 1

Substituting Eqs. 1 and 2 in Definition 4, we can derive a relationship between α and β values that alter a nominal task model T while meeting a deviation demand $\sigma(t_a)$ at a given time interval t_a as follows:

$$\beta = \frac{\sigma(t_a) - \left(\left\lfloor \dfrac{t_a}{p-\alpha} \right\rfloor - \left\lfloor \dfrac{t_a}{p} \right\rfloor \right) e}{\left\lfloor \dfrac{t_a}{p-\alpha} \right\rfloor} \tag{3}$$

The allowed deviation from the nominal dbf is bounded by $[\sigma_l(t_a), \sigma_u(t_a)]$. By replacing $\sigma(t_a)$ by $\sigma_l(t_a)$ in Eq. 3, we can establish a relationship between a lower bound for the parameter β_l, and the possible values of α. In a similar manner, we can replace $\sigma(t_a)$ by $\sigma_u(t_a)$ to obtain the upper bound β_u.

Figure 2 illustrates how we can use the relationships described above to obtain a feasibility region for the values of α and β given a certain $\sigma(t_a)$. The figure shows a plot of β as a function of α, in addition to the resulting β_l and β_u. The dashed straight lines delimit the valid intervals for α and β according to Definitions 2 and 3, respectively. The lines for β_l and β_u intersect at the point $(\alpha, \beta) = (p, -e)$. We restrict the lower bound of α to $-p$, so the range of allowed α values from Definition 2 changes to $[-p,\ p]$. Considering the limits β_l and β_u and the restrictions over the parameters, we can obtain a feasibility region (shown in shaded green) for the valid combinations of α and β that will allow to keep the altered demand within predefined boundaries.

To illustrate the theoretical foundations, we present the following example with concrete task parameters that we will use throughout the rest of the paper.

Example 1. Consider a sporadic task with parameters $e = 0.375$ and $p = d = 0.5$. Find the feasibility region for α and β such that the demand of the altered task at $t_a = 30$ remains within a range of $\pm 10\%$ of the nominal demand.

Figure 2 shows the computed upper bound β_u and lower bound β_l with respect to valid values for α by applying Eq. 3 to the demand of the task in Example 1. The resulting feasibility region for the variations in parameters is shaded green. When drawing a vertical straight line for a given value of α, any value of β within that region will ensure that the resulting demand from the altered system will remain within the specified variations.

4   Asymptotic Analysis for Task Alteration Parameters

This section describes how variations in α and β change over increasing time intervals t to meet the specified demand bounds. We use Eq. 3 to establish the relation between β and the time interval t for a given α. Similarly, for a given β, the equation defines the relation between α and time interval t. Analyzing the change of β and α as the time interval t increases gives us an insight into the change of permissible system parameters alteration over different time intervals.

To compute these asymptotic bounds, we need to apply a transformation to Eq. 3 using approximations that are valid for asymptotic values of time intervals.

First, we relate the decrease in period α to the period p using a variable k, where $\alpha = k \times p$ such that $k \in (-\infty, 1[$. In other words, the variable k is a ratio of the decrease in period α with respect to the nominal period p. Second, we relate t to both p and α by defining c where $t \approx c\ (p - \alpha)$ assuming c is some factor much larger than $(p - \alpha)$. Hence, $t \approx c\ p\ (1 - k)$ as well.

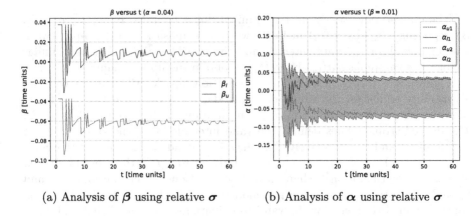

(a) Analysis of β using relative σ (b) Analysis of α using relative σ

Fig. 3. Asymptotic analysis for the β and α using relative σ

We evaluate these approximation as $t \to \infty$. We obtain the limit of the floor operator using the Squeeze Theorem of Limits [10], which allows us to find $\lim_{x \to \infty} f(x)$ where $f(x)$ is bounded by $g(x)$ and $h(x)$, $g(x) \le f(x) \le h(x)$ as follows:

$$\lim_{x \to \infty} g(x) \le \lim_{x \to \infty} f(x) \le \lim_{x \to \infty} h(x) \tag{4}$$

Applying Eq. 4 to the definition of floor function, $c - 1 \le \lfloor c \rfloor < c$, we deduce that $\lim_{c \to +\infty} c - 1 = c$ and $\lim_{c \to +\infty} c = c$, and as a result:

$$\lim_{c \to +\infty} \lfloor c \rfloor = c \tag{5}$$

Similarly, since $(1 - k)$ is a constant. We obtain the following result in Eq. 6. Combining Eqs. 5 and 6 allow for transforming Eq. 3 to obtain β.

$$\lim_{c \to +\infty} \lfloor c\,(1 - k) \rfloor = c\,(1 - k) \tag{6}$$

Asymptotic Analysis for Variation in Execution Time. β We consider $\sigma(t)$ values that can be defined relatively to the nominal demand dbf(t). Let us define σ as a fraction f of the nominal demand dbf(t). For example, the demand variation bound can be set to be $\pm 10\%$ of the nominal demand at any given interval t. In this case, to compute the asymptotic values we use Eq. 7 as follows:

$$\sigma(t) = f\ \mathrm{dbf}(t) = f \left\lfloor \frac{t}{p} \right\rfloor e \tag{7}$$

Using $\sigma(t)$ from Eq. 7, the asymptotic values of a function $\beta_v(t)$ that varies with t can be derived as follows:

$$
\begin{aligned}
\lim_{t\to+\infty} \beta_v(t) &= \lim_{t\to+\infty} \frac{f\left\lfloor \frac{t}{p} \right\rfloor e - \left(\left\lfloor \frac{t}{p-\alpha} \right\rfloor - \left\lfloor \frac{t}{p} \right\rfloor\right)e}{\left\lfloor \frac{t}{p-\alpha} \right\rfloor} \\
&= \lim_{c\to+\infty} \frac{f\left\lfloor \frac{cp(1-k)}{p} \right\rfloor e - \left(\left\lfloor \frac{c(p-\alpha)}{p-\alpha} \right\rfloor - \left\lfloor \frac{cp(1-k)}{p} \right\rfloor\right)e}{\lfloor c \rfloor} \\
&= \lim_{c\to+\infty} \frac{f\lfloor c(1-k) \rfloor e - (\lfloor c \rfloor - \lfloor c(1-k) \rfloor)e}{\lfloor c \rfloor} \\
&= \lim_{c\to+\infty} \frac{fc(1-k)e - (c - c(1-k))e}{c} \\
&= -ke + f(1-k)e
\end{aligned}
\tag{8}
$$

Figure 3a shows the boundaries β_u and β_l when $\sigma(t) \in [0.9*\mathrm{dbf}(t), 1.1*\mathrm{dbf}(t)]$ in Example 1 for an arbitrary value $\alpha = 0.04$. Using Eq. 8, we find the asymptotic values for the boundaries are $\beta_l \approx -0.064$ and $\beta_u \approx 0.0045$. The figure shows that the boundary curve smooths as t increases due to the diminishing effect of the floor operator in Eq. 7.

Asymptotic Analysis for Variation in Period. α For a given value of β, we study how a varying function $\alpha_v(t)$ changes over time interval t by obtaining the relation between $\alpha_v(t)$ and t from Eq. 3 as follows:

$$
Z = \left\lfloor \frac{t}{p - \alpha_v(t)} \right\rfloor = \frac{\sigma + \left\lfloor \frac{t}{p} \right\rfloor e}{e + \beta}
\tag{9}
$$

Unlike the analysis for the values of $\beta_v(t)$, defining a precise relation between $\alpha_v(t)$ and t for a given β is not a straightforward operation. Since the inverse of the floor operator is undefined, we cannot obtain a closed formula for $\alpha_v(t)$. Instead, we restrict the analysis to obtain conservative bounds for the range of $\alpha_v(t)$ values that satisfy Eq. 9. To do this, we can apply the range property of the floor operator [11], which states the following:

$$
\lfloor x \rfloor = m \iff m \le x < m + 1
\tag{10}
$$

Using the property in (10), we can describe a range for the values of $\alpha\,v(t)$ as:

$$
p - \frac{t}{Z} \le \alpha_v(t) < p - \frac{t}{Z+1}, \text{ with } Z = \frac{\sigma + \left\lfloor \frac{t}{p} \right\rfloor e}{(e + \beta)}
\tag{11}
$$

Substituting σ for the specified demand variation bounds σ_l and σ_u in the obtained inequality, we can obtain the relation of the corresponding boundaries for $\alpha_v(t)$ versus time interval t for a given β. Note that each boundary for σ leads to a feasible range of $\alpha_v(t)$, so we define Z_u and Z_l, which we obtain replacing σ_u and σ_l in the term Z defined in Eq. 9, respectively. Substituting Z by Z_u and Z_l in Eq. 11 yields two inequalities with four boundaries which can be bounded by the $\alpha_v(t)$ in Eq. 12. Now, we show the asymptotic values for both boundaries when the demand variation bound σ is defined as a function of nominal demand and we visualize these results in Fig. 3b.

$$p - \frac{t}{Z_l} \le \alpha_v(t) < p - \frac{t}{Z_u + 1} \tag{12}$$

We consider $\sigma(t)$ values that are relative to the nominal demand dbf(t) where the variation of the demand is constrained by a given range $[\sigma_l, \sigma_u]$ that changes over time intervals t. Using the transformation from Eq. 7, the asymptotic values for α can be computed using the boundaries in Eq. 11 again as follows starting with the left-hand side in Eq. 13 then the right-hand size in Eq. 14:

$$p - \frac{t}{Z} = p - \frac{c\,p\,(1-k)}{\frac{f\,c\,(1-k)\,e + c\,(1-k)\,e}{e\,+\beta}} = p - \frac{c\,p\,(1-k)(e\,+\beta)}{c\,(1-k)\,e\,(1+f)} = p - \frac{p\,(e\,+\beta)}{e\,(1+\,f)} \tag{13}$$

$$p - \frac{t}{Z+1} = p - \frac{cp(1-k)}{\frac{c(1-k)e(1+f)+(e+\beta)}{e+\beta}} = p - \frac{cp(1-k)(e+\beta)}{c(1-k)e(1+f)+(e+\beta)} \tag{14}$$

Then taking the limit as t goes to ∞ for Eq. 13 yields the same equation, however, for Eq. 14, we obtain the asymptotic value as follows:

$$\lim_{c \to +\infty} \frac{cp(1-k)}{\frac{c(1-k)e(1+f)+(e+\beta)}{e+\beta}} = \lim_{c \to +\infty} \frac{p(1-k)(e+\beta)}{e(1-k)(1+f) + \frac{(e+\beta)}{c}} = \frac{p(1+\beta)}{e(1+f)} \tag{15}$$

Thus, we conclude that asymptotically, both sides of the inequality will converge to the same limit. According to the Squeeze Theorem, α can be defined asymptotically in this case as:

$$\alpha \approx p - \frac{p\,(e+\beta)}{e(1+f)} \tag{16}$$

Figure 3b shows the boundaries for α_u and α_l when $\sigma(t) \in [0.9 * \text{dbf}(t), 1.1 * \text{dbf}(t)]$ in Example 1 for an arbitrary value $\beta = 0.01$. Using Eq. 16, we find the asymptotic values for the boundaries are $\alpha_l \approx -0.07$ and $\alpha_u \approx 0.03$. The boundaries in Fig. 3 shows the importance of the asymptotic analysis since we can observe that these asymptotic limits are not necessarily the tightest over the time interval t. As a result, this analysis provides the designer with a tool to assess the validity of the calculated robustness bounds versus increasing t values.

In the following section, we apply the theoretical analysis to an application of interest by tackling the problem statement introduced in Sect. 1, which aims at assessing the robustness of data-driven trace mining approach that uses arrival-curves models for a deployed real-time system.

5   Application: Robustness Assessment for Empirical Arrival-Curves Models

In this section, we evaluate the hypothesis that an empirical arrival curve can be represented as linear demand-bound functions of the assumed task model in this paper, and as a result, we perform robustness evaluation for the arrival-curves models using the presented theoretical foundations.

The procedure of robustness assessment for the empirical arrival-curve model follows these steps: (a) abstract an arrival-curves model to a sporadic task model as in Sect. 2, (b) obtain the relation that describes the feasibility region of the allowed alteration for the task model which corresponds to a variation in the arrival behavior shown by the empirical model as in Sect. 3, (c) evaluate the approach feasibility by quantifying the effect of approximating the curves to a linear demand-bound function of a sporadic task under an EDF scheduler which we demonstrate in this section.

5.1   Representing Arrival Curves as Demand-Bound Functions

A model of empirical arrival-curves is an aggregate for the curves computed over a set of multiple traces collected from the system [22]. In our application, we consider a model that is comprised of the mean of arrival curves describing the maximum counts of events within variable window sizes, in addition to two boundary curves that described a confidence interval for that mean. Figure 4a shows the arrival-curves model of a specified QNX event computed using a set of traces that represent the normal behavior of a real-time system, we discuss the experimental setup later in this section.

In Sect. 2, the mathematical foundation uses a task model of a sporadic task using the dbf under an EDF scheduler. As a result, we obtain a demand function, which we can approximate by a line passing through the origin. Similarly, an empirical arrival curve representing a maximum count is a function whose non-decreasing curve starts at the origin [22]. Now, we can introduce the methodology that relates both the arrival curve and the demand-bound function.

We apply Linear Regression [17] to obtain the line that best fits an empirical arrival curve. We offset the fitted line to pass by the origin, and as a result, it can be analogous to a demand-bound function. Later in this section, we quantify the negligible error introduced by this process. For example, Fig. 4b shows the fitted regression lines for the mean arrival curve and the two confidence interval curves after being offset to pass by the origin. The linearity of the curves makes them a good pick for our demonstration.

The regression lines in Fig. 4b are now analogous to a nominal dbf(t) with an upper and lower variation bound to the demand σ_l and σ_u respectively which are both functions of t. In other words, we can define a sporadic task which demands e execution time units every p time interval whose demand-bound function can be approximated by an empirical arrival curve counting a maximum of e instances of an event in a trace every sliding window of p time units.

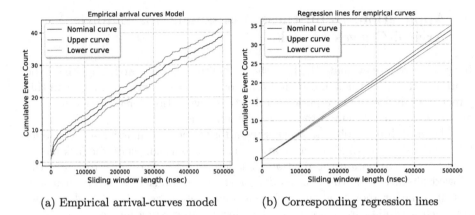

(a) Empirical arrival-curves model   (b) Corresponding regression lines

Fig. 4. Fitting empirical arrival-curves model to demand-bound functions

5.2   Robustness Assessment Using Task Alteration Parameters

In order to enable the analysis presented in the previous sections to the robustness assessment of empirical arrival curves, we use the task model assumed in Sect. 2 to map the task parameters and its variations to the slopes of the regression lines obtained in Fig. 4b. We denote these slopes as, S for the slope of the regression line for the mean curve, S_u, and S_l for the slopes of the regression lines for both confidence interval curves. We compute these slopes as follows:

$$S = \frac{e}{p}, \quad S_u = \frac{e + \beta_u}{p - \alpha_u}, \quad S_l = \frac{e + \beta_l}{p - \alpha_l} \tag{17}$$

Equation 17 defines the relation between task parameters e and p and the regression slopes. We obtain the relations between the variation of parameters α and β from Eq. 3 using the definitions of S_u and S_l as follows:

$$\beta_u = \frac{\sigma_u - \left(\left\lfloor \frac{t_a\, S_u}{e + \beta_u} \right\rfloor - \left\lfloor \frac{t_a\, S}{e} \right\rfloor \right) e}{\left\lfloor \frac{t_a\, S_u}{e + \beta_u} \right\rfloor}, \quad \beta_l = \frac{\sigma_l - \left(\left\lfloor \frac{t_a\, S_l}{e + \beta_l} \right\rfloor - \left\lfloor \frac{t_a\, S}{e} \right\rfloor \right) e}{\left\lfloor \frac{t_a\, S_l}{e + \beta_l} \right\rfloor}$$

$$\tag{18}$$

The above equations provide the relation between bounds on β versus execution time e. To define the relation between α and the period p, we substitute e by $S \times p$ from Eq. 17:

$$\alpha_u = p - \frac{e + \beta_u}{S_u}, \quad \alpha_l = p - \frac{e + \beta_l}{S_l} \tag{19}$$

The above set of equations provide the relations between the parameters e and p, and the corresponding alterations β and α. The relations evaluate the alteration that would cause a deviation σ to the dbfs obtained by approximating the fitted regression lines of the empirical arrival-curves model. Analogously, β and α now describe the permissible variation to the arrival-curves model, i.e., the count of events of the corresponding sliding window interval of observance.

Now, we present an application to demonstrate how to use these relations to assess the robustness of a model for a real-time system. We exploit the proposed approach by obtaining the feasibility region for the permissible task parameter variations of the mapped task model through the approximation of the empirical arrival curves to demand-bound functions.

5.3   Evaluation on QNX Traces from UAV

The dataset traces are generated from an unmanned aerial vehicle (UAV) running the real-time operating system QNX Neutrino 6.4. The UAV was developed at the University of Waterloo, received the Special Flight Operating Certificate (SFOC), and flew real mapping and payload-drop missions in Nova Scotia and Ontario. The traces are collected using the tracing facility *tracelogger*. A trace entry is a timestamped kernel event that shows the type of an event generated while running a specific process on a specified CPU core. In this section, we represent an arrival-curves model for a specific QNX event THREAD THRUNNING that marks every start of a thread execution for a specified process proc/boot/procnto-instr. To evaluate the robustness of the example model in Fig. 4a, we perform the following steps:

(a) **Compute Regression Slopes.** We obtain the slopes of the fitted regression lines for the mean arrival curve and its confidence interval. It is advisable to assess the adjusted R squared of the regression model. The metric measures the goodness of the linear fit to evaluate whether the assumption that the model is linear was valid [17]. In our example, the slopes of the lines in Fig. 4b can be obtained as $S = 6 : 76 \times 10^{-5}, S_u = 7 : 01 \times 10^{-5}$ and $S_l = 6 : 52 \times 10^{-5}$. The adjusted R squared is 98% indicating a good linear fit.

(b) **Choose Task Parameters.** Next step is to specify the task parameters e and p in order to obtain the relation between α and β from Eqs. 18 and 19. However, the provided empirical arrival-curves model cannot be used to obtain the e and p values. This comes from the fact that the slopes of fitted regression lines can represent any underlying task model satisfying the relation $S = \frac{e}{p}$.

Therefore, to obtain reasonable values for e and p, we need to choose p that is a small fraction of t_a to obtain the asymptotic values for α and β, in other words, we aim to maximize the factor c defined in Sect. 4. Additionally, the choice of p or e can be arbitrarily guided by domain knowledge of the system under scrutiny. The other parameter can be estimated using the relation $S = \frac{e}{p}$ from Eq. 17 upon deciding on the value of p or e. In our example, we choose an arbitrary value $t_a = 4 \times 10^{-5}$ that captures a sufficient number of trace events. Then, we choose $p = 0.001 \times t_a = 400$, and as a result, we compute $e = S$ x $p = 0.027$.

(c) Obtain Demand Variation Bound. The last parameters needed to obtain the relation between α and β are σ_u and σ_l. The σ parameter defines the difference between the fitted confidence interval curves after offsetting them to pass by the origin $(0,0)$. Note that σ optimally can be expressed as $\sigma = (\text{dbf}' + \text{intercept}') - (\text{dbf} + \text{intercept})$, but we discard the difference between both intercepts as the error resulting from that approximation is negligible. For the example in Fig. 4b, we measure $\sigma_u = -\sigma_l = \sigma'$ where $\sigma' = 0.957$ at $t_a = 4 \times 10^{-5}$.

(d) Apply Feasibility Region Formulas. To obtain the estimated feasibility region for α and β, we plot the values of β_u and β_l for a valid range of α values using the slopes of fitted regression lines from Eq. 18. For the actual feasibility region, we plot the values of β_u and β_l versus α using Eq. 3. Figure 5 shows the overlay of both feasibility regions using the arrival-curves model and the actual task model which, similarly to the illustration in Fig. 2, describe the permissible values of α and the corresponding bounds on β. The negligible error between both the actual and estimated feasibility regions validates that the approximation of a linear empirical arrival-curves model to the assumed demand-bound function is reasonable.

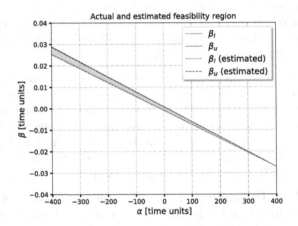

Fig. 5. Feasibility region for representative parameters β, α

The case study shows an example of an arrival-curves model that characterizes the behavior of QNX kernel event on a real-time system. The empirical model can now be represented as the demand-bound function of an equivalent task model whose parameters alteration can be bounded. The boundaries describe the robustness of the model as it quantifies the variation captured in the underlying normal behavior of the system. Such quantification provides designers a valuable tool on how robust the model is, and allows for comparing different models by assessing the feasibility regions of the task parameter variation.

6   Discussion

6.1   Linearity Assumption for Arrival Curves

We showed that having an empirical model that can be best approximated by a regression line minimizes the error between the actual and the estimated feasibility region. However, the linearity assumption might not hold for other arrival-curves models. For example, mode-switching [19] yields an increasing arrival curve but with horizontal gaps that correspond to the mode switches, because of the lack of events arrival versus the increasing sliding window size.

6.2   Compositionality and Empirical Arrival Curves

We presented an empirical arrival-curves model that corresponds to a single QNX event, however, our work can be extended by using compositionality [6, 24] to combine the task models describing empirical arrival curves originating from multiple events into a system-level task model. In this case, the robustness evaluation can be performed on a system-level which considers inter- and intra-event interactions in contrast to the evaluation using event-level models.

6.3   Handling Heterogeneous Task Parameters

Finding the feasibility region for the permissible task variation becomes a more complex problem if there exist different parameters α_i and β_i of heterogeneous tasks. One reason is that the mathematical foundation presented in our work assumes that the variations of nominal parameters for multiple tasks are independent. In practice, the tasks of a given real-time system might not encounter the same alteration, and in this case, translating such complex interaction into a single demand-bound function, using compositionality for example, might be a solution that would enable extending our work to multiple dependent tasks.

6.4   Iterative Model Assessment for Anomaly Detection

In anomaly detection, it is essential to evaluate whether the model is good enough during the training process. Our approach can be integrated with the model training procedure, such that the model is iteratively evaluated as new traces are added. A designer can limit the model tolerance to a given specification that relates α and β as represented in the feasibility region, and then a certification procedure can assess the overlap of this region and the computed one.

7   Related Work on Sensitivity Analysis

Our work in this paper assumes that the demand boundaries of a given task are defined and aims to find the feasible task parameters that would not exceed such demand. Contrarily, research work in the domain of schedulability analysis aims to study whether a given set of tasks can be scheduled, i.e., meet the task demand without exceeding a given deadline, using different scheduling methods [2, 15, 25]. However, in the domain of scheduling, the analysis in this paper can be closely related to sensitivity analysis.

Sensitivity analysis [20, 21, 29, 31] studies how much change to task parameters, i.e., execution time or task period, will not violate scheduling constraints. The early work on sensitivity analysis [14] computed the maximum variation of all execution time for a given set of tasks that keep a system schedulable for a rate-monotonic scheduler. Further work considered parameters other than execution time, for example, the authors in [3] presents a feasibility space for task deadlines to meet the constraint of schedulability. Authors in [29–31] study the sensitivity analysis for EDF scheduling through the computation of optimal task parameters such that a given system remains schedulable. Particularly, [29] applied sensitivity analysis considering a varying task execution and [30] considered the case when the task period can be varied, while [31] assumed a fixed ratio between relative deadline and period. Our work considers a novel scope by obtaining feasibility regions for the permissible variation of task parameters, without restricting such variation to a single task variation parameter, to meet defined constraints on the increase and decrease to task demand rather than the schedulability condition.

8   Conclusion

This paper presents an approach to evaluate the robustness of empirical arrival-curves models that characterize the behavior of real-time systems. We derive theoretical bounds on task parameter alteration permissible by the demand variation represented in the demand-bound function of a sporadic task with an implicit deadline under an EDF scheduler. We demonstrate the feasibility of the approach through an abstraction of an empirical arrival-curves model to a demand-bound function of the assumed task model. We evaluate the approach on the arrival-curves models constructed from QNX operating system events that describe the behavior of a real-time system.

Acknowledgments. This work was supported by grants FONDECYT 11160375 and CONICYT-Basal Project FB0008.

References

1. Ahrendts, L., Ernst, R., Quinton, S.: Exploiting execution dynamics in timing analysis using job sequences. IEEE Des. Test **35**(4), 16–22 (2018). https://doi.org/10.1109/MDAT.2017.2746638
2. Baruah, S.K., Mok, A.K., Rosier, L.E.: Preemptively scheduling hard-real-time sporadic tasks on one processor. In: Real-Time Systems Symposium, 11th Proceedings, pp. 182–190. IEEE (1990). doi:https://doi.org/10.1109/REAL.1990.128746

3. Bini, E., Buttazzo, G.: The space of EDF deadlines: the exact region and a convex approximation. Real-Time Syst. **41**(1), 27–51 (2009). https://doi.org/10.1007/s11241-008-9060-7
4. Cardenas, A.A., Stakhanova, N.: Analysis of metrics for classification accuracy in intrusion detection. In: Empirical Research for Software Security, pp. 173–199. CRC Press (2017). https://doi.org/10.1201/9781315154855
5. Carvajal, G., Salem, M., Benann, N., Fischmeister, S.: Enabling rapid construction of arrival curves from execution traces. IEEE Des. Test **35**(4), 23–30 (2018). https://doi.org/10.1109/MDAT.2017.2771210
6. Chakraborty, S., Künzli, S., Thiele, L.: A general framework for analysing system properties in platform-based embedded system designs. In: DATE, vol. 3, p. 10190 (2003). https://doi.org/10.1109/DATE.2003.1253607
7. Chandola, V., Banerjee, A., Kumar, V.: Anomaly detection for discrete sequences: a survey. IEEE Trans. Knowl. Data Eng. **24**(5), 823–839 (2012). https://doi.org/10.1109/TKDE.2010.235
8. Jazdi, N.: Cyber physical systems in the context of industry 4.0. In: 2014 IEEE International Conference on Automation, Quality and Testing, Robotics, pp. 1–4. IEEE (2014). https://doi.org/10.1109/AQTR.2014.6857843
9. Juba, B., Musco, C., Long, F., Sidiroglou-Douskos, S., Rinard, M.C.: Principled sampling for anomaly detection. In: NDSS (2015). https://doi.org/10.14722/ndss.2015.23268
10. Knapp, A.W.: Basic Real Analysis. Springer, Boston (2005). https://doi.org/10.1007/0-8176-4441-5
11. Knuth, D.E., Graham, R.L., Patashnik, O., et al.: Concrete Mathematics. Adison Wesley, Boston (1989)
12. Lampka, K., Forsberg, B., Spiliopoulos, V.: Keep it cool and in time: with runtime monitoring to thermal-aware execution speeds for deadline constrained systems. J. Parallel Distrib. Comput. **95**, 79–91 (2016). https://doi.org/10.1016/j.jpdc.2016.03.002
13. Le Boudec, J.-Y., Thiran, P. (eds.): Network Calculus. LNCS, vol. 2050. Springer, Heidelberg (2001). https://doi.org/10.1007/3-540-45318-0
14. Lehoczky, J., Sha, L., Ding, Y.: The rate monotonic scheduling algorithm: exact characterization and average case behavior. In: Real Time Systems Symposium, 1989, Proceedings, pp. 166–171. IEEE (1989). https://doi.org/10.1109/REAL.1989.63567
15. Liu, C.L., Layland, J.W.: Scheduling algorithms for multiprogramming in a hard-real-time environment. J. ACM (JACM) **20**(1), 46–61 (1973). https://doi.org/10.1145/321738.321743
16. Milenkoski, A., Vieira, M., Kounev, S., Avritzer, A., Payne, B.D.: Evaluating computer intrusion detection systems: a survey of common practices. ACM Comput. Surv. (CSUR) **48**(1), 12 (2015). https://doi.org/10.1145/2808691
17. Neter, J.: Applied linear regression models
18. Neukirchner, M., Axer, P., Michaels, T., Ernst, R.: Monitoring of workload arrival functions for mixed-criticality systems. In: IEEE 34th Real-Time Systems Symposium (RTSS). pp. 88–96, December 2013. https://doi.org/10.1109/RTSS.2013.17
19. Neukirchner, M., Lampka, K., Quinton, S., Ernst, R.: Multi-mode monitoring for mixed-criticality real-time systems. In: 2013 International Conference on Hardware/Software Codesign and System Synthesis (CODES+ ISSS), pp. 1–10. IEEE (2013). https://doi.org/10.1109/CODES-ISSS.2013.6659021

20. Punnekkat, S., Davis, R., Burns, A.: Sensitivity analysis of real-time task sets. In: Shyamasundar, R.K., Ueda, K. (eds.) ASIAN 1997. LNCS, vol. 1345, pp. 72–82. Springer, Heidelberg (1997). https://doi.org/10.1007/3-540-63875-X_44

21. Racu, R., Jersak, M., Ernst, R.: Applying sensitivity analysis in real-time distributed systems. In: Real Time and Embedded Technology and Applications Symposium. RTAS 2005. 11th IEEE. pp. 160–169. IEEE (2005). https://doi.org/10.1109/RTAS.2005.10

22. Salem, M., Crowley, M., Fischmeister, S.: Anomaly detection using inter-arrival curves for real-time systems. In: 2016 28th Euromicro Conference on Real-Time Systems (ECRTS), pp. 97–106. IEEE (2016). https://doi.org/10.1109/ECRTS.2016.22

23. Schleich, B., Anwer, N., Mathieu, L., Wartzack, S.: Shaping the digital twin for design and production engineering. CIRP Ann. **66**(1), 141–144 (2017). https://doi.org/10.1016/j.cirp.2017.04.040

24. Shin, I., Lee, I.: Compositional real-time scheduling framework. In: Real-Time Systems Symposium, 2004. Proceedings. 25th IEEE International, pp. 57–67. IEEE (2004). https://doi.org/10.1109/REAL.2004.15

25. Spuri, M.: Analysis of deadline scheduled real-time systems (1996)

26. Tavallaee, M., Stakhanova, N., Ghorbani, A.A.: Toward credible evaluation of anomaly-based intrusion-detection methods. IEEE Trans. Syst. Man Cybern. Part C (Appl. Rev.) **40**(5), 516–524 (2010). https://doi.org/10.1109/TSMCC.2010.2048428

27. Vestal, S.: Fixed-priority sensitivity analysis for linear compute time models. IEEE Trans. Software Eng. **20**(4), 308–317 (1994). https://doi.org/10.1109/32.277577

28. Wandeler, E., Thiele, L., Verhoef, M., Lieverse, P.: System architecture evaluation using modular performance analysis: a case study. Int. J. Softw. Tools Technol. Transfer **8**(6), 649–667 (2006). https://doi.org/10.1007/s10009-006-0019-5

29. Zhang, F., Burns, A., Baruah, S.: Sensitivity analysis for EDF scheduled arbitrary deadline real-time systems. In: 2010 IEEE 16th International Conference on Embedded and Real-Time Computing Systems and Applications (RTCSA), pp. 61–70. IEEE (2010). https://doi.org/10.1109/RTCSA.2010.12

30. Zhang, F., Burns, A., Baruah, S.: Sensitivity analysis of task period for EDF scheduled arbitrary deadline real-time systems. In: 2010 3rd IEEE International Conference on Computer Science and Information Technology (ICCSIT), vol. 3, pp. 23–28. IEEE (2010). https://doi.org/10.1109/ICCSIT.2010.5564885

31. Zhang, F., Burns, A., Baruah, S.: Task parameter computations for constraint deadline real-time systems with EDF scheduling. In: 2010 International Conference on Computer Design and Applications (ICCDA), vol. 3, pp. V3–553. IEEE (2010). https://doi.org/10.1109/ICCDA.2010.5541363

Property-Driven Timestamps Encoding for Timeprints-Based Tracing and Monitoring

Rehab Massoud[1]([✉]), Hoang M. Le[1], and Rolf Drechsler[1,2]

[1] University of Bremen, 28359 Bremen, Germany
{massoud,hle,drechsler}@informatik.uni-bremen.de
[2] German Research Center of Artificial Intelligence DFKI GmbH, Bremen, Germany

Abstract. Timeprints are temporal regularly-logged signatures, describing a signal's temporal behavior. They have been recently used in on-chip signals tracing and temporal properties checking. Timeprints are generated by aggregations of encoded timestamps marking where signal changes took place. This paper describes different timestamps encoding mechanisms, and shows how some system's temporal properties can be used to create more efficient timestamps. The efficiency of a timestamps-encoding is introduced in terms of the number of collisions in the timeprints-reconstruction solution space. We show how using property-based timestamps encoding reduces the number of such collisions, leading to better chances capturing unexpected behaviors.

Keywords: Timeprints · Timestamps-encoding · Trace-cycles

1 Introduction

In Real-Time (RT) and Cyber-Physical Systems (CPS), non-intrusive cycle-accurate execution tracing is at the top of designers and operators wish-list – if it is affordable. The barrier to accurate traces' logging is: first that these traces are generally infinite, and generated with very high rates; if we get enough ports to log them, storing and processing them are still inherently problematic. Practically, it is always possible to erase old traces that are not needed anymore. But still, the speed of today's ICs – reaching several Gigahertz – result in unmanageably huge logs quickly, making traces very tricky to store, even for few seconds. Second, the ports' capabilities are also limited by the number of pins that can be assigned in a chip and by the pads physical characteristics. Digital logging speeds can not exceed the maximum on-chip clock, so the amount of bits that can be logged per clock-cycle is constrained by the available logging pins. Similarly, it is hard to store useful duration of operation's data on on-chip

This work is supported by the DAAD, University of Bremen (SyDe graduate school and CRDF) and the BMBF grant SELFIE (grant no. 01IW16001).

ⓒ Springer Nature Switzerland AG 2019
E. André and M. Stoelinga (Eds.): FORMATS 2019, LNCS 11750, pp. 41–58, 2019.
https://doi.org/10.1007/978-3-030-29662-9_3

trace buffers, due to their huge amount. Many systems-specific work-around techniques exist to provide accurate logs with relative efficiency, like [1–3,12], but they are very customized, and hence cannot be extended to any generic on-chip signal. Except for [12], all these methods are strictly limited to design-time, as they require physical tracers and/or debuggers to be attached to the chip, and still incur huge logs per second, which makes continuously capturing normal operation periods non-achievable.

Timeprints have been introduced in [9] as a light-weight check-trace, logged all over the execution for a specific on-chip signal. Timeprints could be generated for a single or multiple signals, as per the designers/auditors choice. Each logged timeprint summarizes information about signals temporal behavior during a trace-cycle. Although timeprints do not have explicitly all the details, they still contain enough data to check exactly and accurately what took place on-chip in many cases. To obtain timeprints, the tracing task is divided into consecutive trace-cycles; and one *timeprint* is logged at the end of each cycle. Timeprints contain information about the exact timings of where the traced signal changed its value, and are generated by encoded timestamps aggregations at the designated change instances. The exact timestamps aggregation into a timeprint is a form of lossy compression, where the exact instances are embedded and need to be retrieved by a *reconstruction* process.

The timestamps-encoding used in generating the timeprints, contributes strongly to the uniqueness/ambiguity of the reconstruction, when retrieving the original timings from a timeprint. Some details about how they affect the tracing (trace-size and reconstruction effort) will be presented next in Sect. 2. There we explain how timeprints are generated and the rule of timestamps encoding in generating them. Then, we give an overview of how temporal properties are used in the reconstruction. In this paper, we explore how these properties can be used to obtain more efficient timestamps' encoding. So, after the background, we give a formulation of the problem of timestamps-encoding generation, in Sect. 3. After the formulation, we present the proposed timestamps-encoding generation algorithms (with and without properties) in Sect. 4. The efficiency measures suggested to compare the different timestamps encodings is then introduced in Sect. 5; and applied to a sample experiment in Sect. 6 for illustrating the effect of using some properties. Finally the paper is concluded in the last section.

2   Background on Timeprints

Run-time verification and monitoring been thoroughly considered in the literature; a recent overview can be found in [4], for example. While Run-time Verification (RV) is capable of checking the temporal properties on-line while the system is in operation; it is limited to those specifications known and formalized at design time. Although some parameterized run-time verification techniques exist, like [11], they are still limited in the sense that they operate on a pre-configuration that is fixed a priori to the monitoring and tracing task itself. This means that after the events have already taken place, the trace at hand (if any) would contain data logged according to a pre-configuration. So, if the trace did not contain enough data about the root-cause of the encountered problem, and a new criteria or a specification that is suspected but was not configured to be traced before hand; there is going to be no way of checking the previous trace already at hand for those newly suspected properties. Of course the new configuration can be implemented in future, where it can capture the suspected case, but there might be no guarantee that the captured suspected case is actually the case that took place in the past, and not just another bug/bad-case. In general if the problem is inconsistent –i.e. sporadic–, there could be no way to capture it again. The availability of a trace that keeps some evidence about executions that took place, and contains non-specified properties would help greatly in identifying such sporadic problems' root-cause.

Timeprints aim at providing specification-independent tracing [9], to enable checking a wide range of temporal properties; including those unknown at design-time. Despite such independence, timeprints can still make use of the known traced signal's temporal properties in the sense described in this paper without much affecting their capabilities to detect/debug unspecified behaviors.

Specifications of behaviors and temporal execution traces can be expressed using different available forms of temporal logic. Temporal properties of systems have been a topic for study from both the perspective of specification efficient pre-description for monitoring, like in [8,10] and from specifications mining and learning perspective, as in [7] and [13]. Here, we limit our focus to the temporal properties over a single trace-cycles for simplicity. Expressing them over generic periods is a subject of our next upcoming work. This focus is also reasonable for a first properties-based timestamps codes generation attempt. It also renders the properties description into a very intuitive and simple task. The drawback of course is the need for a translation layer between system level properties (over generic periods) and trace-cycle properties.

In the next subsection, we describe how timeprints are generated. Then, the temporal properties that could be utilized to obtained better timestamps encoding are defined.

2.1 Timeprint Generation

To generate a trace of timeprints of a signal, first: the continuous signal execution trace is divided into trace-cycles; where the first trace-cycle would start at reset or at a defined-check point, and the value of the timeprints is initialized to 0. A trace-cycle length m is defined before the system's deployment; i.e. before tracing starts. A sample intermediate trace-cycle is depicted in Fig. 1. Within a trace-cycle, an encoded time-stamp is assigned to every clock-cycle; for the ith clock-cycle the corresponding code is denoted by $TS(i)$ in the figure. An example of a possible timestamps encoding is shown at the right of Fig. 1. A typical timestamps-encoding would contain m timestamps-codes, each of bit-width b_i, that can be fixed as in the figure. As the traced signal changes its value, a change marker triggers the aggregation of the corresponding timestamp code to the *timeprint TP*. In the example the aggregation function is *XOR*.

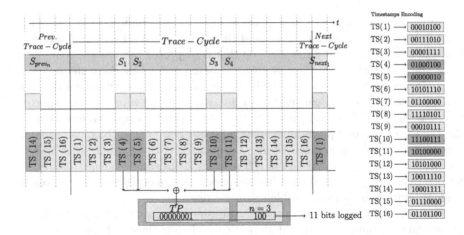

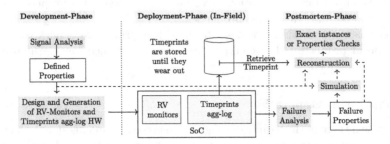

Fig. 1. An intermediate trace-cycle, with its respective timeprint

So TP at the bottom of Fig. 1, is the result of XORing $TS(4)$, $TS(5)$, $TS(10)$, and $TS(11)$. At the end of each trace-cycle, the timeprint value that exists in the timeprint's register is logged; and the tracing continues: XORing the codes, where changes happen. The given encoding in the example is generated by checking some randomly generated codes, for linear independence from each other. Details of the generation algorithm will be given in Sect. 4.

In this paper we fix the aggregation function to XOR, the trace-cycle length to m and the timestamps encoding (code) bit-width to b.

Fig. 2. Timeprints Life Cycle, from [9].

The decision about the trace-cycle characteristics (trace-cycle length, time-prints's width and timestamps encoding) happens at the the signal analysis phase, as at the top left of Fig. 2. The signal analysis is also expected to result in the system's defined properties, from which the decision about which run-time monitors are going to be implemented is taken. A timeprint is an aggregation of timestamps that summarizes the temporal behavior. That is logged by aggregation hardware on-chip (within some System on Chip SoC) or attached to the ports/pins where the tracing is needed. During deployment, a change in the signal values triggers the corresponding timestamp aggregation into the timeprints. At the end of each trace-cycle, the fixed size timeprint is logged; together with the number of changes counted in the trace-cycle. The number of bits needed to log the number of changes is $\lceil log(m-1) \rceil$. This keeps the amount of logging small and constant over time $(b + \lceil log(m-1) \rceil)$.[1] If a problem happened for which its root-cause need to be analyzed or for which an accurate trace is required, the relevant timeprints are retrieved. The failure analysis results in what we call *Failure Properties*, which expresses the visible problematic behavior of the system. To retrieve the accurate timing, (at postmortem) we retrieve exact instances of events from the timeprint via a *Reconstruction*, as in Fig. 2. The reconstruction might use simulation to help aligning the timeprints to the system's visible behavior. All the optional paths are marked by dashed lines.

2.2 Temporal Properties

Timeprints are considered abstractions of the exact temporal execution; but the details lost by a timeprint's abstraction, are retrievable in most of the cases. We do not compromise accuracy during the aggregation process, as most traditional abstractions. Rather, we overlook data that are already known (verified) and hence can be used in the reconstruction. We describe those in terms of *Temporal Properties*, and add them to the reconstruction to decrease the ambiguity. For example, the details that can be retrieved by simulation and alignment to the timeprints trace are not considered lost, because simulation's input can be used in the reconstruction.

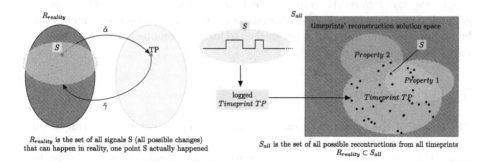

$R_{reality}$ is the set of all signals S (all possible changes) that can happen in reality, one point S actually happened

S_{all} is the set of all possible reconstructions from all timeprints
$R_{reality} \subset S_{all}$

Fig. 3. Timeprints as Abstractions

---

[1] If the signal change rate is known to be below certain limit the number of bits needed to describe the number of changes can still be less than $log(m-1)$. This $log(m-1)$ bits already covers the case of m changes as we aggregate timeprints recursively, i.e. the last timeprint of a trace-cycle is the initial value of the timeprint for the new trace-cycle; hence, if m=0 and the timeprint value changed, it means m changes took place, and if m=0 and the timeprint value is the same, then there has been zero changes in that trace-cycle.

Figure 3 shows the idea behind retrieval of the accurate timing via the reconstruction process; with the help of temporal properties. At the left, the timeprints reconstruction without properties is depicted. A point $S \in R_{Reality}$ corresponds to a specific timing changes in the traced signal that took place on-chip. We call each such a point *Signal S*. This signal would cause the aggregation of some encoded timestamps into the corresponding abstraction, or *Timeprint TP*. This aggregation and logging of the timeprint and the number of changes can be seen as a function $\tilde{\alpha}$ in a Galois insertion, and the reconstruction as $\tilde{\gamma}$, see [9] and the formulation section for more details.

Each point in the timeprints' reconstruction space (on the right of Fig. 3) corresponds to a possible accurate timing that could have led to the timeprint at hand. In the figure, one can see how the ambiguity (many possible accurate timings that could have led to the same timeprints) resulting from the reconstruction process is mitigated via properties. The exclusion of non-real solutions by properties-sets as in the figure corresponds to pruning the search space in the timeprints reconstruction space, as in Fig. 3. The number of solutions can be really huge for large trace-cycle sizes, if properties are not used [5]. This is why the properties usage proposed in [9], is essential to render the whole method acceptable. Ideally, as in Fig. 3, the reconstruction which considers the properties ends up with a unique signal/timing (the intersection of the 3 sets). But this of course might not always be guaranteed; and defining metrics to judge the timeprints efficiency is under development.

In this paper, we suggest using the temporal properties, not only for reconstruction, but also for the generation of the timestamps encoding itself. For this purpose, we need to define briefly what do we mean by a property here. As the focus here is mainly about timing, properties in our context would be temporal properties that relates the timings of events happening within a trace-cycle. In general, if relations between events span more than one trace-cycle, they still can be mapped to some adjacent trace-cycles; so focusing on one trace-cycle does not limit the results presented here.

3   Formulation

The choice of the timestamps has influence on the ambiguity occurring within the logging procedure and thus on the time needed to reconstruct the original signal timings. Intuitively, a sparse choice of timestamps allows only for few possibilities to sum up to the timeprint. It decreases the number of the reconstructed solutions, making it easier to find all of them. However, we can only allow sparsity up to a certain extent as the number of logged bits would grow.

Ideally, we would choose an timestamp encoding that avoids ambiguity at all. This can be achieved by constructing an encoding $TS : [1..m] \rightarrow \mathbb{F}_2^b$, where $TS(1), \ldots, TS(m)$ are linearly independent vectors. Then, reconstructing from the logged timeprint would have a unique solution and it can be obtained quite fast. For example, an *one-hot encoding* would be of this type, and the timeprint would exactly correspond to the signal-changes themselves; i.e. zero solving time.

However, choosing m linearly independent vectors requires that the dimension of $\mathbb{F}_2^b$ is m, hence $b = m$. But this means that the number of bits we need to log depends linearly on m, contradicting our goal to establish a space-efficient logging procedure.

The basic idea behind the timestamps encoding, is to achieve a trade-off in the choice of timestamps by requiring linear independence only up to a depth d. That means each subset of timestamps $T \subseteq TS([1..m])$ of size d is linearly independent. As d grows, the number of solutions to the reconstruction problem decreases, but the number of logged bits b required increases. Computing TS with smallest b given m and d is still an open problem for future research. In this paper we give various algorithms, in the case $d = 4$ and approximate TS and b using a practical heuristic (see Sect. 4).

In the next subsection, we give a formulation of the timestamps encoding (generation) problem before listing the algorithms.

3.1   Timestamps Generation Problem

The required timestamps encoding, as a target, is an ordered set of b-wide bitvectors of m elements. We denote this set be TS. An element of this set can be accessed by an index i, as $TS(i)$, where $TS(i)$ is the ith bitvector, and it represents the code corresponding to the ith clock-cycle inside the trace-cycle. Changes happening to the traced signal, over *trace-cycles* of *length* m, with $m \in \mathbb{N}$, which we simply call *signal*. A *signal* is a map $S : [1..m] \rightarrow \{0,1\}$, where $S(i) = 1$ when a change takes place in the i-th clock-cycle. The logged timeprint TP, is the returned log entry (TP, k) from the aggregation function TP, where $TP = \sum_{i:S(i)=1} TS(i)$ and $k = |\{i \mid S(i) = 1\}|$, representing the number of changes in the signal. We enumerate all signals that represents all possible changes can happen in m-long trace-cycle by σ_m; hence all $S_i \in \sigma$.

Problem: Timestamps Generation 1 (TSG)
Input: trace-cycle length m, bit width $b \in N, log[m] < b < m$, property P.
Task: Find TS, such that: $\forall$ signals $S_i \in \sigma_m$ where $S_i \models P$, $\forall S_{j(j \neq i)} \models P, TP(S_j) \neq TP(S_i)$, where $TP(S_k) = \sum_{i:S_k(i)=1} TS(i)$.

Where a property P is a temporal property defined over S. Another variant of the TSG problem is the one that is limited in the choices of the possible timestamps to a predefined TS.

Problem: Timestamps Generation 2 (TSG)
Input: trace-cycle length m, bit width $b \in N, log[m] < b < m$, property P and input TS_{in}.
Task: Find $TS' \subseteq TS$, such that: $\forall$ signals $S_i \in \sigma_m$ where $S_i \models P$, $\forall S_{j(j \neq i)} \models P, TP(S_j) \neq TP(S_i)$, where $TP(S_k) = \sum_{i:S_k(i)=1} TS(i)$.

An example of the properties is linear independence of degree N; where the property P can be expressed as: that every signal S_i has exactly N ones; or

$|S_i| = N$ has a unique timeprint TP. We denote linear independence of degree N by LI-N.

4 Timestamp Generation Algorithms

In this section, we introduce different practical approaches, which we used to tackle the timestamps encoding/generation problem.

In the next subsections, five different generation methods are explained using:

(1) an SMT solver: we describe the linear independence of degree 4 (LI-4) to the SMT solver and ask for a set of m encoded timestamps of width b,
(2) random generation: starting from a seed, each random integer generated is checked for LI-4 and the required encoding width is then trimmed,
(3) incremental generation: similar to random generation, but starting from 1, and incrementing by one each time for a new choice that is checked then for LI4; the result is the minimum (smallest) possible vectors (time-stamped codes) satisfying a set of conditions,
(4) greedy algorithm: here an algorithm is presented for obtaining the set of fixed width b encoding timestamps, satisfying LI-4, here the full length of these are obtained irrespective of m, and
(5) a composed properties-Based Generation, that takes a set of timestamps as input, and produces a subset of it that fulfills certain property.

For each of these, after describing the algorithm, we present also how the properties can be used in within or at the to of it, for properties-aware timestamps-encoding generation process.

4.1 SMT-Based Time-Stamps Generation

To describe the problem of TSG using an SMT solver, we used bit vector theory and array theory to describe the array of encoded timestamps. LI-4, is encoded as follows: each aggregated 2 entries corresponding to 2 different timestamps-codes, would result in a different aggregation than that of any other 2 different array entries.

As an example of how an SMT solver can be used to generate the time-stamps, the details of the generation for $N = 2$ is illustrated in this section. The exact same criteria can be applied to higher N. Z3 [6] was used to apply the conditions:

For $N \leqslant 2$ (and using XOR gates to merge the time-stamps), the condition (besides the time-stamps' uniqueness) would be:

$$\forall i,j,k,l, [TS_i \oplus TS_j \neq TS_k \oplus TS_l], \tag{1}$$

$$\text{where } (0 < i, j, k, l \leqslant M) \wedge i \neq j \wedge k \neq l$$
$$\wedge (i = k \Rightarrow j \neq l)$$
$$\wedge (j = l \Rightarrow i \neq k)$$
$$\wedge (i = l \Rightarrow j \neq k)$$
$$\wedge (j = k \Rightarrow i \neq l)$$

Similar conditions can be derived for higher N.

The resultant SMT instance is:

$$
\begin{aligned}
&(exists \ ((ts\_var \ (Array \ (\_BitVec3)(\_BitVec6))))) \\
&(forall \ ((k \ (\_BitVec3)) \\
&(l \ (\_BitVec3))(m \ (\_BitVec3))(n \ (_BitVec3))) \\
&(let((A1(and \quad (not(= k \quad l)) \quad (not(= n \quad m)) \\
&\qquad\qquad (=> (= k \quad m)(not(= l \quad n))) \\
&\qquad\qquad (=> (= l \quad n)(not(= k \quad m))) \\
&\qquad\qquad (=> (= k \quad n)(not(= l \quad m))) \qquad\qquad (2) \\
&\qquad\qquad (=> (= l \quad m)(not(= k \quad n))))) \\
&(A2(not(= \quad (bvxor \\
&(select \ ts\_var \ k)(select \ ts\_var \ l)) \\
&\qquad (bvxor \\
&(select \ ts\_var \ m)(select \ ts\_var \quad n)))))) \\
&(=> A1 \quad A2))))
\end{aligned}
$$

which reads as: first, we assume the time-stamps are contained in an array called ts_var, representing a variable array which the SMT solver tries to find a solution for. In this example, we generate time-stamps of width 6 (i.e. array elements are 6 bits wide bitvectors). We generate 8 time-stamps for a trace-cycle of length 8. Hence, this array has an index of length 3 to address it's elements. The statement $A1$ expresses uniqueness of the pair of indexes of each pair of time-stamps. Namely, for every two different indexes of time-stamps to be XORed (k, l), k does not equal l and to compare the result to the result of any other pair of time-stamps of indexes (m, n), where also $m \neq n$, if $k = m$, this implies that l must be$\neq n$ to make (m, n) a different pair, and similarly goes all the other implications to ensure the uniqueness of pairs of time-stamps. When this uniqueness $(A1)$ is satisfied, this implies $A2$, which is that the two results of XORing those two pairs of time-stamps (indexed by (k, l) and (m, n)) are different (not equal, in the SMT formula 2). This implication should hold for all k, l, m, n and we assert that there is a time-stamps array ts_var that fulfils this condition. A solution that the SMT solver finds for this formula gives a list of 8 time-stamps that are guaranteed to give different timeprints (here results of XOR's), for any 2 different time instances.

An alternative encoding of the LI-4 condition, would be to encode all the XOR results into an array of distinct elements.

Unfortunately, this method does not scale. It becomes very expensive to use for more than 16 clock-cycles long (array size). While it takes about $\tilde{1}0\,$s for trace length of 16 clock-cycles, it takes around 10 h for 32 clock-cycles. All those measurements are taken on a machine with Intel Core™ i7 CPU@ 2.67 GHz with 8 GiB memory.

4.2 Random-Based Time-Stamps Generation

Random number generators can be used to generate the time-stamps faster. Each newly generated time-stamp is checked to be fulfilling the condition in Eq. 1. If this is satisfied, the results of XORing the new time-stamp with all previously existing time-stamps is added into a List, to check the next randomly generated time-stamp against, and this goes on. The generation is illustrated in Algorithm 1.

Algorithm 1. Random Time-stamps Generation Algorithm

    Data: *initialize   random − seed*
    Data: *ListOfXORListisempty*
1 $TS_0 = rand()$
2 **for** i *in* $1 \longrightarrow M$ **do**
3     $TS_i = rand()$
4   **while** *IsThereCollision(TS_i)* **do**
5        $TS_i = rand()$
       /* where IsThereCollision(TS_i) is shown below   */
6 *IsThereCollision(TS_i)* {
7 **for** j *in* $0 \longrightarrow i$ **do**
8   **if** *IsRepeated($TS_i \oplus TS_j$)* **then**
       /* where IsRepeated checks whether $TS_i \oplus TS_j$ has been obtained
         before in the XORList, and TempXORList   */
9   BackTrack(RemoveTempXORListFromXORList) return *True*
10   **else**
11   AddToTempXORList($TS_i \oplus TS_j$)
12 *ConfirmAddToTempXORList*
13 return *false*
14 }

Notice that in line 9, backtracking is needed to the last ensured *ListOfXORed* content, when a collision is detected; not to add a non-actually-existing XOR results, from a time-stamp that has become rejected after the collision detection.

This method is much faster than using an SMT solver and the minimal time-stamps generation, mentioned in the next subsection. Time-stamps for trace-cycle's lengths of thousands of clock-cycles can be generated in seconds or few minutes at most on a machine with Intel Core^{TM} i7 CPU@ 2.67 GHz with 8 GiB memory. However, this method does not properly detect if there are no possible solutions to the given constraints; the designer should thus be sure that the method should eventually terminate.

4.3 Incremental Time-Stamps Generation

This method is very similar to the random generation, but instead of randomly generating the time-stamp, before checking them, the latest time-stamp candidate is constantly incremented (by one). Afterwards, the new time-stamp candidate is checked whether it fulfills the conditions or not (in which case the time-stamp is incremented and checked again). This method takes longer time than the random generation but remains faster than the SMT solver and can create time-stamps for trace-cycles of a thousand clock-cycles in less than a day on the same machine mentioned before.

Although this method seems to be providing the minimal size of time-stamps, it is still possible to provide the same size with random generation because we know from the number of possible permutations how many bits are needed to present them. However, non standard size random generators have to be manually developed. So this last method turned out to be the preferred solution for custom bitvector sizes that are not available in the standard C data-types.

After the above-mentioned generation, the time-stamps are utilized to mark each clock-cycle within the trace-cycle. By the time a given signal is toggled, the corresponding time-stamp is XORed into the timeprint, and logged at the end of the trace-cycle. At a host computer that this logged timeprint is transmitted to, the exact instances of change, which triggered the corresponding time-stamps into the XOR-aggregate described earlier, then need to be recovered.

4.4 Greedy Algorithm

This algorithm is similar to the incremental algorithm. It starts from scratch and iterates over all possible timestamps in increasing order (i.e. treating them as integer values). Then, it greedily adds a new timestamp to the set of selected timestamps, if doing so does not violate the property under consideration (e.g. LI-4). Due to some optimizations such as look-ahead elimination of timestamps that are guaranteed to violate the property, this algorithm is much faster than the incremental one. It also generates a maximum m timestamps that could be generated of width b, satisfying the property.

4.5 Properties Based Generation

After obtaining a set of Timestamps by linear, incremental or greedy algorithm, a filtration of the results by removing those who do not produce a unique timeprint is possible. The resultant timestamps set would be resilient not only to this property it was filtered based on but also might perform better when the signal satisfies other related properties.

5 Assessment

To assess the efficiency of the algorithms presented, we have first to define a criteria to evaluate the quality of an ordered set of timestamps. One parameter that can be considered a measure, for example, is the bit width b of the timestamp. The smaller b is, the less logs are going to be incurred, and hence the better a time-stamp encoding is. When a system designer wants to add timeprints based tracing to their system, the first criteria to define is the length of a trace-cycle m (or at least $m_{min} \leq m \leq m_{max}$), which represents the target timestamps set size. Longer trace-cycles result in less logging effort –as one fixed width timeprint is logged at the end of each trace-cycle–. However, in general, longer trace-cycles means harder (bigger) reconstruction problem size and may require bigger b to make the reconstruction process reasonable for the expected number of changes that could happen within a trace-cycle. A typical range of acceptable trace-cycle length is in the range of hundreds to thousands. If we can find better trace reconstruction algorithms than the one we have now, [9], we can further increase m.

As in the formulation of the algorithms that encode the timestamps in a trace-cycle, the target is usually to find a maximum trace-cycle length for a fixed b for efficient logging.

When using a set of timestamps, we can assess its performance based on a number of measures. For example, the number of collisions they produce when reconstructing both generic signals; and reconstructing signals related to the properties similar to those they were generated to accommodate. The measures we shall cover here are:

- The run time of the timestamps encoding generation algorithm. Although the algorithm is usually run once, and the result is hard encoded in the hardware. As the problem is very hard, is still important that the run time is not prohibitive.
- How good the generated encoding is able to distinguish between different signals. A perfect encoding (one-bit hot encoding) would be able to distinguish between all S. But this would lead to $b = m$, which destroys the basic idea of *timeprints: having compressed logs*. The quality of the generated encoding is measured by the number of collisions in the reconstruction made using it.
- How long the encoded timestamps generated by an algorithm could be. Some algorithms can generated a maximum encoding (maximum m) for a given b; while others are limited by a given b and m.
- How a specific encoding affects the reconstruction time.

5.1 Algorithms Run-Time

In order to compare algorithms' run times (in Table 1), we tried all the algorithms with $m = 1024$ and b given as 32 when it is passed as input to the algorithm, and when it is indicated as an output, the value is the one reached by reaching the required 1024 timestamps. Since the comparison is not fully possible due to how

Table 1. Comparison between different Timestamps Encoding Algorithms, generating 1024 timestamps, or for an input of 1024 timestamps (in LI4-to-LI6)

Algorithm	Alg.2	b	m_{max}	Run-Time	new m
Inc-Index	-	output	input	~ 0	-
Random	-	input	input	~ 0	-
SMT-LI4	-	input	input (limiting)	timeout	-
Inc-LI4	-	output	input (limiting)	6 h 51 min 6.037 s	-
Ran-LI4	-	input	input	59 min 24.473 s	-
Greedy-LI4	-	output	output	17 min 53.622 s	-
LI4-to-LI6	Inc-L14	input	output	20 min 51.181 s	79
$m_{in}=1024$	Ran-L14	input	output	19 h 33 min 53.949 s	214
	Greedy-L14	input	output	9 min 5.284 s	71

the different algorithms work, we can still give here a qualitative comparison of the run-time, and whether they have the b, m parameters as input or output.

In Table 1, first rows gives six direct algorithms run-times. **Inc-index** in the first row is just using the index i of a timestamp $TS(i)$ as the coded timestamp. These codes are not for any practical usage, but they are meant to act as a reference to judge properties-usage over a generated set of timestamps versus another. **Random** in the second row is a trivial generated codes, without any checks. It is also used a reference to compare other methods, or properties-based methods to. **SMT-LI4** is the SMT based generation of a set of timestamps that has linear independence of degree 4; which was described in Sect. 4.1. **Inc-LI4** is the incremental generation algorithm described in Sect. 4.3. **Random-LI4** is the algorithm described in Sect. 4.2. **Greedy-LI4** is the algorithm described in Sect. 4.4. The part labeled by **LI4-to-LI6** shows the run time for generating a set of linear independent timestamps of degree 6 from a set that is already generated by any of the three LI4 methods (Inc-LI4, Random-LI4, and Greedy-LI4). For these sets we have a new length m of the newly generated timestamps set. The generated sets are of smaller size because the timestamps that do not fulfill the LI6 condition are removed. Notice that the surviving timestamps from the Random-LI4 are much more than those surviving from other algorithms; but they also took much longer time to be generated.

5.2   Encoding with Properties

The tables below shows the number of reduced timestamps in the case of applying some properties; for example the property that n consecutive changes happened; we denote them by P3, P4, ... Pn. The reduced timestamps (out of 1000) applying Pn are shown in table (a). Table (b)[2] shows the number of remaining timestamps

---

[2] Inc-Ind-k: means the incremental code **Inc-Index** with increments of weight k.

Table 2. Reduction in timestamps (a) and the number of remaining timestamps in reference to the original input set (b).

		P3	P4	P5	P6	P7	P8
Inc-Index		0	791	0	731	0	335
Random		0	0	0	0	0	0
Inc-LI4	-	2	18	0	13	0	11
Ran-LI4	-	0	0	0	0	0	0
Greedy-LI4	-	2	24	0	13	0	9
Comb-LI4-LI6	Inc-LI4	-	0	0	0	0	0
	Ran-LI4	-	0	0	0	0	0
	Greedy-LI4	-	5	0	7	0	9

(a) Reduction in m for different P_n

	D1b2	D2b2	D1b3	D2b3
Inc-Ind-1	15/200	12/200	70/200	81/200
Inc-Ind-3	151/200	114/200	112/200	125/200
Inc-Ind-7	149/200	112/200	149/200	174/200
Random-8	193/200	185/200	143/200	143/200

(b) The number of remaining timestamps in m after applying properties of different "constant delays (1,2,1,2) between 2 and 3 changes" consecutively

after applying the properties in each column. Notice that odd number of changes in the properties is very useful in both types of properties, as it does not cause reduction in the number of timestamps even for incremental codes.

In Table 2a, it could be seen how the greedy algorithm results still contains collisions when it comes to consecutive occurrences of changes.

6   Case-Study

We illustrate the whole process of timeprints based tracing and properties checking to the sensors and braking data of an autonomous driving donkey-car; the one in Fig. 4. The car was equipped with three ultrasonic sensors and four servo motors for the brakes, one at each wheel[3].

Fig. 4. Donkey car

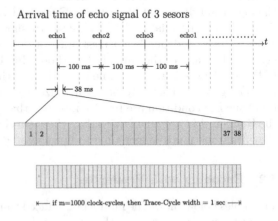

Fig. 5. Sensor data in a trace-cycle

---

[3] This set-up was already existing in our research-group within the bachelor's-project DRIVE, and the data was obtained upon request from the students.

The car has been equipped with three ultrasonic sensors, each is configured to fire every 300 ms, and they were set up to fire in row, separated by 100 ms each. As can be seen in the Fig. 4, the 3 sensors are considered redundant; they will either all had an echo for the fired signal, or not. The difference in their orientation is minimum, and is adjustable in our set-up. The accurate time at which the echo of the fired signal is received, reflects the time taken for the signal to be reflected, and hence if it is smaller than certain threshold it would mean that the car has to start using the brakes to stop enough before it hits the obstacle. The accurate relative difference between the 3 echo signals received can also say something about at which direction exactly is the obstacle; especially if their orientation was different from each other.

To trace accurately the signal's echo time, we trace the signal at the pin "echo" of the sensor, which is raised high (i.e. to 1) by the sensor when it sends the sonic burst, and then goes low when it receives its echo. An echo would be received anyway, but if it was received before 38 ms, it means there is an obstacle closer than the range of about 5–6 m, and the distance can be calculated from the delay. If it was received at 38 ms, it means that the obstacle is relatively far away (more than 6 m away). In our set-up because the car is moving slowly and the room is already small, the car considers braking only when the echo is received before 20 ms. Each sensor receives a fire command from software each 300 ms, and replies back raising a pin high and then low when it receives the echo or when the 38 ms expires. As a designer's trace-related choice, we choose to combine all the signals together (3 firing signals + 3 echos received), as already one pin indicates the firing and the echo reception; and tracing each pin separately would mean logging three timeprints instead of one. We also know that the sensors send their signals in an interleaving manner; which makes it mostly possible to know which echo belongs to which sensor. Possibility remains, that sometimes due to different shifts in the firing times overlaps may occur. But even these shifts can be described as properties and used to point these out in many cases.

To illustrate using properties, we first use the clear example of the basic property of: 3 changes would occur separated by 100 ms, each followed by another change within 38 ms; see Fig. 5. Accumulated delays (shifts due to non accurate firings) also can be modeled, but will not be discussed here to keep the illustration simple. This property can be used to encode shorter timestamps that performs better than those who do not consider such property. But first before we delve into using properties, we show how to decide about the timestamps-set size (trace-cycle length and timestamps bit-width) in the first place. We clarify this more in the following.

Trace-Cycle Length. First, we have to decide about a trace-cycle size. Because the property is going to be described in terms of changes happening (or not happening) at consecutive clock-cycles within a trace-cycle. An echo transmitted and received from one sensor would cause 2 changes at the clock-cycles where it was raised high, and then at where it was made low. Here we assume it is enough to know when the signal is received within 1 ms resolution. The decision about tracing-precision should depend mainly on the system needs. Here for example: it depend on the allowed time to stop and the distance, the car is allowed to drive before it completely stops, starting from the moment and position it detects an obstacle. One msec accuracy corresponds to 17 cm error range in the distance of the obstacle at the moment it was detected. So, a clock-cycle of 1 ms is suitable. Choice of trace-cycle length of 100–1000 clock-cycles (i.e. 0.1 to 1 s) is in the desired range from hundreds to thousand; for small log size and reasonable timeprint-reconstruction time. What affects the exact choice of the trace-cycle length is the number of changes encountered inside one cycle; because this affects hugely both the ambiguity and reconstruction time; so we discuss it next.

Number of Changes in a Trace-Cycle. If we choose a 1000 clock-cycles trace-cycle, we shall have ≤20 changes corresponding to firing and receiving the echo signals of the three sensors over 1 s. If we choose 0.1 s trace-cycle's length (100 clock-cycles), we'll have about 2 changes per trace-cycle, which is very few (makes it for example more efficient to just use the index and not to use any encoding at all). For a 200 clock-cycles trace-cycle, the index would need at least 8 bits, and for 4 changes that are expected within such trace-cycle a log would be 32 bits or even more if shifts lead to more changes. So at 200 clock-cycles, using encoding starts to make sense. In the following we will use both lengths: 200 and 1000 to illustrate the choice of the upcoming design options.

Using Properties. For example, here because we are getting one pair change separated by 38 clock-cycles every $\sim$ 100 ms, we can make the encoding more robust (produces unique results) for occurrences separated by less than 38 clock-cycles; like those in Table 2(b): D38b2, D37b2, D36b2... etc. Notice that any delay between 2 changes is already covered by LI-4, but these properties can be applied to other simple encodings like Index-k and Random-16/24 to make them produce unique results in these cases. One can choose to encode D100b10, D101b10, D102b10 and D103b10, for the 1000 trace-cycle. These properties encode the consecutive 10 firings within such trace cycle, within 100, 101, 102 and 103 ms distance (of no change, i.e. zeros) between them; as these delays have been seen frequently in heuristics. Encoding a property over a trace-cycle means modeling all its possible occurrences within the trace-cycle.

Notice that applying different properties has to be done recursively, until the set of timestamps saturates, and with keeping in memory removed timestamps-codes that might be returned back if the base-timestamp –based on which they were removed– was itself removed. Saturation means that no removals to be done in the set because of violations of the properties. Of course to return a timestamp from such state it has to be checked recursively, to make sure it does not brake any of the previously checked properties. The list of remaining timestamps is checked at every stage, and is considered fulfilling the properties when all the properties-checks cannot remove any more timestamps from the list. An algorithm has been implemented to apply the above properties recursively. But it shall be published later after being checked for wider range of properties.

Generating Timestamps. For trace-cycles of lengths from 200 maximum timestamps bit-width should be 32, to make more efficient than logging the indexes. Less than this, we can try Inc-Index-k with applying the above mentioned properties. Inc-Index-1 would lead to the smallest bit-width if applied correctly. A faster way to reach the set of timestamps fulfilling these properties is to use a list of randomly generated timestamps and check them recursively. Random of width 8 would be too small even for 200 clock-cycles. 16 and 24 would be reasonable to try. An LI4 fulfilling timestamps set (satisfies linear independence of degree 4, either generated with random, incremental or greedy) would be already fulfilling all the delay between 2 properties (Dxb2). So to these LI4 fulfilling sets we can apply to them only the Dxb10 properties to enhance their performance (would then produce unique results).

7   Conclusion

We presented an overview of how some simple temporal properties can be used in enhancing the generation of timestamps encoding used in the timeprints-based monitoring. Using temporal properties in the case study shows the plausibility and potential of obtaining timestamps that produces more unique results. This is a new way to look at the timestamps encoding, i.e. before we only focused on linear independence, which was not easy to extend beyond the 4th degree. Now by applying properties to existing timestamps-sets, we can obtain timestamps that are more capable pf producing unique results in the cases that are known to take place. Here, we simply have made more scattering of the similar solutions that could co-inside, and avoided having them mapped to the same timeprint.

References

1. ARM CoreSight and ETM (2018). http://www.arm.com
2. (2018). https://www.ghs.com/products/supertraceprobe.html
3. (2018). www2.lauterbach.com/pdf/main.pdf
4. Bartocci, E., et al.: Specification-based monitoring of cyber-physical systems: a survey on theory, tools and applications. In: Bartocci, E., Falcone, Y. (eds.) Lectures on Runtime Verification. LNCS, vol. 10457, pp. 135–175. Springer, Cham (2018). https://doi.org/10.1007/978-3-319-75632-5_5
5. Chini, P., Massoud, R., Meyer, R., Saivasan, P.: Fast witness counting. CoRR abs/1807.05777 (2018). http://arxiv.org/abs/1807.05777
6. de Moura, L., Bjørner, N.: Z3: an efficient SMT solver. In: Ramakrishnan, C.R., Rehof, J. (eds.) TACAS 2008. LNCS, vol. 4963, pp. 337–340. Springer, Heidelberg (2008). https://doi.org/10.1007/978-3-540-78800-3_24
7. Giantamidis, G., Tripakis, S.: Learning moore machines from input-output traces. In: Fitzgerald, J., Heitmeyer, C., Gnesi, S., Philippou, A. (eds.) FM 2016. LNCS, vol. 9995, pp. 291–309. Springer, Cham (2016). https://doi.org/10.1007/978-3-319-48989-6_18
8. Maler, O., Nickovic, D., Pnueli, A.: Checking temporal properties of discrete, timed and continuous behaviors. In: Avron, A., Dershowitz, N., Rabinovich, A. (eds.) Pillars of Computer Science. LNCS, vol. 4800, pp. 475–505. Springer, Heidelberg (2008). https://doi.org/10.1007/978-3-540-78127-1_26

9. Massoud, R., Le, H.M., Chini, P., Saivasan, P., Meyer, R., Drechsler, R.: Temporal tracing of on-chip signals using timeprints. In: Design Automation Conference DAC-19 (2019). https://doi.org/10.1145/3316781.3317920
10. Mehrabian, M., et al.: Timestamp temporal logic (TTL) for testing the timing of cyber-physical systems. ACM Trans. Embed. Comput. Syst. **16**(5s), 169:1–169:20 (2017). https://doi.org/10.1145/3126510
11. Schumann, J., Moosbrugger, P., Rozier, K.Y.: R2U2: monitoring and diagnosis of security threats for unmanned aerial systems. In: Bartocci, E., Majumdar, R. (eds.) RV 2015. LNCS, vol. 9333, pp. 233–249. Springer, Cham (2015). https://doi.org/10.1007/978-3-319-23820-3_15
12. Park, S.B., Hong, T., Mitra, S.: Post-silicon bug localization in processors using instruction footprint recording and analysis (ifra). In: TCADIC (2009)
13. Vazquez-Chanlatte, M., Deshmukh, J.V., Jin, X., Seshia, S.A.: Logical clustering and learning for time-series data. In: Majumdar, R., Kunčak, V. (eds.) CAV 2017. LNCS, vol. 10426, pp. 305–325. Springer, Cham (2017). https://doi.org/10.1007/978-3-319-63387-9_15

Mixed-Time Signal Temporal Logic

Thomas Ferrère[1], Oded Maler[2], and Dejan Ničković[3]([✉])

[1] IST Austria, Klosterneuburg, Austria
[2] VERIMAG, University of Grenoble Alpes, Grenoble, France
[3] AIT Austrian Institute of Technology, Vienna, Austria
dejan.nickovic@ait.ac.at

Abstract. We present Mixed-time Signal Temporal Logic (STL-MX), a specification formalism which extends STL by capturing the discrete/continuous time duality found in many cyber-physical systems (CPS), as well as mixed-signal electronic designs. In STL-MX, properties of components with continuous dynamics are expressed in STL, while specifications of components with discrete dynamics are written in LTL. To combine the two layers, we evaluate formulas on two traces, discrete- and continuous-time, and introduce two interface operators that map signals, properties and their satisfaction signals across the two time domains. We show that STL-MX has the expressive power of STL supplemented with an implicit T-periodic clock signal. We develop and implement an algorithm for monitoring STL-MX formulas and illustrate the approach using a mixed-signal example.

1 Introduction

Cyber-physical systems (CPS) typically combine together components with *continuous* dynamics (analog components, sensors, actuators) and components with *discrete* dynamics (digital controllers, software, firmware). Models of (most) components with discrete dynamics operate in discrete (clocked) time and manipulate values in a finite domain. In contrast, components with continuous dynamics are modeled as operating in continuous time over real-valued variables. The interaction between these two classes of heterogeneous components is typically done via *converters*, which allow passing from one time and value domain to another. For instance, analog and digital components in an analog mixed-signal (AMS) design can be integrated by inserting *analog-to-digital* (A/D) and *digital-to-analog* (D/A) converters providing the necessary interface, as illustrated in Fig. 1.[1] The time and value domain differences between analog and digital components pose difficult design and verification challenges.

While correctness evidence is imposed for safety-critical CPS applications (see for example the automotive standard ISO 26262 [14]), CPS verification remains an important bottleneck in the development process, resulting in up to

---

[1] This is a simplification of the AMS setting: not all interaction between analog and digital components goes through A/D and D/A conversions.

© Springer Nature Switzerland AG 2019
E. André and M. Stoelinga (Eds.): FORMATS 2019, LNCS 11750, pp. 59–75, 2019.
https://doi.org/10.1007/978-3-030-29662-9_4

70% of the project effort. Verification of CPS in industry is almost exclusively based on *simulation*, where each scenario can take several hours of simulation time. Simulation traces are typically observed by verification engineers for correctness, resulting in a manual, ad-hoc and error-prone process.

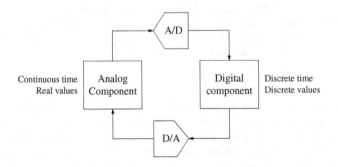

Fig. 1. A typical scenario in AMS design.

Specification-based monitoring is a pragmatic, yet rigorous approach for systematic simulation-based verification. *Signal Temporal Logic* (STL) [18,19] is a declarative specification language for describing properties of CPS behaviors. As an extension of the real-time temporal logics MTL [17] and MITL (*Metric Interval Temporal Logic* [2]), STL allows us to reason about real-time properties of real-valued signals. STL and its extensions have been used to specify and reason about properties of systems coming from Industry 4.0, semiconductor, automotive, avionics, medical devices and system and synthetic biology domains – see the survey [4] for a detailed list of references.

While STL effectively provides support for combining Boolean and real-valued signal properties, the time domain remains continuous for *all* signals. Such specifications are not fully aligned with the actual practice in development and integration of CPS where designers of discrete dynamics components often reason about time in terms of clock ticks, and hence the natural logic to express digital properties is a discrete-time temporal logic. It would be extremely counterproductive if verification engineers, due to few continuous/discrete dynamics interface properties, would have to transform all digital properties to dense time. We propose a simple and transparent solution in which both time models can co-exist. We illustrate the class of properties that motivate us via the following example.

Example 1. Consider the following stabilization property for a CPS system with sampling period $T = 200$. Whenever a discrete signal *cmd* is set up by the digital controller from false to true, the absolute value of a continuous signal x in an analog component must become lower than 1 within 600 time units and remain continuously within that range for at least 300 time units. This informal specification is illustrated in Fig. 2.

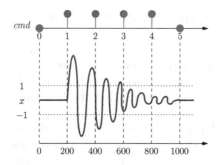

Fig. 2. Illustration of a stabilization specification.

We propose *Mixed-time Signal Temporal Logic* (STL-MX) as a specification language that extends STL to express properties both in terms of discrete logical time (clock ticks) and dense real time. In essence, STL-MX consists of two layers: (1) the standard discrete-time temporal logic LTL [22] for specification of digital component properties; and (2) STL for specification of analog component behaviors. To combine the two layers, we split the trace into a continuous-time and discrete-time part, and introduce two time-mapping operators @^{cd} and @^{dc} that formalize the conversions between continuous-time and discrete-time formulas and signals. We then study the expressiveness of this formalism and show that STL-MX can be effectively embedded into STL when provided with an explicit sampling signal. We present an implementation of the monitoring algorithm for STL-MX and demonstrate the utility of mixed-time specifications on a case study from the AMS domain.

Related Work. The main inspiration for this paper comes from the work that introduces digital clocks into LTL [11]. That work does not consider continuous interpretation of time, in contrast to this paper.

In the past years, there has been a rich body of work on various extensions of MTL and STL. There, continuous-time specification languages were extended with various quantitative semantics [1,9,12,13,15]. In particular, STL was then extended with support for time-frequency properties [10] and freeze quantification [8]. A first-order logic of signals [3] has been recently developed as a generalization of STL and STL with freeze quantification. None of these extensions considers both discrete and continuous time interpretation of the logic at the same time.

The problem of different time domains has been also studied in other domains. Ptolemy [5] provides a prototyping and simulation environment for modelling heterogeneous systems that combine different models of computations. We also mention the GEMOC initiative [6] that is promoting coordinated use of modelling languages with possibly different models of computation, and hence time domains.

2   Mixed-Time Signal Temporal Logic

In this section we introduce the syntax of STL-MX and its semantics over both discrete-time and continuous-time signals. Since we are interested in monitoring we focus on signals of bounded duration. Without loss of generality we assume all digital signals in the circuit to range over the Booleans and analog signals to range over the reals.

Let $\mathbb{D}$ be a value domain, typically $\mathbb{B}$ or $\mathbb{R}$. A discrete-time signal w is a function $w : \{0, 1, \ldots, s\} \to \mathbb{D}$ for $s > 0$. A continuous-time signal u is a function $u : [0, r) \to \mathbb{D}$ for $r > 0$. We denote by $|w|$ and $|u|$ the *length* of signals w and u, respectively. In the rest of this paper, we use $r = |u|$ and $s = |w|$. Relative to u and v, a *sampling* $\tau : \{0, 1, \ldots, s\}$ is a monotonically increasing sequence of times $0 = \tau[0] < \tau[1] < \cdots < \tau[r] < s \in \mathbb{R}_{\geq 0}$. A sampling indicates the times at which the discrete values are read. We say that the sampling τ is *periodic* (with period $T \in \mathbb{R}_{>0}$) when $\tau[i] = iT$ for all $i \in \{0, 1, \ldots, s\}$.

A sequence of disjoint non-empty intervals $I_0 \cdot I_1 \cdots I_k$ is a time partition compatible with a finitely-varying continuous-time Boolean signal x if (1) $\bigcup_{0 \leq j \leq k} I_j = [0, |x|)$ and (2) Each I_j is of the form (t_j, t_{j+1}), $[t_j, t_{j+1})$, $(t_j, t_{j+1}]$ or $[t_j, t_{j+1}]$ such that $t_j \leq t_{j+1}$, $\forall t, t' \in I_j$, $x(t) = x(t')$. The *coarsest time partition* associated with x satisfies the additional property: (3) Whenever $t \in I_j$ and $t' \in I_{j+1}$ then $x(t) \neq x(t')$.

Let $P = \{p_1, \ldots, p_m\}$ be a set of Boolean variables and let $X = \{x_1, \ldots, x_n\}$ be a set of real valued variables. A constraint over X is a predicate of the form $x \prec c$, where $x \in X$, $\prec \in \{<, \leq, =, \geq, >\}$ and $c \in \mathbb{Q}$. A *mixed-time signal temporal logic* (STL-MX) formula ψ is either a continuous-time formula α or a discrete-time formula φ defined over X and P according to the following grammar[2]

$$\alpha ::= x \prec c \mid \neg\alpha \mid \alpha_1 \lor \alpha_2 \mid \alpha_1 \mathcal{U}_I \alpha_2 \mid \alpha_1 \mathcal{S}_I \alpha_2 \mid @^{\mathrm{dc}}(\varphi)$$
$$\varphi ::= p \mid \neg\varphi \mid \varphi_1 \lor \varphi_2 \mid \bigcirc\varphi \mid \ominus\varphi \mid \varphi_1 \mathcal{U}\varphi_2 \mid \varphi_1 \mathcal{S}\varphi_2 \mid @^{\mathrm{cd}}(\alpha)$$

where $\bigcirc$, $\ominus$, $\mathcal{U}$ and $\mathcal{S}$ are temporal *next*, *previous*, *until* and *since* operators, $p \in P$, $x \in X$, $c \in \mathbb{Q}$ and I is an interval of the form $[a, b]$, $[a, b)$, $(a, b]$, (a, b), $[a, \infty)$ or (a, ∞) where $0 \leq a < b$ are rational numbers.

We can define other usual operators $\Diamond_I$ (*eventually*), $\Box_I$ (*always*), $\Diamondslash_I$ (*once*), and $\boxminus_I$ (*historically*) as syntactic abbreviations with $\Diamond_I \varphi := \mathsf{true}\mathcal{U}_I\varphi$, $\Box_I \varphi := \neg\Diamond_I \neg\varphi$, and likewise for past operators – discrete time syntax can be enriched with corresponding constructs. Note that timing interval subscripts may be omitted in when equal to $[0, +\infty)$.

Example 2. We formalize the stabilization property from Example 1 by the following STL-MX formula:

$$\Box(((\ominus \neg cmd) \land cmd) \to @^{\mathrm{cd}}(\Diamond_{[0,600]} \Box_{[0,300]}(|x| < 1)))$$

---

[2] We use the same symbols for Boolean and temporal connectives in both continuous-time and discrete-time formulas. The distinction between the two layers is defined by the context. Note that each valid formula is classified unambiguously as discrete-time or continuous-time.

Let w be a discrete-time m-dimensional Boolean signal and u be a continuous-time real-valued n-dimensional signal, which we assume such that $u_\tau[i] \in [0, r)$ for all $i \in \{0, 1, \ldots, s\}$. We denote by $\pi_p(w)$ and $\pi_x(u)$ the respective projections of w and u on variables p and x. Conversely, for w and w' over the same time domain we denote by $w\|w'$ the pairing of signals w and w', such that $\pi_v(w\|w') = \pi_v(w)$ when variable v is a dimension of w and $\pi_v(w\|w') = \pi_v(w')$ when v is a dimension of w'. Finally, we use $\oplus$ for the Minkowski sum of intervals, that is, $[a_1, b_1] \oplus [a_2, b_2] = [a_1 + a_2, b_1 + b_2]$.

In what follows, we assume a sampling τ given independently and globally defined. The semantics of a discrete-time STL-MX formula φ with respect to signals w and u is described via the satisfaction relation $(w, u, i) \models^d \varphi$, indicating that signals w and u satisfy φ at discrete time index i. Similarly, the semantics of a continuous-time STL-MX formula α with respect to signals w and u is described via the satisfaction relation $(w, u, t) \models^c \alpha$, indicating that signals w and u satisfy α at time t. These relations are defined recursively below.

$$(w, u, i) \models^d p \quad\leftrightarrow \pi_p(w)[i] = 1$$
$$(w, u, i) \models^d \neg\varphi \quad\leftrightarrow (w, u, i) \not\models^d \varphi$$
$$(w, u, i) \models^d \varphi_1 \vee \varphi_2 \leftrightarrow (w, u, i) \models^d \varphi_1 \text{ or } (w, u, i) \models^d \varphi_2$$
$$(w, u, i) \models^d \bigcirc\varphi \quad\leftrightarrow i < |w| \text{ and } (w, u, i+1) \models^d \varphi$$
$$(w, u, i) \models^d \ominus\varphi \quad\leftrightarrow i > 0 \text{ and } (w, u, i-1) \models^d \varphi$$
$$(w, u, i) \models^d \varphi_1\mathcal{U}\varphi_2 \leftrightarrow \exists i \le i' < |w| \text{ s.t. } (w, u, i') \models^d \varphi_2 \text{ and}$$
$$\forall i \le i'' < i', (w, u, i'') \models^d \varphi_1$$
$$(w, u, i) \models^d \varphi_1\mathcal{S}\varphi_2 \leftrightarrow \exists 0 \le i' \le i \text{ s.t. } (w, u, i') \models^d \varphi_2 \text{ and}$$
$$\forall i' < i'' \le i, (w, u, i'') \models^d \varphi_1$$
$$(w, u, i) \models^d @^{cd}(\alpha) \leftrightarrow (w, u, \tau[i]) \models^c \alpha$$

$$(w, u, t) \models^c x \prec c \quad\leftrightarrow \pi_x(u)[t] \prec c$$
$$(w, u, t) \models^c \neg\alpha \quad\leftrightarrow (w, u, t) \not\models^c \alpha$$
$$(w, u, t) \models^c \alpha_1 \vee \alpha_2 \leftrightarrow (w, u, t) \models^c \alpha_1 \text{ or } (w, u, t) \models^c \alpha_2$$
$$(w, u, t) \models^c \alpha_1\mathcal{U}_I\alpha_2 \leftrightarrow \exists t' \in (t \oplus I) \cap [0, |u|) \text{ s.t. } (w, u, t') \models^c \alpha_2 \text{ and}$$
$$\forall t'' \in (t, t'), (w, u, t'') \models^c \alpha_1$$
$$(w, u, t) \models^c \alpha_1\mathcal{S}_I\alpha_2 \leftrightarrow \exists t' \in (t \ominus I) \cap [0, |u|) \text{ s.t. } (w, u, t') \models^c \alpha_2 \text{ and}$$
$$\forall t'' \in (t', t), (w, u, t'') \models^c \alpha_1$$
$$(w, u, t) \models^c @^{dc}(\varphi) \leftrightarrow (w, u, \mathrm{argmax}_{i \in \{0,1,\ldots,s\}}\tau[i] \le t) \models^d \varphi$$

We use $(w, u) \models \psi$ as a shorthand for $(w, u, 0) \models^d \psi$ or $(w, u, 0) \models^c \psi$ according to the type of ψ. Based on these definitions and given a pair (w, v) we associate with each discrete-time formula φ and a continuous-time formula α their respective Boolean *satisfaction signals* w_φ and u_α such that for all $i \in \{0, 1, \ldots, s\}$ and $t \in [0, r)$, $w_\varphi[i] = 1$ iff $(w, u, i) \models^d \varphi$ and $u_\alpha[t] = 1$ iff $(w, u, t) \models^c \alpha$.

As we see, temporal operators inherit their semantics from LTL and STL. The semantics of new interface operators $@^{cd}$ and $@^{dc}$ are illustrated in Fig. 3.

We remark that the choice of whether the top level STL-MX formula is continuous-time or discrete-time is typically application-dependent. Expressing a property of a discrete-time component (e.g. a controller) that drives another

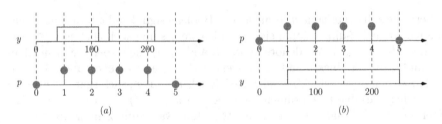

Fig. 3. Semantics of (a) $p = @^{cd}(y)$ and (b) $y = @^{dc}(p)$ for $T = 50$.

continuous-time component (e.g. a plant) usually results in a discrete-time top-level formula, and vice versa.

We now point out some properties of this logic. We say that two discrete-time formulas φ_1 and φ_2 are *equivalent*, denoted by $\varphi_1 \sim \varphi_2$ if for all signals u, w and time indexes i we have $(w, u, i) \models^d \varphi_1 \leftrightarrow (w, u, i) \models^d \varphi_2$. The equivalence between continuous-time formulas is defined similarly. It should be obvious that by converting a discrete-time formula into a continuous-time one, and in turn converting it back to a discrete-time formula we do not alter the meaning of the original formula. We illustrate this observation with the continuous-time signal (i.e. propositional formula) $y = @^{dc}(p)$ from Fig. 3(b) obtained by converting the discrete-time signal p – it is clear that translating y back to a discrete-time signal yields p.

Proposition 1. *Any discrete-time formula φ satisfies* $@^{cd}(@^{dc}(\varphi)) \sim \varphi$.

This stems directly from the fact that any time index $i \in \{0, 1, \ldots, s\}$ verifies $\mathrm{argmax}_{j \in \{0,1,\ldots,n\}} \tau[j] \leq \tau[i] = i$. Conversely, for some time $t \in \mathbb{R}$ we generally do not have $\tau_{\mathrm{argmax}_{j \in \{0,1,\ldots,n\}} \tau[j] \leq t} = t$ hence nothing can be said of $@^{dc}(@^{cd}(\alpha))$ as compared with α, perhaps except for being a piecewise-constant approximation of its satisfaction signals.

Notwithstanding, time mapping operators commute with propositional connectives. For instance, first negating the propositional formula y from Fig. 3(a) and than coverting it to a discrete time formula is equivalent to first converting y to a discrete time formula and then doing the negation.

Proposition 2. *The following equivalences hold for any discrete-time formulas $\varphi, \varphi_1, \varphi_2$ and continuous-time formulas $\alpha, \alpha_1, \alpha_2$:*

$$@^{dc}(\neg\varphi) \sim \neg @^{dc}(\varphi) \qquad @^{dc}(\varphi_1 \vee \varphi_2) \sim @^{dc}(\varphi_1) \vee @^{dc}(\varphi_2)$$
$$@^{cd}(\neg\alpha) \sim \neg @^{cd}(\alpha) \qquad @^{cd}(\alpha_1 \vee \alpha_2) \sim @^{cd}(\alpha_1) \vee @^{cd}(\alpha_2)$$

Checking these facts is straightforward, let us for instance prove the first equivalence. Taking w, u some discrete and continuous signals and a time instant t, we have $(w, u, t) \models^c @^{dc}(\neg\varphi) \leftrightarrow (w, u, \mathrm{argmax}_{j \in \{0,1,\ldots,n\}} \tau[j] \leq t) \models^d \neg\varphi \leftrightarrow (w, u, \mathrm{argmax}_{j \in \{0,1,\ldots,n\}} \tau[j] \leq t) \not\models^d \varphi \leftrightarrow (w, u, t) \not\models^c @^{dc}(\varphi) \leftrightarrow (w, u, t) \models^c \neg @^{dc}(\varphi)$.

As expected, temporal operators do not enjoy such properties. The following section may provide more insight in this respect.

3 Expressivity

STL-MX has similar expressive power as STL when supplemented by a "digital clock", as we show in the following.

Let w be a discrete signal. We say that a continuous signal w^τ is the *right-continuation* of w when $w^\tau[t] = w[\text{argmax}_{j\in\{0,1,\dots,n\}}\tau[j] \le t]$ for all $t \in [0, r)$. Note that on discrete Boolean signals, the interpretation of $@^{dc}$ is exactly right-continuation with period T. Conversely, the interpretation of $@^{cd}$ is the sampling of continuous signals at *absolute* times $\tau[i]$, $i \in \{0, 1, \dots, s\}$. For this purpose, let us introduce a special continuous Boolean signal clk with the following definition:

$$\text{clk} : t \mapsto \begin{cases} 1 & \text{when } t = \tau[i] \text{ for some } i \in \{0, 1, \dots, s\} \\ 0 & \text{otherwise} \end{cases}$$

Following definitions of Sect. 2, let us define STL to be continuous-time STL-MX formulas without discrete-time sub-formulas. For a continuous signal u, a time t, and an STL formula α the standard STL semantics reads $(\emptyset, u, t) \models^c \alpha$.

We now inductively define a syntactical mapping σ from STL-MX to STL formulas:

$$\sigma(p) = p \qquad\qquad\qquad \sigma(@^{cd}(\alpha)) = \neg\text{clk}\,\tilde{\mathcal{S}}(\text{clk} \wedge \sigma(\alpha))$$
$$\sigma(\bigcirc \varphi) = \neg\text{clk}\,\mathcal{U}(\text{clk} \wedge \sigma(\varphi)) \qquad\qquad \sigma(\neg\varphi) = \neg\sigma(\varphi)$$
$$\sigma(\ominus \varphi) = \neg\text{clk}\,\mathcal{S}(\text{clk} \wedge \sigma(\varphi)) \qquad\qquad \sigma(\varphi_1 \vee \varphi_2) = \sigma(\varphi_1) \vee \sigma(\varphi_2)$$
$$\sigma(\varphi_1 \mathcal{U} \varphi_2) = \sigma(\varphi_2) \vee (\sigma(\varphi_1)\,\mathcal{U}_{(0,+\infty)}\sigma(\varphi_2))$$
$$\sigma(\varphi_1 \mathcal{S} \varphi_2) = \sigma(\varphi_2) \vee (\sigma(\varphi_1) \wedge \sigma(\varphi_1)\,\mathcal{S}_{(0,+\infty)}(\sigma(\varphi_2)\,\mathcal{S}_{(0,+\infty)}\text{true}))$$

$$\sigma(x \prec c) = x \prec c \qquad\qquad\qquad \sigma(@^{dc}(\varphi)) = \sigma(\varphi)$$
$$\sigma(\alpha_1 \mathcal{U}_I \alpha_2) = \sigma(\alpha_1)\mathcal{U}_I\sigma(\alpha_2) \qquad\qquad \sigma(\neg\alpha) = \neg\sigma(\alpha)$$
$$\sigma(\alpha_1 \mathcal{S}_I \alpha_2) = \sigma(\alpha_1)\mathcal{S}_I\sigma(\alpha_2) \qquad\qquad \sigma(\alpha_1 \vee \alpha_2) = \sigma(\alpha_1) \vee \sigma(\alpha_2)$$

This mapping is such that an STL-MX formula ψ is satisfied by some signal if and only if its STL translation is satisfied by the right-continuation of the discrete signal, paired with the original continuous signal and the clock. Note that in STL p is associated with a continuous-time satisfaction signal.

Example 3. The stabilization property (2) is mapped into the following STL formula.

$$\Box((\neg\text{clk}\,\mathcal{S}(\text{clk} \wedge \neg cmd)) \wedge cmd) \rightarrow (\neg\text{clk}\,\tilde{\mathcal{S}}(\text{clk} \wedge \Diamond_{[0,600]}\Box_{[0,300]}|x < 1|))$$

Theorem 1. *Let w be a discrete-time signal and let u be a continuous-time signal. Taking w^τ as the right-continuation of w, we have:*

1. for any discrete-time STL-MX formula φ and $i \in \mathbb{N}$

$$(w, u, i) \models^d \varphi \quad \textit{iff} \quad (\emptyset, w^\tau\|u\|\text{clk}, \tau[i]) \models^c \sigma(\varphi)$$

2. *for any continuous-time* STL-MX *formula* α *and* $t \in \mathbb{R}_{\geq 0}$

$$(w, u, t) \models^c \alpha \quad \text{iff} \quad (\emptyset, w^\tau \| u \| \text{clk}, t) \models^c \sigma(\alpha)$$

Proof. (1) and (2) are shown conjointly by induction on the formula structure. For propositions in P we have $\pi_p(w^\tau)[\tau[i]] = \pi_p(w)[i]$ from the definition of w^τ. Boolean connectives naturally commute with the right-continuation operation as seen in Proposition 2. Now looking at the $\bigcirc$ operator, we can check that for a discrete-time formula φ and a discrete signal w, the right-continuation of $^w\bigcirc \varphi$ requires that w_φ holds at the previous discrete time value. Operator $\ominus$ is symmetrical. The discrete *until* does not pose any problem. For the discrete *since*, note that its continuous counterpart $\mathcal{S}_{(0,\infty)}$ has *left*-continuous semantics. Notably, rather than looking for a witness of φ_2 at some time t' in the past, we look for a time t' such that φ_2 holds immediately before; this is done by the formula $\sigma(\varphi_2)\,\mathcal{S}_{(0,+\infty)}\text{true}$. Concerning operator $@^{\text{dc}}$, the translation states the continuous formula α was true on the previous clock tick. For pure continuous-time operators, semantics are unchanged so we only apply recursively the translation to treat possible discrete sub-formulas. Finally, the $@^{\text{cd}}$ operator performs a right-continuation operation, hence we only need to translates discrete-time formulas it applies to.

Corollary 1. *For a periodic sampling $\tau[i] = iT$, the satisfaction of an* STL-MX *formula by a signal reduces (in polynomial time) to the satisfaction of an* STL *formula.*

Proof. A T-periodic clock is definable in STL by the formula

$$\delta_T := \text{clk} \wedge \Box(\text{clk} \to (\Box_{(0,T)} \neg\text{clk} \wedge \Diamond_{(0,T]} \text{clk}))$$

Assuming such a clock signal, we may impose on any Boolean signal p to be a T-period right-continuation signal using the formula

$$\gamma_p := \Box \left(\begin{array}{l} ((\neg p\,\mathcal{S}_{(0,+\infty)}\text{true} \wedge p) \to \text{clk}) \;\wedge\; ((p\,\mathcal{S}_{(0,+\infty)}\text{true} \wedge \neg p) \to \text{clk}) \\ \wedge\; (p \to p\,\mathcal{U}_{(0,+\infty)}\text{true}) \;\wedge\; (\neg p \to \neg p\,\mathcal{U}_{(0,+\infty)}\text{true}) \end{array} \right)$$

The two first conjuncts ensure that left-discontinuities can only occur on clock ticks, while the last two conjuncts enforce right-continuity. Now given some STL-MX formula ψ, we construct the STL formula

$$\psi' := \sigma(\psi) \wedge \delta_T \wedge \bigwedge_{p \in P} \gamma_p$$

It follows from Theorem 1 that ψ is satisfied if and only if ψ' is satisfied. Clearly the size of ψ' is linear in the size of ψ.

4   Monitoring STL-MX

In this section, we present the monitoring procedure for STL-MX. Like previous work on STL monitoring [21], our procedure is closely related to the idea of *temporal testers* advocated in [16,24] for discrete time and dating, in fact, back to [23]. These are *acausal* transducers that realize the semantics of the temporal logic operators as follows. For an operator OP interpreted over time domain $\mathbb{T}$, the temporal tester $\mathcal{T}_{\text{OP}}$ takes as input a Boolean $\mathbb{T}$-signal y and outputs another Boolean signal y' such that if y is the satisfaction signal of some formula φ then y' is the satisfaction signal of OPφ. For example the tester for *next* in discrete time realizes a forward shift, that is, $y'[i] = y[i+1]$. A temporal tester for a compound temporal logic formula φ is obtained by composing temporal testers for the basic operators, following the parse tree of the formula.

Testers have been proposed for several temporal logics, in particular for LTL [24] and MITL [20]. The monitoring procedure for STL described in [19] follows closely the temporal testers paradigm although the transduction function is computed directly on signals, without explicit construction of automata as in [20]. The compositional structure of temporal testers allows us to fully separate the monitoring of the LTL and STL components of an STL-MX formula and reuse existing results. We focus in this paper on the construction of temporal testers for the two additional operators @^{cd} and @^{dc} that interface discrete and continuous time. We refer the reader to [19,20,24] for details regarding the other operators. A high-level overview of the procedure as applied to the stabilization formula (2) is provided in Fig. 4.

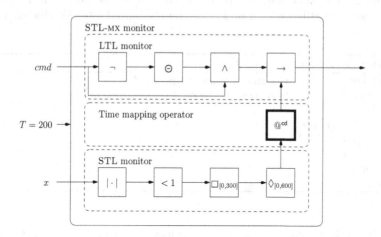

Fig. 4. Monitor based on temporal testers for formula (2).

The temporal tester $\mathcal{T}_{@^{\text{cd}}}$, realizing the semantics of the @^{cd} operator, takes as input a continuous-time Boolean signal u, and outputs a discrete-time Boolean signal w obtained by sampling u at multiples of T. The computation, based on a time partition $I_0 \cdot I_1 \cdots I_n$ compatible with u, is illustrated in Algorithm 1.

Algorithm 1. Temporal tester $\mathcal{T}_{@^{cd}}$.

Require: Continuous Boolean signal u, a sampling period T
Ensure: Discrete Boolean signal $w = @^{cd}(u)$
1: $k \leftarrow 0$
2: **for** $j = 0$ to n **do**
3:    **while** $\tau[k] \in I_j$ **do**
4:       $w[k] \leftarrow u(I_j)$
5:       $k \leftarrow k + 1$
6:    **end while**
7: **end for**
8: **return** w

Proposition 3. *Given a satisfaction signal y of a continuous-time formula α, a time index i, we have that $\mathcal{T}_{@^{cd}}(y)[i] = 1$ if and only if the satisfaction signal $u_{@^{cd}(\alpha)}[i] = 1$.*

The temporal tester $\mathcal{T}_{@^{dc}}$, realizing the semantics of the $@^{dc}$ operator, takes as input a discrete Boolean signal w and outputs a continuous-time Boolean signal u which "extends" the value of w at every time index i by holding it throughout the interval $[\tau[i], \tau[i+1])$. The procedure for computing $\mathcal{T}_{@^{dc}}$ is illustrated in Algorithm 2. Note that the time partition created by the procedure is not the coarsest one compatible with u and it can be minimized later for efficiency.

Algorithm 2. Temporal tester $\mathcal{T}_{@^{dc}}$.

Require: Discrete Boolean signal w, sampling period T
Ensure: Continuous Boolean signal u, the right continuation of w
1: $k \leftarrow 0$
2: **for** $j = 0$ to $|w|$ **do**
3:    $I_k \leftarrow [\tau[j], \tau[j+1])$
4:    $u[I_k] \leftarrow w[j]$
5: **end for**
6: **return** u

Proposition 4. *Given a discrete-time Boolean signal p, a time t and a sampling period T, we have that $\mathcal{T}_{@^{dc}}(p)[t] = 1$ if and only if the satisfaction signal $w_{@^{dc}(p)}[t] = 1$.*

For every other operator OP in the syntax, we already dispose of a transducer $\mathcal{T}_{OP}$ with the corresponding lemma. We can now state the main result that our monitoring procedure computes the appropriate satisfaction signals.

Theorem 2. *Let w and u be discrete-time and continuous time-signals and let T be a sampling period. Then*

1. *For a discrete-time* STL-MX *formula φ, $\mathcal{T}_\varphi(w, u) = w_\varphi$;*
2. *For a continuous-time* STL-MX *formula α, $\mathcal{T}_\alpha(w, u) = u_\alpha$.*

We implemented the monitoring procedure for STL-MX formulas, following the structure shown in Fig. 4 and applying STL-MX operations directly to discrete-time and continuous-time signals. The implementation consists of three layers: an LTL monitor, an STL monitor and the time mapping operations. Keeping the separation between the three layers allows us to monitor not only STL-MX specifications, but also its LTL and STL subsets for purely digital and analog applications, respectively. The implementation was written in C++ for GNU/Debian Linux x86 machines.

5   Case Study

We applied the monitoring implementation for STL-MX to verify basic properties of a simplified model of a $\Delta\text{-}\Sigma$ modulator, a basic component in analog to digital conversion. The circuit has an analog input, and a clocked digital output for typical integration in an ADC circuit. It is composed of the following building blocks: subtractor, integrator, threshold, and pulse generator. The overall architecture appears at Fig. 5.

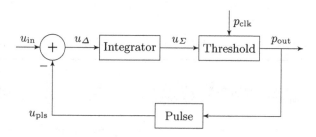

Fig. 5. Block diagram for the $\Delta\text{-}\Sigma$ modulator

The input voltage is first summed with the negated output of the control loop. The resulting voltage is integrated over time; when a value superior to a constant v_0 is reached, a threshold crossing is detected and we see a rising edge in the output. This signal is used to generate a pulse which is subtracted from the input, closing the loop. The effect is that during this pulse the integral sharply goes back below the threshold, and the cycle goes on. In addition, a clock is introduced so as to facilitate synchronization of the digital output. It is placed at the threshold detection level; rather than precisely detecting a crossing we simply test for crossings on clock edges. Here is a short mathematical description of the idealized components realizing this behavior:

$$u_\Delta[t] = u_{\text{in}}[t] - u_{\text{pls}}[t] \qquad \text{(substractor)}$$

$$u_\Sigma[t] = A \cdot \int_0^t u_\Delta[t'] \, dt' \qquad \text{(integrator)}$$

$$p_{\text{out}}[i] = \begin{cases} 1 \text{ if } u_\Sigma[iT] \geq v_0 \\ 0 \text{ otherwise} \end{cases} \qquad \text{(threshold)}$$

$$u_{\text{pls}}[t] = \begin{cases} v_1 \text{ if } p_{\text{out}}[\lfloor\frac{t}{T}\rfloor - 1] = 0 \text{ and } p_{\text{out}}[\lfloor\frac{t}{T}\rfloor] = 1 \\ \quad \text{and } t - \lfloor\frac{t}{T}\rfloor \cdot T \leq T_{\text{pls}} \\ v_0 \text{ otherwise} \end{cases} \qquad \text{(pulse)}$$

where $T = 3.2\,\mu s$ is the period. We can see that in our model, the output is clocked with a frequency of $312\,500\,Hz$. The integrator gain is set to $A = 10^5$, the voltage threshold is $v_0 = 0.0\,V$. The pulse generator outputs piecewise constant signals, with high voltage of $v_1 = 3.3\,V$ and hold time of $T_{\text{pls}} = 2.5\,\mu s$. We have implemented the circuit as a mixed-signal model using Mentor Graphics' Questa ADMS [7] and simulated it against a variety of input signals. The simulation traces thus generated have been monitored with respect to STL-MX properties by our implementation of the procedure described in this paper.

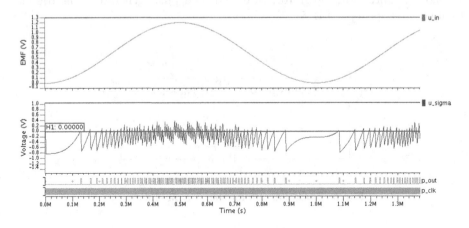

Fig. 6. Simulation trace (w_1, u_1) extracted with $u_{\text{in}} : t \mapsto 0.6\cos(1000 \cdot 2\pi \cdot t) + 0.6$.

We start with the following safety property:

Property 1. When we observe a rise in the output, the voltage out of the integrator has to return to a value below the threshold at the next clock tick.

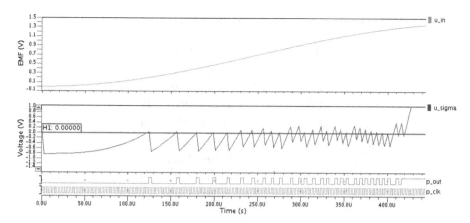

Fig. 7. Simulation trace (w_2, u_2) extract with $u_{\text{in}} : t \mapsto 0.7 \cos(1000 \cdot 2\pi \cdot t) + 0.7$

This property is expressed in STL-MX as:

$$\psi_1 := \Box((\ominus \neg p_{\text{out}} \wedge p_{\text{out}}) \rightarrow \bigcirc @^{\text{cd}} u_{\Sigma} < v_0)$$

The specification ψ_1 would be used during the integration steps of the design cycle so as to check that the input applied to the Δ-Σ modulator has a range conforming to its sampling capabilities.

First we simulate the design with a sinusoidal input at rate 1 kHz and amplitude 0.6 V; this gives us the trace (w_1, u_1) of Fig. 6. The circuit appears to behave adequately, and we have $(w_1, u_1) \models \psi_1$. When we modify slightly the input by setting the amplitude to 0.7 V; the simulation produces the trace (w_2, u_2) of Fig. 7. We can detect a failure of our second property around 420 μs, as the signal u_{Σ} goes back above v_0 within a single clock period. In our implementation the signal u_{Σ} would then indefinitely stay above the threshold, stalling the modulation. The algorithm that concludes that $(u_2, w_2) \not\models \psi_1$.

The Δ-Σ modulator should also verify some some functional specifications, for instance:

Property 2. When the input voltage is above 1.05 V for 12.8 μs the output must have a sequence of two consecutive spikes starting over that time frame.

Such a property, which can be used during the design phase of the Δ-Σ modulator itself, ia expressed as the following STL-MX formula:

$$\psi_2 := \Box(\Box_{[0,12.8]} u_{\text{in}} > 1.05 \rightarrow \Diamond_{[0,12.8]} @^{\text{cd}}(\neg p_{\text{out}} \wedge \bigcirc p_{\text{out}} \wedge \bigcirc^2 \neg p_{\text{out}} \wedge \bigcirc^3 p_{\text{out}}))$$

We test this specification on our design for several inputs of the form $t \mapsto A_1 \cos(f_1 \cdot 2\pi \cdot t) + A_2 \cos(f_2 \cdot 2\pi \cdot t) + B$ with $A_1 + A_2 + B = 1.2$ and f_1, f_2 ranging from 500 Hz to 10 kHz. The property is satisfied as long as the frequency in the input stays small; on the other hand rapidly varying signals introduce quantization uncertainty, and the property no longer holds. In all 6 simulation scenarios, we were able to show that ψ_2 is satisfied.

Table 1. STL-MX monitoring execution times.

Property	Sim. nb.	u_Σ	u_{in}	p_{out}	time (ms)
ψ_1	1	20 470		727	143
ψ_1	2	2 771		58	104
ψ_2	3		26 207	971	45
ψ_2	4		27 926	971	50
ψ_2	5		29 495	971	51
ψ_2	6		31 298	1 212	58
ψ_2	7		32 133	1 212	59
ψ_2	8		33 005	1 212	61

In Table 1, we present the evaluation of the STL-MX implementation to the Δ-Σ modulator case study. The experiments were done on an Intel Core i7-2620M CPU @ 2.7 GHz machine with 8 GB of RAM with the Windows 7 Enterprise operating system. The implementation was executed on Ubuntu 13.04 Linux operating system running on the Windows VMware Player 5.0.2 virtual machine. The table shows for a given STL-MX property, the size of the input signals in terms of the number of samples and the execution for monitoring the property, measured in milliseconds. The evaluation results show that the monitoring procedure induces minimal overhead, since for both properties ψ_1 and ψ_2, the time needed to monitor input of size ranging between $21,000$ and $35,000$ samples never exceeded 150 milliseconds.

Finally, we compare the STL-MX specification ψ_2 to the STL specification $\psi_2' = \sigma(\psi_2)$, where

$$\psi_2' := \Box(\Box_{[0,12.8]}\, u_{in} > 1.05 \rightarrow \Diamond_{[0,12.8]}(\neg p_{out} \wedge (\neg clk\, \mathcal{U}\,(clk \wedge p_{out}))) \wedge$$
$$(\neg clk\, \mathcal{U}\, clk \wedge (\neg clk\, \mathcal{U}\,(clk \wedge \neg p_{out}))) \wedge$$
$$(\neg clk\, \mathcal{U}\, clk \wedge (\neg clk\, \mathcal{U}\,(clk \wedge (\neg clk\, \mathcal{U}\,(clk \wedge p_{out}))))))$$

This example demonstrates the potential value of explicitly separating the two time domains in specifications, which results in formulas that are more succinct and easier to read.

6 Concluding Remarks

We have introduced very useful syntactic and semantic constructs that provide for co-existence of discrete and continuous-time specifications for runtime monitoring of CPS and mixed signal designs. This work is a first step toward a framework for system-wide specification-based verification, covering both discrete-time, bounded-value and continuous-time, real-valued domains. We studied the theoretical properties of this mixed-time logic STL-MX and extended a monitoring framework to handle these two time domains. We demonstrated the usability of the methodology and tool on a case-study. As for the future one may think of the following directions:

1. Automatic insertion of $@^{cd}$ and $@^{dc}$ conversion operators based on type inference so as to facilitate further the expression of properties by the user;
2. Studying other conversion operators, more sophisticated than the currently used periodic sample and hold. For example, the truth value of a discrete-time signal at i can be based on integrating values at continuous time in some interval around iT. One can also think of event-based conversion in asynchronous style, unlike this work that focused on clocked digital components;
3. Studying a tighter interaction between the monitoring procedure and the simulators that generate the heterogeneous traces.
4. Equpping STL-MX with quantitative semantics. We expect that adding quantitative semantics based on the infinity norm to STL-MX shall be straightforward. However, we will need to investigate whether the basic properties of the language would be still preserved under this quantitative semantics. In addition, it would be an interesting challenge to add a more cumulative or average-based semantics to the specification language.

Acknowledgments. This research was supported in part by the Austrian Science Fund (FWF) under grants 27 S11402-N23 (RiSE/SHiNE) and Z211-N23 (Wittgenstein Award), and by the Productive 4.0 project (ECSEL 737459). The ECSEL Joint Undertaking receives support from the European Union's Horizon 2020 research and innovation programme and Austria, Denmark, Germany, Finland, Czech Republic, Italy, Spain, Portugal, Poland, Ireland, Belgium, France, Netherlands, United Kingdom, Slovakia, Norway.

References

1. Akazaki, T., Hasuo, I.: Time robustness in MTL and expressivity in hybrid system falsification. In: Kroening, D., Păsăreanu, C.S. (eds.) CAV 2015. LNCS, vol. 9207, pp. 356–374. Springer, Cham (2015). https://doi.org/10.1007/978-3-319-21668-3_21
2. Alur, R., Feder, T., Henzinger, T.: The benefits of relaxing punctuality. J. ACM **43**(1), 116–146 (1996). https://doi.org/10.1145/227595.227602
3. Bakhirkin, A., Ferrère, T., Henzinger, T.A., Nickovic, D.: The first-order logic of signals: keynote. In: Proceedings of the International Conference on Embedded Software, EMSOFT 2018, Torino, Italy, September 30 - October 5, 2018, p. 1 (2018). https://doi.org/10.1109/EMSOFT.2018.8537203
4. Bartocci, Ezio, et al.: Specification-based monitoring of cyber-physical systems: a survey on theory, tools and applications. In: Bartocci, Ezio, Falcone, Yliès (eds.) Lectures on Runtime Verification. LNCS, vol. 10457, pp. 135–175. Springer, Cham (2018). https://doi.org/10.1007/978-3-319-75632-5_5
5. Buck, J.T., Ha, S., Lee, E.A., Messerschmitt, D.G.: Ptolemy: a framework for simulating and prototyping heterogenous systems. Int. J. Comput. Simul. **4**(2), 155–182 (1994)

6. Combemale, B., et al. (eds.): Joint Proceedings of the First International Workshop On the Globalization of Modeling Languages (GEMOC 2013) and the First International Workshop: Towards the Model Driven Organization (AMINO 2013) Co-located with the 16th International Conference on Model Driven Engineering Languages and Systems (MODELS 2013), Miami, USA, September 29 - October 04, 2013, CEUR Workshop Proceedings, vol. 1102. CEUR-WS.org (2013). http://ceur-ws.org/Vol-1102
7. Graphics Corporation, M.: Questa ADMS. http://www.mentor.com/products/fv/advance_ms/
8. Dluhos, P., Brim, L., Safránek, D.: On expressing and monitoring oscillatory dynamics. In: HSB, pp. 73–87 (2012). https://doi.org/10.4204/EPTCS.92.6
9. Donzé, A., Maler, O.: Robust satisfaction of temporal logic over real-valued signals. In: Chatterjee, K., Henzinger, T.A. (eds.) FORMATS 2010. LNCS, vol. 6246, pp. 92–106. Springer, Heidelberg (2010). https://doi.org/10.1007/978-3-642-15297-9_9
10. Donzé, A., Maler, O., Bartocci, E., Nickovic, D., Grosu, R., Smolka, S.: On temporal logic and signal processing. In: Chakraborty, S., Mukund, M. (eds.) ATVA 2012. LNCS, pp. 92–106. Springer, Heidelberg (2012). https://doi.org/10.1007/978-3-642-33386-6_9
11. Eisner, C., Fisman, D., Havlicek, J., McIsaac, A., Van Campenhout, D.: The definition of a temporal clock operator. In: Baeten, J.C.M., Lenstra, J.K., Parrow, J., Woeginger, G.J. (eds.) ICALP 2003. LNCS, vol. 2719, pp. 857–870. Springer, Heidelberg (2003). https://doi.org/10.1007/3-540-45061-0_67
12. Fainekos, G.E., Pappas, G.J.: Robustness of temporal logic specifications. In: Havelund, K., Núñez, M., Roşu, G., Wolff, B. (eds.) FATES/RV -2006. LNCS, vol. 4262, pp. 178–192. Springer, Heidelberg (2006). https://doi.org/10.1007/11940197_12
13. Fainekos, G.E., Pappas, G.J.: Robustness of temporal logic specifications for continuous-time signals. Theor. Comput. Sci. 410(42), 4262–4291 (2009). https://doi.org/10.1016/j.tcs.2009.06.021
14. ISO 26262:2011: Road Vehicles - Functional Safety. ISO, Geneva, Switzerland
15. Jakšić, S., Bartocci, E., Grosu, R., Ničković, D.: Quantitative monitoring of STL with edit distance. In: Falcone, Y., Sánchez, C. (eds.) RV 2016. LNCS, vol. 10012, pp. 201–218. Springer, Cham (2016). https://doi.org/10.1007/978-3-319-46982-9_13
16. Kesten, Y., Pnueli, A.: A compositional approach to CTL* verification. Theor. Comput. Sci. 331(2–3), 397–428 (2005). https://doi.org/10.1016/j.tcs.2004.09.023
17. Koymans, R.: Specifying real-time properties with metric temporal logic. Real-time Syst. 2(4), 255–299 (1990). https://doi.org/10.1007/BF01995674
18. Maler, O., Nickovic, D.: Monitoring temporal properties of continuous signals. In: Lakhnech, Y., Yovine, S. (eds.) FORMATS/FTRTFT -2004. LNCS, vol. 3253, pp. 152–166. Springer, Heidelberg (2004). https://doi.org/10.1007/978-3-540-30206-3_12
19. Maler, O., Nickovic, D.: Monitoring properties of analog and mixed-signal circuits. STTT 15(3), 247–268 (2013). https://doi.org/10.1007/s10009-012-0247-9
20. Maler, O., Nickovic, D., Pnueli, A.: From MITL to timed automata. In: Asarin, E., Bouyer, P. (eds.) FORMATS 2006. LNCS, vol. 4202, pp. 274–289. Springer, Heidelberg (2006). https://doi.org/10.1007/11867340_20
21. Maler, O., Nickovic, D., Pnueli, A.: Checking temporal properties of discrete, timed and continuous behaviors. In: Avron, A., Dershowitz, N., Rabinovich, A. (eds.) Pillars of Computer Science. LNCS, vol. 4800, pp. 475–505. Springer, Heidelberg (2008). https://doi.org/10.1007/978-3-540-78127-1_26

22. Manna, Z., Pnueli, A.: Temporal Logic. Springer, New York (1992). https://doi.
    org/10.1007/978-1-4612-0931-7_3
23. Michel, M.: Computation of temporal operators. Logique et Analyse **110–111**,
    137–152 (1985)
24. Pnueli, A., Zaks, A.: On the merits of temporal testers. In: Grumberg, O., Veith,
    H. (eds.) 25 Years of Model Checking. LNCS, vol. 5000, pp. 172–195. Springer,
    Heidelberg (2008). https://doi.org/10.1007/978-3-540-69850-0_11

Timed Systems

A State Class Construction
for Computing the Intersection of Time
Petri Nets Languages

Éric Lubat, Silvano Dal Zilio$^{(\boxtimes)}$, Didier Le Botlan, Yannick Pencolé,
and Audine Subias

LAAS-CNRS, Université de Toulouse, CNRS, INSA, Toulouse, France
{eric.lubat,silvano.dalzilio,didier.lebotlan,
yannick.pencole,audine.subias}@laas.fr

Abstract. We propose a new method for computing the language intersection of two Time Petri nets (TPN); that is the sequence of labels in
timed traces common to the execution of two TPN. Our approach is
based on a new product construction between nets and relies on the State
Class construction, a widely used method for checking the behaviour of
TPN. We prove that this new construct does not add additional expressive power, and yet that it can leads to very concise representation of the
result. We have implemented our approach in a new tool, called Twina.
We report on some experimental results obtained with this tool and show
how to apply our approach on two interesting problems: first, to define
an equivalent of the twin-plant diagnosability methods for TPN; then as
a way to check timed properties without interfering with a system.

Keywords: Time Petri nets · Model checking · State classes ·
Realtime systems modeling and verification

1 Introduction

Formal languages, and the problem of efficiently checking intersection between
languages, play an important role in formal verification. For instance, automata-
theoretic approaches to model-checking often boils down to a language emptiness problem; that is finding whether there is a trace, in a system, that is also
"in the negation of a property" [25]. Similarly, in the study of Discrete Event
Systems [28], basic control-theoretic properties are often expressed in terms of
language properties and language composition. We consider examples of these
two problems at the end of this paper.

In this context, there is a large body of research where systems are expressed
using Petri nets (PN). Indeed, PN are well-suited for modelling notions such as
concurrency or causality in a very compact way; and they can be used for verification by building a Labeled Transition System out of them. Just as important,
PN come equipped with a structural construct for *synchronous composition*, that

© Springer Nature Switzerland AG 2019
E. André and M. Stoelinga (Eds.): FORMATS 2019, LNCS 11750, pp. 79–95, 2019.
https://doi.org/10.1007/978-3-030-29662-9_5

coincides with language intersection when the set of labels of the nets are equal. Unfortunately, the situation is not as simple when we consider extensions of Petri nets that deal with time.

In this paper, we propose a new method for computing the language intersection of two *Time Petri nets* (TPN) [10,26]. This problem is quite complex and is hindered by two main problems. First, the state space associated with a TPN is typically infinite when we work with a dense time model; that is when time delays can be arbitrarily small. Therefore we need to work with an abstraction of their transition system. Second, there is no natural way to define the (structural) composition of two transitions that have non-trivial time constraints (meaning different from the interval $[0, \infty[$). These problems limit the possibility for compositional reasoning on TPN.

A solution to the first problem was proposed by Berthomieu and Menasche in [9], where they define a state space abstraction based on *state classes*. This approach is used in several model-checking tools, such as Romeo [22] and Tina [12] for instance. In the following, we propose a simple solution to overcome the second problem. Our approach is based on an extension of TPN with a dedicated product operator, called *Product TPN*, that can be viewed as an adaptation of Arnold-Nivat synchronization product [3] to the case of TPN. We show that it is possible to extend the state class construction to this new extension, which gives an efficient method for computing the intersection of two TPN when the nets are bounded.

Verification of Time Petri Nets. In the following, we consider TPN where transitions may have observable labels. In this context, an *execution* is the timed-event word obtained by recording the transitions that have been fired together with the delays between them. Our goal is to provide a method for symbolically computing the set of executions that are common to two labeled TPN. Without time, it is well-known that we can compute the language of a net from its marking graph. This gives a Labeled Transition System (LTS); an automaton that is finite as soon as the net is bounded. Likewise, we can compute the (language) intersection of two timed nets by computing the LTS of their *synchronous composition*, denoted $N_1 \| N_2$ thereafter. Actually, like in the untimed case, we are more interested by the *synchronous product* of two languages, rather than by their intersection.

The situation is quite different when we take time into account. Indeed, we may have fewer traces with a TPN than with the corresponding, "untimed" net (the one where timing constraints are deleted). This is because timing constraints may prevent a transition from firing, but never enable it. One solution to recover a finite abstraction of the state space is to use the *State Class Graph* (SCG) construction. Actually, SCG is an umbrella term for a family of different abstractions, each tailored to a different class of properties, or to a different extension of TPN. The first such construction, called *Linear State Class Graph* (LSCG) [9], is based on *firing domains*, that is the delays before a transition can fire. The LSCG preserves the set of reachable markings of a net as well as its language; which is exactly what is needed in our case. This is also the construction that we use in Sect. 3.

In the following we also mention the *Strong SCG* construction (SSCG) [11], based on *clock domains*, that is the duration for which a transition has been enabled. The SSCG preserves more information than the linear one. For example, we can infer from clocks when two transitions are enabled "at the same time", meaning we can handle priorities. The added expressiveness of the strong construction comes at a cost; the SSCG (for a given net) has always more classes than the corresponding LSCG, sometimes by a very large amount. (We give some examples of this in Sect. 6.) This is why we prefer to use the LSCG when possible.

Related Works and Review of Existing Methods. A motivation for our work is that we cannot rely on a synchronous product of TPN. Indeed, a major limitation with TPN is that there are no sensible way to define the composition of "non-trivial" transitions, and therefore no sensible way to define the synchronous composition of "non-composable" TPN; we say that *a transition is trivial* when it is associated to the time interval $[0, \infty[$ and that a net is *composable* when all its observable transitions are trivial. (We illustrate the problem at the end of Sect. 2). Likewise we cannot rely on the product of their SCG either. Indeed, the product of two SCG provides an over-approximation of the expected result, since it cannot trace time dependencies between events from different nets.

The situation is not the same with other "timed models". A notable example is *Timed Automata* [2], an extension of finite automata with variables, also called clocks, whose values progress synchronously as time elapses. Timed Automata (TA) can use boolean conditions on clocks to guard transitions and as local invariants on states. It is also possible to reset a clock when "firing" a transition. The classical product operation on finite automata can be trivially extended to TA: we only need to use the conjunction of guards, invariants and resets where needed. This provides a straightforward method for computing the (language) intersection of two TA, and also a trivial proof that the class of languages accepted by a TA are closed under intersection. Another related work is based on the definition of *Timed Regular Expressions* [4], that provides a timed analogue of Kleene Theorem for TA.

These results seem to promote Timed Automata as an algebraic model of choice for reasoning about timed words, and many works have studied the relation between TPN and TA. (On another note, we can remark that even a slight change in semantics may complicate the product construction; see for instance the case with signal-event languages [16].) For instance, Cassez and Roux [19] propose a structural encoding of TPN into TA that preserves the semantics in the sense of timed bisimulation, and therefore that preserves timed language acceptance. This encoding generates one automata and one clock for every transition in the TPN and can be extended in order to accommodate strict timing constraints; that is static time intervals that have a finite, open bound. Later, Bérard et al. [7,15] showed that TPN and TA are indeed equivalent with respect to language acceptance, but that TA are strictly more expressive in terms of weak timed bisimulation ($\approx$). These results are based on semantic encodings from TPN into TA and from TA into TPN that can be chained together to build an encoding from a TPN to an equivalent composable one. A similar result is also found in [27], which provides a structural encoding from a TPN, N, into a composable TPN that is of size linear with respect to N. But none of these encodings handle timing constraints that are bounded and right-open.

One of the main difference between TA and TPN is that, with TA, we can loose the ability to fire a transition just by waiting long enough (until some guards become false). The same behaviour can be observed with TPN when we add a notion of priorities. In particular, Berthomieu et al. [10,11] prove that (bounded) TPN with priorities are very close to TA, in the sense of $\approx$. They also define an extension of TPN [27] with *inhibitor arcs* between transitions (similar to priorities) and a dual notion of *permission arcs*. In this extension, called IPTPN, a net can always be transformed into a composable one. (We show an example of this construction in Sect. 5).

All these results can be used to define three different methods for computing the intersection of TPN. A first method is to use the structural translation from TPN to TA given in [19] and then to use the product construction on TA. This encoding is at the heart of the tool Romeo [22] and has been used to build a TCTL model-checker for TPN (which, incidentally, relies on the "product" of a net with observers for the formulas). Unfortunately, to the best of our knowledge, it is not possible to analyse the product of two nets with Romeo and therefore we have not been able to experiment with this method. Moreover, this approach is closer in spirit to the SSCG construction.

A second method is to use the (combination of) encodings defined in [15] to replace a TPN with an equivalent, composable one. Unfortunately, this construction relies on a semantic encoding that requires the computation of the entire symbolic state space of the net, and is only applicable on net that have closed timing constraints; meaning that we cannot use constraints of the form $[l, h[$ for example. While this method is not usable in practice, it could be used to prove expressiveness results. For example, it gives a proof that the set of TPN with closed timing constraints is closed under intersection; something we silently admitted until now.

A third method also relies on generating composable nets as a preprocessing step. In this case, the idea is to use the IPTPN of [27]. Like in the first method, the main drawback of this approach is that we need to use the strong SCG construction, which means that we could compute much more classes than with a method based on the LSCG. We describe the experimental results obtain with this method in Sect. 6.

Outline of the Paper and Contributions. In the next section we define the semantics of TPN and provide the technical background necessary for our work. Section 3 contains the semantics of Product TPN, while our two main results are given in Sects. 4 and 5, where we show that it is possible to extend the State Class Graph construction to the case of Product TPN and that this extension does not add additional expressiveness power. By construction, our method can be applied even when the TPN are not bounded and without any restrictions on the timing constraints.

We have implemented our approach in a new tool, called Twina [21] Before concluding, we report (Sect. 6) on some experimental results obtained with this tool. We also show some practical applications for our approach on two problems: first, to define an equivalent of the twin-plant diagnosability methods for TPN; then as a way to check timed properties without interfering with a system.

2   Time Petri Nets and Other Technical Background

A *Time Petri Net* (TPN) is a net where each transition, t, is decorated with a (static) time interval $\mathbf{I}_s(t)$ that constrains the time at which it can fire. A transition is enabled when there are enough tokens in its input places. Once enabled, transition t can fire if it stays enabled for a duration θ that is in the interval $\mathbf{I}_s(t)$. In this case, t is said *time enabled*.

A TPN is a tuple $\langle P, T, \mathbf{Pre}, \mathbf{Post}, m_0, \mathbf{I}_s \rangle$ in which: $\langle P, T, \mathbf{Pre}, \mathbf{Post} \rangle$ is a net (with P and T the set of places and transitions); $\mathbf{Pre}$, $\mathbf{Post} : T \to P \to \mathbb{N}$ are the precondition and postcondition functions; $m_0 : P \to \mathbb{N}$ is the initial marking; and $\mathbf{I}_s : T \to \mathbb{I}$ is the *static interval function*. We use $\mathbb{I}$ for the set of all possible time intervals. To simplify our presentation, we only consider the case of closed intervals of the form $[l, h]$ or $[l, +\infty[$, but our results can be extended to the general case. TPN can be *k-safe*, which means the net has at most $k + 1$ reachable markings. A *safe* TPN usually 1-safe.

We consider that transitions can be tagged using a countable set of labels, $\Sigma = \{a, b, \dots\}$. We also distinguish the special constant ϵ (not in Σ) for internal, silent transitions. In the following, we use a global labeling function $\mathcal{L}$ that associates a unique label in $\Sigma \cup \{\epsilon\}$ to every transition[1]. The alphabet of a net is the collection of labels (in Σ) associated to its transitions.

A Semantics for TPN Based on Firing Domains. A *marking* m of a net $\langle P, T, \mathbf{Pre}, \mathbf{Post} \rangle$ is defined as a function $m : P \to \mathbb{N}$ from places to natural numbers. A transition t in T is *enabled* at m if and only if $m \geqslant \mathbf{Pre}(t)$ (we use the pointwise comparison between functions) and $\mathcal{E}(m)$ denotes the set of transitions enabled at m.

A *state* of a TPN is a pair $s = (m, \varphi)$ in which m is a marking, and $\varphi : T \to \mathbb{I}$ is a mapping from transitions to time intervals, also called *firing domains*. Intuitively, if t is enabled at m, then $\varphi(t)$ contains the dates at which t can possibly fire in the future. For instance, when t is newly enabled, it is associated to its static time interval $\varphi(t) = \mathbf{I}_s(t)$. Likewise, a transition t can fire immediately only when 0 is in $\varphi(t)$ and it cannot remain enabled for more than its timespan, *i.e.* the maximal value in $\varphi(t)$.

For a given delay θ in $\mathbb{Q}_{\geq 0}$ and ι in $\mathbb{I}$, we denote $\iota - \theta$ the time interval ι shifted (to the left) by θ:, e.g. $[l, h] - \theta = [\max(0, l - \theta), \max(0, h - \theta)]$. By extension, we use $\varphi \dot{-} \theta$ for the partial function that associates the transition t to the value $\varphi(t) - \theta$. This operation is useful to model the effect of time passage on the enabled transitions of a net.

---

[1] We may assume that there is a countable set of all possible transitions (identifiers) and that different nets have distinct transitions.

The following definitions are quite standard, see for instance [7,10]. The semantics of a TPN is a (labeled) Kripke structure $\langle S, S_0, \rightarrow \rangle$ with only two possible kinds of actions: either $s \xrightarrow{a} s'$, meaning that the transition $t \in T$ is fired from s with $\mathcal{L}(t) = a$; or $s \xrightarrow{\theta} s'$, with $\theta \in \mathbb{Q}_{\geq 0}$, meaning that time θ elapses from s. A transition t can fire from the state (m, φ) if t is enabled at m and firable instantly. When we fire a transition t from state (m, φ), a transition k (with $k \neq t$) is said to be *persistent* if k is also enabled in the marking $m - \mathbf{Pre}(t)$, that is if $m - \mathbf{Pre}(t) \geqslant \mathbf{Pre}(k)$. The other transitions enabled after firing t are called *newly enabled*.

Definition 1 (Semantics). *The semantics of a TPN N, with N the net $\langle P, T, \mathbf{Pre}, \mathbf{Post}, m_0, \mathbf{I}_s \rangle$, is the Timed Transition System (TTS) $[\![N]\!] = \langle S, s_0, \rightarrow \rangle$ where S is the smallest set containing s_0 and closed by $\rightarrow$, where:*

- *$s_0 = (m_0, \varphi_0)$ is the initial state, with m_0 the initial marking and $\varphi_0(t) = \mathbf{I}_s(t)$ for every t in $\mathcal{E}(m_0)$;*
- *the state transition relation $\rightarrow \subseteq S \times (\Sigma \cup \{\epsilon\} \cup \mathbb{Q}_{\geq 0}) \times S$ is the relation such that for all state (m, φ) in S:*
  - *(i) if t is enabled at m, $\mathcal{L}(t) = a$ and $0 \in \varphi(t)$ then $(m, \varphi) \xrightarrow{a} (m', \varphi')$ where $m' = m - \mathbf{Pre}(t) + \mathbf{Post}(t)$ and φ' is a firing function such that $\varphi'(k) = \varphi(k)$ for any persistent transition and $\varphi'(k) = \mathbf{I}_s(k)$ elsewhere.*
  - *(ii) if $\theta \leqslant \varphi$*
    $\forall k \in Enabled(m), \theta \leq max\varphi(k)$ then $(m, \varphi) \xrightarrow{\theta} (m, \varphi \dot{-} \theta)$.

Transitions in the case (i) above are called *discrete transitions*; those labelled with delays (case (ii)) are the *continuous*, or time elapsing, transitions. Like with nets, we say that the alphabet of a TTS is the set of labels, in Σ, associated to discrete actions. Using labels, we can define the product of two TTS by extending the classical definition for the product of finite automata.

Definition 2 (Product of TTS). *Assume $S_1 = \langle S_1, s_1^0, \rightarrow_1 \rangle$ and $S_2 = \langle S_2, s_2^0, \rightarrow_2 \rangle$ are two TTS with respective alphabets Σ_1 and Σ_2. The product of S_1 by S_2 is the TTS $S_1 \| S_2 = \langle (S_1 \times S_2), (s_1^0, s_2^0), \rightarrow \rangle$ such that $\rightarrow$ is the smallest relation obeying the following rules:*

$$\frac{s_1 \xrightarrow{\alpha}_1 s_1' \quad \alpha \in (\Sigma_1 \setminus \Sigma_2) \cup \{\epsilon\}}{(s_1, s_2) \xrightarrow{\alpha} (s_1', s_2)} \qquad \frac{s_2 \xrightarrow{\alpha}_2 s_2' \quad \alpha \in (\Sigma_2 \setminus \Sigma_1) \cup \{\epsilon\}}{(s_1, s_2) \xrightarrow{\alpha} (s_1, s_2')}$$

$$\frac{s_1 \xrightarrow{\alpha}_1 s_1' \quad s_2 \xrightarrow{\alpha}_2 s_2' \quad \alpha \neq \epsilon}{(s_1, s_2) \xrightarrow{\alpha} (s_1', s_2')}$$

Executions, Traces and Equivalences. An *execution* of a net N is a sequence in its semantics, $[\![N]\!]$, that starts from the initial state. It is a time-event word over the alphabet containing both labels (in $\Sigma \cup \{\epsilon\}$) and delays. Continuous transitions can always be grouped together, meaning that when $(m, \varphi) \xrightarrow{\theta} (m, \varphi')$

and $(m, \varphi') \xrightarrow{\theta'} (m, \varphi'')$ then necessarily $(m, \varphi) \xrightarrow{\theta + \theta'} (m, \varphi'')$ (and the firing domain φ' is uniquely defined from φ and θ). Based on this observation, we can always consider executions of the form $\sigma \stackrel{\text{def}}{=} \theta_0 a_0 \theta_1 a_1 \ldots$ where each discrete transition is preceded by a single time delay. By contrast, a *trace* is the untimed word obtained from an execution when we keep only the discrete actions. Then the language of a TPN is the set of all its (finite) traces.

By definition, the language of a TPN is prefix-closed; and it is regular when the net is bounded [9]. It is also the case [27] that the "intersection" of two nets N_1 and N_2—the traces obtained from (pairs of) executions common to the two nets—are exactly the traces in the TTS product $[\![N_1]\!] \parallel [\![N_2]\!]$. Our goal, in the next section, is to define a product operation, $N_1 \times N_2$, that is a *congruence*, meaning that $[\![N_1 \times N_2]\!]$ should be equivalent to $[\![N_1]\!] \parallel [\![N_2]\!]$.

Language equivalence would be too coarse in this context. In this paper, we will instead prefer (a weak version of) timed bisimulation, which rely on a weak version of the transition relation $s \stackrel{\alpha}{\Rightarrow} s'$ (with α an action in $\Sigma \cup \{\epsilon\} \cup \mathbb{Q}_{\geq 0}$ and θ a delay in $\mathbb{Q}_{\geq 0}$) defined from the following set of rules:

$$\frac{}{s \stackrel{\epsilon}{\Rightarrow} s} \qquad \frac{s \stackrel{\epsilon}{\Rightarrow} s' \quad s' \stackrel{\alpha}{\Rightarrow} s'' \quad s'' \stackrel{\epsilon}{\Rightarrow} s'''}{s \stackrel{\alpha}{\Rightarrow} s'''} \qquad \frac{s \stackrel{\theta}{\Rightarrow} s' \quad s' \stackrel{\theta'}{\Rightarrow} s''}{s \xrightarrow{\theta + \theta'} s''}$$

Definition 3 (Behavioural Equivalence). *Assume $G_1 = \langle S_1, s_1^0, \rightarrow_1 \rangle$ and $G_2 = \langle S_2, s_2^0, \rightarrow_2 \rangle$ are two TTS. A binary relation $\mathcal{R}$ over $S_1 \times S_2$ is a weak timed bisimulation if and only if $s_1^0 \, \mathcal{R} \, s_2^0$ and for all actions α and pair of states $(s_1, s_2) \in \mathcal{R}$ we have: (1) if $s_1 \stackrel{\alpha}{\Rightarrow} s_1'$ then there exists s_2' such that $s_2 \stackrel{\alpha}{\Rightarrow} s_2'$ and $s_1' \, \mathcal{R} \, s_2'$; and conversely (2) if $s_2 \stackrel{\alpha}{\Rightarrow} s_2'$ then there exists s_1' such that $s_1 \stackrel{\alpha}{\Rightarrow} s_1'$ and $s_1' \, \mathcal{R} \, s_2'$. In this case we say that G_1 and G_2 are timed bisimilar, denoted $G_1 \approx G_2$, and we use $\approx$ for the union of all timed bisimulations $\mathcal{R}$.*

Timed bisimulation is preserved by product [27], meaning that for all TTS G, G_1 and G_2 we have $G_1 \approx G_2$ implies $(G \| G_1) \approx (G \| G_2)$. In the following we say that two nets are bisimilar, denoted $N_1 \approx N_2$, when $[\![N_1]\!] \approx [\![N_2]\!]$.

Example. We give two examples of TPN with alphabet $\{a, b\}$ in Fig. 1. Executions for the net N_1 (left) include time-event words of the form $\theta_0 a \theta_1 b$ (and their prefix) provided that $\theta_1 \geq 1$. Executions for the net N_2 (middle) include time-event words of the form $\theta_2 a \theta_3 b$ and $\theta_3 b \theta_2 a$ (and their prefix) provided that $\theta_3 \leq 1$. If we consider executions that are in the product of both nets, we find all executions of the form $\theta_0 a$, with the constraint $\theta_0 \leq 1$. We also have one execution of the form $\theta_0 a \theta_1 b$ provided that $\theta_0 + \theta_1 \leq 1$ and $\theta_1 \geq 1$. This corresponds to the case where event a fires exactly at date 0; any other case eventually leading to a *time deadlock* (a situation where time cannot progress). In the same figure (right), we display the "untimed" synchronous product $N_1 \| N_2$. It is clear that there are no possible choice of time constraint for transition $t_3 \times t_1$ that could lead to a net bisimilar to $[\![N_1]\!] \parallel [\![N_2]\!]$. This is a simple example of the "non-composability" of Time Petri nets.

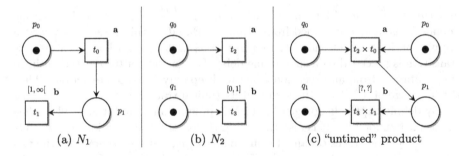

Fig. 1. Two examples of TPN and their (failed, untimed) product.

3   Product TPN and Their Semantics

We propose an extension of TPN with a *synchronous product* operation between TPN, $\times$, in the style of Arnold-Nivat synchronization of processes [3]. Our goal is to obtain a congruent composition operator, in the sense that $[\![N_1 \times N_2]\!] \approx [\![N_1]\!] \, \| \, [\![N_2]\!]$. A *product TPN*, or PTPN, is a TPN $\langle P, T, \mathbf{Pre}, \mathbf{Post}, \mathbf{I}_s \rangle$ augmented with two projections, $\#_1$ and $\#_2$, such that the following properties hold:

- there are two sets $\#_1 P$ and $\#_2 P$ that partition the set of places P.
- there are two sets $\#_1 T$ and $\#_2 T$ that partition the set of transitions T.
- all the pre- and post-conditions of a transition in $\#_i T$ are places in $\#_i P$: if $t \in \#_i T$ and $\mathbf{Pre}(t)(p) > 0$ or $\mathbf{Post}(t)(p) > 0$ then $p \in \#_i P$.

Basically, this means that a PTPN N is the superposition of two distinct, non-interconnected components, that we call $\#_1 N$ and $\#_2 N$ for short.

Definition 4 (Product of TPN). *The product $N_1 \times N_2$ of two disjoint TPN N_1 and N_2 (such that $P_1 \cap P_2 = T_1 \cap T_2 = \emptyset$) is the PTPN obtained from the juxtaposition, preserving labels, of N_1 and N_2 with the two trivial projections $\#_i P = P_i$ and $\#_i T = T_i$ for all $i \in 1..2$.*

With our notations, a PTPN N is equivalent to the composition $(\#_1 N) \times (\#_2 N)$. In the following, we use the notation $\#_i m$ to denote the restriction of a marking m to the places in $\#_i P$ and similarly with $\#_i \varphi$ and the transitions in $\#_i T$. By convenience, $\#_i(m, \varphi)$ denotes the state $(\#_i m, \#_i \varphi)$ and we use $\#_i \Sigma$ for the alphabet of net $\#_i N$.

To ease the presentation, we limit the composition to only two components (instead of a sequence) and we do not define the equivalent of "synchronization vectors". As a result, we do not define the product over PTPN. This could be added, at the cost of more burdensome notations, but it is not needed in our applications (Sect. 6). This is also why we have the same limitations in our implementation [21].

Labels are not necessarily partitioned, so the same label can be shared between the two components of a product. We denote $\Sigma_{1,2}$ the set $(\#_1 \Sigma \cap \#_2 \Sigma)$

of labels occurring on "both sides" of a PTPN. We should also need the notation Σ_1 for the set $(\#_1 \Sigma \setminus \#_2 \Sigma) \cup \{\epsilon\}$ of labels that can occur in $\#_1$ concurrently with $\#_2$ (and similarly for Σ_2). The semantics for PTPN relies largely on the semantics of TPN but makes a particular use of labels.

Definition 5. *The semantics of a PTPN $\langle P, T, \mathbf{Pre}, \mathbf{Post}, m_0, \mathbf{I}_s \rangle$, with projections $\#_1$ and $\#_2$, is the TTS $[\![N]\!]_\times = \langle S, s_0, \mapsto \rangle$ such that $s_0 = (m_0, \varphi_0)$ is the same initial state than in the TPN semantics $[\![N]\!]$, and $\mapsto$ is the transition relation with actions in $\Sigma \cup \{\epsilon\} \cup \mathbb{Q}_{\geq 0}$ such that:*

$$\frac{\alpha \in \mathbb{Q}_{\geq 0} \qquad s \xrightarrow{\alpha} s' \in [\![N]\!]}{s \xmapsto{\alpha} s'} \qquad \frac{t \in T \quad \mathcal{L}(t) = \alpha \notin \Sigma_{1,2} \qquad s \xrightarrow{\alpha} s' \in [\![N]\!]}{s \xmapsto{\alpha} s'} \qquad \frac{a = \mathcal{L}(t_1) = \mathcal{L}(t_2) \quad t_i \in \#_i T \qquad \#_i s \xrightarrow{a} \#_i s' \in [\![\#_i N]\!] \quad i \in 1..2}{s \xmapsto{a} s'}$$

The only new case is for pairs of transitions, t_1 and t_2, from different components but with the same label: $\mathcal{L}(t_1) = \mathcal{L}(t_2) = a$. This is the equivalent of a synchronization. Indeed the premisses entail that both t_1 and t_2 can fire immediately, and the effect is to fire both of them simultaneously. As a side effect, our choice of semantics entails that a transition on a "shared label" (in $\Sigma_{1,2}$) is blocked until we find a matching transition, with the same label, on the opposite component. This may introduce a new kind of time deadlock that has no direct equivalent in a TPN: when a transition has to fire urgently (hence time cannot progress) while there are no matching transition that is time-enabled.

It is the case that the reachable states, in $[\![N]\!]_\times$, are a subset of the states in $[\![N]\!]$. This is because we may forbid a synchronization on a shared label, but never create new opportunities to fire a transition. We also have a more precise result concerning the semantics of a PTPN and the product of its components.

Theorem 1. *The TTS $[\![N]\!]_\times$ is isomorph to the product $[\![\#_1 N]\!] \parallel [\![\#_2 N]\!]$.*

Proof. By induction on the shortest path from the initial state, s_0, to a reachable state s in $[\![N]\!]_\times$ and then a case analysis on the possible transitions from s. □

4   Construction of the State Class Graph for PTPN

We give a brief overview of the LSCG construction for a PTPN $N = \langle P, T, \mathbf{Pre}, \mathbf{Post}, m_0, \mathbf{I}_s \rangle$. In the following, we use the notation α_t^s and β_t^s for the left and right endpoints of interval $\mathbf{I}_s(t)$. For the sake of simplicity, we only consider inequalities that are non-strict (our definitions can be extended to the more general case) and assume that $\beta - \alpha = \infty$ when β is infinite.

A *state class* C is a pair (m, D), where m is a marking and D is a *domain*; a (finite) system of linear inequalities on the firing dates of transitions enabled at m. We will use variable x_i in D to represent the possible firing time of transition t_i. In the Linear SCG construction [8,9], we build an inductive set of classes C_σ, where $\sigma \in T^*$ is a sequence of discrete transitions firable from the initial state.

Intuitively, the class $C_\sigma = (m, D)$ collects all the states reachable from the initial state by firing schedules of support sequence σ. For example, the initial class C_ϵ is (m_0, D_0) where D_0 is the domain defined by the static time constraints in φ_0, that is: $\alpha_i^s \leq x_i \leq \beta_i^s$ for all t_i in $\mathcal{E}(m_0)$.

The efficiency of the SCG construction relies on several factors: (1) First, we can restrict to domains D that are *difference systems*, that is a sequence of constraints of the form $\alpha_i \leq x_i \leq \beta_i$ and $x_i - x_j \leq \gamma_{i,j}$, where each variable in $(x_i)_{t_i \in \mathcal{E}(m_0)}$ corresponds to an enabled transition (and $i \neq j$). (2) Next, we can always put domains in *closure form*, meaning that each bounds α, β and γ are the tightest preserving the solution set of D. Hence we can encode D using a simple vector of values. This data structure, called *Difference Bound Matrix* (DBM), is unique to all the domains that have equal solution set. Hence testing class equivalence is decidable and efficient. (3) Finally, if $C_\sigma = (m, D)$ is defined and t is enabled at m, we can incrementally compute the coefficients of the DBM D', the domain obtained after firing t from C_σ, from the coefficients of D.

We only consider the new case where we simultaneously fire a pair of transitions (t_i, t_j) from a class (m, D). We assume that the resulting marking is m'. First, we need to check that both transitions can eventually fire. This is the case only if the condition $\gamma_{t,k} \geq 0$ is true for all $t \in \{i, j\}$ and k enabled at m (with $k \neq t$). In this case, the resulting domain D' can be obtained by following a short number of steps, namely:

1. add the constraints $x_i = x_j$ and $x_i \leq x_k$ to D, for all $k \notin \{i, j\}$ (since t_i, t_j must fire at the same date and before any other enabled transition);
2. introduce new variables x_k' for all transitions enabled in m', that will become the variables in D', and add the constraint $x_k' = x_k - x_i$ if t_k is persistent or $\alpha_k^s \leq x_k' \leq \beta_k^s$ if t_k is newly enabled;
3. eliminate all the variables from D relative to transitions in conflict with t_i, t_j and put the resulting system in normal form.

Except for step 1 above, with the constraint that $x_i = x_j$, this is exactly the procedure described in [8] for plain TPN. When both transitions (t_i, t_j) can fire, it is possible to completely eliminate all occurrences of the "unprimed" variables x_k in D' and the result is a DBM. Which is exactly what is needed in our case.

We can draw two useful observations from this result. First, we can follow the same procedure with any number of equality constraints, and still wind up with a DBM. Therefore it would be possible to fire more than two transitions simultaneously. Second, we have an indirect proof that forcing the synchronization of transitions is strictly less constraining than using priorities (because it is not possible to use the LSCG construction with priorities), something that was not obvious initially.

5   Expressiveness Results

It is not obvious that PTPN add any expressive power compared to TPN. On the one hand, the semantics of a PTPN N is quite close to the semantics of its components. In particular, $[\![N]\!]_\times = [\![N]\!]$ when there are no shared labels ($\Sigma_{1,2} = \emptyset$). Moreover, in a PTPN like in a TPN, it is not possible to lose the ability of firing a transition just by waiting long enough; a behaviour that distinguishes TPN from TA, or from TPN with priorities for instance. On the other hand, PTPN introduces new kind of time deadlocks which are affected by time delays (see our example at the end of Sect. 2). Next, we prove that the two models are equally expressive (up-to $\approx$) when all timing constraints are either infinite or closed on the right (in which case we say the net is *right-closed*).

Theorem 2. *Given a safe, right-closed PTPN N, we can build a safe, composable TPN N', whose size is linear with respect to N, such that $[\![N]\!]_\times \approx [\![N']\!]$.*

For the sake of brevity, we only sketch the proof. We rely on two auxiliary properties and on an encoding from TPN into *composable* net; meaning an equivalent net where all timing constraints have been "moved" to silent transitions. We find such result in [27, Def. 9], which provides a construction to build a composable net $\mathscr{T}_1(N)$ from every safe and right-closed TPN N. Our restrictions on N in Theorem 2 come from this construction, as is our result on the size of N'.

Our first auxiliary property, (L1), compare the product of composable TPN with their synchronous product, namely: if N_1 and N_2 are composable TPN then $[\![N_1 \times N_2]\!]_\times \approx [\![N_1 \| N_2]\!]$. Property (L1) derives directly from the construction of the product $N_1 \| N_2$ of composable TPN. Indeed, with composable nets, the fusion of transitions sharing a common label are unaffected by continuous transitions. Hence they have the same behaviour in $N_1 \times N_2$ than in $N_1 \| N_2$. (And this is the only place where the semantics of the two nets may diverge.)

Next, we use an equivalent of the congruence property for PTPN, (L2): given two pairs of TPN (N_1, N_2) and (M_1, M_2) such $N_1 \approx N_2$ and $M_1 \approx M_2$ we have that $[\![N_1 \times M_1]\!]_\times \approx [\![N_2 \times M_2]\!]_\times$. Property (L2) can be proved by defining a "candidate relation", $\mathcal{R}$, which contains the pair (s_0, s'_0) of initial states of $N_1 \times M_1$ and $N_2 \times M_2$; then proving that $\mathcal{R}$ is a weak timed bisimulation. A suitable choice for $\mathcal{R}$ is to take the smallest relation such that $(s_1 \uplus s'_1) \mathcal{R} (s_2 \uplus s'_2)$ whenever $s_1 \approx s_2$ and $s'_1 \approx s'_2$. Then the proof follows by simple case analysis.

Finally, we use construction $\mathscr{T}_1$ (above) to build composable TPN from the nets $\#_1 N$ and $\#_2 N$ and to define $N' \stackrel{\text{def}}{=} \mathscr{T}_1(\#_1 N) \| \mathscr{T}_1(\#_2 N)$. By property of $\mathscr{T}_1$ we have $\#_i N \approx \mathscr{T}_1(\#_i N)$ for all $i \in 1..2$. Hence by (L2) and (L1) we have $[\![N]\!]_\times = [\![\#_1 N \times \#_2 N]\!]_\times \approx [\![\mathscr{T}_1(\#_1 N) \times \mathscr{T}_1(\#_2 N)]\!]_\times \approx [\![\mathscr{T}_1(\#_1 N) \| \mathscr{T}_1(\#_2 N)]\!]$. The property follows by transitivity of $\approx$.

Our proof gives a constructive method to build a net N' with (at most) four extra transitions and places, compared to N, for each non-trivial labeled transition. We can use the SCG of N' to compute the language of N (and to compute the intersection of two nets when we choose $N = N_1 \times N_2$). Unfortunately this approach does not scale well. For example, the composition of the two nets given in Fig. 1 has 16 classes with this method instead of only 3 with our approach (and the intermediary TPN has 11 places and 7 transitions). Likewise, for the simple example in Fig. 4 we have a net with 25 places, 211 transitions and 1 389 classes instead of simply 3 classes with PTPN.

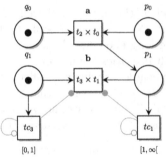

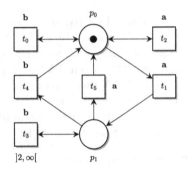

Fig. 2. Example of IPTPN

Fig. 3. TPN for the delay property

Another limitation of this approach are the restrictions imposed on the timing constraints of N. Indeed, to the best of our knowledge, there are no equivalent of construction $\mathscr{T}_1$ in the case of "right-open" transitions.

Composable Time Petri nets using IPTPN. Berthomieu et al. [27] define an extension of TPN with "inhibition and permission" that provides another method for building composable nets. With this extension, it is always possible to build a composable IPTPN from a TPN. For example, Fig. 2 displays the IPTPN corresponding to the "product" of the two nets in Fig. 1. In this construction, we create a silent, extra-transition tc_i for every non-trivial observable transition t_i. These transitions cannot fire (they self-inhibit themselves with an ——o arc) but "record the timing constraints" of the transition they are associated with. Then a permission arc (——•) is used to transfer these constraints on the (product of) labeled transitions.

Tina provides a SCG construction for IPTPN but, like with the addition of priorities, it is necessary to use the strong construction in this case. We use the encoding into IPTPN we just sketched above in our experiments.

6   Experimental Results and Possible Applications

We have implemented the state class construction for PTPN in a tool called Twina [21] that can generate the LSCG of both "plain" and product TPN. The tool and models mentioned here are available online at https://projects.laas.fr/twina/, with instructions on how to reproduce our results.

Performances Compared with IPTPN. We compare the results obtained with PTPN and an encoding into IPTPN, which appears to be the best alternative among the three methods mentioned in Sect. 1. By default, Twina uses option -W, that computes the Linear SCG of a net. We also provide option -I to compute the LSCG for the product of two nets using the construction defined in Sect. 4. We use the same syntax for nets in Twina than in Tina [12]. In particular, our method can be used with nets that are not 1-safe and without any restriction on the timing constraints (so we accept right-open transitions). We also allow read- and inhibitor-arcs with the same semantics than in Tina. We

Table 1. Comparing the PTPN and IPTPN methods

MODEL	EXP.	Twina (LSCG)		IPTPN (SSCG)		RATIO
		STATES	TRANS.	STATES	TRANS.	
jdeds	plain	26	42	28	45	8%
jdeds	twin	544	1 144	706	1 432	30%
jdeds	obs	57	103	64	115	12%
train3	plain	3 101	7 762	5 051	13 027	63%
train3	twin	1 453 393	5 415 838	4 018 109	15 702 687	176%
train3	obs	6 202	16 614	10 102	27 801	63%
train4	plain	10 319	27 153	16 841	45 717	63%
train4	twin	20 954 198	79 768 434	57 567 538	229 935 082	175%
train4	obs	20 638	58 367	33 682	98 015	63%
plant	plain	2 696 558	7 359 339	4 628 698	12 870 710	72%
plant	twin	1 300	3 183	1 633	3 996	26%
plant	obs	5 715 293	15 639 336	9 790 043	27 215 355	71%
wodes	plain	2 554	6 080	5 363	13 047	110%
wodes	twin	55 402	155 586	151 352	426 928	173%
wodes	obs	5 767	13 506	14 663	34 508	154%
wodes232	plain	20 388	88 122	32 382	140 969	59%
wodes232	twin	39 588 981	304 246 211	339 165 870	2 552 685 724	757%
wodes232	obs	106 043	434 712	226 269	888 042	113%

compare the size of the LSCG with the results obtained using IPTPN and Tina in Table 1. The results are reported with the sizes of the SCG in number of classes and edges; we also give the ratio of classes saved between the LSCG and the SSCG. So a 100% ratio means twice as much states in the strong SCG.

We use different models for our benchmarks: *jdeds* is an example taken from [23] extended with time; *train* is a modified version of the train controller example in [13] with an additional transition that corresponds to a fault in the gate; *plant* is the model of a complex automated manufacturing system from [32]; *wodes* is the WODES diagnosis benchmark of Giua (see e.g. [18]) with added timed constraints. For each model, we give the result of three experiments: *plain* where we compute the SCG of the net, alone; *twin* where we compute the intersection between the TPN and a copy of itself with some transitions removed; and *obs* where we compute the intersection of the net with a copy of the TPN in Fig. 3. We explain the relevance of the last two constructions just afterwards.

We see that, in some of our examples, there is a large difference between the size of the LSCG and the size of the SSCG for the same example. This was one of our main reason for developing a specific tool. This is important since, on the extreme case, we can have a quadratic blow-up in the number of classes

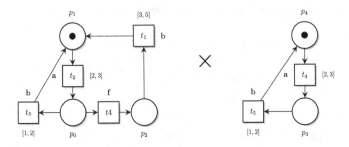

Fig. 4. Product of a TPN N_f (left) and its "twin" N_o (right) for the fault f.

when analysing a twin product. (This is almost the case in example jdeds.) We also observe that, on model plant-twin, the size of the intersection may be much smaller than the size of one of the component alone; 1300 classes compared to 2 million. This is to be expected, since the intersection may have only one class. Nonetheless this emphasizes the need to have methods that can build the intersection on the fly, without computing a symbolic representation for each component first.

Diagnosability and the Twin Plant Method. One possible application of Twina—and our initial motivation for this work—is to check *fault diagnosability* [29] in systems modelled as TPN [5,17]. In this context, a system is described as a TPN with a distinguished unobservable event f that models a fault. (Any transition labelled with f is faulty.) Fault f is diagnosable if it is always possible to detect when a faulty transition has fired, in a finite amount of time, just by looking at the observable flow of events [31]. Under the assumptions that the system does not generate Zeno executions, and that any possible execution is not infinitely unobservable, one way to check diagnosability is to look for infinite *critical pairs* [20]. A critical pair consists of a couple of infinite executions of the TPN, one faulty the other one not, that have equal timed observations. Then fault f is diagnosable if no such pair exists. By using Twina, we aim at checking diagnosability by adapting the *twin-plant* method [24] to TPN. The idea is to make two copies of the same system, one with the fault, N_f, and the other without it, N_o, and to relabel all unobservable events to avoid collisions. Then checking for the existence of an infinite critical pair amounts to finding an infinite execution with f in the product $N_o \times N_f$.

We give an example of this construct in Fig. 4 where a and b are both observable. In system N_f, fault f is not diagnosable if we do not consider time, as we always observe b after an a in both faulty and non-faulty executions. Now considering the observation of time, f is diagnosable as the date of b is always discriminant. In the intersection of N_f and N_o, every execution where transition t_4 fires leads to a time deadlock. Indeed, in this case, we must wait at least 3 to fire transitions t_1 and at most 2 to fire t_5 (and both have label b).

The twin-plant construction is quite useful and we provide an option to directly build a twin TPN in our tool (option -twin). This is the construction we use in our experiments for Table 1. In this case, we can generate a LTS for the twin plant and check that every fault eventually leads to a deadlock in the product, meaning that the system is diagnosable. For instance using a LTL model-checker and a property such as $(\Diamond f) \Rightarrow (\Diamond \text{dead})$ [23]. We also provide a dedicated algorithm (option -diag) to check this property on-the-fly. When the system is not diagnosable, it allows us to find a counter-example before exploring the whole behaviour of the twin-plant.

Observer-Based Verification. Another application of our product construction is model checking TPN, in much the same way some "observer-based" verification techniques rely on the product of a system with an observer [1,30]. The idea is to express a property as the language of an observer, O, then check the property on the system N by looking at the behaviour of $N \times O$. A major advantage of this approach is that there is no risk to disrupt the system under observation, which is not always easy to prove with other methods.

We give an example of observer in Fig. 3. In this net, sequences of events a and b may occur in any order and at any date. On the other hand, the only way to fire t_3 is to "find" two successive occurrences of a and b with a delay (strictly) bigger than 2. Hence we can check if such behaviour is possible in a system, N, by checking whether t_3 can fire in $N \times O$. This is the problem we consider in the *obs* experiments of Table 1. We only consider one small example here. Nonetheless, the same approach could be used to check more complex timed properties. This will be the subject of future works.

7   Conclusion

We propose an extension of TPN with a product operation in the style of Arnold-Nivat. The semantics of our extension is quite straightforward. What is more surprising is that it is possible to adapt the LSCG construction to this case—which means that we do not need the equivalent of clocks or priorities—and that this extension does not add any expressive power. This is a rather promising result, complexity-wise, since it means that we can hope to adapt the same optimization techniques than with "plain" TPN, such as specific symmetry reduction techniques for instance [14].

We have several opportunities for extending our work. Obviously we can easily extend our product to a sequence of nets and add a notion of "synchronization vectors". This could lead to a more compositional framework for TPN, in the style of the BIP language [6]. Another promising application of our approach would be to extend classical results from the theory of supervisory control to the context of TPN. We already mentioned a possible application for diagnosability (which was the initial motivation for our work). A next step could be to study the "quotient" of two TPN language—the dual of the product—which can be used to reason about the controlability of a system and that is at the basis of many compositional verification methods, such as Assume-Guarantee for example.

Acknowledgments. The authors are grateful to Thomas Hujsa and Pierre-Emmanuel Hladik for their valuable comments. We also want to thank Bernard Berthomieu, without whom none of this would have been possible; our work is a tribute to the versatility and the enduring qualities of the state class construction that he pioneered more than 30 years ago.

References

1. Abid, N., Dal Zilio, S., Le Botlan, D.: A formal framework to specify and verify real-time properties on critical systems. Int. J. Crit. Comput. Based Syst. (IJCCBS) **5**(1/2) (2014). https://doi.org/10.1504/IJCCBS.2014.059593
2. Alur, R., Dill, D.L.: A theory of timed automata. Theoret. Comput. Sci. **126**(2) (1994). https://doi.org/10.1016/0304-3975(94)90010-8
3. Arnold, A.: Nivat's processes and their synchronization. Theor. Comput. Sci. **281**(1–2) (2002). https://doi.org/10.1016/S0304-3975(02)00006-3
4. Asarin, E., Caspi, P., Maler, O.: Timed regular expressions. J. ACM **49**(2) (2002). https://doi.org/10.1145/506147.506151
5. Basile, F., Cabasino, M.P., Seatzu, C.: Diagnosability analysis of labeled time Petri net systems. IEEE Trans. Autom. Control **62**(3) (2017). https://doi.org/10.1109/TAC.2016.2588736
6. Basu, A., Bozga, M., Sifakis, J.: Modeling heterogeneous real-time components in BIP. In: Software Engineering and Formal Methods (SEFM). IEEE (2006). https://doi.org/10.1109/SEFM.2006.27
7. Bérard, B., Cassez, F., Haddad, S., Lime, D., Roux, O.H.: Comparison of the expressiveness of timed automata and time Petri nets. In: Pettersson, P., Yi, W. (eds.) FORMATS 2005. LNCS, vol. 3829, pp. 211–225. Springer, Heidelberg (2005). https://doi.org/10.1007/11603009_17
8. Berthomieu, B., Diaz, M.: Modeling and verification of time dependent systems using time Petri nets. IEEE Trans. Softw. Eng. **17**(3) (1991). https://doi.org/10.1109/32.75415
9. Berthomieu, B., Menasche, M.: An enumerative approach for analyzing time Petri nets. In: Proceedings IFIP (1983)
10. Berthomieu, B., Peres, F., Vernadat, F.: Bridging the gap between timed automata and bounded time Petri nets. In: Asarin, E., Bouyer, P. (eds.) FORMATS 2006. LNCS, vol. 4202, pp. 82–97. Springer, Heidelberg (2006). https://doi.org/10.1007/11867340_7
11. Berthomieu, B., Peres, F., Vernadat, F.: Model checking bounded prioritized time Petri nets. In: Namjoshi, K.S., Yoneda, T., Higashino, T., Okamura, Y. (eds.) ATVA 2007. LNCS, vol. 4762, pp. 523–532. Springer, Heidelberg (2007). https://doi.org/10.1007/978-3-540-75596-8_37
12. Berthomieu, B., Ribet, P.O., Vernadat, F.: The tool TINA-construction of abstract state spaces for Petri nets and time Petri nets. Int. J. Prod. Res. **42**(14), 2741–2756 (2004)
13. Berthomieu, B., Vernadat, F.: State class constructions for branching analysis of time Petri nets. In: Garavel, H., Hatcliff, J. (eds.) TACAS 2003. LNCS, vol. 2619, pp. 442–457. Springer, Heidelberg (2003). https://doi.org/10.1007/3-540-36577-X_33
14. Bourdil, P.A., Berthomieu, B., Dal Zilio, S., Vernadat, F.: Symmetry reduction for time Petri net state classes. Sci. Comput. Program. **132**(2) (2016). https://doi.org/10.1016/j.scico.2016.08.008

15. Bérard, B., Cassez, F., Haddad, S., Lime, D., Roux, O.H.: When are timed automata weakly timed bisimilar to time Petri nets? Theoret. Comput. Sci. **403**(2–3) (2008). https://doi.org/10.1016/j.tcs.2008.03.030
16. Bérard, B., Gastin, P., Petit, A.: Intersection of regular signal-event (timed) languages. In: Asarin, E., Bouyer, P. (eds.) FORMATS 2006. LNCS, vol. 4202, pp. 52–66. Springer, Heidelberg (2006). https://doi.org/10.1007/11867340_5
17. Cabasino, M.P., Giua, A., Lafortune, S., Seatzu, C.: A new approach for diagnosability analysis of Petri nets using verifier nets. IEEE Trans. Autom. Control **57**(12) (2012). https://doi.org/10.1109/TAC.2012.2200372
18. Cabasino, M.P., Giua, A., Seatzu, C.: Discrete event diagnosis using Petri nets. In: ICINCO-ICSO (2009)
19. Cassez, F., Roux, O.H.: Structural translation from time Petri nets to timed automata. J. Syst. Softw. **79**(10) (2006). https://doi.org/10.1016/j.jss.2005.12.021
20. Cimatti, A., Pecheur, C., Cavada, R.: Formal verification of diagnosability via symbolic model checking. In: IJCAI (2003)
21. Dal Zilio, S.: TWINA: a realtime model-checker for analyzing Twin-TPN (2019). https://projects.laas.fr/twina/
22. Gardey, G., Lime, D., Magnin, M., Roux, O.H.: Romeo: a tool for analyzing time Petri nets. In: Etessami, K., Rajamani, S.K. (eds.) CAV 2005. LNCS, vol. 3576, pp. 418–423. Springer, Heidelberg (2005). https://doi.org/10.1007/11513988_41
23. Gougam, H.E., Pencolé, Y., Subias, A.: Diagnosability analysis of patterns on bounded labeled prioritized Petri nets. Discrete Event Dyn. Syst. **27**(1) (2017). https://doi.org/10.1007/s10626-016-0234-5
24. Jiang, S., Huang, Z., Chandra, V., Kumar, R.: A polynomial algorithm for testing diagnosability of discrete-event systems. IEEE Trans. Autom. Control **46**(8) (2001). https://doi.org/10.1109/9.940942
25. Kupferman, O., Vardi, M.Y., Wolper, P.: An automata-theoretic approach to branching-time model checking. J. ACM (JACM) **47**(2) (2000). https://doi.org/10.1145/333979.333987
26. Merlin, P.M.: A study of the recoverability of computing systems. Ph.D. thesis, Department of Information and Computer Science, University of California (1974)
27. Peres, F., Berthomieu, B., Vernadat, F.: On the composition of time Petri nets. Discrete Event Dyn. Syst. **21**(3) (2011). https://doi.org/10.1007/s10626-011-0102-2
28. Ramadge, P.J., Wonham, W.M.: The control of discrete event systems. Proc. IEEE **77**(1), 81–98 (1989). https://doi.org/10.1109/5.21072
29. Sampath, M., Sengupta, R., Lafortune, S., Sinnamohideen, K., Teneketzis, D.: Diagnosability of discrete-event systems. IEEE Trans. Autom. Control **40**(9), 1555–1575 (1995). https://doi.org/10.1109/9.412626
30. Toussaint, J., Simonot-Lion, F., Thomesse, J.P.: Time constraint verification methods based on time Petri nets. In: Workshop on Future Trends of Distributed Computing Systems. IEEE (1997). https://doi.org/10.1109/FTDCS.1997.644736
31. Tripakis, S.: Fault diagnosis for timed automata. In: Formal Techniques in Real-Time and Fault-Tolerant Systems (FTRTFT) (2002). https://doi.org/10.1007/3-540-45739-9_14
32. Wang, X., Mahulea, C., Silva, M.: Diagnosis of time Petri nets using fault diagnosis graph. IEEE Trans. Autom. Control **60**(9) (2015). https://doi.org/10.1007/978-3-642-15297-9_12

Stability and Performance Bounds in Cyclic Networks Using Network Calculus

Anne Bouillard[(✉)] [iD]

Nokia Bell Labs France, 91620 Nozay, France
anne.bouillard@nokia-bell-labs.com

Abstract. With the development of real-time systems and of new wireless communication technologies having strong requirements on latencies and reliability, there is a need to compute deterministic performance bounds in networks. This paper focuses on the performance guarantees and stability conditions of networks with cyclic dependencies in the network calculus framework.

Two kinds of techniques exist: backlog-based techniques compute backlog bounds for each server, and obtain good stability bounds to the detriment of the performance bounds; flow-based techniques compute performance bounds for each flow and obtain better performance bounds for low bandwidth usage, but poor stability conditions.

In this article, we propose a unified framework that combines the two techniques and improve at the same time stability conditions and performance bounds in the classical linear model. To do this, we first propose an algorithm that computes tight backlog bounds in trees for a set of flows at a server, and then develop a linear program based on this algorithm that computes performance bounds for cyclic networks. An implementation of these algorithms is provided in the Python package NCBounds and is used for numerical experiments showing the efficiency of the approach.

Keywords: Network calculus · Cyclic networks · Linear programming

1 Introduction

New wireless communication technologies (5G) aim at providing deterministic services, with strong requirements on buffer occupancy, latency and reliability. For example, Time-Sensitive Networks (TSN) is part of the 802.1 working group [27], whose potential application to industrial and automotive networks. Critical embedded systems also become more and more complex and it becomes a necessity to compute accurate worst-case performance guarantees.

Network Calculus is a (min,plus)-based theory that computes global performance bounds from a local description of the network. These performances are the maximum backlog at a server of end-to-end delay of a flow. Examples

A. Bouillard is part of the LINCS (www.lincs.fr).

É. André and M. Stoelinga (Eds.): FORMATS 2019, LNCS 11750, pp. 96–113, 2019.
https://doi.org/10.1007/978-3-030-29662-9_6

of applications are switched network [16], Video-on-Demand [20]... It has been very useful for analysis large embedded networks such as AFDX (Avionics Full Duplex) [13], and more recently, it has been used to model the behavior of TSN [21].

In most applications, such as AFDX, only feed-forward topologies are used. One reason is the difficulty of deriving good deterministic performance bounds in networks with cyclic dependencies. However, allowing cycles in networks would result in a better bandwidth usage and more flexible communications [1]. As a consequence, there is a strong need to design efficient methods for computing precise deterministic performance bounds in cyclic networks, which is the aim of this paper.

State of the art. Recent works have focused on computing tight performance bounds in feed-forward networks. It is proved in [10] that the problem is NP-hard for general feed-forward topologies. Bondorf *et al.* propose in [5,6] an approximation scheme based on finding a *good* decomposition of the problem and compute performance bounds on this decomposition, while in [17], Geyer and Bondorf use Recurrent Neural Networks to find this decomposition in tree networks.

A lot of efforts has been put on the analysis of sub-classes of networks, namely sink-trees and tandems. Schmitt *et al.* introduce in [24] the concept of *Pay multiplexing only once* (PMOO) showing at the same time the difficulties in computing tight performance bounds in tandem networks, and exhibiting tight bounds in sink-trees. In [10,12], it is proved that computing tight performance bounds in tandem networks can be done in polynomial time.

The stability of a network is still an open problem in network calculus. The most classical method for computing performance guarantees in cyclic networks is to use the *fix-point* or *time-stopping* method first presented by Cruz in [15]. A sufficient condition for stability is obtained as the existence of a fix point in an equation derived from the network description. This technique has recently been applied by Amari and Mifdaoui in [2] to ring networks, using the *multidimensional convolution* for PMOO in tandem networks first developed in [9].

Another classical result is the stability of the ring for any bandwidth usage under 100%, which is proved by Tassiulas and Georgiadis in [26] for work-conserving links and generalized in [18]. The stability condition in [2] is only 50% of the bandwidth usage in the uniform ring, performance in [2] are better in small bandwidth usages.

Other research directions focus on the FIFO policy. Rizzo and Le Boudec find sufficient condition for the stability in FIFO networks in [23]; Andrews shows in [3,4] that the FIFO policy can be unstable at arbitrary small utilization rates.

Finally, some techniques have also been introduced to stabilize networks: Starobinski *et al.* propose in [22,25] the *turn-prohibition* method that breaks the cyclic dependencies by forbidding some paths of length 2. This ensures both stability and connectivity. Another solution is to add regulators, named shapers, after each server. In [19], Le Boudec shows that introducing shapers allows the control of the worst-case performances.

Contributions. In this paper, we study the problem of stability in networks with cyclic dependencies in the network calculus formalism, unifying the approaches of the time-stopping method and of the backlog-based method of [18, 26]. As in most of the above references, we restrict ourselves to the linear model: when arrival curves are token-bucket and the service curves rate-latency. This approach includes several steps:

1. generalizing the recent algorithm of [12] that computes exact worst-case delays in a tandem network. It now enables to compute the worst-case backlog of a server for any subset of flows crossing that server in tree networks. As a matter of fact, the algorithm in [12] can be deduced from this new algorithm, while the reverse is not true;
2. improving the time-stopping technique. Performance bounds are computed as the solution of a linear program, allowing more expressiveness that the fix-point method. This improvement combines with backlogged-based method, and in particular, the stability of the ring is proven without the additional technical assumption used in [18];
3. providing the Python package `NCBounds` [11] that contains this algorithm, some variants and state-of-the-art techniques.

The rest of the paper is organized as follows: in Sect. 2, we recall the network calculus basics. Then in Sect. 3, we give our algorithm that computes exact worst-case backlog in tree networks. Next in Sect. 4, we present a linear program to compute sufficient conditions for the stability of networks and prove the stability of some networks. Finally, we compare them through numerical experiments in Sect. 5.

2   Network Calculus Framework

In this section, we present the necessary material needed for the rest of the paper. A more complete presentation of the network calculus framework can be found in the reference books [8, 14, 18]. We use the notation $\mathbb{N}_n$ for $\{1, \ldots, n\}$.

2.1   Data Flows and Server

Data Processes and Arrival Curves. Flows of data are represented by cumulative processes. More precisely, if A represents a flow at a certain point in the network, $A(t)$ is the amount of data of that flow that crosses that point in the time interval $[0, t)$, with the convention $A(0) = 0$. The processes are non-decreasing and left-continuous. We denote by $\mathcal{F}$ the set of such functions.

A flow A is constrained by the arrival curve α, or is α-constrained, if

$$\forall s, t \in \mathbb{R}_+ \text{ with } s \leq t, \quad A(t) - A(s) \leq \alpha(t - s).$$

In the following we will consider *leaky-bucket* functions: $\gamma_{b,r} : 0 \mapsto 0; \ t \mapsto b + rt$, if $t > 0$. The *burst* b can be interpreted as the maximal amount of data that can arrive simultaneously and the *arrival rate* r as a maximal long-term arrival rate of data.

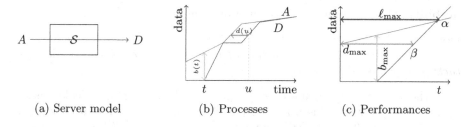

(a) Server model   (b) Processes   (c) Performances

Fig. 1. Server model and worst-case performances.

Servers and Service Curves. An n-server $\mathcal{S} \subseteq \mathcal{F}^n \times \mathcal{F}^n$ (illustrated for $n = 1$ in Fig. 1a) is a relation between n arrival processes $(A_i)_{i=1}^n$ and n departure processes $(D_i)_{i=1}^n$ such that $A_i \geq D_i$ for all $i \in \mathbb{N}_n$. The latter inequality models the causality of the system (no data is created inside the system).

The role of a service curve is to constrain the relation between the inputs of a server and its outputs. Several types of service curves have been defined in the literature (see [18]), and we here only focus on the strict service curve. Intuitively, a strict service curve gives the minimum amount of service provided to the arrival processes provided the system is not empty. More formally, an interval I is a *backlogged period* for $(A, D) \in \mathcal{F} \times \mathcal{F}$ if $\forall u \in I$, $A(u) > D(u)$.

We say that $\beta \in \mathcal{F}$ is a *strict service curve* for 1-server $\mathcal{S}$ if

$$\forall (A, D) \in \mathcal{S}, \quad A \geq D \quad \text{and } \forall \text{ bckl. per. } (s, t], \ D(t) - D(s) \geq \beta(t - s). \quad (1)$$

In the following we will use the *rate-latency* service curves: $\beta_{R,T} : t \mapsto R(t - T)_+$, where T is the *latency* until the server has to become active and R is its minimal *service rate* after this latency.

A n-server $\mathcal{S}$ offers a strict service curve β if, seen as a 1-server, $\mathcal{S}$ offers β to $\sum_{i=1}^m A_i$ and $\sum_{i=1}^m D_i$ for all $((A_i), (D_i)) \in \mathcal{S}$. We call the flow with arrival process $\sum_{i=1}^m A_i$ the aggregate flow of flows $1, \ldots, n$. We assume no knowledge about the service policy in this system (except that it is FIFO per flow).

2.2 Performance Guarantees in a Server

Backlog and Delay. Let $\mathcal{S}$ be a 1-server and $(A, D) \in \mathcal{S}$. The backlog of that server at time t is $b(t) = A(t) - D(t)$. The worst-case backlog is then $b_{\max} = \sup_{t \geq 0} b(t)$.

We denote $b_{\max}(\alpha, \beta)$ the maximum backlog that can be obtained for an α-constrained flow crossing a server with strict service curve β. For example, we have $b_{\max}(\gamma_{b,r}, \beta_{R,T}) = b + rT$ if $r \leq R$.

The delay of data exiting at time t is $d(t) = \sup\{d \geq 0 \mid A(t - d) - D(t)\}$. The worst-case delay is then $d_{\max} = \sup_{t \geq 0} d(t)$.

We denote $d_{\max}(\alpha, \beta)$ the maximum delay that can be obtained for an α-constrained flow crossing a server with strict service curve β. For example, we have $d_{\max}(\gamma_{b,r}, \beta_{R,T}) = T + \frac{T}{R}$ if $r < R$.

Backlog and delay are illustrated on Figs. 1b and c.

Stability. Our main interest is the network stability.

Definition 1 (Server stability). *Consider a server offering a strict service curve β and crossed by an α-constrained flow. This server is said stable if its backlogged periods are bounded.*

If the service curve is rate-latency $\beta_{R,T}$ and the arrival curve leaky-bucket $\gamma_{b,r}$, then a server is stable if and only if $R > r$, as the length of a backlogged period is $\sup\{t > 0 | \alpha(t) > \beta(t)\}$ and is $\ell_{\max}(\gamma_{b,r}, \beta_{R,T}) := \frac{b+RT}{R-r}$ in that case.

This definition involves r and R only. The stability is insensitive to b and T, that only influence the server's performance. This also explains why we restrict in this paper to these types of curves: if a more general arrival (resp. service) curve can be and upper bounded by some token-bucket (resp. rate-latency) functions with the same rate, then the stability sufficient conditions that we compute in this paper are not impacted by the approximation by token bucket and rate latency functions.

2.3   Network Model

Consider a network composed of n servers numbered from 1 to n and crossed by m flows named $f_1, \ldots, f_m$, such that

- each server j guarantees a strict service curve β_j;
- each flow f_i is α_i-constrained and circulates along an acyclic path $\pi_i = \langle \pi_i(1), \ldots, \pi_i(\ell_i) \rangle$ of length ℓ_i.

We call the model *linear* when arrival curves are leaky-bucket and the service curve rate-latency.

For a server j, we define $\mathrm{Fl}(j) = \{i \mid \exists \ell, \ \pi_i(\ell) = j\}$ the set of indices of the flows crossing server j.

We denote by $\mathcal{N}$ this network. The induced graph $G_{\mathcal{N}} = (\mathbb{N}_n, \mathbb{A})$ is the directed graph whose vertices are the servers and the set of arcs is

$$\mathbb{A} = \{(\pi_i(k), \pi_i(k+1)) \mid i \in \mathbb{N}_m, k \in \mathbb{N}_{\ell_i - 1}\}.$$

As we will focus on the performances in server n, we can assume without loss of generality that the network is connected and has a unique final strictly connected component.

Tree Networks. If the induced graph $G_{\mathcal{N}}$ has out-degree 1 for each vertex except node n is 1 and out-degree 0 for vertex n, then $\mathcal{N}$ is called a *tree*. In that case, we denote by $j^\bullet$ the unique successor of server j and assume that $j < j^\bullet$, with the convention $n^\bullet = n + 1$. The set of predecessors of a vertex is $^\bullet j = \{k \mid k^\bullet = j\}$. There exists at most one path between two vertices j and k, denoted $j \rightsquigarrow k$, and if there exists such a path, $^{\bullet j}k$ is the predecessor of k on this path. Figure 2 illustrates the notations of the network model.

Finally we can extend the notion of stability to networks.

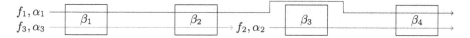

Fig. 2. Example of a tree-networks with 3 flows and 4 servers. To illustrate the notations, we have $\pi(1) = \langle 1, 2, 4 \rangle$, $\mathrm{Fl}(4) = \{1, 2\}$, $4^{\bullet} = \{2, 3\}$, $4^{\bullet_1} = 2$, and $1 \leadsto 4 = \langle 1, 2, 4 \rangle$.

Definition 2 (Local stability). *A network $\mathcal{N}$ is locally stable if all its servers are stable using the initial arrival curves:*

$$\forall j \in \mathbb{N}_n, \quad \ell_{\max}\Big(\sum_{i \in \mathrm{Fl}(j)} \alpha_i, \beta_j \Big) < \infty.$$

Definition 3 (Global stability). *A network is globally stable if the backlogged periods of each server are uniformly bounded.*

It is well-known that if a network is globally stable, then it is locally stable. The converse is true for feed-forward networks, but not in general.

3   Worst-Case Backlog in Trees

In this section, we focus on tree networks and give an algorithm to compute exact worst-case backlog in the linear model. Then we compare with the existing approaches.

3.1   Algorithm

The algorithm presented in this paragraph is a generalization of the one given in [12] with the following differences:

1. our algorithm computes a worst-case backlog at a server;
2. it can be applied to compute the worst-case backlog at a server for any set of flows crossing this server;
3. it is valid for any tree topology.

The two algorithms and their proof are based on the same ideas, and due to the space limitation, we do not present the complete proof here.

Theorem 1. *Consider a stable tree network with n servers offering a rate-latency strict service curves β_{R_j, T_j}, and m flows with leaky-bucket arrival curves γ_{b_i, r_i}. Let I be a subset of flows crossing server n. Then there exists $(\rho_j)_{j \in \mathbb{N}_n}$ and $(\varphi_i)_{i \in \mathbb{N}_n}$ such that the worst-case backlog at server n for flows in I is*

$$B = \sum_{j=1}^{n} \rho_j T_j + \sum_{i=1}^{m} \varphi_i b_i, \tag{2}$$

where the coefficients ρ_j and φ_i depend only on r_i and R_j and are computed by Algorithm 1. This algorithm runs in time $O(n^2 + m)$.

If there is only one flow for each possible source/destination pair, then $m \leq n^2/2$ and the algorithm runs is $O(n^2)$.

We call $I \subseteq \mathbb{N}_m$ the set of flows of interest, and use the following additional notations:

- $r_j^k = \sum_{i \in \mathrm{Fl}(j) \setminus I, \pi_i(\ell_i)=k} r_i$ is the arrival rate at server j for all flows ending at server k and crossing server j that are not of interest;
- $r_j^* = \sum_{i \in I \cap \mathrm{Fl}(j)} r_i$ is the arrival rate of the flows of interest that cross server j.

Algorithm 1. Worst-case backlog algorithm

---

1 **begin**
2 $\quad \xi_n^n \leftarrow r_n^*/R_n - r_n^n$;
3 $\quad Q = \mathbf{queue}(^\bullet n)$;
4 $\quad$ **while** $Q \neq \emptyset$ **do**
5 $\quad\quad j = Q[0]$;
6 $\quad\quad k \leftarrow n$;
7 $\quad\quad$ **while** $\xi_{j\bullet}^k > (r_j^* + \sum_{\ell \in k^\bullet \leadsto n} \xi_{j\bullet}^\ell \cdot r_j^\ell)/(R_j - \sum_{\ell \in j \leadsto k} r_j^\ell)$ **do**
8 $\quad\quad\quad \xi_j^k \leftarrow \xi_{j\bullet}^k$;
9 $\quad\quad\quad k \leftarrow {}^{\bullet j}k$;
10 $\quad\quad$ **for** ℓ from j to k **do** $\xi_j^\ell \leftarrow (r_j^* + \sum_{\ell' \in k^\bullet \leadsto n} \xi_{j\bullet}^{\ell'} \cdot r_j^{\ell'})/(R_j - \sum_{\ell \in j \leadsto k} r_j^{\ell'})$;
11 $\quad\quad Q \leftarrow \mathbf{enqueue}(\mathbf{dequeue}(Q,j),{}^\bullet j)$;
12 $\quad$ **for** j from 1 to n **do** $\rho_j \leftarrow r_j^* + \sum_{\ell \in j \leadsto n} \xi_j^\ell r_j^\ell$;
13 $\quad$ **for** i from 1 to m **do**
14 $\quad\quad$ **if** $i \in I$ **then** $\varphi_i \leftarrow 1$;
15 $\quad\quad$ **else** $\varphi_i \leftarrow \xi_{\pi_i(1)}^{\pi_i(\ell_i)}$;

Proof (Sketch). The proof is in two steps. First we show that there is a worst-case trajectory (*i.e.* a set of arrival and departure processes satisfying all arrival and service curve constraints and reaching the worst-case backlog at a time denoted $t_{n+1} = t_{n\bullet}$) satisfying the following properties:

(P_1) The service policy is SDF (shortest-to-destination-first): priority is given to flows that stop at the server with the smallest number.

(P_2) For each server j, there is a unique backlogged period $(t_j, t_{j\bullet}]$, where the service offered is as small as possible. After and before this backlogged period, the server transmits data instantaneously.

(P_3) The arrival cumulative process of flow f_i entering the system at server j (*i.e.* $\pi_i(1) = j$) is maximal from t_j, the start of the backlogged period of server j (it is $\alpha_i(t - t_j)$ for all $t > t_j$ and 0 otherwise. Intuitively, the backlog does not increase if the cross-traffic is delayed).

(P_4) Data from the flows of interest in I have the lowest priority and are instantaneously served by server j at time $t_{j\bullet}$ (if they cross server j) and are all in server n at time t_{n+1}.

The second step is to find a worst-case trajectory. The first step allows us to reduce the space of the trajectories, and in fact only the dates $(t_j)_{j \in \mathbb{N}_n}$ remain to optimize. This is done by a backward induction on the servers. The choice of date t_j is equivalent to choosing which flows (hence the quantity of data) will be transmitted instantaneously by server j to its successor, so that the backlog in the final server is maximized. □

The worst-case delay of a flow (main results of [12]) can be deduced from the worst-case backlog when I is reduced to this flow.

Corollary 1. *Suppose that flow 1 crosses server n. Then the worst-case delay of flow 1 starting at server j and ending at server n is*

$$\Delta = \frac{B - b_1}{r_1} + \frac{\xi_j^n b_1}{r_1},$$

where B and ξ_j^n are the worst-case backlog and coefficient obtained from Algorithm 1 when $I = \{1\}$.

Interpretation of ξ. The parameter ξ_j^ℓ can be interpreted as the contribution of data crossing server j and exiting at server ℓ contribute to increase the backlog of the flows of interest at server n. For example, consider server n, and suppose that for the flows not of interest, the backlog transmitted from server $n - 1$ to server n and from flows entering at server n at time t_{n-1} is b. Denote by r_n^n the arrival rate of these flows. These data have the highest priority. All data from these flows are served after a time $t = t_n - t_{n-1} = T_n + \frac{b + r_n^n T_n}{R_n - r_n^n}$ (we have $b + r_n^n t = R_n(t - T)_+$). During this time, data created by the flows of interest, at rate r_n^*, can be divided in two parts: $r_n^* T_n$ induced by server n's latency and $r_n^* \frac{b + r_n^n T_n}{R_n - r_n^n}$ induced by the interference of the other flows, which explains the equality $\xi_n^n = \frac{r_n^*}{R_n - r_n^n}$. The interpretation is similar for the other servers. The complexity of the formula and the comparison of line 7 corresponds to searching the downstream bottleneck.

3.2   Backlog and Arrival Curves for Aggregation of Flows

In this paragraph, we show how to use our algorithm to compute arrival curves for the aggregation of flows, and how this can be used to improve the performances bounds computed: Theorem 2 is the base for our backlogged based approach and Theorem 3 improves the performance bounds by combining flows and backlog.

Theorem 2. *With the same notations and assumptions as in Theorem 1, the arrival curve of the departure functions from server n for flows in I is $\gamma_{B, \sum_{i \in I} r_i}$.*

This theorem is a generalization to networks and for several flows of the classical result that characterizes the arrival curve of a departure process (see [8, Theorem 5.3] for example).

Consider a tree network as above and the following assumptions:

- $I = \{f_1, \ldots, f_k\}$ is a set of flows all entering the network at server j, that have respective arrival curves γ_{b_i, r_i}. Data of each flow f_i can arrive at rate at least r_i independently of the other flows;
- the arrival process of the aggregation of the flows in I is constrained by the arrival curve $\gamma_{b,r}$, with $r = \sum_{i \in I} r_i$;
- B is a performance of the tree network (backlog at its root or delay of a flow), and $(\varphi_i)_{i \in I}$ are the computed with Algorithm 1.

In the rest of the paper, the assumption that each flow f_i can arrive at rate r_i independently of the other flows is satisfied, because the servers can serve data instantaneously and any service policy is possible.

Theorem 3. *With the notations and assumptions above,*

$$B \leq \sup\{\sum_{i=1}^{k} \varphi_i x_i + C \mid x_i \leq b_i \ and \ \sum_{i \in I} x_i \leq b\},$$

where C is a constant including the contribution of all flows not in I and of all latencies.

Proof. From property (P_3), the arrival processes A_i of $f_i \in I$ are maximal from time t_j, the start of backlogged period of server j. Then data from flow f_i can arrive at rate r_i at least. As this is also the maximal long-term arrival rate, there exists $x_i \leq b_i$ such that $A_i(t) - A_i(t_j) \leq x_i + r_i(t - t_j)$, and that $\limsup_t A_i(t) - A_i(t_j) - r_i(t - t_j) \geq x_i$. We then have the inequality $B \leq \sum_{i=1}^{k} \varphi_i x_i + C$.
But we also have

$$\sum_{i \in I} A_i(t) - A_i(t_j) \leq b + \sum_{i \in I} r_i(t - t_j),$$

so $\sum_{i \in I} x_i \leq b$. As a consequence, the performance of the system can be bounded by $B \leq \sup\{\sum_{i=1}^{k} \varphi_i x_i + C \mid x_i \leq b_i \ and \ \sum_{i \in I} x_i \leq b\}$. $\square$

3.3   Examples and Comparison with the State of the Art

We compare our performance bounds with the state of the art for two models that have been widely studied in the literature: the sink-tree from [7,24] and the tandem networks (PMOO technique from [2,9]).

Sink-trees are tree topologies where the destination of every flow is the root (node n). In this special case, each iteration of the external loop (lines 5–11) can be performed in constant time (there is only one test to perform). Moreover, the number of flows is at most the number of servers. As a consequence, our algorithm can be performed in $O(n)$.

To compute the maximum backlog at the root, every flow is a flow of interest, so $\varphi_i = 1$ for each flow i and $\rho_j = r_j^* = \sum_{i \in \mathrm{Fl}(j)} r_i$. It is easy to check that the formula is the same as in [7, Theorem 14].

Fig. 3. Left: sink-tree, Right: tandem.

Table 1. Comparison of delay bounds.

	ξ_2^2	ξ_1^2	ξ_1^1	Algorithm 1	[9, Cor. 25]	[7, Th. 18, 15]	[24, Sec. V]
f_1	$\frac{r}{2R-r}$	$\frac{r}{R}$	$\frac{2r}{2R-r}$	$T+\frac{b}{R}+\frac{b+rT}{2R-r}$	$2T+\frac{2b+rT}{R}$	$2T+\frac{2b+rT}{R}$	$T+\frac{b}{R}+\frac{b+rT}{2R-r}$
f_2	$\frac{r}{2R-r}$	$\frac{r}{2R-r}$	$\frac{r^2}{(R-r)(2R-r)}$	$\frac{2b+(2R+r)T}{2R-r}$	∞	$\frac{2b+(2R+r)T}{2R-r}$	∞
f_3	$\frac{r}{R-r}$	$\frac{r}{R-r}$	$\frac{r}{R-r}$	$\frac{2(TR+b)}{R-r}$	$\frac{2(TR+b)}{R-r}$	∞	∞
f_4	$\frac{r}{R-r}$	$\frac{r}{R-r}$	$\left(\frac{r}{R-r}\right)^2$	$\frac{R(TR+b)}{(R-r)^2}+\frac{b}{R-r}$	∞	∞	∞

Table 1 shows the values of ξ_i^j for the two examples of Figs. 3 and flows $f_1,\dots,f_4$, where all flows are constrained by the arrival curve $\gamma_{b,r}$, and the comparison of the worst-case delay obtained in this case against other techniques. We write "∞" when no specific mean is provided to compute de performance.

We see that our algorithm is strictly more general than the study of some specific topologies in several ways: of course we can handle tree topologies that strictly contains tandem and sink-tree networks. But, it can also compute performances for flows of interest that do not cross *all* the servers, which only [7] does for sink-trees.

The PMOO bound gives the tight performance in the tandem network, but not in the sink-tree. The tandem here is quite specific, as all the coefficients ξ_i^j are the same. Our guess is that the PMOO formula is an upper bound of the bounds found by our algorithm, obtained by replacing ξ_i^j by $\max_{i,j} \xi_{i,j}$. So equality occurs when all the coefficients are the same.

4   Computing Performances in Cyclic Networks

In this section, we generalize the fix-point method, also known as time-stopping, that is used to compute the worst-case performance bounds in networks with cyclic dependencies. The principle of this method is to *split* the paths of the flows into sub-paths in order to obtain an acyclic network, for which it is possible to compute performance bounds, in particular output arrival curves at the end of each sub-path. Then to retrieve performance guarantees of the original network, a fix-point on the arrival curves is computed: an output arrival curve at the end of a sub-path is the arrival curve at the start of the next sub-path. Details on this approach can be found in [8,18].

In this section we generalize this approach to take advantage of the results derived in Sect. 3.2. In Sect. 4.1, we present a linear program computing worst-case performance bounds and in Sect. 4.2, we show the stability of the ring and slightly more general networks.

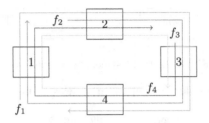

Fig. 4. Ring network with $n = 4$.

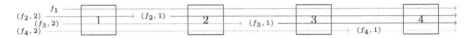

Fig. 5. Uniform tandem network with $n = 4$.

4.1 Decomposition in Trees and Linear Program

We apply the time-stopping method when decomposing the network into trees. The graph of the network $G_\mathcal{N}$ can be transformed into a forest by removing a set of arcs $\mathbb{A}^r$. In the network, each flow f_i that traverse removed arcs is *split* into several flows $(f_i, 1), (f_i, 2), \ldots, (f_i, m_i)$ of respective paths in $(\mathbb{N}_i, \mathbb{A} - \mathbb{A}^r)$, $\pi_{i,1} = \langle \pi_i(1), \ldots, \pi_i(k_1) \rangle$, $\pi_{i,2} = \langle \pi_i(k_1 + 1), \ldots, \pi_i(k_2) \rangle$,..., $\pi_{i,m_i} = \langle \pi_i(k_{m_i} + 1), \ldots, \pi_i(\ell_i) \rangle$, where $(\pi_i(k_j+1), \pi_i(k_j)) \in \mathbb{A}^r$. Figure 4 represents a ring of length 4. One can choose $\mathbb{A}^r = (4, 1)$, and flows f_2, f_3, f_4 can be decomposed into $(f_i, 1)$ and $(f_i, 2)$, $i \in \{2, 3, 4\}$, as depicted in Fig. 5.

Consider $\mathcal{N}^{\mathrm{FF}}$, the feed-forward network obtained after this transformation and let us focus on two kinds of arrival curves:

- the arrival curve of each flow (f_i, k), denoted $\alpha_{i,k}$;
- the arrival curve of the aggregation of flows crossing each removed arc of $\mathbb{A}^r$, and denoted λ_a, and that we call arrival curve of arc a.

If all these arrival curves are known and finite, then the performance bounds can be computed for every flow.

In the original network $\mathcal{N}$, all these arrival curves are *a priori* not known, except $\alpha_{i,1} = \alpha_i$, but we can write equations where these arrival curves are the unknowns. More precisely, suppose that the network is stable and denote $\alpha_{i,k}$ the *best* arrival curve (that is, the minimum arrival curves among all the possible arrival curves) of flow k at server $p_{i,k}(1)$ and λ_a the *best* arrival curve of arc a. From Theorems 2 and 3, there exist functions $F_{i,k}$ and F_a such that

$$\alpha_{i,k} \le F_{i,k}((\alpha_s)_{s \in S}, (\lambda_a)_{a \in \mathbb{A}^r}) \quad \text{and} \quad \lambda_a \le F_{i,k}((\alpha_s)_{s \in S}, (\lambda_a)_{a \in \mathbb{A}^r}),$$

with $S = \{(i, k), i \in \mathbb{N}_m, 1 < k \le m_i\}$.

Using vector notation, with $(\boldsymbol{\alpha}, \boldsymbol{\lambda}) = ((\alpha_s)_{s \in S}, (\lambda_a)_{a \in \mathbb{A}^r})$ and $\mathbf{F} = (F_s)_{s \in S \cup \mathbb{A}^r}$, one can write, $(\boldsymbol{\alpha}, \boldsymbol{\lambda}) \le \mathbf{F}(\boldsymbol{\alpha}, \boldsymbol{\lambda})$ and the following theorem holds.

Theorem 4. *Set* $\mathcal{C} = \{(\alpha, \lambda) \mid (\alpha, \lambda) \leq \mathbf{F}(\alpha, \lambda)\}$ *and* $(\tilde{\alpha}, \tilde{\lambda}) = \sup\{(\alpha, \lambda) \mid (\alpha, \lambda) \in \mathcal{C}\}$. *If* $(\tilde{\alpha}, \tilde{\lambda})$ *is finite, then* $\mathcal{N}$ *is globally stable and for all* s, $\tilde{\alpha}_s$ *is an arrival curve for flow* s *and for all* $a \in \mathbb{A}^r$, $\tilde{\lambda}_a$ *for arc* a.

The proof of this theorem is nearly the same as that of [8, Theorem 12.1].

In the linear model, the arrival rate of each arrival curve remains the same as the original flow, and we only have to compute the burst b_s of each flow s, and B_a is the backlog at each arc in $\mathbb{A}^r$. A sufficient condition for the stability can be expressed as a linear problem. Consider $\mathcal{L}$ the following set of linear constraints:

$$
\mathcal{L} = \left\{
\begin{array}{ll}
b_s \leq \sum_{s' \in S} \varphi^s_{s'} x^s_{s'} + C_s, & \forall s \in S \\
B_a \leq \sum_{s' \in S} \varphi^a_{s'} x^a_{s'} + C_a, & \forall a \in \mathbb{A}^r \\
0 \leq x^s_{s'} \leq b_{s'}, & \forall s' \in S, s \in S \cup \mathbb{A}^r \\
\sum_{s' \in a} x^s_{s'} \leq B_a, & \forall a \in \mathbb{A}^r, s \in S \cup \mathbb{A}^r
\end{array}
\right\},
$$

where we write $(i, k) \in a$ if flows $(f_i, k - 1)$ and (f_i, k) have been split by arc a and where $\varphi^s_{s'}$ are the coefficient obtained by Algorithm 1 with flow(s) of interests $s \in S \cup \mathbb{A}^r$ and C_s the contribution of the latencies.

Theorem 5. *If* $\mathcal{L}$ *is bounded, then the system is stable.*

This is a rephrasing of Theorem 4, using the linear constraints given in Theorem 3: constraints $\{b_s \leq \sum_{s' \in S} \varphi^s_{s'} x^s_{s'} + C_s, 0 \leq x^s_{s'} \leq b_{s'}, \forall s' \in S, \sum_{s' \in a} x^s_{s'} \leq B_a, \forall a \in \mathbb{A}^r\}$ represent the constraints for computing the backlog of flow s, as in Theorem 3 applied to flow s, and similarly $\{B_a \leq \sum_{s' \in S} \varphi^a_{s'} x^a_{s'} + C_a, 0 \leq x^a_{s'} \leq b_{s'}, \forall s' \in S, \sum_{s' \in a'} x^a_{s'} \leq B_{a'}, \forall a' \in \mathbb{A}^r\}$ are the constraints coming from Theorem 3 applied to computing the worst-case backlog at arc a.

A linear program to compute a performance bound of the system (worst-case delay or worst-case backlog) is then

$$
\begin{array}{ll}
\text{Maximize :} & \sum_{s' \in S} \varphi_s y_s + C \\
\text{Constraints :} & \sum_{s \in a} y_s \leq B_a, \quad \forall a \in \mathbb{A}^r, \\
& 0 \leq y_s \leq b_s, \quad \forall s' \in S, \\
& \mathcal{L}.
\end{array}
$$

The linear program has $O(c^2)$ variables and constraints, with $c = |S| + |\mathbb{A}^r|$, and c constraints require using the quadratic Algorithm 1, which can be costly. The next paragraph shows two ways to relax the problem to respectively $O(|S|)$ and $O(|\mathbb{A}^r|)$ variables and constraints.

Flow-Based and Backlog-Based Linear Programs. The linear program we just wrote combines two techniques usually used separately for cyclic networks: the first one uses the time-stopping technique to compute the characteristics of each flow at servers it crosses, and we call them flow-based. The second one computes worst-case backlog in each server, similar to [18,26], and we call them backlog-based.

The set $\mathcal{L}$ can be simplified into $\mathcal{L}_F$ and $\mathcal{L}_B$ to derive respectively flow-based and backlog-based bounds: it suffices to respectively keep the flow related constraints (first and third lines of $\mathcal{L}$) for $\mathcal{L}_F$ and the arc related constraints (second and fourth lines of $\mathcal{L}$) for $\mathcal{L}_B$. Of course, larger performance bounds will be obtained, but we will see in Sect. 5 that these linear programs already improve the flow-based or backlog-based bounds.

As $\varphi_{s'}^s$ are non-negative, variables $x_{s'}^s$ become useless, and we finally obtain:

$$\mathcal{L}_F = \left\{ \begin{array}{l} b_s \leq \sum_{s' \in S} \varphi_{s'}^s x_{s'}^s + C_s, \forall s \in S \\ 0 \leq x_{s'}^s \leq b_{s'}, \forall s' \in S, s \in S \cup \mathbb{A}^r \end{array} \right\}$$
$$= \left\{ b_s \leq \sum_{s' \in S} \varphi_{s'}^s b_{s'}^s + C_s, \forall s \in S \right\},$$

and

$$\mathcal{L}_B = \left\{ \begin{array}{l} B_a \leq \sum_{s' \in S} \varphi_{s'}^a x_{s'}^a + C_a, \forall a \in \mathbb{A}^r \\ \sum_{s' \in a} x_{s'}^s \leq B_a \forall a \in \mathbb{A}^r, s \in S \cup \mathbb{A}^r \end{array} \right\}$$
$$= \left\{ B_a \leq \sum_{a' \in \mathbb{A}^r} (\max_{s' \in a'} \varphi_{s'}^a) B_{a'} + C_a, \forall a \in \mathbb{A}^r \right\}.$$

4.2   Stability of the Ring

Consider a ring with n servers. Its induced graph is $\mathcal{G}$ with $\mathbb{A} = \{(i, i+1), i \leq n-1\} \cup \{(n,1)\}$. The transformation into a tree is a tandem network obtained by removing arc $(n,1)$. Flows are decomposed in either one flow if $\pi_i(1) < \pi_i(\ell_i)$ or two flows otherwise: flow $(f_i, 1)$ has path $\langle \pi_i(1), \ldots, n \rangle$ and flow $(f_i, 2)$ has path $\langle 1, \ldots, \pi_i(\ell_i) \rangle$.

Theorem 6. *The ring is stable under local stability condition.*

Proof. The ring is stable if the set $\mathcal{L}_B$ is bounded, that is, if $\varphi_s^{(n,1)} < 1$ for all $s \in S = \{(i,2) \mid \forall i$ such that $\pi_i(1) > \pi_i(\ell_i)\}$.

To compute B_a, the flows of interest are flows $(i,1)$, so $\varphi_{(i,2)}^a = \xi_1^{\pi_i(\ell_i)}$.

Observe from Algorithm 1 how ξ_j^ℓ are computed: because of the local stability, $R_n > r_n^n + r_n^*$, so $\xi_n^n < 1$. Now assume that $\xi_{j\bullet}^k < 1$ (lines 7–9). Either $\xi_j^k = \xi_{j\bullet}^k < 1$, or $\xi_j^\ell = (r_j^* + \sum_{\ell' \in k\bullet \leadsto n} \xi_{j\bullet}^\ell r_j^{\ell'})/(R_j - \sum_{\ell \in j \leadsto k} r_j^\ell) \leq (r_j^* + \sum_{\ell' \in k\bullet \leadsto n} r_j^{\ell'})/(R_j - \sum_{\ell \in j \leadsto k} r_j^\ell) < 1$, from the local stability condition. As a consequence, for all j and ℓ, $\xi_j^\ell < 1$ and $\max_{s \in S} \varphi_s^{(n,1)} < 1$, which ends the proof.   □

This result has already been proved under stronger assumptions: in [26], servers are constant-rate servers and in [18], servers have a maximal service rate. Our method is not specific to the ring topology, so we can hope to improve the stability conditions for more general topologies.

Stability of Hierarchical Cycles. A straightforward generalization is when the network only has disjoint cycles: each non trivial strongly connected component of the network is a ring. In this case, the stability can be established by induction: perform a topological ordering of the cycles, and compute performances at the outputs of each cycle in this topological order.

Unfortunately, our linear program is not enough to prove the stability of other classes of networks, and we will see in the next section that the stability condition established for a network composed of two rings is stronger than the local stability.

5   Numerical Evaluation

In this section, we compare our approach with the state of the art on several examples. The first one is the ring already defined. Indeed, the ring is the topology which has been studied in [2] and [26]. To demonstrate the generality of our algorithm, we also take the example of a network composed of two rings, but we can only compare this example with the most naive methods of [15, 18]. The different approaches have been implemented in the Python Package NCBounds [11]. Note that the implementation of the package aims at clarity rather than efficiency.

The following approaches are compared.

- **SFA**: the fix-point approach described in [18, Section 6.3.2] computes a fix-point in the performances of each flow at each server it crosses;
- **PMOO**: the fix-point approach described in [2] that is exemplified on the uniform ring;
- **BB**: the backlog bound of [18, Theorem 6.4.1];
- **LP$_\mathbf{F}$**: the flow-based linear programming approach using the $\mathcal{L}_F$ (that can be compared to **SFA** and **PMOO**);
- **LP$_\mathbf{B}$**: the backlog-based linear programming approach using $\mathcal{L}_B$ (that can be compared to **BB**);
- **LP$_\mathbf{F+B}$**: the linear programming approach using all constraints $\mathcal{L}$.

5.1   Uniform Ring Example

Consider a uniform ring network as described in Fig. 4 composed of n servers and n flows of length n. Each server has a service rate $R = 100\,Mb.s^{-1}$ and latency of $1ms$, the maximum burst of each flow is $1Mb$. The arrival rate depends on the utilization rate $u \in [0,1]$ and is $r = \frac{uR}{n}$.

We first compare the stability region for each method that do not stabilize the ring, namely **SFA**, **PMOO** and **LP$_\mathbf{F}$**. Figure 6a depicts the stability region when the number of servers varies from 2 to 100. As expected, **PMOO** provides better bounds than **SFA**, and **LP$_\mathbf{F}$** improves the stability region. As conjectured in [2], the stability region with **PMOO** converges to a utilization rate of 0.5. The stability region of **LP$_\mathbf{F}$** seem to converge to $2 - \sqrt{2} \simeq 0.58$, hence already providing approximately 18% improvement of the stability region over flow-based methods.

Now we fix the number of servers $n = 10$, and compare the worst-case backlogs of flow 1 at server 10 (Fig. 6b). We choose backlog over delay because **BB** is more suited to this performance, and computing delays would lead to even worse performances. We observe the same stability bounds as above for the three flow-based methods. The stability of the ring is experimentally verified by the

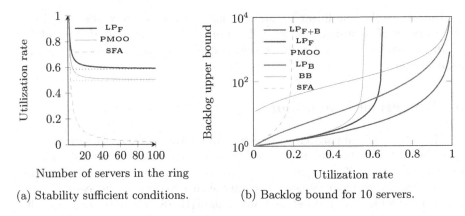

(a) Stability sufficient conditions.   (b) Backlog bound for 10 servers.

Fig. 6. Comparisons with the uniform ring.

three other methods. The more constraints we add in the linear programming approach, the tighter the backlog bound, hence $\mathbf{LP_{F+B}}$ is a better bounds than $\mathbf{LP_F}$ and $\mathbf{LP_B}$. Second, $\mathbf{LP_F}$ also beats **PMOO**. This could be seen as surprising as **PMOO** computes tight bounds for uniform tandems. The difference can be explained by the more general applicability of Algorithm 1 stated in Sect. 3.3: exact worst-case performances can be computed for a flow that *do not cross all servers*, hence the network is decomposed into fewer elements, which induces less pessimism in the performance bounds. $\mathbf{LP_B}$ also beats **BB**. This is quite logical, as the formula uses fewer parameters that the linear program.

5.2 Two-Ring Example

We now consider a network composed of two rings of length n, as depicted in Fig. 7a with $n = 4$. Each flow has length n and circulates along one of the two rings ($2n$ flows), and the description of the servers and flows is the same as above, except that the central server has service rate $2R$. Figure 7b compares the performances obtained with the three **LP** methods against **SFA**, the only other method that can be applied to non-ring networks. We see that the stability region and the performances are improved. In this case, we do not obtain the stability (which is an open issue), but $\mathbf{LP_{F+B}}$ strictly improve the stability region ($u \leq 0.76$) of both $\mathbf{LP_F}$ ($u \leq 0.75$) and $\mathbf{LP_B}$ ($u \leq 0.73$), while the two latter methods do not compare performance-wise.

Backlog Vs delay. Finally, Figs. 8a and 8b depict the delays of flow 1 in the same experimental settings as above. From Corollary 1, the delay is obtained from the backlog by a linear transformation. Consequently, the comparisons remain similar. Still, one can notice that the backlog-based bound is not very good at low utilization rate.

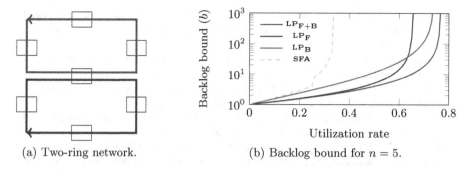

(a) Two-ring network.   (b) Backlog bound for $n = 5$.

Fig. 7. Comparisons with the two-ring network.

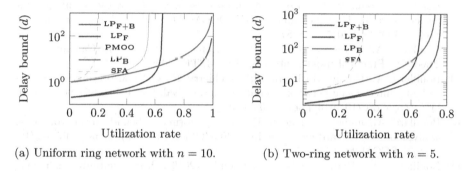

(a) Uniform ring network with $n = 10$.   (b) Two-ring network with $n = 5$.

Fig. 8. Delay bounds.

6   Conclusion

In this article, we gave an algorithm to compute tight worst-case performances in tree-networks and a linear program to compute worst-case performances in general topologies. This approach outperforms the existing approaches both for the stability condition and the performances.

One open question is the choice of the decomposition of the network, the influence of this choice on the stability region and bounds obtained. One way to choose a good decomposition could be to follow the approach of [17] and use neural networks.

Finally, we assumed arbitrary multiplexing, and future work includes adapting the result to specific service policies, such as FIFO, priorities, or generalized processor sharing.

References

1. Amari, A., Mifdaoui, A., Frances, F., Lacan, J., Rambaud, D., Urbain, L.: AeroRing: avionics full duplex ethernet ring with high availability and QoS management. In: ERTS (2016)

2. Amari, A., Mifdaoui, A.: Worst-case timing analysis of ring networks with cyclic dependencies using network calculus. In: RTCSA, pp. 1–10 (2017). https://doi.org/10.1109/RTCSA.2017.8046319

3. Andrews, M.: Instability of FIFO in session-oriented networks. In: Proceedings of SODA 2000 (2000)

4. Andrews, M.: Instability of FIFO in the permanent sessions model at arbitrarily small network loads. In: Proceedings of SODA 2007 (2007)

5. Bondorf, S., Nikolaus, P., Schmitt, J.B.: Quality and cost of deterministic network calculus - design and evaluation of an accurate and fast analysis. In: ACM SIGMETRICS (2017). https://doi.org/10.1145/3078505.3078594

6. Bondorf, S., Nikolaus, P., Schmitt, J.B.: Quality and cost of deterministic network calculus - design and evaluation of an accurate and fast analysis. Proc. ACM Meas. Anal. Comput. Syst. (POMACS) 1(1), 34 (2017). https://doi.org/10.1145/3084453

7. Bondorf, S., Schmitt, J.B.: Boosting sensor network calculus by thoroughly bounding cross-traffic. In: Proceedings of INFOCOM 2015 (2015). https://doi.org/10.1109/INFOCOM.2015.7218387

8. Bouillard, A., Boyer, M., Corronc, E.L.: Deterministic Network Calculus: From Theory to Practical Implementation, Wiley-ISTE (2018)

9. Bouillard, A., Gaujal, B., Lagrange, S., Thierry, E.: Optimal routing for end-to-end guarantees using network calculus. Perform. Eval. 65(11–12), 883–906 (2008). https://doi.org/10.1016/j.peva.2008.04.008

10. Bouillard, A., Jouhet, L., Thierry, E.: Tight performance bounds in the worst case analysis of feed forward networks. In: INFOCOM 2010 (2010). https://doi.org/10.1109/INFCOM.2010.5461912

11. Bouillard, A.: Python package ncbounds (2019). https://github.com/nokia/NCBounds

12. Bouillard, A., Nowak, T.: Fast symbolic computation of the worst-case delay in tandem networks and applications. Perform. Eval. 91, 270–285 (2015). https://doi.org/10.1016/j.peva.2015.06.016

13. Boyer, M., Navet, N., Olive, X., Thierry, E.: The PEGASE project: precise and scalable temporal analysis for aerospace communication systems with network calculus. In: ISOLA 2010 (2010). https://doi.org/10.1007/978-3-642-16558-0_13

14. Chang, C.S.: Performance Guarantees in Communication Networks. TNCS. Springer-Verlag, London (2000). https://doi.org/10.1007/978-1-4471-0459-9

15. Cruz, R.: A calculus for network delay, part II: network analysis. IEEE Trans. Inf. Theor. 37(1), 132–141 (1991). https://doi.org/10.1109/18.61110

16. Cruz, R.: Quality of service guarantees in virtual circuit switched networks. IEEE J. Sel. Areas Commun. 13, 1048–1056 (1995). https://doi.org/10.1109/49.400660

17. Geyer, F., Bondorf, S.: DeepTMA: predicting effective contention models for network calculus using graph neural networks. In: (INFOCOM) (2019). https://doi.org/10.1109/INFOCOM.2019.8737496

18. Le Boudec, J.-Y., Thiran, P. (eds.): Network Calculus. LNCS, vol. 2050. Springer, Heidelberg (2001). https://doi.org/10.1007/3-540-45318-0

19. Le Boudec, J.: A theory of traffic regulators for deterministic networks with application to interleaved regulators. IEEE/ACM Trans. Netw. 26(6), 2721–2733 (2018). https://doi.org/10.1109/TNET.2018.2875191

20. McManus, J.M., Ross, K.W.: Video-on-demand over ATM: constant-rate transmission and transport. IEEE J. Sel. A. Commun. 14(6), 1087–1098 (1996). https://doi.org/10.1109/49.508280

21. Mohammadpour, E., Stai, E., Mohiuddin, M., Boudec, J.L.: Latency and backlog bounds in time-sensitive networking with credit based shapers and asynchronous traffic shaping. In: 30th International Teletraffic Congress, pp. 1–6. ITC (2018). https://doi.org/10.1109/ITC30.2018.10053

22. Pellegrini, F.D., Starobinski, D., Karpovsky, M.G., Levitin, L.B.: Scalable cycle-breaking algorithms for gigabit ethernet backbones. In: Proceedings IEEE INFO-COM (2004). https://doi.org/10.1109/INFCOM.2004.1354641

23. Rizzo, G., Boudec, J.Y.L.: Stability and delay bounds in heterogeneous networks of aggregate schedulers. In: Proceedings of INFOCOM 2008 (2008). https://doi.org/10.1109/INFOCOM.2008.208

24. Schmitt, J., Zdarsky, F., Fidler, M.: Delay bounds under arbitrary multiplexing: when network calculus leaves you in the lurch ... In: INFOCOM 2008 (2008). https://doi.org/10.1109/INFOCOM.2008.228

25. Starobinski, D., Karpovsky, M.G., Zakrevski, L.: Application of network calculus to general topologies using turn-prohibition. In: Proceedings IEEE INFOCOM (2002). https://doi.org/10.1109/INFCOM.2002.1019365

26. Tassiulas, L., Georgiadis, L.: Any work-conserving policy stabilizes the ring with spatial re-use. IEEE/ACM Trans. Netw. 4(2), 205–208 (1996). https://doi.org/10.1109/INFOCOM.1994.337631

27. Time-sensitive networking task group. http://www.ieee802.org/1/pages/tsn.html

ParetoLib: A Python Library for Parameter Synthesis

Alexey Bakhirkin, Nicolas Basset, Oded Maler,
and José-Ignacio Requeno Jarabo[✉] [ID]

VERIMAG, CNRS and Université Grenoble-Alpes, Grenoble, France
{alexey.bakhirkin,bassetni,requenoj}@univ-grenoble-alpes.fr

Abstract. This paper presents ParetoLib, a Python library that implements a new method for inferring the Pareto front in multi-criteria optimization problems. The tool can be applied in the parameter synthesis of temporal logic predicates where the influence of parameters is monotone. ParetoLib currently provides support for the parameter synthesis of standard (STL) and extended (STLe) Signal Temporal Logic specifications. The tool is easily upgradeable for synthesizing parameters in other temporal logics in the near future. An example illustrates the usage and performance of our tool. ParetoLib is free and publicly available on Internet.

1 Introduction

This paper presents ParetoLib, a Python library that implements a new method for inferring the Pareto front for multi-criteria optimization problems: this front is the boundary between the set $\overline{X}$ of valid solutions and its complement $\underline{X}$ in a multi-dimensional parameter space X. We consider that the predicate that holds true in $\overline{X}$ and false in $\underline{X}$ is only accessible via an oracle that answers membership queries $\vec{x} \in \overline{X}$?. Another assumption is that the influence of every parameter value is monotone, i.e., increasing a parameter value can change the value of the predicate from "false" to "true", but not the other way around, which is the case for a range of optimization and parameter synthesis problems.

Given such a setting, ParetoLib learns a rectangular approximation of the Pareto front by repeatedly calling the oracle on different parameter valuations. The algorithm implemented in ParetoLib is based on a generalization of binary search to multi-dimensional parameter spaces. For a somewhat contrived example, a set of valid solutions defined by the polynomial inequality $a^2 + b^2 \geq 1$ and under the assumption that $a \geq 0, b \geq 0$, ParetoLib constructs an approximate representation of the Pareto front that corresponds to the surface of the sphere portion $a^2 + b^2 = 1, a \geq 0, b \geq 0$.

The theory associated to the present tool paper is presented in [3]. A preliminary version of the algorithm was proposed in [8]. The algorithm defined

---

Oded Maler passed away at the beginning of September 2018. This work was initiated by him [8] continued with and finished by the rest of us.

© Springer Nature Switzerland AG 2019
É. André and M. Stoelinga (Eds.): FORMATS 2019, LNCS 11750, pp. 114–120, 2019.
https://doi.org/10.1007/978-3-030-29662-9_7

there was implemented in [11], and applied to parameter synthesis for Signal Temporal Logic (STL [9]) in [12,13]. ParetoLib implements three main contributions with respect to these works. First, our tool implements a new version of the algorithm that converges faster to the Pareto front than the previous one in multi-dimensional spaces with dimension higher than 3. Second, ParetoLib supports parallel computation. Third, our tool provides a generic interface for connecting with external tools that will act as oracles for guiding the learning process. Therefore, ParetoLib can be easily extended to implement parameter synthesis in different domains based on different decision procedures.

ParetoLib currently implements parameter synthesis for standard and extended STL specifications [2]. Given a parameterized STL specification (e.g., $F_{[0,a]}x \leq b$) and an execution trace of some system, ParetoLib finds the optimal combinations of parameters (i.e., a and b), such that the trace satisfies the formula. The tool relies on an external STL runtime monitor. An example with a extended STL specification illustrates the usage and performance of our tool.

2   ParetoLib Library

2.1   Main Features

ParetoLib is a Python library that is free and publicly available on Internet [4]. It has been implemented following the software engineering standards, suggestions and best practices for this language, including a brief documentation and a set of illustrative examples of how to use it. The library is compatible with Python 2.7, 3.4 or higher; and it is PEP 8 compliant. The code has been exhaustively tested, reaching a coverage of more than 90% of the code in the module devoted to the sequential approximation of the monotone partitions and boundary. It also supports multi-core CPUs in order to take advantage of concurrent processing. ParetoLib implements the original discovery algorithm presented in [8,11] as well as a new smarter version shown in [3]. The algorithm introduced in [3] outperforms the previous one in inferring the Pareto front of multi-dimensional spaces when the number of dimensions is higher than 3. The new method still suffers from the curse of dimensionality, but it can be used to extract information for high dimensional models by combining solutions from several low-dimensional sub-problems (see [12,13] for a similar approach).

The design of ParetoLib separates the interface to the external decision procedure from the implementation of the multi-dimensional search (Fig. 1). The implementation of multi-dimensional search is unique, and it is responsible for constructing the approximation of the Pareto front, based on which parameter valuations make the predicate valid and which do not. Parameter valuations are treated abstractly, as points in multi-dimensional space, disregarding their positions and roles in the predicate.

An adaptor to an external decision procedure, named oracle, is responsible for getting from the user a parameterized predicate, extracting from it the set of parameters, and, given a parameter valuation, instantiating the parameters and sending the resulting query to the decision procedure. It is also responsible

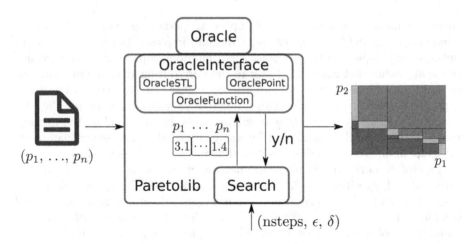

Fig. 1. Diagram showing the interaction between the tool components.

for relaying extra inputs to the decision procedure when necessary. For example, when using ParetoLib for STL parameter synthesis, the oracle is responsible for relaying the input trace(s) to the runtime monitor. ParetoLib allows the users to implement their own oracles and has several built in:

- Two oracles that interface with STL runtime monitors: *OracleSTL* interacts with AMT 2.0 [10], and *OracleSTLe* interacts with StlEval [1]. These oracles are used to perform STL parameter synthesis.
- Two oracles that interface with built-in procedures: *OracleFunction* checks whether a point satisfies a set of polynomial constraints, and *OraclePoint* stores a cloud of pre-defined Pareto points in a NDTree [7]. They may be used for test purposes.

2.2   Interaction with Signal Temporal Logic

The StlEval [1] tool is selected as the STL runtime monitor for running the experiments of parameter synthesis for STL formulas in ParetoLib (Sect. 3). StlEval allows to evaluate formulas in an extension of STL [2] over signals with piecewise-constant interpolation. It also allows to compute robustness [5,6] of STL formulas. Its specification language supports a number of operations:

- standard STL operators: "always", "eventually", "until", etc;
- pre-processing operations: scaling, adding, subtracting, shifting signals, etc;
- computing minimum and maximum of a signal over a sliding window;

For example, the formula: (<= (On (0 10) (- (Max x) (Min x))) 0.1) asserts that the difference between the maximum and minimum of the signal x on the interval from now to 10 time points into the future is not greater than 0.1. Although the particulars of the specification language are not important for ParetoLib, in the experiments our specifications use some features that are unique to StlEval and are not present in AMT 2.0. StlEval also provides several interfaces to the users:

- Command line interface that allows to read a signal and evaluate one or more formulas over it.
- Interactive command interface that allows to send commands to a running instance of StlEval via standard input and get results via standard output (similarly to how some SMT solvers implement SMTLIB command language).
- C++ API via a static or shared library with access to all functions and data structures.
- C API via a static or shared library with access to select functions and data structures.

ParetoLib can use either the interactive command interface or the C API, the latter being marginally more efficient.

3   Running ParetoLib

3.1   Configuring the Oracle

The core of the library is the algorithm implementing the multi-dimensional search of the Pareto boundary. It is implemented by the module Pare-toLib.Search, which encapsulates the complexity of the procedure in three functions (i.e., *Search2D*, *Search3D* and *SearchND*) depending on the dimension of the search space. The algorithm is compatible for spaces of any dimension, and for any oracle defined according to the ParetoLib.Oracle template. A set of running examples can be found in the doc/examples folder of the tool website. Listing 1.1 presents one of these usage examples. Some of the remarkable input parameters of the learning process are the following:

- xspace: the space that contains the upper (feasible) and lower (unfeasible) parts, listed by the min and max possible values for each dimension (i.e., corners).
- oracle: the external knowledge repository that guides the learning process.
- epsilon: a real number representing the maximum desired distance between a discovered point x of the space and a real point y of the Pareto front.
- delta: a real number representing the maximum area/volume contained in the border (i.e., *don't know* region) that separates the upper and lower parts; delta is used as a stopping criterion for the learning algorithm (volume(border) < delta).
- max_step: the maximum number of iterations that the algorithm will execute in case of the stopping condition *delta* is not reached yet; equivalent to the number of inferred Pareto points.
- opt_level: an integer specifying which version of the learning algorithm to use (i.e., 0, 1 or 2; use 2 for fast convergence).
- parallel: boolean that specifies if the user desires to take advantage of the multithreading capabilities of the computer.

Listing 1.1. Example

```
from ParetoLib.Oracle.OracleSTLe import OracleSTLeLib
from ParetoLib.Search.Search import Search2D, EPS, DELTA, STEPS
# File containing the definition of the Oracle
nfile='Tests/Oracle/OracleSTLe/2D/stabilization.txt'
# Definition of the n-dimensional space
min_x, min_y = (0.0, 0.0)
max_x, max_y = (300.0, 1.0)
oracle = OracleSTLeLib()
oracle.from_file(nfile, human_readable=True)
rs=Search2D(ora=oracle,min_cornerx=min_x,min_cornery=min_y,
            max_cornerx=max_x,max_cornery=max_y,epsilon=EPS,
            delta=DELTA,max_step=STEPS,opt_level=0,parallel=False)
```

Oracles must be initialized either when creating the object or by reading a configuration file. The configuration parameters depend on the decision procedure and the external tool that the oracle instance hides. For instance, *OracleSTLeLib* is a subclass of *OracleSTLe* that interacts with the StlEval tool via the C API. It requires (1) a textual file with the parametriced STL formula, (2) a textual file specifying the parameters of the STL equation, and (3) a signal file that is compliant with the StlEval tool format.

3.2 Saving and Plotting the Results

The result of the learning process is saved in a *ResultSet* object, a data structure that divides the search space in three subspaces: the upper part, the lower part, and a border that contains the Pareto front. The size of the gap between the upper and lower parts depends on the accuracy of the learning process, which can be tuned arbitrarily small by the *epsilon* and *delta* parameters during the invocation of the learning method by the user. The ResultSet class provides functions for:

- Testing the membership of a point x to any of the parts.
- Plotting 2D and 3D spaces.
- Exporting/Importing the results to text and binary files.

Figures 2b–c show the image produced by ParetoLib when analyzing the stabilization of a decaying signal (Fig. 2a). The green side represents the upper part and the red side is the lower part. The blue gap between the two parts corresponds to the *don't know* region. The stabilization property is specified as a parametric STL formula:

(F (0 p1) (G (0 inf) (< (On (0 inf) (- (Max x) (Min x))) p2)))

meaning that whatever point of reference we chose, within p_1 time units, signal x will stabilize and the amplitude will fall below $0.5 \cdot p_2$, where p_1 and p_2 are parameters. The boundary represents the limit between feasible and unfeasible valuations (p_1, p_2). Blue dot in Fig. 2c shows the valuations that stabilize the signal after the first peak. For this example, ParetoLib requires less than 2.4 s for computing 500 steps using a single core of a PC with Intel Core i7-8650U CPU,

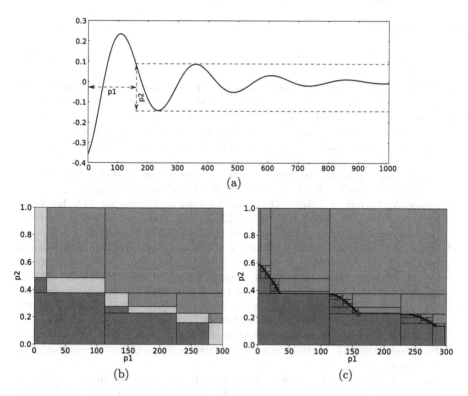

Fig. 2. Damped oscillation (a) and the inferred Pareto front for the stabilization property after 5 (b) and 500 steps (c). (Color figure online)

32 GB RAM and Python 2.7. Approximately, 45% of the cost corresponds to the execution time of the oracle (i.e., 9600 accumulated calls to the StlEval solver). Another 45% belongs to printing log traces on the terminal, and the remaining 10% is the overhead introduced by the searching algorithm.

4   Conclusion

In this paper we present ParetoLib, a Python library for multi-criteria optimization that implements a multi-dimensional extension of binary search. It can be used to solve a range of optimization problems; in particular we apply it for parameter synthesis in Signal Temporal Logic. ParetoLib implements a number of improvements over the previous work. First, it offers a novel search algorithm that shows faster convergence than pre-dating algorithms. Second, it supports parallel computations in multi-core CPU's. Third, it provides a generic interface for connecting with external, domain-specific decision procedures. In future, we would like to further ameliorate the features and performance of the tool. In particular, we plan to upgrade ParetoLib for supporting the parametric identification of more temporal logics.

References

1. Bakhirkin, A.: StlEval, STL Evaluator (2019). https://gitlab.com/abakhirkin/StlEval
2. Bakhirkin, A., Basset, N.: Specification and efficient monitoring beyond STL. In: Vojnar, T., Zhang, L. (eds.) TACAS 2019. LNCS, vol. 11428, pp. 79–97. Springer, Cham (2019). https://doi.org/10.1007/978-3-030-17465-1_5
3. Bakhirkin, A., Basset, N., Maler, O., Requeno, J.I.: Learning Pareto Front and Application to Parameter Synthesis of STL (2019). https://hal.archives-ouvertes.fr/hal-02125140, technical report
4. Basset, N., Maler, O., Jarabo, J.I.R.: ParetoLib library (2018). https://gricad-gitlab.univ-grenoble-alpes.fr/verimag/tempo/multidimensional_search
5. Donzé, A., Ferrère, T., Maler, O.: Efficient robust monitoring for STL. In: Sharygina, N., Veith, H. (eds.) CAV 2013. LNCS, vol. 8044, pp. 264–279. Springer, Heidelberg (2013). https://doi.org/10.1007/978-3-642-39799-8_19
6. Donzé, A., Maler, O.: Robust Satisfaction of temporal logic over real-valued signals. In: Chatterjee, K., Henzinger, T.A. (eds.) FORMATS 2010. LNCS, vol. 6246, pp. 92–106. Springer, Heidelberg (2010). https://doi.org/10.1007/978-3-642-15297-9_9
7. Jaszkiewicz, A., Lust, T.: ND-Tree-based update: a fast algorithm for the dynamic non-dominance problem. IEEE Trans. Evol. Comput. **22**(5), 778–791 (2018). https://doi.org/10.1109/TEVC.2018.2799684
8. Maler, O.: Learning Monotone Partitions of Partially-Ordered Domains (Work in Progress), July 2017. https://hal.archives-ouvertes.fr/hal-01556243, working paper or preprint
9. Maler, O., Nickovic, D.: Monitoring temporal properties of continuous signals. In: Lakhnech, Y., Yovine, S. (eds.) FORMATS/FTRTFT -2004. LNCS, vol. 3253, pp. 152–166. Springer, Heidelberg (2004). https://doi.org/10.1007/978-3-540-30206-3_12
10. Ničković, D., Lebeltel, O., Maler, O., Ferrère, T., Ulus, D.: AMT 2.0: qualitative and quantitative trace analysis with extended signal temporal logic. In: Beyer, D., Huisman, M. (eds.) TACAS 2018. LNCS, vol. 10806, pp. 303–319. Springer, Cham (2018). https://doi.org/10.1007/978-3-319-89963-3_18
11. Vazquez-Chanlatte, M.: Multidimensional thresholds (2018), https://github.com/mvcisback/multidim-threshold
12. Vazquez-Chanlatte, M., Deshmukh, J.V., Jin, X., Seshia, S.A.: Logical clustering and learning for time-series data. In: Majumdar, R., Kunčak, V. (eds.) CAV 2017. LNCS, vol. 10426, pp. 305–325. Springer, Cham (2017). https://doi.org/10.1007/978-3-319-63387-9_15
13. Vazquez-Chanlatte, M., Ghosh, S., Deshmukh, J.V., Sangiovanni-Vincentelli, A., Seshia, S.A.: Time-Series learning using monotonic logical properties. In: Colombo, C., Leucker, M. (eds.) RV 2018. LNCS, vol. 11237, pp. 389–405. Springer, Cham (2018). https://doi.org/10.1007/978-3-030-03769-7_22

Linear and Non-linear Systems

Piecewise Robust Barrier Tubes for Nonlinear Hybrid Systems with Uncertainty

Hui Kong[1]([✉]), Ezio Bartocci[3], Yu Jiang[4], and Thomas A. Henzinger[2]

[1] Max-Planck-Institute for Software Systems, Kaiserslautern, Germany
hkong@mpi-sws.org
[2] IST Austria, Klosterneuburg, Austria
[3] TU Wien, Vienna, Austria
[4] Tsinghua University, Beijing, China

Abstract. Piecewise Barrier Tubes (PBT) is a new technique for flow-pipe overapproximation for nonlinear systems with polynomial dynamics, which leverages a combination of barrier certificates. PBT has advantages over traditional time-step based methods in dealing with those nonlinear dynamical systems in which there is a large difference in speed between trajectories, producing an overapproximation that is time independent. However, the existing approach for PBT is not efficient due to the application of interval methods for enclosure-box computation, and it can only deal with continuous dynamical systems without uncertainty. In this paper, we extend the approach with the ability to handle both continuous and hybrid dynamical systems with uncertainty that can reside in parameters and/or noise. We also improve the efficiency of the method significantly, by avoiding the use of interval-based methods for the enclosure-box computation without loosing soundness. We have developed a C++ prototype implementing the proposed approach and we evaluate it on several benchmarks. The experiments show that our approach is more efficient and precise than other methods in the literature.

1 Introduction

Hybrid systems (HS) [21] are a suitable mathematical framework to model dynamical systems with both discrete and continuous dynamics. This formalism has been successfully adopted to design cyber-physical systems (CPS) whose behavior is characterized by an embedded software monitoring and/or controlling a physical substratum. Formal verification of HS has indeed a practical impact in engineering by assuring important safety-critical requirements at design-time.

This research was supported in part by the Austrian Science Fund (FWF) under grants S11402-N23, S11405-N23 (RiSE/SHiNE), ADynNet (P28182), and Z211-N23 (Wittgenstein Award) and the Deutsche Forschungsgemeinschaft project 389792660-TRR 248.

E. André and M. Stoelinga (Eds.): FORMATS 2019, LNCS 11750, pp. 123–141, 2019.
https://doi.org/10.1007/978-3-030-29662-9_8

Despite the great effort to advance the state-of-the-art, reachability analysis of HS remains one of the most challenging verification tasks. Although the problem of reachability analysis is in general undecidable [21] for HS, in the last decade several efficient and scalable semidecidable approaches have been proposed to analyse HS with linear dynamics [14, 15, 19, 22, 23, 36, 41].

HS with nonlinear ordinary differential equations (ODEs) remains still very challenging to solve because these ODEs do not have a closed form solution in general. One common strategy to tackle this problem is to compute an over-approximation (also called flowpipe) that contains all the possible trajectories originating from an initial set of states within a bounded-time horizon [1, 6, 9–11]. If the overapproximation does not intersect with the unsafe set of states, then the system is safe. However, if the overapproximation is too coarse, it may intersect the unsafe set of states only due to the approximation errors and then the verdict about safety may be inconclusive. Thus, one of the main problem to address is *how to efficiently compute tight over-approximations of the reachable set of states for nonlinear continuous and hybrid systems*.

To overcome this problem, in a recent paper [24], we have introduced the notion of Piecewise Barrier Tubes (PBT), a new flowpipe overapproximation for nonlinear systems with polynomial dynamics. The main idea of this approach is that for each segment of a flowpipe, it constructs a coarse box that is big enough to contain the segment and then it computes in the box a set of barrier functions [26, 34] which work together to form a tube surrounding the flowpipe.

PBT has advantages over traditional time-step based methods in dealing with those nonlinear dynamical systems in which there is a large difference in speed between trajectories, producing a tight over-approximation that is time independent. However, the approach in [24] cannot handle uncertainty and hybrid systems. In addition, the use of interval method for enclosure-box computation reduces its efficiency.

In this paper, we extend the approach with the ability to handle both continuous and hybrid dynamical systems with uncertainty which can reside in parameters and/or noise. We improve the efficiency of the method significantly, by avoiding the use of interval method for enclosure-box computation without loosing soundness. We have developed a C++ prototype implementing the proposed approach and we evaluate it on several benchmarks. The experiments show that our approach is more efficient and precise than other methods proposed in the literature.

The other existing techniques used to compute a bounded flowpipe are mainly based on interval method [32] or Taylor model [4]. Interval method is quite efficient even for high dimensional systems [32], but it suffers from the *wrapping effect* that arises due to an uncontrollable growth of the interval enclosure that accumulates overapproximation errors. The use of Taylor model is more precise because it uses a vector of polynomials plus a vector of small intervals to symbolically represent the flowpipe. However, checking the intersection with the unsafe region requires generally the use of interval method that brings back the wrapping effect. In particular, the wrapping effect can explode easily when the flowpipe segment over a time interval is stretched drastically due to a large difference in speed between individual trajectories.

Only recently, tools such as CLRT [9,10], Flow* [6], MathSAT SMT solver [7,8], HySAT/iSAT [12], dReach [27], C2E2 [11] and CORA [1], have made some progresses in verifying nonlinear continuous and hybrid models. Some of these tools [7,12,27] are based on decision procedures that overcome the theoretical limits in nonlinear theories over the reals. The main idea is to encode the reachability problem for nonlinear systems as first-order logic formulas over the real numbers. A satisfiability modulo theories (SMT) solver implementing such procedures can return either a verdict of unsatisfiability when the unsafe region is not reached or an inconclusive verdict [12,27] such as δ-sat if the problem is satisfiable given a certain precision δ (the same problem may result unsatisfiable by increasing the precision). However, in the case of unsatisfiability these tools generally do not provide a reachable set representation that explains the verdict. Other techniques for reachability analysis of nonlinear systems include invariant generation [25,31,38,39,42], abstraction and hybridization [2,5,16,28,33,37].

The paper is organized as follows. Section 2 presents the necessary preliminaries. Section 3 shows how to compute robust barrier certificates using linear programming, while in Sect. 4 we present our approach to address the reachability analysis problem of nonlinear continuous and hybrid systems with uncertainty. Section 5 provides our experimental results.

2 Preliminaries

In this section, we recall some concepts used throughout the paper. We first clarify some notation conventions. If not specified otherwise, we use boldface lower case letters to denote vectors, we use $\mathbb{R}$ for the real numbers field and $\mathbb{N}$ for the set of natural numbers, and we consider multivariate polynomials in $\mathbb{R}[x]$, where the components of x act as indeterminates. In addition, for all the polynomials $B(c, x)$, we denote by c the vector composed of all the c_i and denote by x the vector composed of all the remaining variables x_i that occur in the polynomial. We use $\mathbb{R}_{\geq 0}$ and $\mathbb{R}_{>0}$ to denote the domain of nonnegative real number and positive real number respectively. With an abuse of notation, we sometimes use $B(x) = 0$ for the semialgebraic set it defines. ∂S denotes the boundary of compact set S.

Next, we present the notation of the Lie derivative, which is widely used in the discipline of differential geometry. Let $f : \mathbb{R}^n \to \mathbb{R}^n$ be a continuous vector field such that $\dot{x}_i = f_i(x)$ where $\dot{x}_i$ is the time derivative of $x_i(t)$.

Definition 1 (Lie derivative). *For a given polynomial $p \in \mathbb{R}[x]$ over $x = (x_1, \ldots, x_n)$ and a continuous system $\dot{x} = f$, where $f = (f_1, \ldots, f_n)$, the **Lie derivative** of $p \in \mathbb{R}[x]$ along f is defined as $\mathcal{L}_f p = \sum_{i=1}^{n} \frac{\partial p}{\partial x_i} \cdot f_i$.*

Essentially, the Lie derivative of p is the time derivative of p, i.e., reflects the change of p over time.

In this paper, we focus on semialgebraic systems with uncertainty, which is described by the following ODE.

$$\dot{x} = f(x(t), u(t)) \tag{1}$$

where f is a vector of polynomial functions, $x(t)$ is a solution of the system, $u(t)$ is the vector of uncertain parameters and/or perturbation and $u(t)$ is Lipschitz continuous. Note that we do not make a distinction between uncertain parameters and perturbation since we deal with them uniformly. Formally, semialgebraic system with uncertainty is defined as follows.

Definition 2 (Semialgebraic system with uncertainty). *A semialgebraic system with uncertainty is a 5-tuple* $\mathcal{M} \overset{def}{=} \langle X, f, X_0, \mathcal{I}, \mathcal{U} \rangle$*, where*

1. *$X \subseteq \mathbb{R}^n$ is the state space of the system $\mathcal{M}$,*
2. *$f \in \mathbb{R}[x, u]^n$ is locally Lipschitz continuous vector function defining the vector flow as in ODE (1),*
3. *$X_0 \subseteq X$ is the initial set, which is semialgebraic [43],*
4. *$\mathcal{I}$ is the invariant or domain of the system,*
5. *$\mathcal{U}$ is a domain for the uncertain parameters and perturbation, i.e., $u(t) \in \mathcal{U}$*

The local Lipschitz continuity guarantees the existence and uniqueness of the differential equation $\dot{x} = f$ locally. A trajectory of a semialgebraic system with uncertainty is defined as follows.

Definition 3 (Trajectory). *Given a semialgebraic system with uncertainty* $\mathcal{M}$*, a **trajectory** originating from a point $x_0 \in X_0$ to time $T > 0$ is a continuous and differentiable function $\zeta(x_0, t) : [0, T] \to \mathbb{R}^n$ such that (1) $\zeta(x_0, 0) = x_0$, and (2) $\exists u(\cdot) : \forall \tau \in [0, T]: \frac{d\zeta}{dt}\big|_{t=\tau} = f(\zeta(x_0, \tau), u(\tau))$, where $u(\cdot) : [0, T] \to \mathcal{U}$. T is assumed to be within the maximal interval of existence of the solution from x_0.*

For ease of readability, we also use $\zeta(t)$ for $\zeta(x_0, t)$ if it is clear from the context.

3   Robust Barrier Certificate by Linear Programming

A barrier certificate for a continuous dynamics system is a real-valued function $B(x)$ such that (1) the initial set and the unsafe set are located on different sides of the hyper-surface $\mathcal{H} = \{x \in \mathbb{R}^n \mid B(x) = 0\}$ respectively, and (2) no trajectory originating from the same side of $\mathcal{H}$ as the initial set can cross through $\mathcal{H}$ to reach the other side. Therefore, the existence of such a function $B(x)$ can guarantee the safety of the system. The above condition can be formalized using an infinite sequence of higher order Lie derivatives [44]. Unfortunately, this formalization cannot be applied directly to barrier certificate computation. Therefore, a couple of sufficient conditions for the above condition have been proposed [17,26,30]. Most recently, based on the sufficient condition in [34], a new approach was proposed to overapproximate the flowpipe of nonlinear continuous dynamical systems using combination of barrier certificates [24].

However, the approach is limited to continuous dynamical systems without uncertainty. To tackle this problem, we extend the approach to deal with continuous and hybrid systems with uncertainty. Similarly, we adopt the same barrier certificate condition as [24], but we introduce the uncertainty in the barrier certificate condition. Note that in order to distinguish it from barrier certificate for dynamical system without uncertainty, we call a barrier certificate satisfying the following condition *robust barrier certificate*.

Theorem 1. *Given an uncertain semialgebraic system* $\mathcal{M} = \langle X, f, X_0, \mathcal{I}, \mathcal{U} \rangle$, *let X_{us} be the unsafe set, the system is guaranteed to be safe if there exists a real-valued function $B(x)$ such that*

$$\forall x \in X_0 : B(x) > 0 \tag{2}$$

$$\forall (x, u) \in \mathcal{I} \times \mathcal{U} : \mathcal{L}_f B > 0 \tag{3}$$

$$\forall x \in X_{us} : B(x) < 0 \tag{4}$$

The most common approach to barrier certificate computation is by SOS programming [26,34]. The idea of this kind of approach is to first relax the original constraints like (2)–(4) into a set of positive semidefinite (PSD) polynomials by applying Putinar representation [35], which is further relaxed by requiring every PSD polynomial has a sum-of-squares decomposition, which can be solved by SOS programming in polynomial time. However, constructing automatically a set of consistent templates for the barrier certificate as well as the auxiliary polynomials is not trivial. In addition, SOS programming method can yield fake solution sometimes due to numerical error.

An alternative to SOS programming based approaches is to use linear programming based approaches. This class of approaches relies on an LP-relaxation to the original constraint. In [3,40], to compute Lyapunov function, an LP-relaxation was obtained by applying Handelman representation to the original constraint. Recently, this kind of LP-relaxation was adopted in [24] to compute piecewise barrier tubes. In [45], an extended version of Handelman representation, called Krivine representation [29], was employed for barrier certificate computation. Compared to Handelman representation, which can only deal with convex polytopes, Krivine representation can deal with more general compact semialgebraic sets. However, Krivine representation requires normalizing the polynomials involved, which is expensive.

In this paper, we adopt the same representation as in [24], i.e., Handelman representation as our LP-relaxation scheme for Theorem 1. We assume that the initial set X_0, the unsafe set X_{us}, the invariant $\mathcal{I}$, the parameter and/or perturbance space are all convex and compact polyhedra, i.e., $X_0 = \{x \in \mathbb{R}^n \mid p_1(x) \geq 0, \cdots, p_{m_1}(x) \geq 0\}$, $\mathcal{I} = \{x \in \mathbb{R}^n \mid q_1(x) \geq 0, \cdots, q_{m_2}(x) \geq 0\}$, $\mathcal{U} = \{u \in \mathbb{R}^l \mid w_1(u) \geq 0, \cdots, w_{m_3}(u) \geq 0\}$ and $X_{us} = \{x \in \mathbb{R}^n \mid r_1(x) \geq 0, \cdots, r_{m_4}(x) \geq 0\}$ where $p_i(x)$, $q_i(x)$, $r_k(x)$ and $w_i(u)$, are all linear polynomials. Then, Theorem 1 can be relaxed as follows.

Theorem 2. *Given a semialgebraic system with uncertainty $\mathcal{M} = \langle X, f, X_0, \mathcal{I}, \mathcal{U} \rangle$, let X_0, X_{us}, $\mathcal{I}$ and $\mathcal{U}$ be defined as above, the system is guaranteed to be safe if there exists a real-valued polynomial function $B(x)$ such that*

$$B(x) \equiv \sum_{|\alpha| \leq M_1} \lambda_\alpha \prod_{i=1}^{m_1} p_i^{\alpha_i} + \epsilon_1 \tag{5}$$

$$\mathcal{L}_f B \equiv \sum_{|\beta| \leq M_2} \lambda_\beta \prod_{i=1}^{m_2} q_i^{\beta_i} \prod_{j=1}^{m_3} w_j^{\beta_{m_2+j}} + \epsilon_2 \tag{6}$$

$$-B(x) \equiv \sum_{|\gamma| \leq M_3} \lambda_\gamma \prod_{i=1}^{m_4} r_i^{\gamma_i} + \epsilon_3 \tag{7}$$

where $\alpha = (\alpha_k), \beta = (\beta_k), \gamma = (\gamma_k)$, $\lambda_\alpha, \lambda_\beta, \lambda_\gamma \in \mathbb{R}_{\geq 0}$, $\epsilon_i \in \mathbb{R}_{>0}$ and $M_i \in \mathbb{N}, i = 1, \cdots, 3$.

Remark 1. Theorem 2 implies that the system $\mathcal{M}$ can be proved to be safe as long as we can find a real-valued polynomial function $B(x)$ such that $B(x)$, $-B(x)$ and $\mathcal{L}_f B$ can be written as a nonnegative combination of the products of the powers of the polynomials defining X_0, X_{us} and $\mathcal{I} \times \mathcal{U}$ respectively. This theorem provides us with a solution to solve barrier certificate by linear programming. Given a polynomial template $B(c, x)$ for $B(x)$, where c is the coefficients of the monomials to be decided in $B(c, x)$, we substitute $B(c, x)$ for $B(x)$ occurring in the conditions (5)–(7) to obtain three polynomial identities in $\mathbb{R}[x]$ with linear polynomials in $\mathbb{R}[c, \lambda]$ as their coefficients, where λ is a vector composed of all the $\lambda_\alpha, \lambda_\beta, \lambda_\gamma$ occurring in (5)–(7). Since (5)–(7) are identities, then all the coefficients of the corresponding monomials on both sides of the identities must be identical. By collecting the corresponding coefficients of the monomials on both sides of the identities and let them equal respectively, we obtain a system S of linear equations and inequalities on c, λ. Now, finding a robust barrier certificate is converted to finding a feasible solution for S, which can be solved by linear programming efficiently. Since the degree of $B(c, x)$ is key to the expressive power of $B(c, x)$, in our implementation, we attempt to solve a barrier certificate from a group of templates with different degrees.

Due to the page limit, we do not elaborate on our algorithm for barrier certificate computation, but we demonstrate how it works in the following example.

Example 1. Given a 2D system defined by $\dot{x} = 2x + 3y + u_1, \dot{y} = -4x + 2y + u_2$, let $X_0 = \{(x, y) \in \mathbb{R}^2 \mid p_1 = x + 100 \geq 0, p_2 = -90 - x \geq 0, p_3 = y + 45 \geq 0, p_4 = -40 - y \geq 0\}$, $\mathcal{I} = \{(x, y) \in \mathbb{R}^2 \mid q_1 = x + 110 \geq 0, q_2 = -80 - x \geq 0, q_3 = y + 45 \geq 0, q_4 = -20 - y \geq 0\}$, $\mathcal{U} = \{(u_1, u_2) \in \mathbb{R}^2 \mid w_1 = u_1 + 50.0 \geq 0, w_2 = 50.0 - u_1 \geq 0, w_3 = u_2 + 50.0 \geq 0, w_4 = 50.0 - u_2 \geq 0\}$ and $X_{us} = \{(x, y) \in \mathbb{R}^2 \mid r_1 = x + 98 \geq 0, r_2 = -90 - x \geq 0, r_3 = y + 24 \geq 0, r_4 = -20 - y \geq 0\}$. Assume $B(c, x) = c_0 + c_1 x + c_2 y$, $M_i = \epsilon_i = 1$ for $i = 1, \cdots, 3$, then we obtain the following polynomial identities according to Theorem 2

$$c_1 + c_2 x + c_3 y - \sum_{i=1}^{4} \lambda_{1i} p_i - \epsilon_1 \equiv 0$$

$$c_2(2x + 3y + u_1) + c_3(-4x + 2y + u_2) - \sum_{j=1}^{4} \lambda_{2j} q_j - \sum_{j=1}^{4} \lambda_{3j} w_j - \epsilon_2 \equiv 0$$

$$- (c_1 + c_2 x + c_3 y) - \sum_{k=1}^{4} \lambda_{4k} r_k - \epsilon_3 \equiv 0$$

where $\lambda_{ij} \geq 0$ for $i, j = 1, \cdots, 4$. If we collect the coefficients of x, y, u_1, u_2 in the above polynomials and let them be 0, we obtain a system S of linear polynomial equations and inequalities over c_i, λ_{ij}. By solving S using linear programming, we obtain a feasible solution with $c_1 = -1263.5, c_2 = -11.5, c_3 = -5.85$.

4   Piecewise Robust Barrier Tubes

The idea of piecewise robust barrier tubes (PRBTs) is to use robust barrier tubes (RBTs) to piecewise overapproximate the flowpipe segments of nonlinear hybrid systems with uncertainty, where each RBT is essentially a cluster of robust barrier certificates which are situated around the flowpipe to form a tight tube enclosing the flowpipe. The basic idea of PRBT computation is shown in Algorithm 1.

4.1   Construction of the Enclosure-Box

A key step in PRBT computation is the construction of enclosure-box for a given compact initial set. Note that here *an enclosure-box is a hyperrectangle that entirely contains a flowpipe segment.* In principle, the smaller the enclosure-box, the easier it is to compute a barrier tube. However, to make full use of the power of nonlinear overapproximation, it is desirable to have as big enclosure-box as possible so that fewer barrier tubes are needed to cover a flowpipe.

In [24], interval method was adopted to build an enclosure-box. However, the main problem with interval method is that the enclosure-box thus computed is usually very small which will result in a big number of barrier tubes for a fixed length of flowpipe. On the one hand, this will lead to an increasing burden on barrier tube computation. On the other hand, the capability of barrier tube in overapproximating complex flowpipe can not be fully released. For these reasons, we choose to use a purely simulation-based approach without losing soundness.

A key concept involved in our simulation-based enclosure-box construction is *twisting of trajectory*, which is a measure of maximal bending of trajectories in a box. For the convenience of presentation, we present the formal definition of twisting of trajectory as follows.

Algorithm 1. PRBT computation

---

input : f: dynamics of the system; X_0: Initial set; $\mathcal{U}$: set of uncertainty; N: number of robust barrier tubes (RBT) in PRBT; (θ_{min}, d_{min}): parameters for simulation

output: PRBT: piecewise robust barrier tube

---

1 PRBT ← empty queue;
2 **while** Length(PRBT) < N **do**
3 $\quad$ [Found, θ, d] ← [$false, \theta_0, d_0$] ;
4 $\quad$ **while** $\theta > \theta_{min}$ **do**
5 $\quad\quad$ E ← construct a coarse enclsoure-box for X_0 by (θ, d)-simulation;
6 $\quad\quad$ [Found, RBT, X_0'] ←compute RBT inside E and obtain a set $X_0' \supseteq (RBT \cap \partial E)$;
7 $\quad\quad$ **if** *not* Found **then**
8 $\quad\quad\quad$ (θ, d) ← $1/2 * (\theta, d)$; // to shrink E
9 $\quad\quad\quad$ continue;
10 $\quad\quad$ **else**
11 $\quad\quad\quad$ PRBT ← Push(PRBT, RBT); // add RBT to the queue of PRBT
12 $\quad\quad\quad$ X_0 ← X_0' ; // update X_0 for computing next RBT
13 $\quad\quad\quad$ break;
14 $\quad$ **if** *not* Found **then** break ;
15 **return** PRBT;

Definition 4 (Twisting of trajectory). *Let $\mathcal{M}$ be a continuous system and $\zeta(t)$ be a trajectory of $\mathcal{M}$. Then, $\zeta(t)$ is said to have a twisting of θ on the time interval $I = [T_1, T_2]$, written as $\xi_I(\zeta)$, if it satisfies that $\xi_I(\zeta) = \theta$, where*

$$\xi_I(\zeta) \overset{def}{=} \sup_{t_1, t_2 \in I} \arccos\left(\frac{\langle \dot{\zeta}(t_1), \dot{\zeta}(t_2) \rangle}{\|\dot{\zeta}(t_1)\|\|\dot{\zeta}(t_2)\|}\right).$$

Then, we have Algorithm 2 to compute enclosure-box.

Remark 2. In this paper, we assume that both X_0 and $\mathcal{U}$ are defined by hyper-rectangles. The basic idea of enclosure-box construction is that, given a continuous dynamical system with uncertainty, we first remove the uncertainty by taking the center point $\boldsymbol{u}_c$ of $\mathcal{U}$ for the dynamics (line 1–2). Then, we sample a set S_0 of points from X_0 for simulation (line 3). Prior to doing simulation for S_0, we first select a point $\boldsymbol{x}_0$ (usually the center point of X_0) to do (θ, d)-simulation to obtain the end point $\boldsymbol{x}_e$ of the simulation (line 7). A (θ, d)-*simulation is a simulation that stops either when the twisting of the simulation reaches θ or when the Euclidean distance between $\boldsymbol{x}_0$ and $\boldsymbol{x}_e$ reaches d.* The motivation to get the end point $\boldsymbol{x}_e$ is that, there are n planes of the form $x_i = \boldsymbol{x}_e^i$ (the i'th element of $\boldsymbol{x}_e$) intersecting at $\boldsymbol{x}_e$, so we want to check if one of the n planes, say P, was hit by all the simulations that start from S_0, and if yes, it is very likely that P cut through the entire flowpipe. Then, we take P as one of the facets of the desired enclosure-box E. In addition, during the simulations, we simultaneously

---

Algorithm 2. Construct enclosure-box

---

input : $f(x, u)$: system dynamics; X_0: initial set; $\mathcal{U}$: uncertain parameters; θ: twisting of simulation; θ_{min}: minimal theta for simulation; d: maximum distance of simulation;

output: E: an enclosure-box containing X_0; P: plane where flowpipe exits ;
G: range of intersection of $Flow_f(X_0)$ with plane P by simulation

---

1   $u_c \leftarrow$ center point of $\mathcal{U}$;
2   $f_c(x) \leftarrow$ the center dynamic $f(x, u_c)$;
3   $S_0 \leftarrow$ sample a set of points from X_0;
4   select a point $x_0 \in S_0$;
5   succ $\leftarrow false$;
6   **while** $\theta \geq \theta_{min}$ **do**
7      $x_e \leftarrow$ end point of (θ, d)-simulation of $f_c(x)$ for x_0;
8   **foreach** x_e^i: *plane in the i'th dimension of x_e* **do**
9   do simulation for all the points in S_0, update G and E;
10   **if** *all the simulations hit x_e^i* **then**
11   P $\leftarrow x_e^i$;
12   succ $\leftarrow true$;
13   **if** succ **then**
14   bloat E s.t $Flow_f(X_0)$ exits from E only through the facet in P;
15   return [E, P, G];
16   **else**
17        $[\theta, d] \leftarrow 1/2 * [\theta, d]$;

---

keep updating (1) the boundary where the simulations can reach and use that range as our candidate enclosure-box E, and (2) the boundary range G where the simulations intersect with the plane $P : x_i = x_e^i$. If we end up finding such a plane P, we will push the other facets of E outwards to make the flowpipe exit only from this specific facet of E. Of course, this objective cannot be guaranteed only by simulation and pushing, we need to further check if the flowpipe does not intersect the other facets of E, which can be done according to Theorem 3.

Theorem 3. *Given an uncertain semialgebraic system $\mathcal{M} = \langle X, f, X_0, \mathcal{I}, \mathcal{U} \rangle$, assume $E \subset \mathcal{I}$ is an enclosure-box of X_0 and F_i is a facet of E. The flowpipe of $\mathcal{M}$ from X_0 does not intersect F_i, i.e, $(Flow_f(X_0) \cap F_i) \cap E = \emptyset$ if there exists a barrier certificate $B_i(x)$ for F_i inside E.*

Remark 3. Theorem 3 can be easily proved by the definition of barrier certificate, which is ignored here. In order to make sure that the flowpipe evades a facet F_i of E, according to Theorem 1, we only need to find a barrier certificate for F_i. In the case of no barrier certificate being found, further bloating to the facet of E will be performed. If bloating facet still end up with failure, we keep shrinking E by setting (θ, d) to $(\theta/2, d/2)$ until barrier certificates are found for all the facet of E or θ gets less than some threshold θ_{min}.

4.2   Computation of Robust Barrier Tube

An ideal application scenario of barrier certificate is when we can prove the safety property using a single barrier certificate. Unfortunately, this is usually not true because the flowpipe can be very complicated so that no polynomial function of a specified degree satisfies the constraint. In the previous subsection, we introduce how to obtain for an initial set X_0 an enclosure-box E in which the system dynamics is simple enough so that a robust barrier certificate $B(\boldsymbol{x})$ can be easily computed. Therefore, we can compute a set of robust barrier certificates, which we call Robust Barrier Tube (RBT), to create a tight overapproximation for the flowpipe provided that there is a set of auxiliary sets serving as unsafe sets. Formally, we define RBT as follows.

Definition 5 (Robust Barrier Tube (RBT)). *Given a semialgebraic system* $\mathcal{M} = \langle X, \boldsymbol{f}, X_0, \mathcal{I}, \mathcal{U} \rangle$, *let* E *be an enclosure-box of* X_0 *and* $X_{AS} = \{X_{AS}^i : X_{AS}^i \subseteq E\}$ *be a set of auxiliary sets (AS), an RBT is a set of real-valued functions* $\Phi = \{B_i(\boldsymbol{x}), i = 1, \cdots, m\}$ *such that for all* $B_i(\boldsymbol{x}) \in \Phi$: *(i)* $\forall \boldsymbol{x} \in X_0$: $B_i(\boldsymbol{x}) > 0$, *(ii)* $\forall (\boldsymbol{x}, \boldsymbol{u}) \in E \times \mathcal{U} : \mathcal{L}_f B_i > 0$, *and (iii)* $\forall \boldsymbol{x} \in X_{AS}^i : B_i(\boldsymbol{x}) < 0$.

The precision of RBT depends closely on the set X_{AS} of ASs. Therefore, to derive a good barrier tube, we need to first construct a set of high quality ASs. The factors that could affect the quality of the set X_{AS} of ASs include (1) the number of ASs, and (2) the position, size and shape of AS. Roughly speaking, the more ASs we have, if positioned properly, the more precise the RBT would be. Regarding the position, size and shape of AS, a desirable AS should (1) be as close to the flowpipe as possible, (2) spread widely around the flowpipe, and (3) be shaped like a shell for the flowpipe. Intuitively, a high quality set of ASs could be shaped like a ring around a human finger so that the barrier tube is tightly confined in the narrow space between the ring and the finger. With the key factors aforementioned in mind, we developed Algorithm 3 for RBT computation.

Remark 4. In principle, the more barrier certificates we use, the better over-approximation we may achieve. However, using more barrier certificates also means more computation time. Therefore, we have to make a trade-off between precision and efficiency. In Algorithm 3, we choose to use RBT consisting of $2(n-1)$ barrier certificates for n dimensional dynamical systems, which means we need to construct $2(n-1)$ ASs. We use the same scheme as in [24] to construct ASs. Recall that we get a coarse region G where the flowpipe intersects with one of the facets of E during the construction of the enclosure-box E. Since G is an $n-1$ dimensional box, the RBT must contain G. Therefore, we choose to construct $2(n-1)$ ASs which are able to form a tight hollow hyper-rectangle around G. The idea is that for each facet G_{ij} of G, we construct an $n-1$ dimensional hyper-rectangle between G_{ij} and E_{ij} as an AS (line 2), where E_{ij} is the $n-1$ dimensional face of E that corresponds to G. Then, we use Algorithm 3 to compute an RBT(line 4). In the **while** loop 3, we try to find the best barrier certificate by adjusting the width of AS (line 5 and 6) iteratively until the difference in width between two consecutive ASs is less than the specified threshold ϵ. To be intuitive, we provide Fig. 1 to demonstrate the process.

Algorithm 3. Compute robust barrier tube

---

input : f: system dynamics; X_0: Initial set; E: enclosure-box of X_0; $\mathcal{U}$: set of uncertainty; P: plane where flowpipe exits from enclosure-box E; G: box approx. of $(\mathrm{P} \cap Flow_f(X_0))$ by simulation; ϵ: difference between AS's (auxiliary set)

output: RBT: barrier tube; X_0': box over-approx. of $(\mathrm{RBT} \cap \mathrm{E})$

---

1 **foreach** G_{ij}: *a facet of* G **do**
2   AS $\longleftarrow$ CreateAS($\mathrm{G}, \mathrm{P}, G_{ij}$);
3   **while** *true* **do**
4          $[found, B_{ij}] \longleftarrow$ ComputeRBC($f, X_0, \mathrm{E}, \mathrm{AS}, \mathcal{U}$);
5   **if** *found* **then** AS' $\longleftarrow$ Expand (AS) ;
6   **else** AS' $\longleftarrow$ Contract (AS) ;
7   **if** Diff(AS', AS) $\leq \epsilon$ **then**
8   break;
9   AS $\longleftarrow$ AS';
10   **if** *found* **then**
11   RBT $\longleftarrow$ Push(RBT, B_{ij});
12   break;
13   **else**
14   return FAIL

15 return SUCCEED;

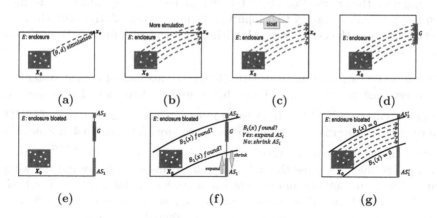

Fig. 1. (a)→(g): demonstration of RBT computation

4.3 PRBT for Continuous Dynamics

The idea of computing PRBT is straightforward. Given an initial set X_0, we first construct a coarse enclosure-box E containing X_0 and then we further compute an RBT inside E to get a much more precise overapproximation for the flowpipe. Meanwhile, we obtain a hyper-rectangle R formed by ASs with a hollow X_0' in the middle. Since the intersection of the RBT and the facet of E is contained entirely in the hollow X_0' of R, we use X_0' as a new initial set and repeat the entire process to compute a PRBT step by step. Since our approach is time independent, the length of a PRBT cannot be measured by the length of time horizon. Hence, in our implementation, we try to compute a specified number of RBTs.

4.4   PRBT for Hybrid Dynamics

To extend our approach with the ability to deal with hybrid systems, we need to handle two problems (i) compute the intersection of RBT and guard set, and (ii) compute the image of the intersection after discrete jump. In general, these two issues can be very hard depending on what kind of guard sets and transitions are defined for the hybrid systems.

In this paper, we make some assumptions on the hybrid systems under consideration. Let a discrete transition τ be defined as follows.

$$\tau_{ll'} = \langle \text{Guard}_{ll'}, \text{Trans}_{ll'} \rangle \tag{8}$$

where l and l' are the locations of the dynamics before and after a discrete transition respectively, $\text{Guard}_{ll'} = \{ x \in \mathbb{R}^n \mid x_i \sim b_i, \sim \in \{\leq, \geq\} \}$ and $\text{Trans}_{ll'} : x' = Ax$, where A is an n-dimensional matrix. Based on this assumption, the problem of computing the intersection of RBT and guard set is reduced to computing the intersection of RBT with a plane of $x_i = b_i$, which can be handled using a similar strategy to computing the intersection of RBT with the facet of enclosure-box. Hence, we have Algorithm 4 to deal with discrete transition of a hybrid system.

Remark 5. The strategy to deal with discrete transitions of hybrid systems is that every time we obtain an enclosure-box E, we first detect whether E intersects with some guard set $\text{Guard}_{11'}$. If no, we proceed with the normal process of PRBT computation. Otherwise, we switch to the procedure of Algorithm 4 in which the input X_0^l is the last state set whose enclosure-box intersects with $\text{Guard}_{11'}$. Since the flowpipe may not cross through the guard plane entirely, we use the while loop in line 2 to compute an overapproximation for the intersection. The basic idea of the while loop is that, given a state set X_0^l, we first construct an enclosure-box E by simulation (line 4), if E intersects with $\text{Guard}_{11'}$, we shrink E by cutting off the part of E that lies in the guard set (line 7). As a result of this operation, the flowpipe could exit from E not only through the guard plane but also through other facets of E. For each of those facets, we compute an overapproximation for its intersection with the flowpipe using simulation and barrier certificate computation (line 8 and 11). In addition, since those intersections X_0^{ij} that do not lie in the guard plane could still reach the guard plane later, we therefore push them into a queue for further exploration.

Algorithm 4. handle discrete transition of hybrid system

---

    input : X_0^l: intermediate initial set at location l; $\mathsf{Guard}_{ll'}$: guard set of transition $\tau_{ll'}$; $\mathsf{Trans}_{ll'}$: image mapping of transition $\tau_{ll'}$
    output: $X_0^{l'}$: image of transition $\tau_{ll'}$

1 $\mathsf{InitQ} \leftarrow \mathsf{Push}(\mathsf{InitQ}, X_0^l)$;
2 **while** InitQ *not empty* **do**
3     $X_0^l \leftarrow \mathsf{Pop}(\mathsf{InitQ})$;
4     $\mathsf{E} \leftarrow$ construct enclosure-box for X_0^l ;
5   **if** $\mathsf{E} \cap \mathsf{Guard}_{ll'} == \emptyset$ **then**
6   continue;
7     $\mathsf{E} \leftarrow \mathsf{E} \cap \overline{\mathsf{Guard}}_{ll'}$;
8     $X_{\Phi \cap \mathsf{E}} \leftarrow$ do simulation and barrier certificate computation to find an overapproximation for the region where the flowpipe Φ intersects with the guard plane $x_i = b_i$;
9     $Q_{\Phi \cap \mathsf{E}} \leftarrow \mathsf{Push}(Q_{\Phi \cap \mathsf{E}}, X_{\Phi \cap \mathsf{E}})$;
10   **foreach** E_{ij}: *facet of* E *except guard plane* **do**
11        $X_0^{ij} \leftarrow$ do simulation and barrier certificate computation to an overapproximation for the region where the barrier tube intersects with E_{ij}; $\mathsf{InitQ} \leftarrow \mathsf{Push}(\mathsf{InitQ}, X_0^{ij})$;
12 $X_{\Phi \cap E} \leftarrow$ box overapprox. $Q_{\Phi \cap E}$;
13 $X_0^{l'} \leftarrow \mathsf{Trans}_{ll'} X_{\Phi \cap E}$;

---

5   Implementation and Experiments

We have developed PRBT, a software prototype written in C++ that implements the concepts and the algorithms presented in this paper. PRBT computes piecewise robust barrier tubes for nonlinear continuous and hybrid systems with polynomial dynamics. We compare our approach in efficiency and precision with the state-of-the-art tools Flow* and CORA using several benchmarks of nonlinear continuous and hybrid systems. Note that since C2E2 does not support uncertainty, so we cannot compare with it. The experiments were carried out on a desktop computer with a 3.6 GHz *Intel 8 Core i7-7700* CPU and 32 GB memory.

5.1 Nonlinear Continuous Systems

We consider six nonlinear benchmark systems with polynomial dynamics for which their models and settings are provided in Table 1.

The experimental results are reported in Table 2. Since our approach is time independent, which is different from Flow* and CORA, to make the comparison fair enough, we choose to compute a slightly longer flowpipe than the other two tools. Note that there are two columns for time for Flow*. The reason why we have an extra time column for Flow* is that it can be very fast and precise to compute the Taylor model for a given system. However, Taylor models cannot be in general applied directly to solve the safety verification problem. Checking

Table 1. Continuous dynamical model definitions

Model	Dynamics	Uncertainty	X_0
Controller 2D	$\dot{x} = d_1 xy + y^3 + 2$ $\dot{y} = d_2 x^2 + 2x - 3y$	$d_1 \in [0.95, 1.05]$ $d_2 \in [0.95, 1.05]$	$x \in [29.9, 30.1]$ $y \in [-38, -36]$
Van der Pol Oscillator	$\dot{x} = y + d_1$ $\dot{y} = y - x - x^2 y + d_2$	$d_1 \in [-0.01, 0.01]$ $d_2 \in [-0.01, 0.01]$	$x \in [1, 1.5]$ $y \in [2.40, 2.45]$
Lotka-Volterra	$\dot{x} = x(1.5 - y) + d_1$ $\dot{y} = -y(3 - x) - d_2$	$d_1 \in [-0.01, 0.01]$ $d_2 \in [-0.01, 0.01]$	$x \in [4.6, 5.5]$ $y \in [1.6, 1.7]$
Buckling Column	$\dot{x} = y + d_1$ $\dot{y} = 2x - x^3 - 0.2y + 0.1 + d_2$	$d_1 \in [-0.01, 0.01]$ $d_1 \in [-0.01, 0.01]$	$x \in [-0.5, -0.4]$ $y \in [-0.5, -0.4]$
Jet Engine	$\dot{x} = -y - 1.5x^2 - 0.5x^3 - 0.5 + d_1$ $\dot{y} = 3x - y + d_2$	$d_1 \in [-0.005, 0.005]$ $d_2 \in [-0.005, 0.005]$	$x \in [1.19, 1.21]$ $y \in [0.8, 1.0]$
Controller 3D	$\dot{x} = 10(y - x) + d_1$ $\dot{y} = x^3 + d_2$ $\dot{z} = xy - 2.667z$	$d_1 \in [-0.001, 0.001]$ $d_2 \in [-0.001, 0.001]$	$x \in [1.79, 1.81]$ $y \in [1.0, 1.1]$ $z \in [0.5, 0.6]$

their intersection with the unsafe set requires their transformation into simpler geometric form (e.g. box), which has an exponential complexity in the number of the dimensions and it needs to be considered in the overall running time.

Remark 6. Table 2 shows us how brutal the reality of reachability analysis of nonlinear systems is and this gets even worse in the presence of uncertainty and large initial set. As can be seen in Table 2, both Flow* and CORA failed to give a solution for half of the benchmarks either due to timeout or due to exception. This phenomenon may be alleviated if smaller initial sets are provided or uncertainty is removed. In terms of computing time T, PRBT does not always outperform the other two tools. Actually, Flow* or CORA can be much faster in

Table 2. Experimental results for benchmark systems. #var: number of variables; T: computing time for flowpipe; TT: computing time including box transformation; N: number of flowpipe segments; D: candidate degrees for template polynomial (for PRBT only); TH: time horizon for flowpipe (for Flow* and CORA only). F/E: failed to terminate under 30 min or exception happened.

Model	#var	PRBT			TH	Flow*			CORA	
		T	N	D		T	TT	N	T	N
Controller 2D	2	35.73	12	3	0.012	48.8	417.64	240	F	1200
Van der Pol	2	221.62	17	4	6.74	23.88	1111.05	135	E	–
Lotka-Volterra	2	30.10	9	4	3.20	6.06	405.32	320	40.30	160
Buckling Column	2	74.02	35	3	14.00	F	–	–	734.81	1400
Jet Engine	2	240.98	18	4	9.50	F	–	–	1.69	190
Controller 3D	3	774.58	20	3	0.55	F	–	–	F	–

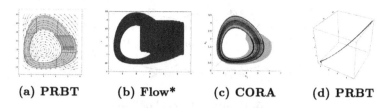

(a) PRBT   **(b) Flow***   **(c) CORA**   **(d) PRBT**

Fig. 2. Lotka-Volterra: (a), (b), (c); controller 3D: (d)

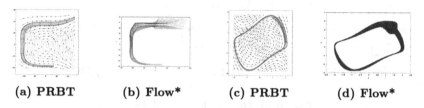

(a) PRBT   **(b) Flow***   **(c) PRBT**   **(d) Flow***

Fig. 3. Controller 2d: (a), (b); Van der Pol Oscillator: (c), (d)

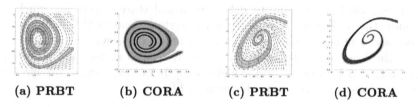

(a) PRBT   **(b) CORA**   **(c) PRBT**   **(d) CORA**

Fig. 4. Buckling Column: (a), (b); Jet Engine: (c), (d)

some cases. However, when the box transformation time for Taylor model was taken into account, the total computing time TT of Flow* increased significantly. One point to note here is that, PRBT, in general, produces a much smaller number N of flowpipe segments than the other two, which means that the time used to check the intersection of flowpipe with the unsafe set can be reduced considerably. In addition, as shown in Figs. 2, 3 and 4, PRBT is more precise than the other two on average.

5.2 Nonlinear Hybrid System

We use the tunnel diode oscillator (TDO) circuit (with different setting) introduced in [20] to illustrate the application of our approach to hybrid system. The two state space variables are the voltage $x_1 = V_C$ across capacitor and the current $x_2 = I_L$ through the inductor. The system dynamics is described as follows,

$$\dot{x}_1 = \frac{1}{C}(-h(x_1) + x_2) \qquad \dot{x}_2 = \frac{1}{L}(-x_1 - \frac{x_2}{G} + V_{in})$$

where $h(x_1)$ describes the tunnel diode characteristic and $V_{in} = 0.3\,\text{V}$, $G = 5\,\text{m}$ Ω^{-1}, $L = 0.5\,\mu\text{H}$ and $C = 2\,\text{pF}$.

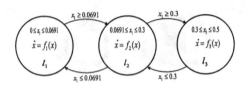

Fig. 5. Hybridized model of TDO

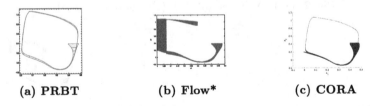

(a) PRBT   (b) Flow*   (c) CORA

Fig. 6. Flowpipe of hybridized TDO

For this model, we want to define an initial state region X_0 which can guarantee the oscillating behaviour for the system. Due to the highly nonlinear behaviour of the system, a common strategy to deal with this model is to use a hybridized model to approximate the dynamics system and then apply formal verification to the hybrid model [13,18]. In our experiment, we use three cubic equations to approximate the curve of $h(x_1)$.

$$h(x_1) = \begin{cases} 0.000847012 + 35.2297x_1 - 395.261x_1^2 + 1372.29x_1^3, \ 0 \le x_1 \le 0.0691 \\ 1.242 - 0.033x_1 - 47.4311x_1^2 + 116.48x_1^3, \ 0.0691 \le x_1 \le 0.3 \\ -16.544 + 139.64x_1 - 389.245x_1^2 + 359.948x_1^3, \ 0.3 \le x_1 \le 0.50 \end{cases}$$

From the piecewise function $h(x_1)$, we can derive a 3-mode hybrid system which is shown in Fig. 5. The system switches between the locations as the value of x_1 changes.

Let the initial set be $X_0 = \{(x_1, x_2) \in \mathbb{R}^2 \mid 0.40 \le x_1 \le 0.48, 0.38 \le x_2 \le 0.39\}$ on location l_3, we compute an overapproximation for the flowpipe using PRBT, Flow* and CORA respectively. As illustrated in Fig. 6, both PRBT and CORA found an invariant with roughly the same precision, which indicates the model oscillates for the initial set, while Flow* ran into an error.

References

1. Althoff, M., Grebenyuk, D.: Implementation of interval arithmetic in CORA 2016. In: Proceedings of ARCH. EPiC Series in Computing, vol. 43, pp. 91–105. Easy-Chair (2017)
2. Asarin, E., Dang, T., Girard, A.: Hybridization methods for the analysis of non-linear systems. Acta Inform. **43**(7), 451–476 (2007)
3. Ben Sassi, M.A., Sankaranarayanan, S., Chen, X., Ábrahám, E.: Linear relaxations of polynomial positivity for polynomial lyapunovfunction synthesis. IMA J. Math. Control. Inf. **33**(3), 723–756 (2015)

4. Berz, M., Makino, K.: Verified integration of odes and flows using differential algebraic methods on high-order taylor models. Reliab. Comput. **4**(4), 361–369 (1998)
5. Bogomolov, S., Schilling, C., Bartocci, E., Batt, G., Kong, H., Grosu, R.: Abstraction-based parameter synthesis for multiaffine systems. In: Piterman, N. (ed.) HVC 2015. LNCS, vol. 9434, pp. 19–35. Springer, Cham (2015). https://doi.org/10.1007/978-3-319-26287-1_2
6. Chen, X., Ábrahám, E., Sankaranarayanan, S.: Flow*: an analyzer for non-linear hybrid systems. In: Sharygina, N., Veith, H. (eds.) CAV 2013. LNCS, vol. 8044, pp. 258–263. Springer, Heidelberg (2013). https://doi.org/10.1007/978-3-642-39799-8_18
7. Cimatti, A., Griggio, A., Irfan, A., Roveri, M., Sebastiani, R.: Experimenting on solving nonlinear integer arithmetic with incremental linearization. In: Beyersdorff, O., Wintersteiger, C.M. (eds.) SAT 2018. LNCS, vol. 10929, pp. 383–398. Springer, Cham (2018). https://doi.org/10.1007/978-3-319-94144-8_23
8. Cimatti, A., Griggio, A., Irfan, A., Roveri, M., Sebastiani, R.: Incremental linearization for satisfiability and verification modulo nonlinear arithmetic and transcendental functions. ACM Trans. Comput. Log. **19**(3), 19:1–19:52 (2018)
9. Cyranka, J., Islam, M.A., Byrne, G., Jones, P., Smolka, S.A., Grosu, R.: Lagrangian reachabililty. In: Majumdar, R., Kunčak, V. (eds.) CAV 2017. LNCS, vol. 10426, pp. 379–400. Springer, Cham (2017). https://doi.org/10.1007/978-3-319-63387-9_19
10. Cyranka, J., Islam, Md.A., Smolka, S.A., Gao, S., Grosu, R.: Tight continuous-time reachtubes for lagrangian reachability. In: Proceedings of CDC 2018: 57th IEEE Conference on Decision and Control. IEEE (2018, to appear)
11. Duggirala, P.S., Mitra, S., Viswanathan, M., Potok, M.: C2E2: a verification tool for stateflow models. In: Baier, C., Tinelli, C. (eds.) TACAS 2015. LNCS, vol. 9035, pp. 68–82. Springer, Heidelberg (2015). https://doi.org/10.1007/978-3-662-46681-0_5
12. Fränzle, M., Herde, C., Teige, T., Ratschan, S., Schubert, T.: Efficient solving of large non-linear arithmetic constraint systems with complex boolean structure. JSAT **1**(3–4), 209–236 (2007)
13. Frehse, G., Krogh, B.H., Rutenbar, R.A.: Verification of hybrid systems using iterative refinement. In: Proceedings of SRC TECHCON 2005, Portland, USA, 24–26 October 2005
14. Frehse, G., et al.: SpaceEx: scalable verification of hybrid systems. In: Gopalakrishnan, G., Qadeer, S. (eds.) CAV 2011. LNCS, vol. 6806, pp. 379–395. Springer, Heidelberg (2011). https://doi.org/10.1007/978-3-642-22110-1_30
15. Girard, A., Le Guernic, C.: Efficient reachability analysis for linear systems using support functions. Proc. IFAC World Congr. **41**(2), 8966–8971 (2008)
16. Grosu, R., et al.: From cardiac cells to genetic regulatory networks. In: Gopalakrishnan, G., Qadeer, S. (eds.) CAV 2011. LNCS, vol. 6806, pp. 396–411. Springer, Heidelberg (2011). https://doi.org/10.1007/978-3-642-22110-1_31
17. Gulwani, S., Tiwari, A.: Constraint-based approach for analysis of hybrid systems. In: Gupta, A., Malik, S. (eds.) CAV 2008. LNCS, vol. 5123, pp. 190–203. Springer, Heidelberg (2008). https://doi.org/10.1007/978-3-540-70545-1_18
18. Gupta, S., Krogh, B.H., Rutenbar, R.A.: Towards formal verification of analog and mixed-signal designs. In: TECHCON (2003)
19. Gurung, A., Ray, R., Bartocci, E., Bogomolov, S., Grosu, R.: Parallel reachability analysis of hybrid systems in xspeed. Int. J. Softw. Tools Technol. Transf., 1–23 (2018, to appear)

20. Hartong, W., Hedrich, L., Barke, E.: Model checking algorithms for analog veri-fication. In: Proceedings of the 39th annual Design Automation Conference, pp. 542–547. ACM (2002)
21. Henzinger, T.A.: The theory of hybrid automata. In: Proceedings of IEEE Sym-posium on Logic in Computer Science, pp. 278–292 (1996)
22. Jiang, Y., Song, H., Wang, R., Gu, M., Sun, J., Sha, L.: Data-centered runtime verification of wireless medical cyber-physical system. IEEE Trans. Ind. Inform. **13**(4), 1900–1909 (2017)
23. Jiang, Y., Wang, M., Liu, H., Hosseini, M., Sun, J.: Dependable integrated clinical system architecture with runtime verification. In: 2017 IEEE/ACM International Conference on Computer-Aided Design (ICCAD), pp. 951–956, November 2017
24. Kong, H., Bartocci, E., Henzinger, T.A.: Reachable set over-approximation for non-linear systems using piecewise barrier tubes. In: Chockler, H., Weissenbacher, G. (eds.) CAV 2018. LNCS, vol. 10981, pp. 449–467. Springer, Cham (2018). https://doi.org/10.1007/978-3-319-96145-3_24
25. Kong, H., Bogomolov, S., Schilling, C., Jiang, Y., Henzinger, T.A.: Safety verifi-cation of nonlinear hybrid systems based on invariant clusters. In: Proceedings of HSCC 2017: the 20th International Conference on Hybrid Systems: Computation and Control, pp. 163–172. ACM (2017)
26. Kong, H., He, F., Song, X., Hung, W.N.N., Gu, M.: Exponential-condition-based barrier certificate generation for safety verification of hybrid systems. In: Shary-gina, N., Veith, H. (eds.) CAV 2013. LNCS, vol. 8044, pp. 242–257. Springer, Heidelberg (2013). https://doi.org/10.1007/978-3-642-39799-8_17
27. Kong, S., Gao, S., Chen, W., Clarke, E.: dReach: δ-reachability analysis for hybrid systems. In: Baier, C., Tinelli, C. (eds.) TACAS 2015. LNCS, vol. 9035, pp. 200–205. Springer, Heidelberg (2015). https://doi.org/10.1007/978-3-662-46681-0_15
28. Krilavicius, T.: Hybrid techniques for hybrid systems. Ph.D. thesis, University of Twente, Enschede, Netherlands (2006)
29. Lasserre, J.B.: Polynomial programming: LP-relaxations also converge. SIAM J. Optim. **15**(2), 383–393 (2005)
30. Liu, J., Zhan, N., Zhao, H.: Computing semi-algebraic invariants for polynomial dynamical systems. In: Proceedings of EMSOFT 2011: the 11th International Con-ference on Embedded Software, pp. 97–106. ACM (2011)
31. Matringe, N., Moura, A.V., Rebiha, R.: Generating invariants for non-linear hybrid systems by linear algebraic methods. In: Cousot, R., Martel, M. (eds.) SAS 2010. LNCS, vol. 6337, pp. 373–389. Springer, Heidelberg (2010). https://doi.org/10.1007/978-3-642-15769-1_23
32. Nedialkov, N.S.: Interval tools for ODEs and DAEs. In: Proceedings of SCAN 2006: the 12th GAMM - IMACS International Symposium on Scientific Computing, Computer Arithmetic and Validated Numerics, pp. 4–4. IEEE (2006)
33. Prabhakar, P., García Soto, M.: Hybridization for stability analysis of switched linear systems. In: Proceedings of HSCC 2016: of the 19th International Conference on Hybrid Systems: Computation and Control, pp. 71–80. ACM (2016)
34. Prajna, S., Jadbabaie, A.: Safety verification of hybrid systems using barrier certifi-cates. In: Alur, R., Pappas, G.J. (eds.) HSCC 2004. LNCS, vol. 2993, pp. 477–492. Springer, Heidelberg (2004). https://doi.org/10.1007/978-3-540-24743-2_32
35. Putinar, M.: Positive polynomials on compact semi-algebraic sets. Indiana Univ. Math. J. **42**(3), 969–984 (1993)

36. Ray, R., Gurung, A., Das, B., Bartocci, E., Bogomolov, S., Grosu, R.: XSpeed: accelerating reachability analysis on multi-core processors. In: Piterman, N. (ed.) HVC 2015. LNCS, vol. 9434, pp. 3–18. Springer, Cham (2015). https://doi.org/10.1007/978-3-319-26287-1_1

37. Roohi, N., Prabhakar, P., Viswanathan, M.: Hybridization based CEGAR for hybrid automata with affine dynamics. In: Chechik, M., Raskin, J.-F. (eds.) TACAS 2016. LNCS, vol. 9636, pp. 752–769. Springer, Heidelberg (2016). https://doi.org/10.1007/978-3-662-49674-9_48

38. Sankaranarayanan, S.: Automatic invariant generation for hybrid systems using ideal fixed points. In: Proceedings of HSCC 2010: the 13th ACM International Conference on Hybrid Systems: Computation and Control, pp. 221–230. ACM (2010)

39. Sankaranarayanan, S., Sipma, H.B., Manna, Z.: Constructing invariants for hybrid systems. In: Alur, R., Pappas, G.J. (eds.) HSCC 2004. LNCS, vol. 2993, pp. 539–554. Springer, Heidelberg (2004). https://doi.org/10.1007/978-3-540-24743-2_36

40. Sankaranarayanan, S., Chen, X., et al.: Lyapunov function synthesis using handelman representations. IFAC Proc. Vol. 46(23), 576–581 (2013)

41. Schupp, S., Ábrahám, E., Makhlouf, I.B., Kowalewski, S.: HyPro: A C++ library of state set representations for hybrid systems reachability analysis. In: Barrett, C., Davies, M., Kahsai, T. (eds.) NFM 2017. LNCS, vol. 10227, pp. 288–294. Springer, Cham (2017). https://doi.org/10.1007/978-3-319-57288-8_20

42. Sogokon, A., Ghorbal, K., Jackson, P.B., Platzer, A.: A method for invariant generation for polynomial continuous systems. In: Jobstmann, B., Leino, K.R.M. (eds.) VMCAI 2016. LNCS, vol. 9583, pp. 268–288. Springer, Heidelberg (2016). https://doi.org/10.1007/978-3-662-49122-5_13

43. Stengle, G.: A Nullstellensatz and a Positivstellensatz in semialgebraic geometry. Mathematische Annalen 207(2), 87–97 (1974)

44. Taly, A., Tiwari, A.: Deductive verification of continuous dynamical systems. In: FSTTCS, vol. 4, pp. 383–394 (2009)

45. Yang, Z., Huang, C., Chen, X., Lin, W., Liu, Z.: A linear programming relaxation based approach for generating barrier certificates of hybrid systems. In: Fitzgerald, J., Heitmeyer, C., Gnesi, S., Philippou, A. (eds.) FM 2016. LNCS, vol. 9995, pp. 721–738. Springer, Cham (2016). https://doi.org/10.1007/978-3-319-48989-6_44

Bounded Model Checking of Max-Plus Linear Systems via Predicate Abstractions

Muhammad Syifa'ul Mufid[1]([✉]), Dieky Adzkiya[2], and Alessandro Abate[1]

[1] Department of Computer Science, University of Oxford, Oxford, UK
{muhammad.syifaul.mufid,alessandro.abate}@cs.ox.ac.uk
[2] Department of Mathematics, Institut Teknologi Sepuluh Nopember,
Surabaya, Indonesia
dieky@matematika.its.ac.id

Abstract. This paper introduces the abstraction of max-plus linear (MPL) systems via predicates. Predicates are automatically selected from system matrix, as well as from the specifications under consideration. We focus on verifying time-difference specifications, which encompass the relation between successive events in MPL systems. We implement a bounded model checking (BMC) procedure over a predicate abstraction of the given MPL system, to verify the satisfaction of time-difference specifications. Our predicate abstractions are experimentally shown to improve on existing MPL abstractions algorithms. Furthermore, with focus on the BMC algorithm, we can provide an explicit upper bound on the completeness threshold by means of the transient and the cyclicity of the underlying MPL system.

1 Introduction

Max-Plus-Linear (MPL) systems are a class of discrete-event systems, with dynamics based on two binary operations (maximisation and addition) over a max-plus semiring. MPL systems are used to model synchronisation phenomena without concurrency. These systems have been used in many areas, such as manufacturing [27], transportation [24], and biological systems [10,18].

Classical analysis of MPL systems is conducted using algebraic approaches [4,24]. Recently, an alternative take based on formal abstractions has been developed to verify MPL systems against quantitative specifications [1] that are general and expressive. The performance and scalability of the abstraction approach has been later improved by employing tropical operations [29] that are native to the max-plus semiring.

This work pushes the envelop on scalability of formal abstractions of MPL systems. We newly apply predicate abstractions (PA) and bounded model checking (BMC) for the verification of MPL systems over time-difference specifications. Predicate abstractions are an abstraction approach that leverages a set of predicates, and have been classically used for software and hardware verification

© Springer Nature Switzerland AG 2019
É. André and M. Stoelinga (Eds.): FORMATS 2019, LNCS 11750, pp. 142–159, 2019.
https://doi.org/10.1007/978-3-030-29662-9_9

[16,21], for the abstraction of programs [6,15], and for reachability analysis of hybrid systems [3].

BMC is a symbolic model checking approach that leverages SAT solvers. The basic idea is to attempt finding counterexamples with a length bounded by some integer. If no counterexamples are found, the length is greedily increased. The approach is sound (counterexamples are correct), and complete (no counterexamples are admitted) whenever a completeness threshold (CT) for the length is reached [8,9]. Whilst there exist results on correct upper-bounds on the CT, in practice BMC is run until the underlying problem becomes intractable.

This paper has two specific contributions. The first contribution is related to the abstraction approach. Moving beyond [1,29], where the abstraction procedures are based on the translation of MPL systems into piecewise affine (PWA) systems, in this work we newly employ PA. Namely, we determine a set of predicates such that the dynamics within each partitioning region is affine. In other words, there is no need to compute PWA systems anymore.

The second contribution is related to the model-checking approach. [1] employs standard model checking to verify the abstract transition system. In this paper, we leverage BMC: notice that PA naturally yield Boolean encodings that can be relevant for the SAT-based BMC procedure. We focus on time-difference specifications. Since we are working on abstractions, counterexample generated by the BMC procedure needs to be checked for spuriousness (cf. Algorithms 5 and 6). Whenever a counterexample is spurious, we refine the abstract transition using the procedure in [2], combined with lazy abstraction [26]. Finally, for the considered time-difference specifications, we show that the CT can be upper-bounded by means of the transient and cyclicity of the concrete MPL system - such bounds are in general tighter than those obtained working on the abstract transition system. As a side result, we provide a few instance of "direct verification", where the model checking of MPL models can be performed straightforwardly for time-difference specifications.

The paper is organised as follows. Section 2 describes the basics of models, abstraction techniques and temporal logic formulae used in this work. It also contains the notion of time-difference over MPL systems. The contributions of this paper are contained in Sects. 3 and 4. Proofs of the propositions and lemmas are provided in the longer version of this paper [30]. The comparison of abstraction procedures is presented in Sect. 5, with PA implemented in C++ and model checking run over NuSMV [11]. We also compare the completeness threshold w.r.t. the transient and cyclicity of MPL systems with those that are computed by NuSMV. The paper is concluded in Sect. 6.

2 Model and Preliminaries

2.1 Max-Plus Linear Systems

By max-plus semiring we understand an algebraic structure $(\mathbb{R}_{\max}, \oplus, \otimes)$ where $\mathbb{R}_{\max} := \mathbb{R} \cup \{\varepsilon := -\infty\}$ and $a \oplus b := \max\{a, b\}$, $a \otimes b := a + b$ $\forall a, b \in \mathbb{R}_{\max}$. The set of $n \times m$ matrices over max-plus semiring is denoted as $\mathbb{R}_{\max}^{n \times m}$.

Two binary operations of a max-plus semiring can be extended to matrices as follows

$$[A \oplus B](i,j) = A(i,j) \oplus B(i,j),$$

$$[A \otimes C](i,j) = \bigoplus_{k=1}^{m} A(i,k) \otimes C(k,j),$$

where $A, B \in \mathbb{R}_{\max}^{n \times m}, C \in \mathbb{R}_{\max}^{m \times p}$. Given $r \in \mathbb{N}$, the max-plus algebraic power of $A \in \mathbb{R}_{\max}^{n \times n}$ is denoted by $A^{\otimes r}$ and corresponds to $A \otimes \ldots \otimes A$ (r times).

A Max-Plus Linear (MPL) system is defined as

$$\mathbf{x}(k+1) = A \otimes \mathbf{x}(k), \tag{1}$$

where $A \in \mathbb{R}_{\max}^{n \times n}$ is the system matrix and $\mathbf{x}(k) = [x_1(k) \ldots x_n(k)]^{\top}$ is the state variables [4]. In particular, for $i \in \{1, \ldots, n\}$, $x_i(k+1) = \max\{A(i,1) + x_1(k), \ldots, A(i,n) + x_n(k)\}$. In applications, $\mathbf{x}$ represents the time stamps of the discrete events, while k corresponds to the event counter. Therefore, it is more convenient to take $\mathbb{R}^n$ (instead of $\mathbb{R}_{\max}^n$) as the state space.

Definition 1 (Precedence Graph [4]). The precedence graph of A, denoted by $\mathcal{G}(A)$, is a weighted directed graph with nodes $1, \ldots, n$ and an edge from j to i with weight $A(i,j)$ if $A(i,j) \neq \varepsilon$. □

Definition 2 (Regular Matrix [24]). A matrix $A \in \mathbb{R}_{\max}^{n \times n}$ is called regular if there is at least one finite element in each row. □

Definition 3 (Irreducible Matrix [4]). A matrix $A \in \mathbb{R}_{\max}^{n \times n}$ is called irreducible if the corresponding precedence graph $\mathcal{G}(A)$ is strongly connected. □

Recall that a directed graph is strongly connected if for two different nodes i, j of the graph, there exists a path from i to j [4,20]. The weight of a path $p = i_1 i_2 \ldots i_k$ is equal to the total weight of the corresponding edges i.e. $|p| = A(i_2, i_1) + \ldots + A(i_k, i_{k-1})$. A circuit, namely a path that begins and ends at the same node, is called *critical* if it has maximum average weight, which is the weight divided by the length of path [4].

Every irreducible matrix $A \in \mathbb{R}_{\max}^{n \times n}$ admits a unique max-plus eigenvalue $\lambda \in \mathbb{R}$, which corresponds to the weight of critical circuit in $\mathcal{G}(A)$. Furthermore, by Proposition 1 next, A satisfies the so-called transient condition:

Proposition 1 (Transient Condition [4]). For an irreducible matrix $A \in \mathbb{R}_{\max}^{n \times n}$ and its corresponding max-plus eigenvalue $\lambda \in \mathbb{R}$, there exist $k_0, c \in \mathbb{N}$ such that $A^{\otimes(k+c)} = \lambda c \otimes A^{\otimes k}$ for all $k \geq k_0$. The smallest such k_0 and c are called the transient and the cyclicity of A, respectively. □

Example 1. Consider a 2×2 MPL system that represents a simple railway network [24]:

$$\mathbf{x}(k+1) = \begin{bmatrix} 2 & 5 \\ 3 & 3 \end{bmatrix} \otimes \mathbf{x}(k). \tag{2}$$

Its max-plus eigenvalue is $\lambda = 4$, whereas the transient and cyclicity for the matrix are $k_0 = c = 2$. □

Any given MPL system can be translated into a Piece-Wise Affine (PWA) system [23]. A PWA system comprises of spatial regions with correspond- ing PWA dynamics. The regions are generated from all possible coefficients $\mathbf{g} = (g_1, \ldots, g_n) \in \{1, \ldots, n\}^n$, which satisfies $A(i, g_i) \neq \varepsilon$ for $1 \leq i \leq n$. As shown in [1], the region corresponding to $\mathbf{g}$ is

$$R_{\mathbf{g}} = \bigcap_{i=1}^{n} \bigcap_{j=1}^{n} \{\mathbf{x} \in \mathbb{R}^n | x_{g_i} - x_j \geq A(i, j) - A(i, g_i)\}. \tag{3}$$

One could check that for each non-empty $R_{\mathbf{g}}$ and $\mathbf{x}(k) \in R_{\mathbf{g}}$, the MPL system (1) can be rewritten as the following affine dynamics:

$$x_i(k + 1) = x_{g_i}(k) + A(i, g_i), \quad i = 1, \ldots, n. \tag{4}$$

Notice that (4) can be expressed as $\mathbf{x}(k+1) = A_{\mathbf{g}} \otimes \mathbf{x}(k)$, where $A_{\mathbf{g}}$ is a region matrix [29] for the coefficient $\mathbf{g}$.

2.2   Time Differences in MPL Systems

We consider delays occurring between events governed by (1). Delays can describe the difference of two events corresponding to the same event counter but at different variable indices (i.e. $x_i(k) - x_j(k)$), or the difference of two con- secutive events for the same index (i.e. $x_i(k+1) - x_i(k)$). This paper focuses on the later case although, in general, the results of this paper can be applied to the former case.

We write the $(k + 1)^{\text{th}}$ time difference for the ith component as $t_i(k) = x_i(k + 1) - x_i(k)$. One can see that

$$t_i(k) = \max_{j^* \in \mathtt{fin}_i} \{x_{j^*}(k) + A(i, j^*)\} - x_i(k), \tag{5}$$

where $\mathtt{fin}_i$ is the set containing the indices of finite elements of $A(i, \cdot)$.[1]

2.3   Transition Systems and Linear Temporal Logic

Definition 4 (Transition System [5]). A transition system is formulated by a tuple $(S, T, I, \mathcal{AP}, L)$, where

- S is a set of states,
- $T \subseteq S \times S$ is a transition relation,
- $I \subseteq S$ is a set of initial states,
- $\mathcal{AP}$ is a set of atomic propositions, and
- $L : S \rightarrow 2^{\mathcal{AP}}$ is a labelling function.   □

---

[1] For the sake of simplicity, we write the elements of $\mathtt{fin}_i$ in a strictly increasing order.

A *path* of TS is defined as a sequence of states $\pi = s_0 s_1 \ldots$, where $s_0 \in I$ and $(s_i, s_{i+1}) \in T$ for all $i \geq 0$. We denote $\pi[i] = s_{i-1}$ as the ith state of π. Furthermore, $|\pi|$ represents the number of transitions in π.

Linear temporal logic (LTL) is one of the predominant logics that are used for specifying properties over the set of atomic propositions [5]. LTL formulae are recursively defined as follows.

Definition 5 (Syntax of LTL [5]). LTL formulae over the set of atomic propositions $\mathcal{AP}$ are constructed according to the following grammar:

$$\varphi := \text{true} \mid a \mid \varphi_1 \wedge \varphi_2 \mid \neg\varphi \mid \bigcirc\varphi \mid \varphi_1 \cup \varphi_2,$$

where $a \in \mathcal{AP}$.   □

The symbol $\bigcirc$ (next) and $\cup$ (until) are called temporal operators. Two additional operators, $\Diamond$ (eventually) and $\square$ (always), are generated via the until operators: $\Diamond\varphi = \text{true} \cup \varphi$ and $\square\varphi = \neg\Diamond\neg\varphi$. We refer to [5] for the semantics of LTL formulae including the satisfaction relation $\models$ over transition systems.

2.4 Abstractions and Predicate Abstractions

Abstractions are techniques to generate a finite and smaller model from a large or even infinite-space (i.e., a continuous-space model, e.g., an MPL system) model. Abstractions can reduce the verification of a temporal property φ over the original model (a *concrete* model with state space S), to checking a related property on a simpler *abstract* model (over $\hat{S}$) [5]. The mapping from S to $\hat{S}$ is called *abstraction function*.

From a (concrete) transition system $TS = (S, T, I, \mathcal{AP}, L)$ and an abstraction function $f : S \rightarrow \hat{S}$, the (abstract) transition system $TS_f = (\hat{S}, T_f, I_f, \mathcal{AP}, L_f)$ is generated from TS as follows: (i) $I_f = \{f(s) \mid s \in I\}$, (ii) $(f(s), f(s')) \in T_f$ if $(s, s') \in T$, and (iii) $L_f(f(s)) = L(s)$, for all $s \in S$.

The important relation between TS and TS_f is that the former is *simulated* by the latter (which is denoted by $TS \preceq TS_f$). In detail, all behaviour on concrete transition system occur on the abstract one. The formal definition of simulation relation can be found in [5, Definition 7.47]. Furthermore, given an LTL formula φ, $TS_f \models \varphi$ implies $TS \models \varphi$ [5,13].

Predicate abstractions [13,17,19,22] denote abstraction methods that use a set of *predicates* $P = \{p_1, \ldots, p_k\}$ to characterise the abstract states. Predicates are identified from the concrete model, and possibly from the specification(s) under consideration. Each predicate p_i corresponds to a Boolean variable b_i and each abstract state $\hat{s} \in \hat{S}$ corresponds to a Boolean assignment of these k Boolean variables [13]. Therefore, we obtain that $|\hat{S}| \leq 2^k$. An abstract state will be labelled with predicate p_i if the corresponding b_i is true in that state. For this reason, predicates also serve as atomic propositions [13].

The predicates are also used to define an abstraction function between the concrete and abstract state spaces. A concrete state $s \in S$ will be related to an abstract state $\hat{s} \in \hat{S}$ iff the truth value of p_i on s equals the value of b_i

on $\hat{s}$. The abstraction function for predicate abstractions is defined as $f(s) = \bigwedge_{i=1}^{k} \text{val}(s, p_i)$, where $\text{val}(s, p_i) = b_i$ if p_i is satisfied in s, otherwise $\neg b_i$.

3 Predicate Abstractions of MPL Systems

3.1 Related Work

The notion of abstractions of an MPL system has been first introduced in [1]: there, it leverages translation of an MPL system into the corresponding PWA system. The resulting abstract states are expressed as Difference-Bound Matrices (DBM). A more efficient procedure for MPL abstractions via max-plus algebraic operations is later discussed in [29].

3.2 Generation of the Predicates

Considering an abstraction via a set of predicates, the first issue is to find appropriate predicates. Recall that related abstraction techniques [1,29] explore the connection between MPL and PWA systems and use DBMs to represent the abstract states. Similarly, predicates here are chosen such that the dynamics in the resulting abstract states are affine as in (3) and can be expressed as DBMs. Following these considerations, the predicates are defined as an inequality $p \equiv x_i - x_j \sim c$ where $\sim \in \{>, \geq\}^2$, $c \in \mathbb{R}$. For simplicity, we may write a predicate as a tuple $p \equiv (i, j, c, s)$ where $s = 1$ if $\sim = \geq$, otherwise $s = 0$. The negation of p then can be written as $\neg p \equiv (j, i, -c, 1 - s)$.

From the PWA region in (3), c can be chosen from the difference of two finite elements of the state matrix $A \in \mathbb{R}_{\max}^{n \times n}$ at the same row. In detail, if $A(k, j) \neq \varepsilon$ and $A(k, i) \neq \varepsilon$ with $i < j$ and $1 \leq k \leq n$, then we get a predicate $(i, j, A(k, j) - A(k, i), 1)$.

Algorithm 1 shows a procedure to generate the predicates from an MPL system. For each $k \in \{1, \ldots, n\}$, P_k is a set of predicates generated from $A(k, \cdot)$. If there are exactly $m > 1$ finite elements at each row of A then $|P_k| = \binom{m}{2}$ and in general $|\bigcup_{k=1}^{n} P_k| \leq n\binom{m}{2}$: indeed, it is possible to get the same predicate from two different rows when $A(k_1, j) - A(k_1, i) = A(k_2, j) - A(k_2, i)$ for $k_1 \neq k_2$.

As mentioned before, predicates can also be associated to given specifications. In this paper, we focus on time-difference specifications that are generated from a set of *time-difference propositions*. For $\alpha \in \mathbb{R}$, we define a time-difference proposition '$t_i \sim \alpha$' to reason the condition that $x_i' - x_i \sim \alpha$. We remove the counter event k for the sake of simplicity.

One can rewrite (5) as $t_i = \max_{j^* \in \text{fin}_i} \{x_{j^*} + A(i, j^*)\} - x_i$. Therefore, from $t_i \sim \alpha$ for $\sim \in \{>, \geq, <, \leq\}$ we have $\max_{j^* \in \text{fin}_i} \{x_{j^*} + A(i, j^*)\} - x_i \sim \alpha$. The number of predicates corresponding to '$t_i \sim \alpha$' is bounded by $|\text{fin}_i|$. For each $j^* \in \text{fin}_i$ we get a predicate $x_{j^*} - x_i \sim \alpha - A(i, j^*)$. However, in case of $i \in \text{fin}_i$, or in other words $A(i, i) \neq \varepsilon$, $x_i - x_i \sim \alpha - A(i, j^*)$ is not a predicate. Algorithm 2 shows how to generate the predicates w.r.t. a time-difference proposition.

---

² In this paper, we always use $p \equiv x_i - x_j \geq c$ as a predicate.

Algorithm 1. Generation of predicates from an MPL system

Input: $A \in \mathbb{R}_{\max}^{n \times n}$,
Output: P_{mat}, a set of predicates
1: **procedure** mpl2pred(A, k) ▷ generation of predicates from the kth row of A
2:    $P_k \leftarrow \emptyset$
3:    $\text{fin}_k := \text{Find}(A(k, \cdot) \neq \varepsilon)$ ▷ fin_k is a vector consisting the index of
4:    **for** $j \in \{2, \ldots, |\text{fin}_k|\}$ finite elements of $A(k, \cdot)$, $\text{fin}_k[i]$ is
5:      **for** $i \in \{1, \ldots, j-1\}$ the ith element of fin_k
6:        $P_k \leftarrow P_k \cup \{(\text{fin}_k[i], \text{fin}_k[j], A(k, \text{fin}_k[j]) - A(k, \text{fin}[i]), 1)\}$
7:      **end**
8:    **end**
9:    **return** P_k
10: **end**

11: **procedure** mpl2pred(A) ▷ generation of predicates from matrix A
12:    $P_{mat} \leftarrow \emptyset$
13:    **for** $k \in \{1, \ldots, n\}$ ▷ generation of predicates for each row of matrix A
14:      $P_{mat} \leftarrow P_{mat} \cup \text{mpl2pred}(A, k)$ and storing the resulting predicates in P_{mat}
15:    **end**
16:    **return** P_{mat}
17: **end**

Algorithm 2. Generation of predicates from a time-difference proposition

---

Input: $A \in \mathbb{R}_{\max}^{n \times n}$, a matrix containing exactly m finite elements in each row
        $t_i \sim \alpha$, a time-difference proposition
Output: P_{time}, a set of predicates
1: **procedure** td2pred$(A, t_i \sim \alpha)$
2:    $P_{time} \leftarrow \emptyset$
3:    $A(i, i) \leftarrow \varepsilon$
4:    $\text{fin}_i \leftarrow \text{Find}(A(i, \cdot) \neq \varepsilon)$
5:    **if** $\sim \in \{>, \geq\}$ **then**
6:      **for** $j^* \in \text{fin}_i$
7:        $P_{time} \leftarrow P_{time} \cup \{(j^*, i, \alpha - A(i, j^*), s)\}$ ▷ s is 0 if $\sim$ is $>$ and s is 1 if $\sim$ is $\geq$
8:      **end**
9:    **else if** $\sim \in \{<, \leq\}$ **then**
10:      **for** $j^* \in \text{fin}_i$
11:        $P_{time} \leftarrow P_{time} \cup \{(i, j^*, A(i, j^*) - \alpha, s)\}$ ▷ each predicate uses operator $>$ or $\geq$
12:      **end**
13:    **end**
14:    **return** P_{time}
15: **end**

3.3 Generation of Abstract States

This section starts by describing the procedure to generate abstract states via a set of predicates. We denote P as the set of predicates generated by Algorithms 1 and 2, i.e. $P = P_{mat} \cup P_{time} = \{p_1, \ldots, p_k\}$. Let $\hat{S}$ be a set of abstract states defined over Boolean variables $B = \{b_1, \ldots, b_k\}$, where the truth value of b_i depends on that of p_i. For each Boolean variable b_i, we define the corresponding DBM as follows: $\text{DBM}(b_i) = \{\mathbf{x} \in \mathbb{R}^n \mid p_i \text{ is true in } \mathbf{x}\}$ and $\text{DBM}(\neg b_i) = \{\mathbf{x} \in \mathbb{R}^n \mid p_i \text{ is false in } \mathbf{x}\}$. One can show that $\text{DBM}(b_i \wedge b_j) = \text{DBM}(b_i) \cap \text{DBM}(b_j)$.

Algorithm 3 shows the steps to generate the abstract states of an MPL system given a set of predicates P. For each $i \in \{1, \ldots, |P|\}$, we manipulate DBMs: the complexity of Algorithm 3 depends on emptiness checking of DBM (line 11), which runs in $\mathcal{O}(n^3)$, where n is the dimension of the state matrix [1]. Therefore, the worst-case complexity of Algorithm 3 is $\mathcal{O}(2^{|P|} n^3)$.

Algorithm 3. Generation of the abstract states from a set of predicates

---

Input: P, a set of predicates $\triangleright P = P_{mat} \cup P_{time}$
Output: $\hat{S}$, a set of abstract states
$\qquad\quad$ D, a partition of $\mathbb{R}^n$ w.r.t. $\hat{S}$ $\triangleright D$ is a set of DBMs
1: **procedure** pred_abs(P)
2: $\quad B \leftarrow \{b_1, \ldots, b_{|P|}\}$ $\triangleright$ a set of Boolean variables
3: $\quad D \leftarrow \{\mathbb{R}^n\}$
4: $\quad \hat{S} \leftarrow \{\texttt{true}\}$
5: $\quad$ **for** $i \in \{1, \ldots, |P|\}$
6: $\qquad \hat{S} \leftarrow \bigcup_{\hat{s} \in \hat{S}} \{\hat{s} \wedge \neg b_i\} \cup \bigcup_{\hat{s} \in \hat{S}} \{\hat{s} \wedge b_i\}$
7: $\qquad D_{neg} \leftarrow \bigcup_{E \in D} \{E \cap DBM(\neg b_i)\}$ $\triangleright$ each DBM in D is intersected with $DBM(\neg b_i)$
8: $\qquad D_{pos} \leftarrow \bigcup_{E \in D} \{E \cap DBM(b_i)\}$ $\triangleright$ both D_{neg} and D_{pos} are set of DBMs
9: $\qquad D \leftarrow D_{neg} \cup D_{pos}$
10: $\qquad D_{temp} \leftarrow \emptyset$ $\triangleright$ temporary variable for D
11: $\qquad \hat{S}_{temp} \leftarrow \emptyset$ $\triangleright$ temporary variable for $\hat{S}$
12: $\qquad$ **for** $j \in \{1, \ldots, |D|\}$
13: $\qquad\quad$ **if** $D[j]$ is not empty **then** $\triangleright$ DBM emptiness check
14: $\qquad\qquad$ **add** $D[j]$ to D_{temp}
15: $\qquad\qquad$ **add** $\hat{S}[j]$ to $\hat{S}_{temp}$
16: $\qquad\quad$ **end**
17: $\qquad$ **end**
18: $\qquad D \leftarrow D_{temp}$
19: $\qquad \hat{S} \leftarrow \hat{S}_{temp}$
20: $\quad$ **end**
21: $\quad$ **return** $(\hat{S}, D)$
22: **end**

3.4 Generation of Abstract Transitions

Having obtained the abstract states, one needs to generate the abstract transitions, which can be obtained via one-step reachability, as described in [1]. Namely, there is a transition from $\hat{s}_i$ to $\hat{s}_j$ if $\mathsf{Im}(\mathsf{DBM}(\hat{s}_i)) \cap \mathsf{DBM}(\hat{s}_j) \neq \emptyset$, where $\mathsf{Im}(\mathsf{DBM}(\hat{s}_i)) = \{A \otimes \mathbf{x} \mid \mathbf{x} \in \mathsf{DBM}(\hat{s}_i)\}$. The computation of $\mathsf{Im}(\mathsf{DBM}(\hat{s}_i))$ corresponds to the image of $\mathsf{DBM}(\hat{s}_i)$ w.r.t. the affine dynamics of $\hat{s}_i$ which has complexity $\mathcal{O}(n^2)$ [29].

However, unlike [29, Algorithm 2], Algorithm 3 does not produce the affine dynamics for each abstract state. For each $\hat{s} \in \hat{S}$, we need to find $\mathbf{g}$ as in (4). One can generate the affine dynamics for $\hat{s} \in \hat{S}$ from the value (either true or false) of $p \in P_{mat}$ on $\hat{s}$. Given a predicate $p \equiv (i, j, c, s)$, we call i and j as the left and right index of p (as $x_i \sim x_j + c$) and denoted them by $\texttt{left}(p)$ and $\texttt{right}(p)$, respectively.

If $p \equiv (i, j, A(k, j) - A(k, i), 1)$ is true in $\hat{s}$, we have $x_i + A(k, i) \geq x_j + A(k, j)$, otherwise $x_j + A(k, j) > x_i + A(k, i)$. Hence, the left index of predicates can be used to determine the affine dynamics. Algorithm 4 provides the procedure to find the affine dynamic associated to $\hat{s} \in \hat{S}$.

For each k, $\texttt{fin}_k$ is computed. Initially, the elements of $\texttt{fin}_k$ are in strictly increasing order. Then, for each predicate $p \in P_k$, we swap the location of $\texttt{left}(p)$ and $\texttt{right}(p)$ whenever p is false on $\hat{s}$. Suppose i is the first element of $\texttt{fin}_k$ after swapping. One could show that $x_i + A(k, i) \sim x_j + A(k, j)$ for all $j \in \texttt{fin}_k \setminus \{i\}$.

Algorithm 4. Generation of the affine dynamics for an abstract state

---

Input: $A \in \mathbb{R}_{\max}^{n \times n}$, a m-regular matrix with $m > 1$
       $\hat{s} \in \hat{S}$, an abstract state
       $P_1, \ldots, P_n$, sets of predicates generated by Algorithm 1
Output: g, the finite coefficient representing the affine dynamics for $\hat{s}$
1: **procedure** get_affine$(A, \hat{s}, P_1, \ldots, P_n)$
2:    **g** $\leftarrow$ zeros$(1, n)$
3:    **for** $k \in \{1, \ldots, n\}$
4:       fin$_k \leftarrow$ Find$(A(k, \cdot) \neq \varepsilon)$ ▷ recall that elements in fin$_k$ is
5:       **for** $p \in P_k$ in strictly-increasing order
6:         **if** p is false in $\hat{s}$ **then**
7:            **swap** left(p) with right(p) in fin$_k$
8:         **end**
9:       **end**
10:     **g**$[k] \leftarrow$ fin$_k[1]$ ▷ insertion of the kth element of **g**
11:    **end**
12:    **return g**
13: **end**

3.5 Model Checking MPL Systems over Time-Difference Specifications: Direct Verification

This section discusses the verification of MPL systems over time-difference specifications. First, we define a (concrete) transition system w.r.t. a given MPL system.

Definition 6 (Transition system associated with MPL system). A transition system TS for an MPL system in (1) is a tuple $(S, T, \mathcal{X}, \mathcal{AP}, L)$ where

- the set of states S is $\mathbb{R}^n$,
- $(\mathbf{x}, \mathbf{x}') \in T$ if $\mathbf{x}' = A \otimes \mathbf{x}$,
- $\mathcal{X} \subseteq \mathbb{R}^n$ is a set of initial conditions,
- $\mathcal{AP}$ is a set of time-difference propositions,
- the labelling function $L : S \rightarrow 2^{\mathcal{AP}}$ is defined as follows: a state $\mathbf{x} \in S$ is labeled by '$t_i \sim \alpha$' if $[A \otimes \mathbf{x} - \mathbf{x}]_i \sim \alpha$, where $\sim \ \in \{>, \geq, <, \leq\}$.   □

We express the time-difference specifications as LTL formulae over a set of time-difference propositions.[3] For instance, $\bigcirc(t_i \leq \alpha)$ represents 'the next time difference for the ith component is $\leq \alpha$' while $\Diamond\Box(t_i \leq \alpha)$ corresponds to 'after some finite executions, the time difference for the ith component is always $\leq \alpha$'. To check the satisfaction of these specifications, we generate the abstract version of MPL system.

    The abstract transition system $TS_f = (\hat{S}, T_f, I_f, P_{mat} \cup P_{time}, L_f)$ for an MPL system is generated via predicate abstraction where P_{mat} and P_{time} is the set of predicates generated by Algorithms 1 and 2, respectively. The (abstract) labelling function L_f is defined over predicates $p \in P_{mat} \cup P_{time}$: for $\hat{s} \in \hat{S}$, $p \in L_f(\hat{s})$ iff p is true in $\hat{s}$. We show the relation between predicates in P_{time} and a time-difference proposition in $\mathcal{AP}$.

Proposition 2. Suppose P_{time} is a set of predicates corresponding to a time-difference proposition '$t_i \sim \alpha$' and an abstract state $\hat{s} \in \hat{S}$.

---

[3] Notice that, in Definition 6 we consider $\mathcal{AP}$ as a set of time-difference propositions.

i. For $\sim \{>, \geq\}$, a (concrete) state $\mathbf{x} \in \mathrm{DBM}(\hat{s})$ is labeled by '$t_i \sim \alpha$' iff at least one predicate in P_{time} is true in $\hat{s}$.
ii. For $\sim \{<, \leq\}$, a (concrete) state $\mathbf{x} \in \mathrm{DBM}(\hat{s})$ is labeled by '$t_i \sim \alpha$' iff all predicates in P_{time} are true in $\hat{s}$. □

Example 2. Suppose we have an MPL system (2) and $\mathcal{AP} = \{t_1 \leq 5\}$. We consider two time-difference specifications $\lozenge(t_1 \leq 5)$ and $\lozenge\square(t_1 \leq 5)$ and a set of initial conditions $\mathcal{X} = \mathbb{R}^2$. By Algorithms 1 and 2, we have $P_{mat} = \{(1, 2, 3, 1), (1, 2, 0, 1)\}$ and $P_{time} = \{(1, 2, 0, 1)\}$. Thus, $P = \{p_1, p_2\}$ where $p_1 \equiv (1, 2, 3, 1)$ and $p_2 \equiv (1, 2, 0, 1)$.

The resulting abstract transition is depicted in Fig. 1. All abstract states are initial. The corresponding LTL formulae for the time-difference specifications are $\lozenge p_2$ and $\lozenge\square p_2$.

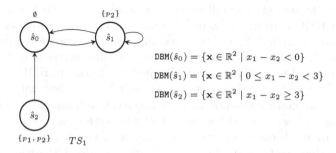

$$\mathrm{DBM}(\hat{s}_0) = \{\mathbf{x} \in \mathbb{R}^2 \mid x_1 - x_2 < 0\}$$
$$\mathrm{DBM}(\hat{s}_1) = \{\mathbf{x} \in \mathbb{R}^2 \mid 0 \leq x_1 - x_2 < 3\}$$
$$\mathrm{DBM}(\hat{s}_2) = \{\mathbf{x} \in \mathbb{R}^2 \mid x_1 - x_2 \geq 3\}$$

Fig. 1. The abstract transition system via predicate abstractions with a time-difference proposition.

It is clear that $TS_1 \models \lozenge p_2$. Therefore, the underlying MPL system satisfies $\lozenge(t_1 \leq 5)$. However, $TS_1 \not\models \lozenge\square p_2$ and we can not conclude whether $\lozenge\square(t_1 \leq 5)$ is false. We will show how to deal with this problem in Sect. 4. □

Direct Verification. In some cases, it is possible to check the satisfaction of time-difference specifications directly, namely without generating the abstraction of the MPL system. We call a time-difference proposition $t_i \sim \alpha$ is a *contradiction* if there is no $\mathbf{x} \in \mathbb{R}^n$ such that $[A \otimes \mathbf{x} - \mathbf{x}]_i \sim \alpha$. On the other hand, $t_i \sim \alpha$ is a *tautology* if all $\mathbf{x} \in \mathbb{R}^n$ satisfy $[A \otimes \mathbf{x} - \mathbf{x}]_i \sim \alpha$.

Proposition 3. Given an MPL system (1) with $A(i, i) = \beta \in \mathbb{R}$.

i. For $\sim \{>, \geq\}$, $t_i \sim \alpha$ is a tautology if $\beta \sim \alpha$.
ii. For $\sim \{<, \leq\}$, $t_i \sim \alpha$ is a contradiction if $\alpha < \beta$. □

The consequence of Proposition 3 is that any time-difference specification defined from a tautology (resp., contradiction) time-difference proposition, is guaranteed to be true (resp., false). For instance, from Example 2, the specification $(t_1 \geq 2)\mathsf{U}(t_2 \geq 3)$ is satisfied, while $\lozenge(t_2 \leq 2)$ is not. As a second instance of direct verification, in the case of irreducible MPL systems, the dissatisfaction of specifications in the form of $\Diamond\Box(t_i \sim \alpha)$ is related to the max-plus eigenvalue of the corresponding system matrix.

Proposition 4. Consider an MPL system characterised by an irreducible matrix $A \in \mathbb{R}_{\max}^{n \times n}$ and a time-difference specification $\Diamond\Box(t_i \sim \alpha)$. Suppose λ is the max-plus eigenvalue of A. The following holds:

i. For $\sim \{>, \geq\}$, if $\lambda < \alpha$ then $\Diamond\Box(t_i \sim \alpha)$ is false.
ii. For $\sim \{<, \leq\}$, if $\lambda > \alpha$ then $\Diamond\Box(t_i \sim \alpha)$ is false.   □

4   Bounded Model Checking of MPL Systems

In this section, we implement bounded model checking (BMC) algorithm to check the satisfaction of time-difference specifications over MPL system. The basic idea of BMC is to find a bounded counterexample of a given length k. If no such counterexample is found, then one increases k by one until a pre-known completeness threshold is reached, or until the problem becomes intractable. The readers are referred to [7–9] for a more detailed description of BMC.

We use NuSMV 2.6.0 [11] via command `check_ltlspec_bmc_onepb` to apply BMC. It performs non-incremental BMC to find a counterexample with length k. If no such bug is present then the command is reapplied for length $k+1$, otherwise we apply spurious checking (cf. Sect. 4.1). In case of non-spurious witness, one can conclude that the time-difference specification is false. Otherwise, we refine the transition system (cf. Sect. 4.2) such that the counterexample is removed and then reapply BMC command for length k. This procedure is repeated until we reach a completeness threshold (cf. Sect. 4.3).

4.1   Checking Spuriousness of Counterexamples

There are two types of k-length bounded abstract counterexamples $\pi = \hat{s}_0 \hat{s}_1 \ldots \hat{s}_k$ in BMC: either no-loop or lasso-shaped paths. The former one can be used to express the violation of invariant properties $\Box p$. A lasso-shaped path is $\pi = \hat{s}_0 \hat{s}_1 \ldots \hat{s}_k$ such that there exists $1 \leq l \leq k$ where $s_{l-1} = s_k$ [8,9]. Although it is finite, it can represent an infinite path $\bar{\pi} = (\hat{s}_0 \hat{s}_1 \hat{s}_{l-1})(\hat{s}_l \ldots \hat{s}_k)^\omega$ where $\hat{s}_{l-1+m} = \hat{s}_{k+m}$ for $m \geq 0$. It can be used to represent the counterexample of LTL formulae with eventuality, such as $\Diamond p$ and $\Diamond\Box p$.

From now, we write a lasso-shaped path as $(\pi_{stem})(\pi_{loop})^\omega$, where $\pi_{stem} = \hat{s}_0 \ldots \hat{s}_{l-1}$ and $\pi_{loop} = \hat{s}_l \ldots \hat{s}_k$. To avoid ambiguity, we consider that the length of a lasso-shaped path is equal to $|\pi_{stem}| + |\pi_{loop}|$.[4] Furthermore, any no-loop path cannot be expressed as a lasso-shaped one. That is, if π is a no-loop path then the states in π are all different.

The spuriousness of no-loop paths can be checked via forward-reachability analysis. In detail, $\pi = \hat{s}_0 \hat{s}_1 \ldots \hat{s}_k$ is not spurious iff the sequence of DBMs

---

[4] Notice a loop-back transition from $\hat{s}_k$ to $\hat{s}_l$ in π_{loop}.

$D_1, \ldots, D_{k+1}$ where $D_1 = \text{DBM}(\hat{s}_0)$ and $D_{i+1} = \text{Im}(D_i) \cap \text{DBM}(\hat{s}_i)$ for $1 \leq i \leq k$, are not empty. Simply put, there exists $\mathbf{x}(0) \in \text{DBM}(\hat{s}_0)$ such that $\mathbf{x}(i+1) = A \otimes \mathbf{x}(i) \in \text{DBM}(\hat{s}_{i+1})$ for $0 \leq i \leq k$. Algorithm 5 summarises the procedure of spuriousness checking for no-loop paths.

Algorithm 5. Spuriousness checking of no-loop paths

Input: $\pi = \hat{s}_0 \hat{s}_1 \ldots \hat{s}_k$, a no-loop path with length of k
Output: b, a boolean value   ▷ $b =$ true iff π is spurious
   D, a set of DBMs

```
1:  procedure is_spurious(π)
2:      b ← false
3:      E ← DBM(π[1])                        ▷ π[i+1] = ŝᵢ for 0 ≤ i ≤ k
4:      D ← {E}                              ▷ E is the first DBM in D
5:      k ← |π| − 1
6:      i ← 1
7:      while (i ≤ k and b == false)
8:          E ← Im(E) ∩ DBM(π[i+1])
9:          if E is empty then
10:             b ← true
11:         else
12:             add E to D                   ▷ E is now the (i+1)ᵗʰ DBM in D
13:         end
14:         i ← i + 1
15:     end
16:     return (b, D)
17: end
```

The spuriousness checking for lasso-shaped paths is computed via Algorithm 6. We use periodicity checking to deal with the infinite suffix $(\pi_{loop})^\omega$. In lines 14–22, we check the spuriousness of $(\pi_{stem})(\pi_{loop})^{it}$ where π_{loop} is repeated it times. If it is not spurious then we check the periodicity of the DBM (line 25). We can conclude that $(\pi_{stem})(\pi_{loop})^\omega$ is not spurious if the periodicity is found. In case of an irreducible MPL system, by Proposition 1, the periodicity is no greater than its cyclicity. On the other hand, after 1000 iterations, if the periodicity cannot be found then the algorithm is stopped with an 'undecided' result.

One can see that the spuriousness checking for no-loop paths (Algorithm 5) is guaranteed to be complete. However, this is not the case for Algorithm 6. In the case of irreducible MPL systems, it is complete due to the fact that the periodicity is related to Proposition 1. However for reducible MPL systems, it is incomplete as it may provide undecided results.

Lemma 1 relates the spuriousness of an abstract path, either no-loop or lasso-shaped path, with the value of transient and cyclicity of an irreducible matrix.

Lemma 1. Consider an irreducible $A \in \mathbb{R}_{\max}^{n \times n}$ with transient k_0 and cyclicity c and the resulting abstract transition system $TS_f = (\hat{S}, T_f, I_f, P_{mat} \cup P_{time}, L_f)$. Suppose that π is a path over TS_f. Then,

i. If π is a no-loop path with $|\pi| \geq k_0 + c$, then it is spurious.
ii. If $\pi = (\pi_{stem})(\pi_{loop})^\omega$ with $|\pi_{stem}| + |\pi_{loop}| > k_0 + c$, then it is spurious. $\square$

Algorithm 6. Spuriousness checking of a lasso-shaped path

Input: $\pi_{stem} = \hat{s}_0\hat{s}_1 \ldots \hat{s}_{l-1}$
    $\pi_{loop} = \hat{s}_l\hat{s}_1 \ldots \hat{s}_k$
Output: b, a boolean value   ▷ b = true iff π is spurious
    D, a set of DBMs

1: **procedure** is_spurious(π_{stem}, π_{loop})
2:     $(b, D) \leftarrow$ is_spurious(π_{stem})
3:     **if** ($b ==$ **true**) **then**
4:         **go to** line 35   ▷ π_{stem} is already spurious
5:     **else**
6:         $l \leftarrow |\pi_{stem}| + 1$ ▷ the number of states in π_{stem}
7:         $E \leftarrow D[l]$ ▷ E is the last DBM in D
8:         $m \leftarrow |\pi_{loop}|$ ▷ the number of states in π_{loop}
9:         $it \leftarrow 0$ ▷ the number of iterations
10:        $p \leftarrow$ **false**   ▷ boolean value to represent the periodicity
11:        **while** ($it \leq 1000$ and $p ==$ **false** and $b ==$ **false**)   ▷ maximum number of
12:            $it \leftarrow it + 1$ iterations is 1000
13:            $i \leftarrow 1$
14:            **while** ($i \leq m$ and $b ==$ **false**)
15:                $E \leftarrow \mathsf{Im}(E) \cap \mathsf{DBM}(\pi_{loop}[i])$
16:                **if** E is empty **then**
17:                    $b \leftarrow$ **true**
18:                **else**
19:                    **add** E to D
20:                **end**
21:                $i \leftarrow i + 1$
22:            **end**
23:            $j, num \leftarrow |D|$ ▷ the number of DBMs in D, notice
24:            **while** ($j - m > l$ and $p ==$ **false** and $b ==$ **false**)   that mod($|D|, m$) $= l$
25:                **if** ($D[j - m] == E$) **then**
26:                    $p \leftarrow$ **true**
27:                **end**
28:                $j \leftarrow j - m$
29:            **end**
30:        **end**
31:        **if** ($it > 1000$ and $p ==$ **false** and $b ==$ **false**) **then**
32:            print 'undecided'
33:        **else**
34:            **return** (b, D)
35:        **end**
36:    **end**
37: **end**

4.2 Refinement Procedure

Provided that the counterexample is spurious, one needs to refine the abstract transition. Instead of adding new predicates as in CEGAR [12], we are inspired by the refinement procedure described in [2, Sec. 3.3]: for each abstract state $\hat{s}$ with more than one outgoing transitions, it partitions $\mathsf{DBM}(\hat{s})$ according to its successors.

Our approach for the refinement procedure is slightly different. We refine the abstract transition based on a spurious counterexample $\pi = \hat{s}_0 \ldots \hat{s}_k$ using the concept of lazy abstraction [26]. This starts by finding a pivot state, namely a state in which the spuriousness starts. Then, it splits the pivot state using the procedure in [2].

Notice that, from Algorithm 5, the pivot state can be found from the number of DBMs we have in D. One could find that $\hat{s}_{|D|-1}$ is a pivot state. On the other hand, from Algorithm 6, a pivot state is $\hat{s}_i$ where $i = |D| - 1$, if $|D| < |\pi_{stem}| + 1$ (the spuriousness is found in π_{stem}), otherwise $i = |\pi_{stem}| + 1 + \text{mod}(D - |\pi_{stem}| - 1, |\pi_{loop}|)$.

With regards to the refined abstract transitions, the labels and affine dynamics for the new abstract states are equal to those of the pivot state. Furthermore, the outgoing (resp. ingoing) transitions from (resp. to) new abstract states are determined similarly using one-step reachability.

Example 3. We use abstract transition in Fig. 1 with specification $\Diamond \Box p_2$. The NuSMV model checker reports a counterexample of length 2: $\pi = \hat{s}_1(\hat{s}_0\hat{s}_1)^\omega$. By Algorithm 6, it is spurious and the pivot state is $\hat{s}_1$. The resulting post-refinement abstract transition is depicted in Fig. 2. $\qquad\qquad\qquad\qquad\square$

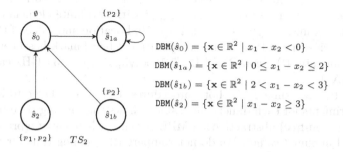

$$\text{DBM}(\hat{s}_0) = \{\mathbf{x} \in \mathbb{R}^2 \mid x_1 - x_2 < 0\}$$
$$\text{DBM}(\hat{s}_{1a}) = \{\mathbf{x} \in \mathbb{R}^2 \mid 0 \le x_1 - x_2 \le 2\}$$
$$\text{DBM}(\hat{s}_{1b}) = \{\mathbf{x} \in \mathbb{R}^2 \mid 2 < x_1 - x_2 < 3\}$$
$$\text{DBM}(\hat{s}_2) = \{\mathbf{x} \in \mathbb{R}^2 \mid x_1 - x_2 \ge 3\}$$

Fig. 2. The refinement of the abstract transition in Fig. 1. The abstract state $\hat{s}_1$ is split into $\hat{s}_{1a}, \hat{s}_{1b}$.

4.3   Upper-Bound on the Completeness Threshold

Given a transition system TS and a specification φ, a completeness threshold is a bound k such that, if no counterexample of φ with length k or less can be found in TS, then φ is satisfied by TS [8,9].

We recall from above that for specific formulae, the completeness threshold is related to the structure of the underlying transition system. For instance, the CT for safety properties of the form $\Box p$ is equal to the *diameter* of transition system: the length of longest shortest distance between two states [7]. Likewise, the CT for liveness specifications in the form of $\Diamond p$ is given by the *recurrent diameter* (the length of loop-free path) [14]. Computing the completeness threshold for general LTL formulae is still an open problem [14].

We show that the CT for (abstract) transition system that generated from an irreducible MPL system is related to the transient and cyclicity of the corresponding matrix.

Lemma 2. Consider an irreducible $A \in \mathbb{R}_{max}^{n \times n}$ with transient k_0 and cyclicity c and the resulting abstract transition system $TS_f = (\hat{S}, T_f, I_f, P_{mat} \cup P_{time}, L_f)$. The CT for TS_f and for any LTL formula φ over $P_{mat} \cup P_{time}$ is bounded by $k_0 + c$. $\qquad\qquad\qquad\qquad\square$

Lemma 2 ensures that the CT is not greater than the sum of the transient and cyclicity of the MPL systems. Looking back to the transition system in Fig. 1, the completeness threshold for $\Diamond p_2$ is 2. In comparison, the transient and cyclicity of matrix in (2) are $k_0 = c = 2$.

By Lemma 2, one could say that the BMC algorithm for irreducible MPL systems is complete for any LTL formula. However, this is not the case for reducible MPL systems, due to the incompleteness of Algorithm 6.

5   Computational Benchmarks

We compare the run-time of the predicate abstractions in this paper with related abstraction procedures in [29], which use max-plus algebraic operations ("tropical abstractions") and are enhanced versions of the earlier work in [1]. For increasing n, we generate matrices $A \in \mathbb{R}_{\max}^{n \times n}$ with two finite elements in each row, each with values ranging between 1 and 10. Location and value of the finite elements are chosen randomly. The computational benchmark has been implemented on an Intel(R) Xeon(R) CPU E5-1660 v3, 16 cores, 3.0 GHz each, and 16 GB of RAM.

We run the experiments for both procedures using C++. Over 10 independents experiments for each dimension, Table 1 shows the running time to generate (specification-free) abstractions of MPL systems, where entry represents the average and maximal values. We do not compare the running time for the generation of abstract transitions because both methods apply the same algorithm.

Table 1. Average and maximal running times of abstraction procedures

n	Tropical abstractions from [29]	Predicate abstractions (this work)
3	$\{0.15, 0.21\}$ [ms]	$\{0.27, 0.38\}$ [ms]
4	$\{0.26, 0.35\}$ [ms]	$\{0.49, 0.72\}$ [ms]
5	$\{0.41, 0.44\}$ [ms]	$\{0.79, 0.88\}$ [ms]
6	$\{1.12, 1.20\}$ [ms]	$\{1.92, 2.10\}$ [ms]
7	$\{2.68, 3.74\}$ [ms]	$\{3.19, 4.60\}$ [ms]
8	$\{8.78, 10.02\}$ [ms]	$\{9.13, 13.74\}$ [ms]
9	$\{32.12, 36.66\}$ [ms]	$\{30.38, 42.02\}$ [ms]
10	$\{0.12, 0.14\}$ [s]	$\{0.11, 0.17\}$ [s]
11	$\{0.57, 0.66\}$ [s]	$\{0.54, 0.81\}$ [s]
12	$\{3.82, 4.67\}$ [s]	$\{2.58, 4.19\}$ [s]
13	$\{23.71, 28.28\}$ [s]	$\{15.80, 28.52\}$ [s]
14	$\{1.39, 1.59\}$ [min]	$\{0.89, 1.27\}$ [min]
15	$\{27.73, 31.06\}$ [min]	$\{4.68, 8.40\}$ [min]

As we can see in Table 1, for large dimensions (beyond 8), the average running time of predicate abstractions is faster than that of tropical abstractions. We recall that the (specification-free) predicate abstractions of MPL systems are computed by Algorithms 1, 2 and 4. Whereas for tropical abstractions, they are computed by [29, Algorithm 2].

We also provide a comparison over values of CT. NuSMV is able to compute CT via an incremental BMC command `check_ltlspec_sbmc_inc -c`. For each bound k, in addition to counterexample searching, it generates a SAT (i.e. boolean satisfiability) problem to verify whether the LTL formula can be concluded to hold. This method of computation of completeness check can be found in [25, 28].

Table 2 shows the comparison of the CT values specified by Lemma 2 and those computed by NuSMV. For dimension of $n \in \{3, 4, 5\}$, we generate 20 random irreducible matrices $A \in \mathbb{R}_{max}^{n \times n}$ with two finite elements in each row. We use the same time-difference specification $\Diamond\Box(t_1 \leq 10)$ for all experiments.

Table 2. The comparison of completeness thresholds.

n	#stf	#($ct_1 < ct_2$)	#($ct_1 = ct_2$)	#($ct_1 > ct_2$)
3	14	0	1	13
4	15	1	0	14
5	14	0	0	14

The 2nd column of Table 2 represents the number of experiments whose the specification $\Diamond\Box(t_1 \leq 10)$ is satisfied. The last three columns describe the comparison of CT. We use ct_1 and ct_2 to respectively denote the CT that computed by NuSMV and Lemma 2. As we can see, the CT upper bounds specified by Lemma 2 are relatively smaller than those computed by NuSMV.

6   Conclusions

This paper has introduced a new technique to generate the abstractions of MPL systems via a set of predicates. The predicates are chosen automatically from system matrix and the time-difference specifications under consideration. Having obtained the abstract states and transition, this paper has implemented bounded model checking to check the satisfaction of time-difference specifications.

The abstraction performance has been tested on a numerical benchmark, which has displayed an improvement over existing procedures. The comparison for completeness thresholds suggests that the cyclicity and transient of MPL systems can be used as an upper bound. Yet, this bound is relatively smaller than the CT bounds computed by NuSMV.

Acknowledgements. The first author is supported by Indonesia Endowment Fund for Education (LPDP), while the third acknowledges the support of the Alan Turing Institute, London, UK.

References

1. Adzkiya, D., De Schutter, B., Abate, A.: Finite abstractions of max-plus-linear systems. IEEE Trans. Autom. Control. **58**(12), 3039–3053 (2013). https://doi.org/10.1109/TAC.2013.2273299
2. Adzkiya, D., Zhang, Y., Abate, A.: VeriSiMPL 2: an open-sourcesoftware for the verification of max-plus-linear systems. Discrete Event Dyn. Syst. **26**(1), 109–145 (2016). https://doi.org/10.1007/s10626-015-0218-x
3. Alur, R., Dang, T., Ivančić, F.: Progress on reachability analysis of hybrid systems using predicate abstraction. In: Maler, O., Pnueli, A. (eds.) HSCC 2003. LNCS, vol. 2623, pp. 4–19. Springer, Heidelberg (2003). https://doi.org/10.1007/3-540-36580-X_4
4. Baccelli, F., Cohen, G., Olsder, G.J., Quadrat, J.P.: Synchronization and Linearity: An Algebra for Discrete Event Systems. Wiley, Chichester (1992)
5. Baier, C., Katoen, J.P.: Principles of Model Checking. MIT Press, Cambridge (2008)
6. Ball, T., Majumdar, R., Millstein, T., Rajamani, S.K.: Automatic predicate abstraction of C programs. In: Proceedings of Programming Language Design and Implementation 2001 (PLDI 2001), vol. 36, pp. 203–213. ACM (2001). https://doi.org/10.1145/381694.378846
7. Biere, A., Cimatti, A., Clarke, E., Zhu, Y.: Symbolic model checking without BDDs. In: Cleaveland, W.R. (ed.) TACAS 1999. LNCS, vol. 1579, pp. 193–207. Springer, Heidelberg (1999). https://doi.org/10.1007/3-540-49059-0_14
8. Biere, A., Cimatti, A., Clarke, E.M., Strichman, O., Zhu, Y., et al.: Bounded model checking. Adv. Comput. **58**(11), 117–148 (2003)
9. Biere, A., Heljanko, K., Junttila, T., Latvala, T., Schuppan, V.: Linear encodings of bounded LTL model checking. Log. Methods Comput. Sci. **2**(5), 1–64 (2006). https://doi.org/10.2168/LMCS-2(5:5)2006
10. Brackley, C.A., Broomhead, D.S., Romano, M.C., Thiel, M.: A Max-plus model of ribosome dynamics during mRNA translation. J. Theor. Biol. **303**, 128–140 (2012). https://doi.org/10.1016/j.jtbi.2012.03.007
11. Cimatti, A., et al.: NuSMV 2: an opensource tool for symbolic model checking. In: Brinksma, E., Larsen, K.G. (eds.) CAV 2002. LNCS, vol. 2404, pp. 359–364. Springer, Heidelberg (2002). https://doi.org/10.1007/3-540-45657-0_29
12. Clarke, E., Grumberg, O., Jha, S., Lu, Y., Veith, H.: Counterexample-guided abstraction refinement. In: Emerson, E.A., Sistla, A.P. (eds.) CAV 2000. LNCS, vol. 1855, pp. 154–169. Springer, Heidelberg (2000). https://doi.org/10.1007/10722167_15
13. Clarke, E., Grumberg, O., Talupur, M., Wang, D.: Making predicate abstraction efficient. In: Hunt, W.A., Somenzi, F. (eds.) CAV 2003. LNCS, vol. 2725, pp. 126–140. Springer, Heidelberg (2003). https://doi.org/10.1007/978-3-540-45069-6_14
14. Clarke, E., Kroening, D., Ouaknine, J., Strichman, O.: Completeness and complexity of bounded model checking. In: Steffen, B., Levi, G. (eds.) VMCAI 2004. LNCS, vol. 2937, pp. 85–96. Springer, Heidelberg (2004). https://doi.org/10.1007/978-3-540-24622-0_9

15. Clarke, E., Kroening, D., Sharygina, N., Yorav, K.: Predicate abstraction of ANSI-C programs using SAT. Form. Methods Syst. Des. **25**(2–3), 105–127 (2004). https://doi.org/10.1023/B:FORM.0000040025.89719.f3

16. Clarke, E., Talupur, M., Veith, H., Wang, D.: SAT based predicate abstraction for hardware verification. In: Giunchiglia, E., Tacchella, A. (eds.) SAT 2003. LNCS, vol. 2919, pp. 78–92. Springer, Heidelberg (2004). https://doi.org/10.1007/978-3-540-24605-3_7

17. Clarke, E.M., Grumberg, O., Long, D.E.: Model checking and abstraction. ACM Trans. Program. Lang. Syst. (TOPLAS) **16**(5), 1512–1542 (1994). https://doi.org/10.1145/186025.186051

18. Comet, J.P.: Application of max-plus algebra to biological sequence comparisons. Theor. Comput. Sci. **293**(1), 189–217 (2003). https://doi.org/10.1016/S0304-3975(02)00237-2

19. Das, S., Dill, D.L., Park, S.: Experience with predicate abstraction. In: Halbwachs, N., Peled, D. (eds.) CAV 1999. LNCS, vol. 1633, pp. 160–171. Springer, Heidelberg (1999). https://doi.org/10.1007/3-540-48683-6_16

20. De Schutter, B.: On the ultimate behavior of the sequence of consecutive powers of a matrix in the max-plus algebra. Linear Algebra Its Appl. **307**(1–3), 103–117 (2000). https://doi.org/10.1016/S0024-3795(00)00013-6

21. Flanagan, C., Qadeer, S.: Predicate abstraction for software verification. In: Proceedings of the 29th Principles of Programming Languages (POPL 2002), vol. 37, pp. 191–202. ACM (2002). https://doi.org/10.1145/503272.503291

22. Graf, S., Saidi, H.: Construction of abstract state graphs with PVS. In: Grumberg, O. (ed.) CAV 1997. LNCS, vol. 1254, pp. 72–83. Springer, Heidelberg (1997). https://doi.org/10.1007/3-540-63166-6_10

23. Heemels, W., De Schutter, B., Bemporad, A.: Equivalence of hybrid dynamical models. Automatica **37**(7), 1085–1091 (2001). https://doi.org/10.1016/S0005-1098(01)00059-0

24. Heidergott, B., Olsder, G.J., Van der Woude, J.: Max Plus at Work: Modeling and Analysis of Synchronized Systems: A Course on Max-Plus Algebra and Its Applications. Princeton University Press, Princeton (2014)

25. Heljanko, K., Junttila, T., Latvala, T.: Incremental and complete bounded model checking for full PLTL. In: Etessami, K., Rajamani, S.K. (eds.) CAV 2005. LNCS, vol. 3576, pp. 98–111. Springer, Heidelberg (2005). https://doi.org/10.1007/11513988_10

26. Henzinger, T.A., Jhala, R., Majumdar, R., Sutre, G.: Lazy abstraction. In: Proceedings of the ACM Symposium on Principles of Programming Languages (POPL 2002), pp. 58–70 (2002). https://doi.org/10.1145/503272.503279

27. Imaev, A., Judd, R.P.: Hierarchial modeling of manufacturing systems using max-plus algebra. In: Proceedings of American Control Conference 2008, pp. 471–476 (2008)

28. Latvala, T., Biere, A., Heljanko, K., Junttila, T.: Simple is better: efficient bounded model checking for past LTL. In: Cousot, R. (ed.) VMCAI 2005. LNCS, vol. 3385, pp. 380–395. Springer, Heidelberg (2005). https://doi.org/10.1007/978-3-540-30579-8_25

29. Mufid, M.S., Adzkiya, D., Abate, A.: Tropical abstractions of max-plus linear systems. In: Jansen, D.N., Prabhakar, P. (eds.) FORMATS 2018. LNCS, vol. 11022, pp. 271–287. Springer, Cham (2018). https://doi.org/10.1007/978-3-030-00151-3_16

30. Mufid, M.S., Adzkiya, D., Abate, A.: Bounded model checking of max-plus linear systems via predicate abstractions. arXiv e-prints arXiv:1907.03564, July 2019

Reachability Analysis for High-Index Linear Differential Algebraic Equations

Hoang-Dung Tran[1], Luan Viet Nguyen[2], Nathaniel Hamilton[1],
Weiming Xiang[1] , and Taylor T. Johnson[1(✉)]

[1] Institute for Software Integrated Systems, Vanderbilt University,
Nashville, TN, USA
taylor.johnson@vanderbilt.edu
[2] University of Pennsylvania, Philadelphia, PA, USA

Abstract. Reachability analysis is a fundamental problem for safety
verification and falsification of Cyber-Physical Systems (CPS) whose
dynamics follow physical laws usually represented as differential equations. In the last two decades, numerous reachability analysis methods
and tools have been proposed for a common class of dynamics in CPS
known as ordinary differential equations (ODE). However, there is lack
of methods dealing with differential algebraic equations (DAE), which is
a more general class of dynamics that is widely used to describe a variety
of problems from engineering and science, such as multibody mechanics,
electrical circuit design, incompressible fluids, molecular dynamics, and
chemical process control. Reachability analysis for DAE systems is more
complex than ODE systems, especially for *high-index* DAEs because they
contain both a *differential part* (i.e., ODE) and *algebraic constraints*
(AC). In this paper, we propose a scalable reachability analysis for a class
of high-index large linear DAEs. In our approach, a high-index linear
DAE is first decoupled into one ODE and one or several AC subsystems
based on the well-known Marz decoupling method utilizing *admissible*
projectors. Then, the *discrete* reachable set of the DAE, represented as
a list of *star-sets*, is computed using simulation. Unlike ODE reachability analysis where the initial condition is freely defined by a user, in
DAE cases, the consistency of the initial condition is an essential requirement to guarantee a feasible solution. Therefore, a thorough check for
the consistency is invoked before computing the discrete reachable set.
Our approach successfully verifies (or falsifies) a wide range of practical,
high-index linear DAE systems in which the number of state variables
varies from several to thousands.

1 Introduction

Reachability analysis for continuous and hybrid systems has been an attractive
research topic for the last two decades since it is an essential problem for verification of safety-critical CPS. In this context, numerous techniques and tools
have been proposed. Reachability analysis using zonotopes [2,21] and support
functions [19,22] are efficient approaches when dealing with linear, continuous

© Springer Nature Switzerland AG 2019
É. André and M. Stoelinga (Eds.): FORMATS 2019, LNCS 11750, pp. 160–177, 2019.
https://doi.org/10.1007/978-3-030-29662-9_10

and hybrid systems. For nonlinear, continuous and hybrid systems, dReal [25] using $\delta-$reachability analysis and Flow* [10] using Taylor model are well-known and efficient approaches. However, these over-approximation based approaches can only conduct a reachability analysis for small and medium scale systems. To deal with large-scale systems, other simulation-based methods have been proposed recently. For linear cases, the simulation-equivalent reachability analysis [5,16] utilizing the *generalized star-set* as the state-set representation has shown an impressive result by successfully dealing with linear systems up to 10,000 state variables. In this approach, the *discrete simulation-equivalent* reachable set of a linear ODE system can be computed efficiently using standard ODE solvers by taking advantage of the superposition property. Another technique applies order-reduction abstraction [23,33,34] in which a large system can be abstracted to a smaller system with bounded error. For nonlinear cases, C2E2 [15,18] utilizing simulation has shown significant improvement on time performance and scalability in comparison with other methods. Recently, a new numerical verification approach has been proposed to verify/falsify the safety properties of CPS with physical dynamics described by partial differential equations [31,35].

Although many methods have been developed for reachability analysis of CPS, most of them mentioned above focus on CPS with ODE dynamics. There is a lack of methodology in analyzing systems with high-index DAE dynamics. It is because the reachability analysis for DAE systems is more complex than ODE systems, especially for *high-index* DAEs because they contain both a *differential part* (i.e., ODE) and *algebraic constraints* (AC). It should be emphasized that there are efficient reachability analysis approaches for DAE systems with index-1 [1,11,13,28]. Dealing with index-1 DAE is slightly different from coping with pure ODE because, with a consistent initial condition, a semi-explicit index-1 DAE can be converted to an ODE. As CPS involving high-index DAE dynamics appear extensively in engineering and science such as multi-body mechanics, electrical circuit design, heat and gas transfer, chemical process, atmospheric physics, thermodynamic systems, and water distribution network [8,17], there is an urgent need for novel reachability analysis methods and tools that can either verify or falsify the safety properties of such CPS. Solving this challenging problem is the main contribution of this research.

The novelty of our approach comes from its objective in dealing with high-index DAE which is a popular class of dynamics that has not been addressed in the existing literature. In this paper, we investigate the reachability analysis for large linear DAE systems with the index up to 3, which appear widely in practice. There are a variety of definitions for the index of a linear DAE. However, throughout the paper, we use the concept of *tractability index* proposed in [26] to determine the index of a linear DAE system. Our approach consists of three main steps (a) decoupling and consistency checking, (b) reachable set computation, and (c) safety verification or falsification; that can be summarized as follows.

The first step is to use the Marz decoupling method [7,26] to decouple a high-index DAE into one ODE subsystem and one or several algebraic constraint (AC) subsystems. The core step in decoupling is constructing a set of admissible projectors which has not previously been discussed deeply in the existing literature. In this paper, *we propose a novel algorithm that can construct such admissible projectors for a linear DAE system with the index up to 3 (most of DAE systems in practice have index from 1 to 3)*. Additionally, we define a *consistent space* for the DAE because, unlike ODE reachability analysis where the initial set of states can be freely defined by a user, to guarantee a numerical solution for the DAE system, the initial state and inputs of such DAE system must be consistent and satisfy certain constraints. It is important to emphasize that the decoupling and consistency checking methods used in our approach can be combined with existing over-approximation reachability analysis methods [2,19] to compute the over-approximated reachable sets for high-index, linear DAE systems with small to medium dimensions.

The second step in our approach is reachable set computation. Since our main objective is to verify or falsify large linear DAEs, we extend ODE simulation-based reachability analysis to DAEs. In particular, we modify the *generalized star-set* proposed in [5] to enhance the efficiency in checking the initial condition consistency and safety for DAEs. From a consistent initial set of states and inputs, the reachable set of a DAE system can be constructed by combining the reachable sets of its subsystems. It is also worth pointing out that the piecewise constant inputs assumption for ODE with inputs used in [5] may lead a DAE system to *impulsive behavior*. Therefore, in this paper, we assume the inputs applied to the system are *smooth functions*. Such the inputs can be obtained by *smoothing* piecewise constant inputs with filters.

The last step in our approach is to verify or falsify the safety properties of the DAE system using the constructed reachable set computed in the second step. In this paper, we consider linear safety specifications. We are interested in checking the safety of the system in a specific direction defined using a directional matrix. Using the modified star-set and the directional matrix, checking the safety property can be solved efficiently as a low-dimensional feasibility linear programming problem. In the case of violation, our approach generates a counterexample trace that falsifies the system safety.

Contribution. The main contributions of the paper are as follows.

1. A novel reachability analysis approach for high-index linear DAE systems developed based on the effective combination of a decoupling method and a reachable set computation using star-set. To the best of our knowledge, this problem has not been addressed in the existing literature.
2. An end-to-end design and implementation of the approach in a Python toolbox, called *Daev*, which is publicly available for verifying high-index linear DAE systems.
3. An extensive evaluation that demonstrates the capability of our approach in verifying/falsifying a wide range of practical, high-index linear DAE systems where the number of state variables varies from several to thousands.

We note that our reachability analysis approach for high-index DAEs based on combining the decoupling technique and existing ODE reachability analysis is extensible and generic. Instead of using star-set, one can use the decoupling technique in a combination of other state-of-the-art ODE reachability analysis tool like SpaceEx and Flow* for specific application purposes. We choose star-set to handle high-index large linear DAEs because of its scalability advantage compared to other ODE reachability analysis tools.

Outline of paper. The remainder of the paper is structured as follows. Section 2 reviews the relevant definitions of a high-index large linear DAE system, and the concept of a modified star-set used to represent its reachable set. Section 3 describes our decoupling approach that can effectively decouple a high-index DAE system into ODE and AC subsystems. Section 4 discusses the consistent condition for the initial states and inputs of a DAE system. Section 5 presents the core algorithms that can efficiently compute reachable set and perform a safety verification/falsification for a high-index large linear DAE system. Section 6 describes the verification results of our approach through a collection of high-index linear DAE system benchmarks. Section 7 concludes the paper and presents future research directions for the proposed work.

2   Preliminaries

2.1   Linear DAE System

We are interested in the reachability analysis of a high-index large linear DAE system described as follows:

$$\Delta: \ E\dot{x}(t) = Ax(t) + Bu(t), \tag{1}$$

where $x(t) \in \mathbb{R}^n$ is the state vector of the system; $E, A \in \mathbb{R}^{n \times n}$, $B \in \mathbb{R}^{n \times m}$ are the system's matrices in which E is *singular*; and $u(t) \in \mathbb{R}^m$ is the input of the system. Let I_n be the n-dimensional identity matrix. The regularity, the tractability index, the admissible projectors, the fixed-step bounded-time simulation, and the bounded-time simulation-equivalent reachable set of the system are defined below.

Definition 1 (Regularity [12]). *The pair (E, A) is said to be regular if $det(sE - A)$ is not identically zero.*

Remark 1. For any specified initial conditions, the regularity of the pair (E, A) guarantees the existence and uniqueness of a solution of the system (1).

Definition 2 (Tractability index [26]). *Assume that the DAE system (1) is solvable, i.e., the matrix pair (E, A) is regular. A matrix chain is defined by:*

$$\begin{aligned} E_0 &= E, \ A_0 = A, \\ E_{j+1} &= E_j - A_j Q_j, \quad A_{j+1} = A_j P_j, \ for \ j \geq 0, \end{aligned} \tag{2}$$

where Q_j are projectors onto $Ker(E_j)$, i.e., $E_j Q_j = 0$, $Q_j^2 = Q_j$, and $P_j = I_n - Q_j$. Then, there exists an index μ such that E_μ is nonsingular and all E_j are singular for $0 \leq j < \mu - 1$. It is said that the system (1) has tractability index-μ. In the rest of the paper, we use the term "index" to state for the "tractability index" of the system.

Definition 3 (Admissible projectors [26]**).** *Given a DAE with tractability index-μ, the projectors* $Q_0, Q_1, \cdots, Q_{\mu-1}$ *in Definition 2 are called admissible if and only if they satisfy the following property:* $\forall j > i,\ Q_j Q_i = 0.$

Definition 4 (Fixed-step, bounded-time simulation). *Given consistent initial state* x_0 *and input* $u(t)$, *a time bound* T, *and a time step* h, *the finite sequence:*

$$\rho(x_0, u(t), h, T = Nh) = x_0 \xrightarrow[0 \le t < h]{u(t)} x_1 \xrightarrow[h \le t < 2h]{u(t)} x_2 \cdots \xrightarrow[(N-1)h \le t < Nh]{u(t)} x_N,$$

is a $(x_0, u(t), h, T)$-*simulation of the DAE system (1) if and only if for all* $0 \le i \le N - 1$, x_{i+1} *is the state of the system trajectory starting from* x_i *when provided with input function* $u(t)$ *for* $ih \le t < (i + 1)h$. *If there is no input,* $u(t) = 0$.

The consistent condition for the initial state x_0 and input $u(t)$ will be discussed in detail in Sect. 4. From the fixed-step, bounded-time simulation of a DAE system, we define the following bounded-time, simulation-equivalent reachable set of the DAE system.

Definition 5 (Bounded-time, simulation-equivalent reachable set). *Given sets of consistent initial state* X_0 *and input* U, *the bounded-time, simulation-equivalent reachable set* $R_{[0,T]}(\Delta)$ *of the system (1) is the set of all states that can be encountered by any* $(x_0, u(t), h, T)$-*simulation starting from any* $x_0 \in X_0$ *and input* $u(t) \in U$.

Let $Unsafe(\Delta) \triangleq Gx \le f$ be the unsafe set of the DAE system (1) in which $x \in \mathbb{R}^n$ is the state vector of the system, $G \in \mathbb{R}^{k \times n}$ is the *unsafe matrix* and $f \in \mathbb{R}^k$ is the *unsafe vector*. Given sets of consistent initial state X_0 and input U, the simulation-based safety verification and falsification problem is defined in the following.

Definition 6 (Simulation-based safety verification and falsification). *The DAE system (1) is said to be "simulationally safe" up to time* T *if and only if its simulation-equivalent reachable set,* $R_{[0,T]}(\Delta)$, *and the unsafe set,* $Unsafe(\Delta)$, *are disjoint, i.e.,* $R_{[0,T]}(\Delta) \cap Unsafe(\Delta) = \emptyset$. *Otherwise, it is simulationally unsafe.*

The DAE system is said to be "simulationally falsifiable" if and only if it is simulationally unsafe and there exists a simulation, $(x_0, u(t), h, T)$, *that leads the initial state,* x_0, *of the system to an unsafe state,* $x_{unsafe} \in Unsafe(\Delta)$.

The main objective of the paper is to compute the simulation-equivalent reachable set, $R_{[0,T]}(\Delta)$, of the DAE system and use it to verify or falsify the safety property of the system. In the rest of the paper, we use the term *reachable set* to stand for *simulation-equivalent reachable set*. Next, we define a *modified star set* which is used as the state-set representation of the DAE system.

2.2   Modified Star Set

In our approach, we use a modified star set to represent the reachable set of the DAE system. The modified star set is slightly different from the generalized star set [5] because it does not have a *center vector* and is only defined on a star's $n \times k$ basis matrix.

Definition 7 (Modified star set). *A modified star set (or simply star) Θ is a tuple $\langle V, P \rangle$ where $V = [v_1, v_2, \cdots, v_k] \in \mathbb{R}^{n \times k}$ is a star basis matrix and P is a linear predicate. The set of states represented by the star is given by:*

$$\llbracket \Theta \rrbracket = \{x \mid x = \Sigma_{i=1}^{k}(\alpha_i v_i) = V \times \alpha, \ P(\alpha) \triangleq C\alpha \leq d\}, \tag{3}$$

where $\alpha = [\alpha_1, \alpha_2, \cdots, \alpha_k]^T$, $C \in \mathbb{R}^{p \times k}$, $d \in \mathbb{R}^p$ and p is the number of linear constraints.

The benefit of the modified star set come from its form given as a *matrix-vector product* which is convenient (in next sections) for checking initial condition consistency and safety properties. In the rest of the paper, we will refer to both the tuple Θ and the set of states $\llbracket \Theta \rrbracket$ as Θ.

To construct the reachable set of the DAE system (1), we decouple the system into $\mu + 1$ subsystems where μ is the index of the DAE system. The underlining technique used in our approach is the Marz decoupling method utilizing admissible projectors which is presented in detail in the following section.

3   Decoupling

In this section, we discuss how to decouple a high-index DAE system into one ODE subsystem and one or several AC subsystems using the matrix chain and admissible projectors defined in the previous section with noticing that the decoupled system and the original one are equivalent, i.e., they have the same solutions. Since we are particularly interested in DAE systems with index up to 3 which happen in most of DAE systems in practice, the proofs of decoupling process for index-1, -2, and -3 are given in detail in the extended version of this paper [32].[1] A generalization of decoupling for a DAE with arbitrary index is presented in [26]. As the construction of admissible projectors used in decoupling has not been discussed clearly in existing literature, in this section, we propose a method and an algorithm to solve this problem.

Lemma 1 (Index-1 DAE decoupling [7,26]). *An index-1 DAE system described by (1) can be decoupled using the matrix chain defined by Eq. (2) as follows:*

---

[1] Available   online: http://www.taylortjohnson.com/research/tran2019formats_extended.pdf.

$$\Delta_1 : \quad \dot{x}_1(t) = N_1 x_1(t) + M_1 u(t), \quad ODE \ subsystem,$$
$$\Delta_2 : \quad x_2(t) = N_2 x_1(t) + M_2 u(t), \quad AC \ subsystem,$$
$$x(t) = x_1(t) + x_2(t),$$
$$x_1(t) = P_0 x(t), \ N_1 = P_0 E_1^{-1} A_0, \ M_1 = P_0 E_1^{-1} B,$$
$$x_2(t) = Q_0 x(t), \ N_2 = Q_0 E_1^{-1} A_0, \ M_2 = Q_0 E_1^{-1} B.$$

Proof is given in the appendix of [32].

Lemma 2 (Index-2 DAE decoupling [7,26]**).** *An index-2 DAE system described by (1) can be decoupled into a decoupled system using the matrix chain defined by Eq. (2) and the admissible projectors in Definition 3 as follows:*

$$\Delta_1 : \quad \dot{x}_1(t) = N_1 x_1(t) + M_1 u(t), \quad ODE \ subsystem,$$
$$\Delta_2 : \quad x_2(t) = N_2 x_1(t) + M_2 u(t), \quad AC \ subsystem \ 1,$$
$$\Delta_3 : \quad x_3(t) = N_3 x_1(t) + M_3 u(t) + L_3 \dot{x}_2(t), \quad AC \ subsystem \ 2,$$
$$x(t) = x_1(t) + x_2(t) + x_3(t),$$
$$x_1(t) = P_0 P_1 x(t), \ N_1 = P_0 P_1 E_2^{-1} A_2, \ M_1 = P_0 P_1 E_2^{-1} B,$$
$$x_2(t) = P_0 Q_1 x(t), \ N_2 = P_0 Q_1 E_2^{-1} A_2, \ M_2 = P_0 Q_1 E_2^{-1} B,$$
$$x_3(t) = Q_0 x(t), \ N_3 = Q_0 P_1 E_2^{-1} A_2, \ M_3 = Q_0 P_1 E_2^{-1} B, \ L_3 = Q_0 Q_1.$$

Proof is given in the appendix of [32].

Lemma 3 (Index-3 DAE decoupling [7,26]**).** *An index-3 DAE system described by (1) can be decoupled into a decoupled system using the matrix chain defined by Eq. (2) and the admissible projectors in Definition 3 as follows:*

$$\Delta_1 : \quad \dot{x}_1(t) = N_1 x_1(t) + M_1 u(t), \quad ODE \ subsystem,$$
$$\Delta_2 : \quad x_2(t) = N_2 x_1(t) + M_2 u(t), \quad AC \ subsystem \ 1,$$
$$\Delta_3 : \quad x_3(t) = N_3 x_1(t) + M_3 u(t) + L_3 \dot{x}_2(t), \quad AC \ subsystem \ 2$$
$$\Delta_4 : \quad x_4(t) = N_4 x_1(t) + M_4 u(t) + L_4 \dot{x}_3(t) + Z_4 \dot{x}_2(t), \quad AC \ subsystem \ 3$$
$$x(t) = x_1(t) + x_2(t) + x_3(t) + x_4(t), \quad where:$$
$$x_1(t) = P_0 P_1 P_2 x(t), \ N_1 = P_0 P_1 P_2 E_3^{-1} A_3, \ M_1 = P_0 P_1 P_2 E_3^{-1} B,$$
$$x_2(t) = P_0 P_1 Q_2 x(t), \ N_2 = P_0 P_1 Q_2 E_3^{-1} A_3, \ M_2 = P_0 P_1 Q_2 E_3^{-1} B,$$
$$x_3(t) = P_0 Q_1 x(t), \ N_3 = P_0 Q_1 P_2 E_3^{-1} A_3, \ M_3 = P_0 Q_1 P_2 E_3^{-1} B, \ L_3 = P_0 Q_1 Q_2,$$
$$x_4(t) = Q_0 x(t), \ N_4 = Q_0 P_1 P_2 E_3^{-1} A_3, \ M_4 = Q_0 P_1 P_2 E_3^{-1} B, \ L_4 = Q_0 Q_1,$$
$$Z_4 = Q_0 P_1 Q_2.$$

Proof is given in the appendix of [32].

It should be noted that the AC subsystems Δ_3 and Δ_4 in Lemmas 2 and 3 are called algebraic constraints, though they contain the derivatives of $x_2(t)$ and $x_3(t)$. This is because the explicit forms of these algebraic constraints can be obtained if we further extend the derivatives using the corresponding ODE subsystems. In addition, one can see that for a DAE system with index-2 or -3, a set of admissible projectors need to be constructed for decoupling. In the following, we give a Proposition and Lemmas that are used to construct such admissible projectors.

Proposition 1 (Orthogonal projector on a subspace). *Given a real matrix* $Z \in \mathbb{R}^{n \times n}$ *such that* $rank(Z) = r < n$, *the Singular-Value Decomposition (SVD) of* Z *has the form:*

$$Z = [L_1 \ L_2] \begin{bmatrix} S_{r \times r} & 0 \\ 0 & 0 \end{bmatrix} \begin{bmatrix} K_1^T \\ K_2^T \end{bmatrix}, \tag{4}$$

where $L_1, K_1 \in \mathbb{R}^{n \times r}$ *and* $L_2, K_2 \in \mathbb{R}^{n \times n-r}$. *Then, the matrix* $Q = K_2 K_2^T$ *is an orthogonal projector on* $Ker(Z)$, *i.e.,* $ZQ = 0$, $Q = Q^T$ *and* $Q^2 = Q$.

Proof is given in the appendix of [32].

For an index-2 or -3 DAE system, using Proposition 1, we can construct a set of projectors of the matrix chain defined in Eq. (2). However, these projectors are not yet admissible, because $Q_j Q_i \neq 0, j > i$. Instead, the admissible projectors can be constructed based on these inadmissible projectors using the following Lemmas.

Lemma 4 (Admissible projectors for an index-2 DAE system). *Given an index-2 DAE system described by (1), let* Q_0 *and* Q_1 *respectively be the orthogonal projectors of* E_0 *and* E_1 *of the matrix chain defined in Eq. (2). The following projectors* Q_0^* *and* Q_1^* *are admissible:* $Q_0^* = Q_0$, $Q_1^* = -Q_1 E_2^{-1} A_1$.

Proof is given in the appendix of [32].

Lemma 5 (Admissible projectors for an index-3 DAE system). *Given an index-3 DAE system described by (1), let* Q_0, Q_1 *and* Q_2 *respectively be the orthogonal projectors of* E_0, E_1 *and* E_2 *of the matrix chain defined in Eq. (2). We define the following projectors and the corresponding new matrices for the matrix chain as:*

$$Q_2' = -Q_2 E_3^{-1} A_2, \quad Q_1' = -Q_1 P_2' E_3^{-1} A_1, \quad E_2' = E_1 - A_1 Q_1', \quad A_2' = A_1 P_1'$$

where $P_2' = I_n - Q_2'$ *and* $P_1' = I_n - Q_1'$. *Let* Q_2'' *be the orthogonal projector on* E_2' *and* $E_3'' = E_2' - A_2' Q_2''$, *then the following projectors* Q_0^*, Q_1^* *and* Q_2^* *are admissible:* $Q_0^* = Q_0$, $Q_1^* = Q_1'$, $Q_2^* = -Q_2''(E_3'')^{-1} A_2'$.

Proof is given in the appendix of [32].

Lemmas 4 and 5 are the constructions of admissible projectors for index-2 and -3 DAE systems. The details of the admissible projectors construction are summarized in the appendix [32]. Next, based on the decoupled DAE system, we discuss the consistent condition of the system and analyze the system behavior under the effect of input functions.

4   Consistency

In this section, we discuss the consistent condition for a DAE system. Using the decoupled DAE system, the consistent condition for the initial state and inputs is derived. Additionally, the piecewise constant assumption on the inputs used in [5] for ODE systems may lead to *impulsive behavior* in high-index DAE systems. To avoid this, we limit our problem to *smooth* and *specific-user-defined* inputs. As a result, DAE systems with inputs can be converted to autonomous DAE systems, where *consistent spaces* for the initial states and inputs can be conveniently defined and checked. Furthermore, the reachable set computation is executed efficiently using a decoupled autonomous DAE system.

Using Lemmas 1, 2, and 3, to guarantee a solution for the DAE system, the initial states and inputs must satisfy the following conditions:

$$
\begin{aligned}
\text{Index-1 DAE}: \quad & x_2(0) = N_2 x_1(0) + M_2 u(0), \\
\text{Index-2 DAE}: \quad & x_2(0) = N_2 x_1(0) + M_2 u(0), \\
& x_3(0) = N_3 x_1(0) + M_3 u(0) + L_3 \dot{x}_2(0), \\
\text{Index-3 DAE}: \quad & x_2(0) = N_2 x_1(0) + M_2 u(0), \\
& x_3(0) = N_3 x_1(0) + M_3 u(0) + L_3 \dot{x}_2(0), \\
& x_4(0) = N_4 x_1(0) + M_4 u(0) + L_4 \dot{x}_3(0) + Z_4 \dot{x}_2(0).
\end{aligned}
\tag{5}
$$

Assuming that the consistent condition is satisfied, Lemmas 2 and 3 indicate the solution of the system involves the derivatives of the input functions $\dot{x}_2(t) = N_2 \dot{x}_1(t) + M_2 \dot{u}(t)$ and $\dot{x}_3(t) = N_3 \dot{x}_1(t) + M_4 \dot{u}(t) + L_3[N_2 \ddot{x}_1(t) + M_2 \ddot{u}(t)]$. In cases where we apply piecewise constant inputs to a high-index DAE system, the impulsive behavior may appear in the system at an exact discrete time point t_k. For example, let $u(t)$ be a step function in $[t_k, t_{k+1})$, then $\dot{u}(t_k) = \delta(t_k)$, where $\delta(t_k)$ is the Dirac function describing an impulse. To avoid such impulsive behavior and do reachability analysis for high-index DAE systems, we limit our approach to smooth inputs which are governed by the following ODE: $\dot{u}(t) = A_u u(t)$, $u(0) = u_0 \in U_0$, where $A_u \in \mathbb{R}^{m \times m}$ is the user-defined input matrix, and U_0 is the set of initial inputs.

Remark 2. By introducing the input matrix A_u, we limit the safety verification and falsification of a high-index DAE system to a class of *specific-user-defined* inputs. If $A_u = 0$, then the input set is a set of constant inputs. We note that designing the input matrix A_u can be seen as the last step in designing a controller for a DAE system to eliminate the impulsive behavior of the closed-loop system which is a fundamental problem in DAE control system [14].

Given a user-defined input matrix A_u, a DAE system described by (1) can be converted to an equivalent autonomous DAE system of the following form:

$$
\bar{E}\dot{\bar{x}}(t) = \bar{A}\bar{x}(t),
\tag{6}
$$

where $\bar{x}(t) = \begin{bmatrix} x(t) \\ u(t) \end{bmatrix} \in \mathbb{R}^{n+m}$, $\bar{E} = \begin{bmatrix} E & 0 \\ 0 & I_m \end{bmatrix}$, $\bar{A} = \begin{bmatrix} A & B \\ 0 & A_u \end{bmatrix} \in \mathbb{R}^{(n+m) \times (n+m)}$

and the state of the original DAE is: $x(t) = \begin{bmatrix} I_n & 0 \end{bmatrix} \bar{x}(t)$.

Similar to the original DAE system, the autonomous DAE system (6) can be decoupled to form one autonomous ODE subsystem and one or several AC subsystems. It should be noted that the autonomous DAE system has the same index as the original one.

We have discussed the conversion of a DAE system with user-defined input to an autonomous DAE system. Next, we derive the *consistent space* for the initial condition of an autonomous DAE system. All previous results apply to these systems given that $u(t) = 0$.

Definition 8 (Consistent Space for an autonomous DAE system). *Consider an autonomous DAE system (Δ) defined in Eq. (1) by letting $u(t) = 0$. From this, we define in the following a "consistent matrix" Γ as:*

Index-1 Δ : $\Gamma = Q_0 - N_2 P_0$, (Q_0, P_0, N_2) *are defined in Lemma 1,*

Index-2 Δ : $\Gamma = \begin{bmatrix} P_0 Q_1 - N_2 P_0 P_1 \\ Q_0 - (N_3 + L_3 N_2 N_1) P_0 P_1 \end{bmatrix}$,

(Q_i, P_i, N_i, L_i) *are defined in Lemma 2,*

Index-3 Δ : $\Gamma = \begin{bmatrix} P_0 P_1 Q_2 - N_2 P_0 P_1 P_2 \\ P_0 Q_1 - (N_3 + L_3 N_2 N_1) P_0 P_1 P_2 \\ Q_0 - [N_4 + L_4(N_3 N_1 + L_3 N_2 N_1^2) + Z_4 N_2 N_1] P_0 P_1 P_2 \end{bmatrix}$,

$(Q_i, P_i, N_i, L_i, Z_4)$ *are defined in Lemma 3,*

then, $Ker(\Gamma)$ is the consistent space of the system Δ, where $Ker(\Gamma)$ denotes the null space of the matrix Γ.

An initial state x_0 is consistent if it is in the consistent space, i.e., $\Gamma x_0 = 0$. The consistent matrix and consistent space is introduced because it is useful and convenient for checking the consistency of an initial set of states represented using a star set. For example, assume that the initial set of states is defined by $\Theta(0) = \langle V(0), P \rangle$, then this set is consistent for all α satisfying the predicate P if $\Gamma V(0) = 0$. This means that we require consistency for all points in the initial set. With a consistent initial set of states, we investigate the reachable set computation and safety verification/falsification of an autonomous DAE system in the next section.

5 Reachability Analysis

5.1 Reachable Set Computation

The reachable set of an autonomous DAE system is constructed by combining the reachable set of all of its decoupled subsystems. The reachable set of all AC subsystems can be derived from the reachable set of the ODE subsystem, which can be computed efficiently using existing ODE solvers. We first discuss the reachable set computation of the ODE subsystem by exploiting its *superposition property*. Then, the reachable set of the autonomous DAE system is constructed conveniently using only matrix addition and multiplication.

Let $\Theta(0) = \langle V(0), P \rangle$ be the initial set of states of an autonomous DAE system defined in (1) by letting $u(t) = 0$. Assume that the initial set of states, $X(0)$, satisfies the consistent condition. After decoupling, the initial set of states of the ODE subsystem $\Theta_1(0)$ is obtained as follows: $\Theta_1(0) = \langle V_1(0), P \rangle$ where $V_1(0) = (\prod_{i=0}^{\mu-1} P_0 \cdots P_{\mu-1}) V(0) = [v_1^1(0) \ v_2^1(0) \ \cdots \ v_k^1(0)]$, μ is the index of the DAE system, and $P_i, (i = 0, \cdots, \mu - 1)$, are defined in Lemma 1 or 2 or 3 corresponding to the index μ.

Then, for any $x_1(0) \in \Theta_1(0)$, we have $x_1(0) = \Sigma_{i=1}^{k} \alpha_i v_i^1(0)$. The solution of the ODE subsystem at time t is given by: $x_1(t) = \Sigma_{i=1}^{k} \alpha_i v_i^1(t) = V_1(t)\alpha$, where $v_i^1(t) = e^{N_1 t} v_i^1(0)$ and $V_1(t) = [v_1^1(t) \ v_2^1(t) \ \cdots \ v_k^1(t)]$. Therefore, the reachable set of the ODE subsystem at anytime t is also a star set defined by $\Theta_1(t) = V_1(t)\alpha$. Using existing ode solvers, we can construct the matrix $V_1(t)$ at anytime t. From $\Theta_1(t)$, the reachable set of the autonomous DAE system can be obtained using the following Lemma.

Lemma 6 (Reachable Set Construction). *Given an autonomous DAE system defined in Eq. (1) where $u(t) = 0$ and a consistent initial set of states $\Theta(0) = \langle V(0), P \rangle$, let $\Theta_1(t) = \langle V_1(t), P \rangle$ be the reachable set at time t of the corresponding ODE subsystem after decoupling. Then, the reachable set $\Theta(t)$ at time t of the system is given by $\Theta(t) = \langle V(t) = \Psi V_1(t), P \rangle$, where Ψ is a "reachable set projector" defined below.*

$$
\begin{aligned}
&\text{Index-1}: \ \Psi = (I_n + N_2), \ N_2 \text{ is defined in Lemma 1,} \\
&\text{Index-2}: \ \Psi = (I_n + N_2 + N_3 + L_3 N_2 N_1), \\
&\qquad (N_{i=1,2,3}, L_3) \text{ are defined in Lemma 2,} \\
&\text{Index-3}: \ \Psi = (I_n + N_2 + N_3 + N_4 + L_3 N_2 N_1 \\
&\qquad\qquad + L_4 N_3 N_1 + L_4 L_3 N_2 N_1^2 + Z_4 N_2 N_1), \\
&\qquad (N_{i=1,2,3,4}, L_{i=3,4}, Z_4) \text{ are defined in Lemma 3.}
\end{aligned} \tag{7}
$$

Proof is given in the appendix of [32].

The reachable set construction of an autonomous DAE system is summarized in the appendix [32]. Next, from the constructed reachable set, we discuss how to verify or falsify the safety property.

5.2 Safety Verification and Falsification

By utilizing the star set to represent the reachable set of a DAE system, the safety verification and falsification problem is solved in the following manner. Let $Unsafe(\Delta) \triangleq Gx \leq f$ be the unsafe set of an autonomous DAE system and assume that we want to check the safety of the system at the time step $t_j = jh$.

This is equivalent to checking $GV(jh)\alpha \leq f$ subject to $P(\alpha) \triangleq C\alpha \leq d$, where $V(jh)$ is the basic matrix of the reachable set $\Theta(jh)$ of the system at time jh computed using the reachable set construction algorithm in the appendix of [32] Combining these constraints, the problem changes to checking the feasibility of the following linear predicate: $\bar{P} \triangleq \bar{G}\alpha \leq \bar{f}$, where $\bar{G} = [(GV(jh))^T \quad C^T]^T$ and $\bar{f} = [f^T \quad d^T]^T$. This can be solved efficiently using existing linear programming algorithms. The verification and falsification algorithm in the appendix of [32] summarizes the steps of verifying or falsifying the safety property of an autonomous DAE system. In the next section, we evaluate our approach using a set of DAE benchmarks with several thousand states.

6   Experimental Results

In this section, we first demonstrate the effectiveness and scalability of our approach via the verification results for several DAE benchmarks [29]. Then, we analyze the time performance of our approach using the index-2, two-dimensional semi-discretized Stokes Equation benchmark [27]. It is worthy of noting that our reachability analysis approach for high-index DAEs is extensible and generic, in the sense that we can combine a decoupling method with other ODE reachability analysis tools such as SpaceEx and Flow*. The verification results of all benchmarks using such combinations with SpaceEx are presented in the appendix [32], which demonstrates the limitations in both timing and scalability performances. Our approach based on the combination of a decoupling method and a reachable set computation using star-set is implemented in a tool called $Daev^2$ using Python and its standard packages numpy, scipy, and mathplotlib. All experiments were done on a computer with the following configuration: Intel Core i7-6700 CPU @ 3.4 GHz 8 Processor, 62.8 GiB Memory, 64-bit Ubuntu 16.04.3 LTS OS.

6.1   Scalability Performance

Table 1 presents the verification results for all high-index DAE system benchmarks using Daev. From the table, we can see that Daev is scalable in verifying large DAE systems with thousands of state variables where the over-approximation approach is not applicable. Moreover, our approach can produce an unsafe trace in the case that a DAE system violates its safety property. An example of unsafe traces of the index-2, interconnected rotating masses system [30] is shown in the appendix [32]. Therefore, our approach is practically useful for falsification of large, linear DAE systems.

6.2   Timing Performance

Next, we investigate the time performance of our approach through the reachability analysis of the index-2, two-dimensional semi-discretized Stokes Equation benchmark.

---

[2] https://github.com/verivital/daev/releases/tag/formats2019.

Table 1. Verification results for all benchmarks using Daev.

Benchmarks	n	Index	Unsafe set	Result	V-T(s)
RL network [24]	3	2	$x_1 \leq -0.2 \wedge x_2 \leq -0.1$	Unsafe	0.184
			$x_1 \geq 0.2$	Safe	0.44
RLC circuit [12]	4	1	$x_1 + x_3 \geq 0.2$	Unsafe	0.224
			$x_4 \leq -0.3$	Safe	1.37
Interconnected rotating mass [30]	4	2	$x_3 \leq -0.9$	Unsafe	0.37
			$x_4 \leq -1.0$	Safe	0.114
Generator [20]	9	3	$x_9 \geq 0.01$	Unsafe	0.4
			$x_1 \geq 1.0$	Safe	0.684
Damped-mass spring [27]	11	3	$x_3 \leq 1 \wedge x_8 \leq 1.5$	Safe	1.06
			$x_8 \leq -0.2$	Unsafe	1.08
PEEC [9]	480	2	$x_{478} \geq 0.05$	Safe	28.84
			$x_{478} \geq 0.01$	Unsafe	28.25
MNA-1 [9]	578	2	$x_1 \geq -0.001$	Safe	192.7
			$x_1 \geq -0.0015$	Unsafe	202.6
MNA-4 [9]	980	3	$x_2 \geq 0.0005$	Safe	1858.4
			$x_2 \geq 0.0002$	Unsafe	1836.04
Stokes-equation [27]	4880	2	$v_x^c + v_y^c \leq -0.04$	Unsafe	3502.3
			$v_x^c \geq 0.2$	Safe	3532.3

Example 1 (Semi-discretized Stokes Equation [27]). This example studies the safety of a Stokes equation that describes the flow of an incompressible fluid in a two-dimensional spatial domain Ω. The mathematical description of the Stokes-equation is given in the appendix [32]. An index-2 DAE system is derived from the Stokes-equation by discretizing the domain Ω by a number of uniform square cells. Let n be the number of discretized segments of the domain on the x- or y-axes, then the dimension of the DAE system is $3n^2 + 2n$. Additionally, we are interested in the velocity along the x- and y- axes, $v_x^c(t)$ and $v_y^c(t)$, of the fluid in the *central cell* of the domain Ω. The unsafe set of the system is defined: $Unsafe \triangleq -v_x^c(t) - v_y^c(t) \leq 0.04$. By increasing the number of cells used to discretize the domain Ω, we can produce an index-2 DAE system with arbitrarily large dimension. We evaluate the time performance of our approach via three scenarios. First, we discuss how the times for decoupling, reachable set computation, and safety checking are affected by changes in the system dimension. Second, we analyze the reachable set computation time along with the *width* of the basic matrix of the initial set $V(0)$, i.e., the number of the initial basic vectors. Finally, because the reachable set of the system is constructed from the reachable set of its corresponding ODE subsystem, which is computed

using ODE solvers as shown in the reachable set construction algorithm in the appendix [32], we investigate the time performance of reachable set computation using different ODE solving schemes. Table 2 presents the verification time, V-T, for the Stokes-equation benchmark with different dimensions. The verification time is broken into three components measured in seconds: decoupling time D-T, reachable set computation time RSC-T, and checking safety time CS-T. Table 2 shows the decoupling and reachable set computation times dominate the time for verification process. In addition, these times increase as the system size grows. The time for checking safety is almost unchanged and very small. This happens because the size of the feasibility problem $\bar{P}$ defined in the verification/falsification algorithm in the appendix [32] is unchanged and usually small when we only check the safety in some specific directions defined by the unsafe matrix G in the algorithm.

Table 2. Verification time of Stokes-equation with different dimensions n.

n	86	321	706	1241	1926	2761
D-T	0.012 s	0.63 s	6.32 s	40.38 s	155.32 s	466.38 s
RSC-T	0.019 s	0.37 s	2.98 s	19.29 s	68.15 s	200.89 s
CS-T	0.0017 s	0.0014 s	0.0015 s	0.0017 s	0.0018 s	0.002 s
V-T	0.0327 s	1.0014 s	9.3015 s	59.6717 s	223.4718 s	667.272 s

Since the reachable set the Stokes-equation benchmark is constructed by simulating its corresponding ODE subsystem with each initial vector of its initial basic matrix, the time for computing the reachable set of the Stokes-equation depends linearly on the number of the initial basic vectors k. Table 3 shows the reachable set computation time, RSC-T, for the Stokes-equation of dimension $n = 321$ versus the number of the initial basic vectors k.

Table 3. Reachable set computation time of Stokes-equation of dimensions $n = 321$ with different number of initial basic vectors k.

k	2	4	6	8	10	12	14
RSC-T	1.9 s	3.41 s	5.01 s	6.71 s	8.3 s	9.9 s	11.44 s

Our approach relies on existing ODE solvers. Therefore, it is interesting to consider how the reachable set computation time performs with different existing ODE solving schemes supported by the *scipy* package such as *vode*, *zvode*, *lsoda*, *dopri5* and *dop853*. All solvers are used with the absolute tolerance $atol = 1e{-}12$ and the relative tolerance $rtol = 1e{-}08$. Figure 1 illustrates the time performance of different schemes and indicates that the *vode*, *dopri5*, and *dop853* are fast schemes that should be used for large DAE systems. In addition, we should avoid using the *lsoda* and *zvode* schemes for large DAE systems due to theirs slow performance.

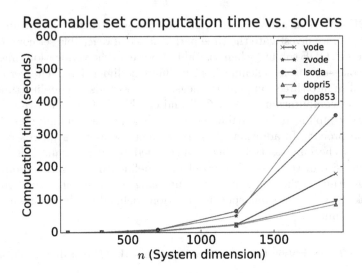

Fig. 1. Reachable set computation time of Stokes-equation using different ode solvers

7   Conclusion and Future Work

We have studied a simulation-based reachability analysis for high-index, linear DAE systems. The experiential results show that our approach can deal with DAE systems with up to thousands of state variables. Therefore, it is useful and applicable to verify or falsify safety-critical CPS involving DAE dynamics. Additionally, the decoupling and the consistency checking techniques used in our approach can be used as a transformation pass for existing over-approximation techniques [2,19] to verify the safety of DAE systems with small and medium dimension.

The reachability analysis for DAE systems with millions of dimensions remains challenging, although recent symbolic state-space representations, such as star sets, that allow for analyzing very large ODEs may also prove pivotal for DAEs [6]. The verification time of our approach depends mostly on the decoupling and the reachable set computation times. Therefore, to enhance the time performance and the scalability of our approach to make it work for million-dimensional DAE systems, both decoupling and reachable set computation techniques need to be improved. A promising application that inspires seeking a such scalable approach is verification and falsification of very large circuits, such as those that may arise in analog/mixed signal (AMS) designs, which are described as high-index DAEs. Transformations from standard circuit languages such as Verilog-AMS or VHDL-AMS to representations as hybrid automata may enable such analyses [3,4].

Acknowledgments. The material presented in this paper is based upon work supported by the National Science Foundation (NSF) under grant numbers CNS 1464311, CNS 1713253, SHF 1527398, and SHF 1736323, the Air Force Office of Scientific Research (AFOSR) through contract numbers FA9550-15-1-0258, FA9550-16-1-0246, and FA9550-18-1-0122. The U.S. government is authorized to reproduce and distribute reprints for Governmental purposes notwithstanding any copyright notation thereon. Any opinions, findings, and conclusions or recommendations expressed in this publication are those of the authors and do not necessarily reflect the views of AFOSR or NSF.

References

1. Althoff, M., Krogh, B.: Reachability analysis of nonlinear differential-algebraic systems. IEEE Trans. Autom. Control **59**(2), 371–383 (2014). https://doi.org/10.1109/TAC.2013.2285751
2. Althoff, M.: An introduction to CORA 2015. In: Proceedings of the Workshop on Applied Verification for Continuous and Hybrid Systems (2015)
3. Bak, S., Beg, O.A., Bogomolov, S., Johnson, T.T., Nguyen, L.V., Schilling, C.: Hybrid automata: from verification to implementation. Int. J. Softw. Tools Technol. Transf. **21**(1), 87–104 (2019). https://doi.org/10.1007/s10009-017-0458-1
4. Bak, S., Bogomolov, S., Johnson, T.T.: HYST: a source transformation and translation tool for hybrid automaton models. In: Proceedings of the 18th International Conference on Hybrid Systems: Computation and Control, pp. 128–133. ACM (2015)
5. Bak, S., Duggirala, P.S.: Simulation-equivalent reachability of large linear systems with inputs. In: Majumdar, R., Kunčak, V. (eds.) CAV 2017. LNCS, vol. 10426, pp. 401–420. Springer, Cham (2017). https://doi.org/10.1007/978-3-319-63387-9_20
6. Bak, S., Tran, H.D., Johnson, T.T.: Numerical verification of affine systems with up to a billion dimensions. In: Proceedings of the 22nd ACM International Conference on Hybrid Systems: Computation and Control, HSCC 2019, pp. 23–32. ACM, New York (2019). https://doi.org/10.1145/3302504.3311792
7. Banagaaya, N., Alì, G., Schilders, W.H.: Index-Aware Model Order Reduction Methods. Springer, Cham (2016). https://doi.org/10.2991/978-94-6239-189-5
8. Byrne, G., Ponzi, P.: Differential-algebraic systems, their applications and solutions. Comput. Chem. Eng. **12**(5), 377–382 (1988)
9. Chahlaoui, Y., Van Dooren, P.: A collection of benchmark examples for model reduction of linear time invariant dynamical systems (2002)
10. Chen, X., Ábrahám, E., Sankaranarayanan, S.: Flow*: an analyzer for non-linear hybrid systems. In: Sharygina, N., Veith, H. (eds.) CAV 2013. LNCS, vol. 8044, pp. 258–263. Springer, Heidelberg (2013). https://doi.org/10.1007/978-3-642-39799-8_18
11. Cross, E.A., Mitchell, I.M.: Level set methods for computing reachable sets of systems with differential algebraic equation dynamics. In: American Control Conference, pp. 2260–2265. IEEE (2008)
12. Dai, L.: Singular Control Systems. Lecture Notes in Control and Information Sciences. Springer, Heidelberg (1989)
13. Dang, T., Donzé, A., Maler, O.: Verification of analog and mixed-signal circuits using hybrid system techniques. In: Hu, A.J., Martin, A.K. (eds.) FMCAD 2004. LNCS, vol. 3312, pp. 21–36. Springer, Heidelberg (2004). https://doi.org/10.1007/978-3-540-30494-4_3

14. Duan, G.R.: Analysis and Design of Descriptor Linear Systems, vol. 23. Springer, New York (2010)
15. Duggirala, P.S., Mitra, S., Viswanathan, M., Potok, M.: C2E2: a verification tool for stateflow models. In: Baier, C., Tinelli, C. (eds.) TACAS 2015. LNCS, vol. 9035, pp. 68–82. Springer, Heidelberg (2015). https://doi.org/10.1007/978-3-662-46681-0_5
16. Duggirala, P.S., Viswanathan, M.: Parsimonious, simulation based verification of linear systems. In: Chaudhuri, S., Farzan, A. (eds.) CAV 2016. LNCS, vol. 9779, pp. 477–494. Springer, Cham (2016). https://doi.org/10.1007/978-3-319-41528-4_26
17. Eich-Soellner, E., Führer, C.: Numerical Methods in Multibody Dynamics, vol. 45. Springer, Wiesbaden (1998). https://doi.org/10.1007/978-3-663-09828-7
18. Fan, C., Qi, B., Mitra, S., Viswanathan, M., Duggirala, P.S.: Automatic reachability analysis for nonlinear hybrid models with C2E2. In: Chaudhuri, S., Farzan, A. (eds.) CAV 2016. LNCS, vol. 9779, pp. 531–538. Springer, Cham (2016). https://doi.org/10.1007/978-3-319-41528-4_29
19. Frehse, G., et al.: SpaceEx: scalable verification of hybrid systems. In: Gopalakrishnan, G., Qadeer, S. (eds.) CAV 2011. LNCS, vol. 6806, pp. 379–395. Springer, Heidelberg (2011). https://doi.org/10.1007/978-3-642-22110-1_30
20. Gerdin, M.: Parameter estimation in linear descriptor systems. Citeseer (2004)
21. Girard, A.: Reachability of uncertain linear systems using zonotopes. In: Morari, M., Thiele, L. (eds.) HSCC 2005. LNCS, vol. 3414, pp. 291–305. Springer, Heidelberg (2005). https://doi.org/10.1007/978-3-540-31954-2_19
22. Guernic, C.L., Girard, A.: Reachability analysis of linear systems using support functions. Nonlinear Anal. Hybrid Syst. 4(2), 250–262 (2010). https://doi.org/10.1016/j.nahs.2009.03.002
23. Han, Z., Krogh, B.H.: Reachability analysis of large-scale affine systems using low-dimensional polytopes. In: Hespanha, J.P., Tiwari, A. (eds.) HSCC 2006. LNCS, vol. 3927, pp. 287–301. Springer, Heidelberg (2006). https://doi.org/10.1007/11730637_23
24. Ho, C.W., Ruehli, A., Brennan, P.: The modified nodal approach to network analysis. IEEE Trans. Circuits Syst. 22(6), 504–509 (1975)
25. Kong, S., Gao, S., Chen, W., Clarke, E.: dreach: δ-reachability analysis for hybrid systems, pp. 200–205 (2015)
26. März, R.: Canonical projectors for linear differential algebraic equations. Comput. Math. Appl. 31(4–5), 121–135 (1996)
27. Mehrmann, V., Stykel, T.: Balanced truncation model reduction for large-scale systems in descriptor form. In: Benner, P., Sorensen, D.C., Mehrmann, V. (eds.) Dimension Reduction of Large-Scale Systems. LNCSE, vol. 45, pp. 83–115. Springer, Heidelberg (2005). https://doi.org/10.1007/3-540-27909-1_3
28. Mitchell, I.M., Susuki, Y.: Level set methods for computing reachable sets of hybrid systems with differential algebraic equation dynamics. In: Egerstedt, M., Mishra, B. (eds.) HSCC 2008. LNCS, vol. 4981, pp. 630–633. Springer, Heidelberg (2008). https://doi.org/10.1007/978-3-540-78929-1_51
29. Musau, P., Lopez, D.M., Tran, H.D., Johnson, T.T.: Linear differential-algebraic equations (benchmark proposal). EPiC Ser. Comput. 54, 174–184 (2018)
30. Schon, T., Gerdin, M., Glad, T., Gustafsson, F.: A modeling and filtering framework for linear differential-algebraic equations. In: 42nd IEEE Conference on Decision and Control. Proceedings, vol. 1, pp. 892–897. IEEE (2003)
31. Tran, H.D., Bao, T., Johnson, T.T.: Discrete-space analysis of partial differential equations. EPiC Seri. Comput. 54, 185–195 (2018)

32. Tran, H.D., Nguyen, L.V., Hamilton, N., Xiang, W., Johnson, T.T.: Reachability analysis for high-index linear differential algebraic equations: extended version. In: 17th International Conference on Formal Modeling and Analysis of Timed Systems (2019)
33. Tran, H.D., Nguyen, L.V., Johnson, T.T.: Large-scale linear systems from order-reduction (benchmark proposal). In: 3rd Applied Verification for Continuous and Hybrid Systems Workshop (ARCH), Vienna, Austria (2016)
34. Tran, H.D., Nguyen, L.V., Xiang, W., Johnson, T.T.: Order-reduction abstractions for safety verification of high-dimensional linear systems. Discrete Event Dyn. Syst. **27**(2), 443–461 (2017)
35. Tran, H.D., Xiang, W., Bak, S., Johnson, T.T.: Reachability analysis for one dimensional linear parabolic equations. IFAC-PapersOnLine **51**(16), 133–138 (2018)

Timed Automata

The Timestamp of Timed Automata

Amnon Rosenmann[(✉)] [iD]

Graz University of Technology, Steyrergasse 30, 8010 Graz, Austria
rosenmann@math.tugraz.at

Abstract. Let eNTA be the class of non-deterministic timed automata with silent transitions. Given $A \in$ eNTA, we effectively compute its timestamp: the set of all pairs (time value, action) of all observable timed traces of A. We show that the timestamp is eventually periodic and that one can compute a simple deterministic timed automaton with the same timestamp as that of A. As a consequence, we have a partial method, not bounded by time or number of steps, for the general language non-inclusion problem for eNTA. We also show that the language of A is periodic with respect to suffixes.

Keywords: Timed automata · Timestamp of timed automata ·
Reachability problem · Language inclusion for timed automata

1 Introduction

Timed automata (TA) are finite automata extended with clocks that measure the time that elapsed since past events in order to control the triggering of future events. They were defined by Alur and Dill in their seminal paper [1] as abstract models of real-time systems and were implemented in tools like UPPAAL [20], Kronos [10], RED [27] and PRISM [19].

A fundamental problem in this area is the reachability problem, which in its basic form asks whether a given location of a timed automaton is reachable from the initial location. The set of states of the system (i.e., locations and valuation to the clocks) is, in general, an infinite uncountable set. However, through the construction of a region automaton, which contains finitely-many equivalence classes of regions [1], the reachability problem becomes a decidable problem (though of complexity PSPACE-complete).

Research on the reachability problem went beyond the above basic question. In [14] it is shown that the problem of the minimum and maximum reachability time is also PSPACE-complete. In another work, [13], which is more of a theoretical nature, the authors show that some problems on the relations between states may be defined in the decidable theory of the domain of real numbers equipped with the addition operation. In particular, the reachability problem between any two states is decidable. For other aspects of the reachability problem, also in the context of variants and extensions of timed automata (e.g. with game and probability characteristics) we refer to [3,5,11,14,17,18,26,28]. In this

© Springer Nature Switzerland AG 2019
E. André and M. Stoelinga (Eds.): FORMATS 2019, LNCS 11750, pp. 181–198, 2019.
https://doi.org/10.1007/978-3-030-29662-9_11

paper we generalize the reachability problem in another direction. We show that the problem of computing the set of all time values on which any observable transition occurs (and thus, a location is reached by an observable transition) is solvable. This set, called the *timestamp* of the automaton A and denoted $\mathbf{TS}(A)$, is more precisely defined to be the set of all pairs (t, a) that appear in the observable timed traces of A. Note that for this definition it does not matter whether we consider infinite runs or finite ones.

We show that the timestamp is in the form of a union of action-labeled open intervals with integral end-points, and action-labeled points of integral values. When the timestamp is unbounded in time then it is eventually periodic.

The set of languages defined by the class DTA of deterministic timed automata is strictly included in the set of languages defined by the class NTA of non-deterministic timed automata [1,16], and the latter is strictly included in the set of languages defined by the class eNTA of non-deterministic timed automata with silent transitions [8]. The fundamental problem of inclusion of the language accepted by a timed automaton A (e.g. the implementation) in the language accepted by the timed automaton B (e.g. the specification) is undecidable for the class NTA but decidable for the class DTA. On the other hand, for special sub-classes or modifications it was shown that decidability exists (see [2,4,6,8, 9,21–24] for a partial list). However, the abstraction (or over-approximation) represented in the form of a timestamp is a discrete object, in which questions like inclusion of timestamps or universality are decidable. In fact, we show that for any given non-deterministic timed automaton with silent transitions, one can construct a simple deterministic timed automaton having the same timestamp.

The computation of the timestamp is done through the construction of a periodic augmented region automaton $\mathfrak{R}^t_{\mathrm{per}}(A)$. It is a region automaton augmented with a global non-resetting clock t and containing periodic regions and periodic transitions: they are defined modulo a time period $L \in \mathbb{N}$. This kind of abstraction demonstrates a periodic nature which is absent, in general, from timed traces: there are timed automata with no timed traces that are eventually periodic (see Example 1). Periodic transitions were introduced in [12], where it was shown that they increase the expressiveness of DTA, though they are less expressive than silent transitions.

The construction of the periodic automaton is preceded by defining the infinite augmented region automaton $\mathfrak{R}^t_{\infty}(A)$, in which the values of the clock t are unbounded. Then, after exhibiting the existence of a pattern that repeats itself every L time units, we fold the infinite automaton into a finite one according to this periodic structure.

Our construction shows that the language of a timed automaton $A \in$ eNTA is periodic with respect to suffixes: for every run ϱ with suffix ς that occurs after passing a fixed computable time there are infinitely-many runs of A with the same suffix ς, but with the suffix shifted in time by multiples of L. Note that this result does not follow from the pumping lemma, which does not hold in general in timed automata [7].

Due to lack of space, some proofs are either sketched or completely missing (for a longer version see [25]).

2   Timed Automata with Silent Transitions

A timed automaton is an abstract model aiming at capturing the temporal behavior of real-time systems. It is a finite automaton extended with a finite set of clocks defined over $\mathbb{R}_{\geq 0}$. It consists of a finite set of *locations* q with a finite set of *transitions* τ between the locations, while time, measured by the clocks, is continuous. A transition at time t can occur only if the condition expressed as a *transition guard* is satisfied at t. The transition is immediate - no clock is advancing in time. However, some of the clocks may be reset to zero.

There are two sorts of transitions: *observable* transitions, which can be traced by an outside observer, and *silent* transitions, which are inner transitions and thus cannot be observed from the outside. There are finitely-many types of observable transitions, each type labeled by a unique *action* $a \in \Sigma$, whereas all the silent transitions have the same label ϵ. In NTA, the class of non-deterministic timed automata, there exist states in which two transitions from the same location q can be taken at the same time and with the same action but to two different locations q' and q''. When this situation cannot happen, the TA is deterministic.

Let $\mathbb{N}_0 := \mathbb{N} \cup \{0\}$ and let $\mathcal{P}(S)$ be the power set of a set S. A transition guard is a conjunction of constraints of the form $c \sim n$, where c is a clock, $\sim \in \{<, \leq, =, \geq, >\}$ and $n \in \mathbb{N}_0$. A formal definition of eNTA is as follows.

Definition 1 (eNTA). *A non-deterministic timed automaton with silent transitions $A \in$ eNTA is a tuple $(\mathcal{Q}, q_0, \Sigma_\epsilon, \mathcal{C}, \mathcal{T})$, where:*

1. *$\mathcal{Q}$ is a finite set of locations and q_0 is the initial location;*
2. *$\Sigma_\epsilon = \Sigma \cup \{\epsilon\}$ is a finite set of transition labels, called actions, where Σ refers to the observable actions and ϵ represents a silent transition;*
3. *$\mathcal{C}$ is a finite set of clock variables;*
4. *$\mathcal{T} \subseteq \mathcal{Q} \times \Sigma_\epsilon \times \mathcal{G} \times \mathcal{P}(\mathcal{C}) \times \mathcal{Q}$ is a finite set of transitions of the form $(q, a, g, \mathcal{C}_{rst}, q')$, where:*
   (a) $q, q' \in \mathcal{Q}$ are the source and the target locations respectively;
   (b) $a \in \Sigma_\epsilon$ is the transition action;
   (c) $g \in \mathcal{G}$ is the transition guard;
   (d) $\mathcal{C}_{rst} \subseteq \mathcal{C}$ is the subset of clocks to be reset.

A clock *valuation* v is a function $v : \mathcal{C} \to \mathbb{R}_{\geq 0}$. We denote by $\mathcal{V}$ the set of all clock valuations and by $\mathbf{d}$ the valuation which assigns the value d to every clock. Given a valuation v and $d \in \mathbb{R}_{\geq 0}$, we define $v + d$ to be the valuation $(v + d)(c) := v(c) + d$ for every $c \in \mathcal{C}$. The valuation $v[\mathcal{C}_{rst}]$, $\mathcal{C}_{rst} \subseteq \mathcal{C}$, is defined to be $v[\mathcal{C}_{rst}](c) = 0$ for $c \in \mathcal{C}_{rst}$ and $v[\mathcal{C}_{rst}](c) = v(c)$ for $c \notin \mathcal{C}_{rst}$.

The *semantics* of $A \in$ eNTA is given by the *timed transition system* $[\![A]\!] = (S, s_0, \mathbb{R}_{\geq 0}, \Sigma_\epsilon, T)$, where:

1. $S = \{(q, v) \in \mathcal{Q} \times \mathcal{V}\}$ is the set of states, with $s_0 = (q_0, \mathbf{0})$ the initial state;
2. $T \subseteq S \times (\Sigma_\epsilon \cup \mathbb{R}_{\geq 0}) \times S$ is the transition relation. The set T consists of
   (a) *Timed transitions (delays):* $(q, v) \xrightarrow{d} (q, v + d)$, where $d \in \mathbb{R}_{\geq 0}$;
   (b) *Discrete transitions (jumps):* $(q, v) \xrightarrow{a} (q', v')$, where $a \in \Sigma_\epsilon$ and there exists a transition $(q, a, g, \mathcal{C}_{rst}, q')$ in T, such that for each clock c, $v(c)$ satisfies the constraints of g regarding c, and $v' = v[\mathcal{C}_{rst}]$.

A (finite) *run* ϱ of $A \in$ eNTA is a sequence of alternating timed and discrete transitions of the form

$$(q_0, \mathbf{0}) \xrightarrow{d_1} (q_0, \mathbf{d}_1) \xrightarrow{a_1} (q_1, v_1) \xrightarrow{d_2} \cdots \xrightarrow{d_k} (q_{k-1}, v_{k-1} + d_k) \xrightarrow{a_k} (q_k, v_k)$$

and *duration* $T = \sum_{j=1}^{k} d_j$. The run ϱ of A induces the *timed trace (timed word)*

$$\lambda = (t_1, a_1), (t_2, a_2), \ldots, (t_k, a_k),$$

with $a_i \in \Sigma_\epsilon$ and $t_i = \Sigma_{j=1}^{i} d_j$. From the latter we can extract the *observable timed trace (observable timed word)*, which is obtained by deleting from λ all the pairs containing silent transitions. Note that when the TA is deterministic then each timed trace refers to a unique run. We remark that we did not include the location invariants in the definition of timed automata since these invariants can be incorporated in the transition guards. We also do not distinguish between accepting and non-accepting locations as they do not change the analysis and results concerning the reachability problems that are dealt with here. Thus, the *language* $\mathfrak{L}(A)$ of A refers here to the set of observable timed traces of A without restricting it to those observable timed traces of runs that end in acceptable locations.

3   The Trail and Timestamp of a Single Path

Given a timed automaton $A \in$ eNTA over s clocks $x_1, \ldots, x_s$, we add to it a non-resetting global clock t that displays absolute time. A finite *path* in A has the form $\gamma = q_0 \tau_1 q_1 \tau_2 \cdots \tau_n q_n$ of alternating locations and transitions, with q_0 the initial location and τ_i a transition between q_{i-1} and q_i, $i = 1, \ldots, n$, that is, a path here refers to the standard definition in a directed graph. A run of the TA induces a *trajectory* in the non-negative part of the $tx_1 \cdots x_s$-space that is a piecewise-linear curve (the discontinuity is the clocks reset).

Definition 2 (Trajectory of a run). *Let $\{t, x_1, \ldots, x_s\}$ be an ordered set of clocks of $A \in$ eNTA. Let ϱ be a run of duration T of A. The trajectory of ϱ is the set of points $(t, x_1, \ldots, x_s)$ in the $tx_1 \cdots x_s$-space visited during ϱ, where $0 \leq t \leq T$.*

Next, we define the *trail* of a path.

Definition 3 (Trail of a path). *The trail of a path γ is the union of the trajectories of all feasible runs along γ, that is, runs that follow the locations and discrete transitions of γ.*

The *trail legs*, the parts of the trail between clocks reset, are in the form of *zones* [15], a conjunction of diagonal constraints $x_i - x_j < n_{ij}$ or $x_i - x_j \leq n_{ij}$, $n_{ij} \in \mathbb{Z}$, bounded by transition constraints $x_i \sim n_i$, where $\sim \in \{<, \leq, =, \geq, >\}$, $n_i \in \mathbb{N}_0$. Each trail leg can be further partitioned into *simplicial trails*, which are (possibly unbounded) parallelotopes consisting of a sequence of *regions* [1] arranged along the directional vector $\mathbf{1} = (1, 1, \ldots, 1)$. Each region $\mathbf{n} + \Delta$ is in the form of an open (unless it is a point) simplex Δ that is a hyper-triangle of dimension $0 \leq d \leq s+1$. The simplex Δ is characterized by the fractional values $\{x_i\}$ of the clock variables, and each point in the simplex satisfies the same fixed ordering of the form

$$0 \preceq_1 \{x_{i_1}\} \preceq_2 \{x_{i_2}\} \preceq_3 \cdots \preceq_s \{x_{i_s}\} < 1, \tag{1}$$

where $\preceq_i \in \{=, <\}$. The integral point $\mathbf{n} \in \mathbb{N}_0^{s+1}$ consists of the integral parts of the values of the clocks $x_0, x_1, \ldots, x_s$, and it indicates the lowest point in the $x_0 \cdots x_s$-space of the boundary of the region. Each region has a unique *immediate time-successor*, which is the next region along the directional vector $\mathbf{1}$, as long as no clock is reset on an event.

Definition 4 (Timestamp of a run). *The* timestamp of a run ϱ *is the set of pairs* $(t_i, a_i) \in \mathbb{R}_{\geq 0} \times \Sigma$ *of the observable timed trace induced by* ϱ.

Definition 5 (Timestamp of a path). *The* timestamp of a path γ of A *is the union of the timestamps of all runs* ϱ *along* γ.

Each instance of a transition along γ is an *event*.

Definition 6 (Timestamp of an event in a path). *The* timestamp of an event *in a path* γ *is the union of the timestamps of that event of all runs along* γ. *It is the part of the timestamp of the path that refers to that event.*

Proposition 1. *The timestamp of each event is either a labeled integral point or a labeled (open, closed or half-open) interval between points m and n, $m < n$, $m \in \mathbb{N}_0$ and $n \in \mathbb{N} \cup \infty$.*

Proof (sketch). It follows from the fact that the trail of each path is composed of simplices as in (1) residing on the integral grid, and such are the intersections with domains defined by transition constraints and projections due to clocks resets. Thus, it suffices to show that the timestamp of a single simplex Δ is of the required form and this follows from the fact that the simplex vertices are of integral value.

An alternative proof is via a linear programming problem over the variables t_i, where t_i represents the time of event i along a path γ, by showing that the minimum and maximum (if not infinite) of the solution set is integral. $\square$

Definition 7 (Timestamp of a timed automaton). *The* timestamp $\mathbf{TS}(A)$ *of a timed automaton A is the set of all pairs (t, a), such that an observable transition with action a occurs at time t in some run of A.*

4   Augmented and Infinite Augmented Region Automaton

4.1   Infinite Augmented Region Automaton

Given a (finite) timed automaton A, the region automaton $\mathfrak{R}(A)$ [1] is a finite *discretized* version of A, such that time is abstracted and both automata define the same untimed language. Each vertex in $\mathfrak{R}(A)$ records a location q in A and a region r, which is either in the form of a simplex (as described in Sect. 3) or an unbounded region, in which the value of at least one of the clocks is $\top$, meaning that it passed the maximal integer value M that appears in the transition guards. The regions partition the space of clock valuations into equivalence classes, where two valuations belong to the same equivalence class if and only if they agree on the clocks with $\top$ value and on the integral parts and the order among the fractional parts of the other clocks. The edges of $\mathfrak{R}(A)$ are labeled by the transition actions, and they correspond to the actual transitions that occur in the runs of A. Using the time-successor relation over the clock regions (see [1]), the region automaton can be effectively constructed. As shown in [1], through the region automaton the questions of reachable locations and states of A and the actions along the (possibly infinitely-many) paths that lead to these locations, i.e. the untimed language of A, become decidable.

Now we define the *infinite augmented region automaton* $\mathfrak{R}^t_\infty(A)$. First, we add to A a clock t that measures absolute time, does not appear in the transition guards, is never reset to 0 and does not affect the runs and timed traced of A. Next, we construct the region automaton augmented with t. The construction is similar to the construction of the standard region automaton with respect to the regular clocks (all clocks except for t) and the maximal bound M, that is, the time regions of each regular clock x_i are $\{0\}, (0,1), \{1\}, (1,2), \ldots, M, > M$, the latter being unbounded and refers to all values of x greater than M. The integration of the clock t is as follows. The construction of regions is as usual by considering the integral parts and the order of the fractional parts of all clocks, including t. The only difference is that the integral part of t is in $\mathbb{N}_0$ and not bounded by M. Thus, the infinitely-many time-regions associated with t are the alternating point and open unit interval: $\{0\}, (0,1), \{1\}, (1,2), \ldots$ (see Fig. 1(b)). Hence, $\mathfrak{R}^t_\infty(A)$ contains information about absolute time that is lacking from the standard region automaton.

Definition 8 (Infinite augmented region automaton). *Given $A \in$ eNTA extended with the clock t that measures absolute time, a corresponding* infinite *augmented region automaton $\mathfrak{R}^t_\infty(A)$ is a tuple $(V, v_0, E, \Sigma_\epsilon)$, where:*

1. *V is an infinite (in general) set of vertices of the form $(q, \mathbf{n}, \Delta)$, where q is a location of A and the pair $(\mathbf{n}, \Delta)$ is a region, with*

$$\mathbf{n} = (n_0, n_1, \ldots, n_s) \in \mathbb{N}_0 \times \{0, 1, \ldots, M, \top\}^s \tag{2}$$

containing the integral parts of the clocks $t, x_1, \ldots, x_s$, and Δ is the simplex defined by the order of the fractional parts of the clocks.

2. $v_0 = (q_0, \mathbf{0}, \mathbf{0})$ *is the initial vertex with q_0 the initial location of A and with all clocks having integral part and fractional part equal to 0.*
3. *E is the set of edges. There is an edge*

$$(q, r) \xrightarrow{a} (q', r') \tag{3}$$

labeled with a in $\mathfrak{R}_\infty^t(A)$ if and only if there is a run of A which contains a timed transition followed by a discrete transition of the form

$$(q, v) \xrightarrow{d} (q, v + d) \xrightarrow{a} (q', v'), \tag{4}$$

such that the clock valuation v over $t, x_1, \ldots, x_s$ represents a point in the region r and the clock valuation v' represents a point in the region r'.
4. *$\Sigma_\epsilon = \Sigma \cup \{\epsilon\}$ is the finite set of actions that are edge labels.*

We note that there may be infinitely-many edges going-out of the same region in $\mathfrak{R}_\infty^t(A)$ (see Fig. 1(b)).

Proposition 2. *For each positive integer n, one can effectively construct the part of $\mathfrak{R}_\infty^t(A)$ which contains all regions with $t \leq n$ and all in-coming edges of these regions.*

The timestamp of the TA A, denoted **TS**(A), is the union of the timestamps of all observable transitions of A, that is, the set of all pairs (t, a), such that an observable transition with action a occurs at time t in some run of A. We define also the timestamp of $\mathfrak{R}_\infty^t(A)$.

Definition 9 (Timestamp of $\mathfrak{R}_\infty^t(A)$). *The timestamp of $\mathfrak{R}_\infty^t(A)$, **TS**$(\mathfrak{R}_\infty^t(A))$, is the union of sets $s \times a$, where s is a time-region of t (an integral point $\{n\}$ or an open unit interval $(n, n+1)$) that is part of a region of a vertex of $\mathfrak{R}_\infty^t(A)$ and $a \in \Sigma$ is a label of an edge of $\mathfrak{R}_\infty^t(A)$ that is directed towards this vertex.*

Proposition 3. TS$(A) = $ **TS**$(\mathfrak{R}_\infty^t(A))$.

Proof. By definition of the infinite augmented region automaton $\mathfrak{R}_\infty^t(A)$, its regions are exactly the clock-regions which are visited by runs of the TA A extended with the clock t. In particular, the time-regions of $\mathfrak{R}_\infty^t(A)$ are the time-regions that are visited by the runs on the extended TA. Thus, **TS**$(A) \subseteq$ **TS**$(\mathfrak{R}_\infty^t(A))$. By Proposition 1, this is an equality since for each open interval $(n, n+1)$ representing absolute time that is visited in some run of A on an action a, the set of all runs of A cover all the points of this interval with the same action a. □

4.2   Augmented Region Automaton

A second construction is the augmented region automaton, denoted $\mathfrak{R}^t(A)$, in which we consider only the fractional part of t and ignore its integral part.

$\mathfrak{R}^t(A)$ is a finite folding of $\mathfrak{R}^t_\infty(A)$, obtained by identifying vertices that contain the same data except for the integral part of t, and the corresponding edges. Thus, t has only two time-regions: $\{0\}$ and $(0,1)$. As a compensation, we assign weights to the edges of $\mathfrak{R}^t(A)$, as explained below.

Definition 10 (Augmented region automaton). *Given a non-deterministic timed automaton with silent transitions $A \in \mathrm{eNTA}$, extended with the absolute-time clock t, a corresponding (finite)* augmented region automaton $\mathfrak{R}^t(A)$ *is a tuple* $(V, v_0, E, \Sigma_\epsilon, W^*)$, *where:*

1. *V is the set of vertices. Each vertex is a triple $(q, \mathbf{n}, \Delta)$, where q is a location of A and the pair $(\mathbf{n}, \Delta)$ is a region, with*

$$\mathbf{n} = (n_1, \ldots, n_s) \in \{0, 1, \ldots, M, \top\}^s \tag{5}$$

containing the integral parts of the clocks $x_1, \ldots, x_s$, and Δ is the simplex defined by the fractional parts of the clocks $t, x_1, \ldots, x_s$.
2. *$v_0 = (q_0, \mathbf{0}, \mathbf{0})$ is the initial vertex.*
3. *E is the set of edges. There is an edge $(q, r) \xrightarrow{a} (q', r')$ labeled with action a if and only if there is a run of A which contains a timed transition followed by a discrete transition of the form $(q, v) \xrightarrow{d} (q, v + d) \xrightarrow{a} (q', v')$, such that, when ignoring the integral part of the time measured by t, the clock valuation v represents a point in the region r and the clock valuation v' represents a point in the region r'.*
4. *$\Sigma_\epsilon = \Sigma \cup \{\epsilon\}$ is the finite set of actions.*
5. *W^* is the set of weights on the edges. Each weight m, possibly marked with '*', is $m = \lfloor t_1 \rfloor - \lfloor t_0 \rfloor \in [0..M]$, where $\lfloor t_1 \rfloor$ is the integral part of the value of t in the target location and $\lfloor t_0 \rfloor$ - in the source location in the corresponding run of A.*

There may be more than one edge between two vertices of $\mathfrak{R}^t(A)$, each one with a distinguished weight. A marked weight m^* represents infinitely-many consecutive values $m, m+1, m+2, \ldots$ as weights between the same two vertices, with m being the minimal value of such a sequence. It refers to a transition to or from a region r in which all regular clocks have passed the maximal integer M appearing in a transition guard as is illustrated in Fig. 1.

The languages $\mathcal{L}(\mathfrak{R}^t(A))$ of $\mathfrak{R}^t(A)$ and $\mathcal{L}(\mathfrak{R}^t_\infty(A))$ of $\mathfrak{R}^t_\infty(A)$ consist of all observable timed traces but, in contrast to the language $\mathcal{L}(A)$ of A, in each pair (t_i, a_i) the time t_i is not exact: it is either an exact integer n or an arbitrary value of an interval $(n, n+1)$ that satisfies $t_i \geq t_{i-1}$. Thus, $\mathcal{L}(\mathfrak{R}^t(A))$ and $\mathcal{L}(\mathfrak{R}^t_\infty(A))$ are less abstract than the untimed language $\mathcal{L}(\mathfrak{R}(A))$ of the region automaton $\mathfrak{R}(A)$ but are more abstract than $\mathcal{L}(A)$: one cannot, in general, distinguish between a transition that occurs without any time delay, e.g. when $x_i \geq 0$, and a transition that demands a time delay, e.g. when $x_i > 0$. When comparing $\mathcal{L}(\mathfrak{R}^t(A))$ and $\mathcal{L}(\mathfrak{R}^t_\infty(A))$ then, since $\mathfrak{R}^t(A)$ may be obtained from $\mathfrak{R}^t_\infty(A)$, it is clear that $\mathcal{L}(\mathfrak{R}^t(A))$ cannot be less abstract than $\mathcal{L}(\mathfrak{R}^t_\infty(A))$. But, in fact, these region automata are equally informative: for each positive integer n, one can

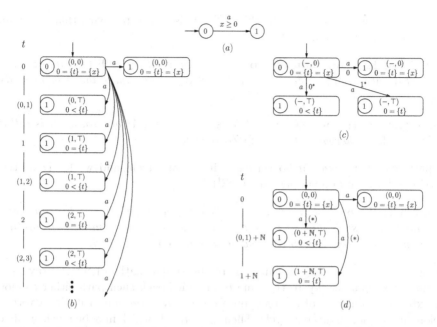

Fig. 1. (a) $A \in$ TA; (b) The infinite augmented region automaton $\mathfrak{R}^t_\infty(A)$; (c) The augmented region automaton $\mathfrak{R}^t(A)$; (d) A periodic augmented region automaton $\mathfrak{R}^t_{per}(A)$. Each rectangle represents a vertex containing the location of A (circled, left), the integral values of t and x (top) and the simplex (bottom).

effectively construct $\mathfrak{R}^t_\infty(A)$ up to time $t = n$, as in Proposition 2, by unfolding $\mathfrak{R}^t(A)$ and recovering absolute time t by summing up the weights of the edges along the taken paths. Indeed, since the transitions in A do not rely on t, by taking the quotient of $\mathfrak{R}^t_\infty(A)$ by 'forgetting' the integral part of t, the only loss of information is the time difference in t between the target and source regions, but then this information is regained in the form of weight on the corresponding edge of $\mathfrak{R}^t(A)$. Thus, we have the following.

Proposition 4. $\mathfrak{L}(\mathfrak{R}^t(A)) = \mathfrak{L}(\mathfrak{R}^t_\infty(A))$.

5   Eventual Periodicity

In this section we address the main topic of this paper: exploring the time-periodic property of TA. In addition to demonstrating its existence, we show how one can actually compute the parameters of a period.

5.1   Non-Zeno Cycles in $\mathfrak{R}^t(A)$

$\mathfrak{R}^t(A)$ is in the form of a finite connected directed graph with an initial vertex. Every edge of $\mathfrak{R}^t(A)$ corresponds to a feasible transition in A (contained in a run of A). In what follows, a 'path' in $\mathfrak{R}^t(A)$ is a directed path that starts at the initial vertex g_0, unless otherwise stated.

Definition 11 (Duration of a path). *Given a path γ in $\mathfrak{R}^t(A)$, its minimal integral duration, or simply duration, $d(\gamma) \in \mathbb{N}_0$ is the sum of the weights on its edges, where a weight m^* is counted as m.*

Definition 12 ((Non)-Zeno cycle). *A cycle of $\mathfrak{R}^t(A)$ of duration 0 is called a Zeno cycle. Otherwise, it is a non-Zeno cycle.*

A path is called *simple* if no vertex of it repeats itself, and we let D be the maximal duration of a simple path in $\mathfrak{R}^t(A)$.

Lemma 1. *There exists a minimal positive integer $t_{\text{nz}} \leq D + 1$, the non-Zeno threshold time, such that every path γ of $\mathfrak{R}^t(A)$ that is of (minimal) duration t_{nz} or more contains a vertex belonging to some non-Zeno cycle.*

In order to compute t_{nz} we can explore the simple paths of $\mathfrak{R}^t(A)$, say in a breadth-first manner, up to the time t_0 in which each such path either cannot be extended to a path of a larger duration or any extension of it hits a vertex belonging to some non-Zeno cycle. Then $t_{\text{nz}} = t_0 + 1$, which may be much smaller than $D + 1$.

5.2 A Period of $\mathfrak{R}^t(A)$

A set S is *minimal* with respect to some property if for every element $e \in S$ the set $S \setminus \{e\}$ does not satisfy the property.

Definition 13 (Covering set of non-Zeno cycles). *A set C of non-Zeno cycles of $\mathfrak{R}^t(A)$ is called a covering set of non-Zeno cycles if every path γ of $\mathfrak{R}^t(A)$ whose duration $d(\gamma)$ is at least t_{nz} intersects a cycle in C in a common vertex.*

Without loss of generality, we may assume that a covering set of non-Zeno cycles is minimal.

Definition 14 (Period of $\mathfrak{R}^t(A)$). *A time period (or just period) L of $\mathfrak{R}^t(A)$ is a common multiple of the set of durations $d(\pi)$, $\pi \in C$, for some fixed (minimal) covering set of non-Zeno cycles C. For convenience, we also set L to be greater than M, unless $\mathfrak{R}^t(A)$ does not contain non-Zeno cycles, in which case we define L to be 0.*

5.3 Eventual Periodicity of $\mathfrak{R}^t_\infty(A)$

Let t_{nz}, C, L be as above, with C fixed. We denote by $\mathfrak{R}^t_\infty(A)|_{t \geq n}$ the subgraph of $\mathfrak{R}^t_\infty(A)$ that starts at time-level n, that is, the set of vertices of $\mathfrak{R}^t_\infty(A)$ with absolute time $t \geq n$ and their out-going edges.

Definition 15 (L-shift in time). *Given a subgraph G of $\mathfrak{R}_\infty^t(A)$, an L-shift in time of G, denoted $G + L$, is the graph obtained by adding the value L to each value of the integral part of the clock t in G and leaving the rest of the data unaltered. We also denote by $V(G) + L$ the L-shift in time for the set of vertices of G, with $v + L$ in case $V = \{v\}$.*

Lemma 2. *If $\mathfrak{R}_\infty^t(A)$ is not bounded in time then*

$$\mathfrak{R}_\infty^t(A)|_{t \geq t_{nz}} + L \subseteq \mathfrak{R}_\infty^t(A)|_{t \geq t_{nz}+L}.$$

Proof. First we show that the inclusion holds for the set of vertices of the above subgraphs. Let γ be a path of $\mathfrak{R}_\infty^t(A)$ which terminates in a vertex $v_1 \in \mathfrak{R}_\infty^t(A)|_{t \geq t_{nz}}$. Let $\gamma' = p(\gamma)$ be the image of γ under the projection to $\mathfrak{R}^t(A)$. If γ contains an edge e_1 whose image $e_1' = p(e_1)$ is labeled by a marked weight m^* then we can replace e_1 by another edge $e_2 \in p^{-1}(e_1')$ whose delay is greater by L than the delay of e_1. So, suppose that e_1 starts in the vertex u_1 and terminates in w_1. Then e_2 starts in u_1 and terminates in the vertex $w_2 = w_1 + L$ and then the path continues as in γ but with an L-shift in time, terminating in the vertex $v_2 = v_1 + L$. Otherwise, no edge of γ' has a marked weight. Since $d(\gamma) \geq t_{nz}$ then by Lemma 1 and the definition of L, γ' contains a vertex v' that belongs to a non-Zeno cycle π and whose duration is a factor of L. Hence, by a 'pumping' argument, we can extend γ' with $L/d(\pi)$ cycles of π that start and end in v' and then reach the vertex $v_2 = v_1 + L$ in the pre-image in $\mathfrak{R}_\infty^t(A)$ of this extended path.

The inclusion of the out-going edges follows from the fact that the out-going edges do not depend on the value of t. □

Let us denote by V_k, $k = 0, 1, 2, \ldots$, the set of vertices

$$V_k = V(\mathfrak{R}_\infty^t(A)|_{t \geq t_{nz}+kL}) \setminus V(\mathfrak{R}_\infty^t(A)|_{t \geq t_{nz}+(k+1)L}).$$

Theorem 1. *If the infinite augmented region automaton $\mathfrak{R}_\infty^t(A)$ is not bounded in time then it is eventually periodic: there exists an integral time $t_{per} > 0$ such that*

$$\mathfrak{R}_\infty^t(A)|_{t \geq t_{per}} + L = \mathfrak{R}_\infty^t(A)|_{t \geq t_{per}+L}.$$

Proof. By Lemma 2, $V_k + L \subseteq V_{k+1}$, for $k \geq 0$. But there is a bound on the number of possible vertices of V_k since t is bounded, hence the sequence V_k eventually stabilizes. The result then follows since for the out-going edges the same argument given in the proof of Lemma 2 holds also here. □

When $\mathfrak{R}_\infty^t(A)$ is finite then we can set t_{per} to be $t_{max} + 1$, where t_{max} is the maximal integral time of $\mathfrak{R}_\infty^t(A)$. By the following proposition, a possible value for t_{per} can be effectively computed when $\mathfrak{R}_\infty^t(A)$ is infinite.

Proposition 5. *if $|V_k| = |V_{k+1}| = |V_{k+2}|$ for some k then we can set $t_{per} = t_{nz} + kL$.*

As is known, a TA may be totally non-periodic in the sense that no single timed trace of it is eventually periodic (see Example 1). However, a special kind of periodicity, which we call *suffix-periodicity*, holds between different timed traces, as shown in the following theorem.

Theorem 2. *If $A \in$ eNTA is not bounded in time then its language $\mathcal{L}(A)$ is suffix-periodic: if $t_r > t_{per}$ and*

$$\lambda = (t_1, a_1), \ldots, (t_{r-1}, a_{r-1}), (t_r, a_r), (t_{r+1}, a_{r+1}), \ldots, (t_{r+m}, a_{r+m})$$

is an observable timed trace of $\mathcal{L}(A)$ then, for each $k \in L\mathbb{Z}$, if $t_r + k > t_{per}$ then there exists an observable timed trace $\lambda' \in \mathcal{L}(A)$ such that

$$\lambda' = (t_1', a_1'), \ldots, (t_s', a_s'), (t_r + k, a_r), (t_{r+1} + k, a_{r+1}), \ldots, (t_{r+m} + k, a_{r+m}).$$

6   Periodic Augmented Region Automaton

After revealing the periodic structure of $\mathfrak{R}_\infty^t(A)$, it is natural to fold it into a finite graph according to this period, which we call *periodic augmented region automaton* and denote by $\mathfrak{R}_{per}^t(A)$. The construction of $\mathfrak{R}_{per}^t(A)$ is done by first taking the subgraph of $\mathfrak{R}_\infty^t(A)$ of time $t < t_{per} + L$ and then folding the infinite subgraph of $\mathfrak{R}_\infty^t(A)$ of time $t \geq t_{per} + L$ onto the subgraph of time $t_{per} \leq t < t_{per} + L$, which becomes the periodic subgraph, as explained below. For an edge e, we denote by $\iota(e)$ and $\tau(e)$ the initial, resp. terminal, vertex of e.

Definition 16 (Periodic augmented region automaton). *Given an infinite augmented region automaton $\mathfrak{R}_\infty^t(A)$ with period L and periodicity starting time t_{per}, a finite projection $p(\mathfrak{R}_\infty^t(A))$ of it, called periodic augmented region automaton and denoted $\mathfrak{R}_{per}^t(A)$, is a tuple $(V, v_0, E, \Sigma_\epsilon, B)$, where:*

1. *V is the set of vertices, with $v_0 = (q_0, \mathbf{0}, \mathbf{0})$ the initial vertex. For each $v \in \mathfrak{R}_{per}^t(A)$, if $u \in p^{-1}(v) \subseteq \mathfrak{R}_\infty^t(A)$ then u equals v in all fields, except possibly for the integral part of t. If $v.\lfloor t \rfloor < t_{per}$ then $u = v$ and v is a regular vertex. Otherwise, v is a periodic vertex, $v.\lfloor t \rfloor$ is written as $n + L\mathbb{N}_0$, for some $t_{per} \leq n < t_{per} + L$, $p^{-1}(v)$ is infinite and $\{u.\lfloor t \rfloor \mid p(u) = v\} = \{n + kL \mid k = 0, 1, 2, \ldots\}$.*

2. *E is the set of edges, which are the projected edges of $\mathfrak{R}_\infty^t(A)$ under the map p. Each edge joining two vertices of $\mathfrak{R}_\infty^t(A)$ is mapped to an edge with the same action label that joins the projected vertices. Some of the edges are marked with a symbol of $B = \{(*), (*+)\}$. The description below is technical and refers to the different types of edges that occur when folding $\mathfrak{R}_\infty^t(A)$: whether the source of the edge is a regular ($\mathbf{R}$) or a periodic ($\mathbf{P}$) vertex (in the latter case the preimage in $\mathfrak{R}_\infty^t(A)$ contains infinitely-many edges, one from each of the preimage vertices), whether it is unmarked ($\mathbf{U}$) or marked ($\mathbf{M}$) (in the latter case there are infinitely-many edges starting from each of the vertices in the preimage source vertices), and finally the plus sign ($+$) represents the case where in the preimage the target vertices are not of value n but $n + L$.*

- **UR:** (unmarked, regular) If $e \in \mathfrak{R}^t_{\text{per}}(A)$ is unmarked and $\iota(e)$ is regular then $\iota(e).\lfloor t \rfloor = n_1 < t_{\text{per}}$, $\tau(e).\lfloor t \rfloor = n_2$ or $\tau(e).\lfloor t \rfloor = n_2 + L\mathbb{N}_0$ and $p^{-1}(e) = \{e'\}$, with $\iota(e').\lfloor t \rfloor = n_1$ and $\tau(e').\lfloor t \rfloor = n_2$.
- **UP:** (unmarked, periodic) If $e \in \mathfrak{R}^t_{\text{per}}(A)$ is unmarked and $\iota(e)$ is periodic then $\iota(e).\lfloor t \rfloor = n_1 + L\mathbb{N}_0$, $\tau(e).\lfloor t \rfloor = n_2 + L\mathbb{N}_0$, $t_{\text{per}} \le n_1, n_2 < t_{\text{per}} + L$ and the preimage of e in $\mathfrak{R}^t_\infty(A)$ are the infinitely-many edges satisfying the following. If $n_1 \le n_2$ then $p^{-1}(e) = \{e' \,|\, \iota(e').\lfloor t \rfloor = n_1 + kL, \tau(e').\lfloor t \rfloor = n_2 + kL, k = 0, 1, 2, \ldots\}$, and if $n_1 > n_2$ then $p^{-1}(e) = \{e' \,|\, \iota(e').\lfloor t \rfloor = n_1 + kL, \tau(e').\lfloor t \rfloor = n_2 + (k+1)L, k = 0, 1, 2, \ldots\}$.
- **MR:** (marked, regular) If $e \in \mathfrak{R}^t_{\text{per}}(A)$ is marked with '$(*)$' and $\iota(e)$ is regular, with $\iota(e).\lfloor t \rfloor = n_1$ and $\tau(e).\lfloor t \rfloor = n_2$ or $n_2 + L\mathbb{N}_0$, then $p^{-1}(e) = \{e' \,|\, \iota(e').\lfloor t \rfloor = n_1, \tau(e').\lfloor t \rfloor = n_2 + kL, k = 0, 1, 2, \ldots\}$, that is, infinitely-many edges starting from the same vertex.
- **MP:** (marked, periodic) If $e \in \mathfrak{R}^t_{\text{per}}(A)$ is marked with '$(*)$' and $\iota(e)$ is periodic, with $\iota(e).\lfloor t \rfloor = n_1 + L\mathbb{N}_0$ and $\tau(e).\lfloor t \rfloor = n_2 + L\mathbb{N}_0$, then its preimage in $\mathfrak{R}^t_\infty(A)$ contains all the edges according to both rules **UP** and **MR**.
- **MP+:** (marked, periodic, shifted) If $e \in \mathfrak{R}^t_{\text{per}}(A)$ is marked with '$(*+)$' then the same rules that apply to an edge marked with '$(*)$' hold, except that the target vertices are of L-shift in time compared to those of an edge marked with '$(*)$'.

3. $\Sigma_\epsilon = \Sigma \cup \{\epsilon\}$ is the finite set of actions.

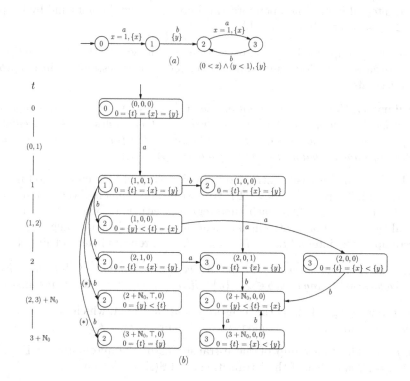

Fig. 2. (a) $A \in \text{TA}$; (b) $\mathfrak{R}^t_{\text{per}}(A)$, a periodic augmented region automaton of A

We remark that instead of periodic time interval of type $[a, b)$ we can define it analogously to be of type $(a, b]$ as in Fig. 1(d), where the periodic time is $(0, 1]$.

Example 1. The TA shown in Fig. 2(a) is taken from [1], where it demonstrates non-periodicity: the time difference between an a-transition and the following b-transition is strictly decreasing along a run. $\mathfrak{R}^t_{\text{per}}(A)$, however, becomes periodic (Fig. 2(b)).

Proposition 6. $\mathfrak{R}^t_{\text{per}}(A)$ *is well-defined and as informative as* $\mathfrak{R}^t_{\infty}(A)$.

7   The Timestamp

Theorem 3. *The timestamp of a TA A is a union of action-labeled integral points and open unit intervals with integral end-points. It is either finite or forms an eventually periodic (with respect to time t) subset of $\mathbb{R}_{\geq 0} \times \Sigma$ and is effectively computable.*

Proof. By Theorem 2, if the timestamp is not finite then it becomes periodic, with period L, after time $t = t_{\text{per}}$. Thus, if it can effectively be computed up to time $t_{\text{per}} + L$, then in order to find whether there is an observable transition with action a at time $t_{\text{per}} + L + t$ one only needs to check the timestamp at time $t_{\text{per}} + (t \mod L)$.

   By Proposition 1, the timestamp up to time $t_{\text{per}} + L$ is a finite number of labeled integral points and open intervals between integral points and by Proposition 2, it is effectively computable.   □

   The timestamp of a TA is an abstraction of its language. However, the timestamp is eventually periodic and computable, hence the timestamp inclusion problem is decidable.

Corollary 1. *Given two timed automata $A, B \in$ eNTA over the same alphabet (action labels), the question of non-inclusion of their timestamps is decidable, thus providing a decidable sufficient condition for the (in general, undecidable) question of non-inclusion of their languages: $\mathcal{L}(A) \not\subseteq \mathcal{L}(B)$.*

   The timestamp is easily extracted from $\mathfrak{R}^t_{\text{per}}$ (in fact, it is enough to take the subgraph of $\mathfrak{R}^t_{\infty}$ up to level $t_{\text{per}} + L$). We just form the union of the time-regions up to level $t_{\text{per}} + L$, where each time-region is either a point $\{n\}$ or an open interval $(n, n + 1)$, along with the labels of the actions of the in-going edges. The timestamp in the interval $t_{\text{per}} \leq t < t_{\text{per}} + L$ then repeats itself indefinitely.

Definition 17. *For each $a \in \Sigma$, let A_a be the restriction of A to a-actions, obtained by substituting each $b \in \Sigma \setminus \{a\}$ with ϵ, representing the silent transition.*

Thus, the language of A_a is the 'censored' language of A, which is the outcome of deleting from each word (timed trace) all pairs (b, t), $b \neq a$.

Example 2. The timestamp of the a-transitions of the automaton of Fig. 2 is $\mathbf{TS}(A_a) = \mathbb{N}$, and that of the b-transitions is $\mathbf{TS}(A_b) = [1, \infty)$.

7.1   Timestamp Automaton

Given a TA A, one can effectively construct a deterministic TA $\tilde{A}$, called a *timestamp automaton* of A with the same timestamp as that of A.

Definition 18 (Timestamp automaton). *Given a timed automaton $A \in$ eNTA, a timestamp automaton $\tilde{A}$ is a deterministic (finite) timed automaton with a single clock and with timestamp identical to that of A. It is the union of the timestamp automata $\tilde{A}_a$, $a \in \Sigma$, having a common initial vertex. Each $\tilde{A}_a$ is in the shape of a linear graph and possibly ending in a simple loop.*

Theorem 4. *Given a timed automaton $A \in$ eNTA, one can effectively construct a timestamp automaton $\tilde{A}$.*

Example 3. Let A be a TA with timestamp

$$\mathbf{TS}(A_a) = (1,3] \cup \{5\} \cup (6 + ([0,2) \cup \{3\} \cup (8,18)) + 21\mathbb{N}_0) \times \{a\},$$
$$\mathbf{TS}(A_b) = [0,1] \cup (2,4) \cup \{5\} \cup (6 + ((0,1) \cup (1,2) \cup (5,6) \cup (8,9)) + 10\mathbb{N}_0) \times \{b\},$$
$$\mathbf{TS}(A_c) = [1,4] \cup \{6\} \cup (10,\infty) \times \{c\}.$$

Then a possible timestamp automaton of A is given in Fig. 3.

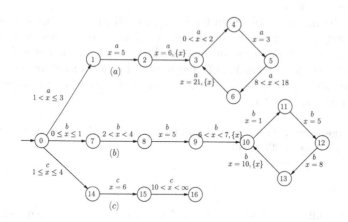

Fig. 3. Timestamp automata of (a) $\mathbf{TS}(A_a)$; (b) $\mathbf{TS}(A_b)$; (c) $\mathbf{TS}(A_c)$

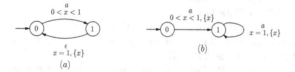

Fig. 4. (a) A non-determinizable $A \in$ eNTA; (b) A timestamp automaton $\tilde{A}$

Example 4. The language of the TA $A \in$ eNTA of Fig. 4(a) is

$$\mathcal{L}(A) = \{(t_0, a), (t_1, a), \ldots, (t_n, a) \mid i < t_i < i + 1, i = 0, \ldots, n - 1, n \in \mathbb{N}_0\}$$

(supposing all locations are 'accepting'). The timestamp of A is the set of all positive non-integral reals: $\mathbf{TS}(A) = \mathbb{R}_{\geq 0} \setminus \mathbb{N}_0$. A is not determinizable. Each transition occurs between the next pair of successive natural numbers. The guard of each such transition must refer to a clock which was reset on some previous integral time. But since all transitions occur on non-integral time, the only clock that can be referred to is a clock x that is reset at time 0 and hence the transition guards need to be of the form $n < x < n + 1$ for each $n \in \mathbb{N}_0$, which makes the automaton infinite. Nevertheless, the timestamp automaton associated with A, seen in Fig. 4(b), is deterministic.

8 Conclusion and Future Research

The timestamp of a non-deterministic timed automaton with silent transitions (eNTA) consists of the set of all action-labeled times at which locations can be reached by observable transitions. The problem of computing the timestamp is a generalization of the basic reachability problem, a fundamental problem in model checking, thus being of interest from the theoretical as well as from the practical point of view. In this paper we showed that the timestamp can be effectively computed, also when the timed automata are non-deterministic and include silent transitions.

One of the major problems in testing and verification of abstract models of real-time systems is the inclusion of the language of one timed automaton in the language of another timed automaton. This problem is, in general, undecidable. Thus, since (non)-inclusion of timestamps of timed automata is a decidable problem, we have a tool which provides a sufficient condition for language non-inclusion in timed automata.

Acknowledgements. This research was partly supported by the Austrian Science Fund (FWF) Project P29355-N35.

References

1. Alur, R., Dill, D.L.: A theory of timed automata. Theor. Comput. Sci. **126**(2), 183–235 (1994). https://doi.org/10.1016/0304-3975(94)90010-8
2. Alur, R., Fix, L., Henzinger, T.A.: Event-clock automata: a determinizable class of timed automata. Theor. Comput. Sci. **211**(1–2), 253–273 (1999). https://doi.org/10.1016/S0304-3975(97)00173-4
3. Alur, R., Kurshan, R.P., Viswanathan, M.: Membership questions for timed and hybrid automata. In: Real-Time Systems Symposium, pp. 254–263 (1998). https://doi.org/10.1109/REAL.1998.739751
4. Alur, R., Madhusudan, P.: Decision problems for timed automata: a survey. In: Bernardo, M., Corradini, F. (eds.) SFM-RT 2004. LNCS, vol. 3185, pp. 1–24. Springer, Heidelberg (2004). https://doi.org/10.1007/978-3-540-30080-9_1

5. Asarin, E., Maler, O.: As soon as possible: time optimal control for timed automata. In: Vaandrager, F.W., van Schuppen, J.H. (eds.) HSCC 1999. LNCS, vol. 1569, pp. 19–30. Springer, Heidelberg (1999). https://doi.org/10.1007/3-540-48983-5_6

6. Baier, C., Bertrand, N., Bouyer, P., Brihaye, T.: When are timed automata determinizable? In: ICALP (2), pp. 43–54 (2009). https://doi.org/10.1007/978-3-642-02930-1_4

7. Beauquier, D.: Pumping lemmas for timed automata. In: Nivat, M. (ed.) FoSSaCS 1998. LNCS, vol. 1378, pp. 81–94. Springer, Heidelberg (1998). https://doi.org/10.1007/BFb0053543

8. Bérard, B., Petit, A., Diekert, V., Gastin, P.: Characterization of the expressive power of silent transitions in timed automata. Fundam. Inform. **36**(2–3), 145–182 (1998). https://doi.org/10.3233/FI-1998-36233

9. Bouyer, P., Dufourd, C., Fleury, E., Petit, A.: Updatable timed automata. Theor. Comput. Sci. **321**(2–3), 291–345 (2004). https://doi.org/10.1016/j.tcs.2004.04.003

10. Bozga, M., Daws, C., Maler, O., Olivero, A., Tripakis, S., Yovine, S.: Kronos: a model-checking tool for real-time systems. In: Hu, A.J., Vardi, M.Y. (eds.) CAV 1998. LNCS, vol. 1427, pp. 546–550. Springer, Heidelberg (1998). https://doi.org/10.1007/BFb0028779

11. Chen, T., Han, T., Katoen, J., Mereacre, A.: Reachability probabilities in Markovian timed automata. In: CDC-ECC, pp. 7075–7080 (2011). https://doi.org/10.1109/CDC.2011.6160992

12. Choffrut, C., Goldwurm, M.: Timed automata with periodic clock constraints. J. Autom. Lang. Comb. **5**(4), 371–403 (2000). https://doi.org/10.25596/jalc-2000-371

13. Comon, H., Jurski, Y.: Timed automata and the theory of real numbers. In: Baeten, J.C.M., Mauw, S. (eds.) CONCUR 1999. LNCS, vol. 1664, pp. 242–257. Springer, Heidelberg (1999). https://doi.org/10.1007/3-540-48320-9_18

14. Courcoubetis, C., Yannakakis, M.: Minimum and maximum delay problems in real-time systems. Form. Methods Syst. Des. **1**(4), 385–415 (1992). https://doi.org/10.1007/BF00709157

15. Daws, C., Tripakis, S.: Model checking of real-time reachability properties using abstractions. In: Steffen, B. (ed.) TACAS 1998. LNCS, vol. 1384, pp. 313–329. Springer, Heidelberg (1998). https://doi.org/10.1007/BFb0054180

16. Finkel, O.: Undecidable problems about timed automata. In: Asarin, E., Bouyer, P. (eds.) FORMATS 2006. LNCS, vol. 4202, pp. 187–199. Springer, Heidelberg (2006). https://doi.org/10.1007/11867340_14

17. Haase, C., Ouaknine, J., Worrell, J.: On the relationship between reachability problems in timed and counter automata. In: Finkel, A., Leroux, J., Potapov, I. (eds.) RP 2012. LNCS, vol. 7550, pp. 54–65. Springer, Heidelberg (2012). https://doi.org/10.1007/978-3-642-33512-9_6

18. Henzinger, T.A., Prabhu, V.S.: Timed alternating-time temporal logic. In: Asarin, E., Bouyer, P. (eds.) FORMATS 2006. LNCS, vol. 4202, pp. 1–17. Springer, Heidelberg (2006). https://doi.org/10.1007/11867340_1

19. Kwiatkowska, M., Norman, G., Parker, D.: PRISM 4.0: verification of probabilistic real-time systems. In: Gopalakrishnan, G., Qadeer, S. (eds.) CAV 2011. LNCS, vol. 6806, pp. 585–591. Springer, Heidelberg (2011). https://doi.org/10.1007/978-3-642-22110-1_47

20. Larsen, K.G., Pettersson, P., Yi, W.: Uppaal in a nutshell. STTT **1**(1–2), 134–152 (1997). https://doi.org/10.1007/s100090050010

21. Lorber, F., Rosenmann, A., Nickovic, D., Aichernig, B.K.: Bounded determinization of timed automata with silent transitions. Real Time Syst. **53**(3), 291326 (2017). https://doi.org/10.1007/s11241-017-9271-x

22. Ouaknine, J., Rabinovich, A., Worrell, J.: Time-bounded verification. In: Bravetti, M., Zavattaro, G. (eds.) CONCUR 2009. LNCS, vol. 5710, pp. 496–510. Springer, Heidelberg (2009). https://doi.org/10.1007/978-3-642-04081-8_33

23. Ouaknine, J., Worrell, J.: On the language inclusion problem for timed automata: closing a decidability gap. In: LICS, pp. 54–63 (2004). https://doi.org/10.1109/LICS.2004.1319600

24. Ouaknine, J., Worrell, J.: Towards a theory of time-bounded verification. In: ICALP (2), pp. 22–37 (2010). https://doi.org/10.1007/978-3-642-14162-1_3

25. Rosenmann, A.: The timestamp of timed automata. arXiv abs/1412.5669v4 (2019). http://arxiv.org/abs/1412.5669

26. Tripakis, S., Yovine, S.: Analysis of timed systems using time-abstracting bisimulations. Form. Methods Syst. Des. **18**(1), 25–68 (2001). https://doi.org/10.1023/A:1008734703554

27. Wang, F.: Efficient verification of timed automata with BDD-like data structures. STTT **6**(1), 77–97 (2004). https://doi.org/10.1007/s10009-003-0135-4

28. Wozna, B., Zbrzezny, A., Penczek, W.: Checking reachability properties for timed automata via SAT. Fundam. Inform. **55**(2), 223–241 (2003)

On the Distance Between Timed Automata

Amnon Rosenmann$^{(\boxtimes)}$ (iD)

Graz University of Technology, Steyrergasse 30, 8010 Graz, Austria
`rosenmann@math.tugraz.at`

Abstract. Some fundamental problems in the class of non-deterministic timed automata, like the problem of inclusion of the language accepted by timed automaton A (e.g., the implementation) in the language accepted by B (e.g., the specification) are, in general, undecidable. In order to tackle this disturbing problem we show how to effectively construct deterministic timed automata A_d and B_d that are discretizations (digitizations) of the non-deterministic timed automata A and B and differ from the original automata by at most $\frac{1}{6}$ time units on each occurrence of an event. Language inclusion in the discretized timed automata is decidable and it is also decidable when instead of $\mathcal{L}(B)$ we consider $\overline{\mathcal{L}(B)}$, the closure of $\mathcal{L}(B)$ in the Euclidean topology: if $\mathcal{L}(A_d) \not\subseteq \mathcal{L}(B_d)$ then $\mathcal{L}(A) \not\subseteq \mathcal{L}(B)$ and if $\mathcal{L}(A_d) \subseteq \mathcal{L}(B_d)$ then $\mathcal{L}(A) \subseteq \overline{\mathcal{L}(B)}$.

Moreover, if $\mathcal{L}(A_d) \not\subseteq \mathcal{L}(B_d)$ we would like to know how far away is $\mathcal{L}(A_d)$ from being included in $\mathcal{L}(B_d)$. For that matter we define the distance between the languages of timed automata as the limit on how far away a timed trace of one timed automaton can be from the closest timed trace of the other timed automaton. We then show how one can decide under some restriction whether the distance between two timed automata is finite or infinite.

Keywords: Timed automata ·
Language inclusion in timed automata ·
Distance between timed automata

1 Introduction

Timed automaton (TA) was introduced by Alur and Dill [1] as an abstract model for real-time systems by extending finite automaton with continuous clocks. When the TAs are non-deterministic then a fundamental problem of language inclusion is, in general, undecidable, for example, whether the set of timed traces of the TA representing the implementation is included in that of the specification. This lead to imposing restrictions on and modifications to non-deterministic TAs in order to achieve decidability (see [2,4–7,12,14,16,17] for a partial list). Another approach was to allow robustness in the language [10] or perturbations in the clocks [3] (see also [8]). The problem is that by allowing a

© Springer Nature Switzerland AG 2019
É. André and M. Stoelinga (Eds.): FORMATS 2019, LNCS 11750, pp. 199–215, 2019.
https://doi.org/10.1007/978-3-030-29662-9_12

fixed imprecision, undecidability problems due to working over continuous time do not vanish.

Digitization of timed systems, where basic decision problems like language inclusion are decidable, was considered, for example, in [11,13,15]. But, as stated in [15], the implementation should be 'closed under digitization' and the specification should be 'closed under inverse digitization' in order to be able to reduce the language inclusion problem from the continuous world to the discretized one. In [19] the authors construct TAs with reset only on integral time and demonstrate the decidability of the language inclusion problem $\mathfrak{L}(A) \subseteq \mathfrak{L}(B)$ in case B is an integer reset TA. In this paper we go further with this approach. The idea is to work in the setting of discretized time, but without restricting or modifying the definition of a TA. The discretization is over intervals which are smaller than 1 time unit so that although we work in the discretized setting we are able to check for exact occurrence of events also outside integral time. For this matter we construct discretized TAs that enable effective comparison of the languages of the original TAs. The discretized TA stays within a distance of $\frac{1}{6}$ time units from the original TA (the distance can, in fact, be as small as we like, in the cost of complexity, but that won't improve our knowledge about the inclusion of the languages of the original automata), a goal that is achieved through the introduction of an additional clock, t, that measures absolute time. Now, instead of comparing directly the language of two TAs, a problem which is in general undecidable, we can compare their discretized TAs and have the following (see Theorem 3): if $\mathfrak{L}(A_d)$, the language of the discretized TA of A, is not included in $\mathfrak{L}(B_d)$, the language of the discretized TA of B, then the same holds for $\mathfrak{L}(A)$ with respect to $\mathfrak{L}(B)$. If, however, $\mathfrak{L}(A_d) \subseteq \mathfrak{L}(B_d)$ then $\mathfrak{L}(A)$ is included in the topological closure of $\mathfrak{L}(B)$.

The next natural question, in case $\mathfrak{L}(A) \not\subseteq \mathfrak{L}(B)$, is how far away is a timed trace of $\mathfrak{L}(A)$ from all timed traces of $\mathfrak{L}(B)$, that is, what is the conformance distance $c(\mathfrak{L}(A), \mathfrak{L}(B))$, the distance of $\mathfrak{L}(A)$ from being conformed with $\mathfrak{L}(B)$). When an untimed word of $\mathfrak{L}(A)$ is not in $\mathfrak{L}(B)$ or when a transition in A which is not bound in time is not met with a similar transition in $\mathfrak{L}(B)$ of the same action label then $c(\mathfrak{L}(A), \mathfrak{L}(B)) = \infty$ and the existence of these cases is decidable. A more challenging question is whether there is a sequence of timed traces of $\mathfrak{L}(A)$ which tend to diverge from $\mathfrak{L}(B)$, causing $c(\mathfrak{L}(A), \mathfrak{L}(B)) = \infty$. For example, it may happen that due to imprecisions or delays in a real system, a TA model is changed to allow wider time intervals around actions compared to the more idealistic previous model. It is then necessary to check whether or not this extended freedom is controlled and the distance between the two TAs stays within a reasonable bound (see [8] regarding an ideal model versus a realistic model). Moreover, an algorithm based on the approach suggested here may find the timed traces that deviate from the allowed distance between two timed languages. Further applications for computing the distance may be when safety properties include time restrictions for specific set of timed traces, given as timed automata, and we want to check these timed traces with respect to the implementation model. In general, in a design of a computerized system, e.g. a network, that contains timing changes, a relaxed equivalence verification may allow bounded perturbations in time that needed to be checked.

Computing the distance between TAs (or their languages), even between discretized TAs, may be quite complex. Here we concentrate on the problem of deciding whether the distance is infinite. It is not clear to us whether this problem is decidable in general, but for a (perhaps) restricted version of it we construct an algorithm that solves it.

2   Timed Automaton

A timed automaton is an abstract model of temporal behavior of real-time systems. It is a finite automaton with *locations* and *transitions* between them, extended with a finite set of (continuous) clocks defined over $\mathbb{R}_{\geq 0}$. A transition at time t can occur only if the condition expressed as a *transition guard* is satisfied at t. A transition guard is a conjunction of constraints of the form $c \sim n$, where c is a clock, $\sim \in \{<, \leq, =, \geq, >\}$ and $n \in \mathbb{N}_0 = \mathbb{N} \cup \{0\}$. Each transition is labeled by some *action* $a \in \Sigma$ and some of the clocks may be reset to zero. In NTA, the class of non-deterministic timed automata, and unlike deterministic TAs, it may occur that two transitions from the same location q can be taken at the same time and with the same action but to two different locations q' and q''.

Definition 1 (Timed automaton). *A non-deterministic timed automaton $A \in \text{NTA}$ is a tuple $(\mathcal{Q}, q_0, \mathcal{F}, \Sigma, \mathcal{C}, \mathcal{T})$, where:*

1. *$\mathcal{Q}$ is a finite set of locations and $q_0 \in \mathcal{Q}$ is the initial location;*
2. *$\mathcal{F} \subseteq \mathcal{Q}$ is the set of accepting locations;*
3. *Σ is a finite set of transition labels, called actions;*
4. *$\mathcal{C}$ is a finite set of clock variables;*
5. *$\mathcal{T} \subseteq \mathcal{Q} \times \Sigma \times \mathcal{G} \times \mathcal{P}(\mathcal{C}) \times \mathcal{Q}$ is a finite set of transitions of the form $(q, a, g, \mathcal{C}_{rst}, q')$, where:*
   - *(a) $q, q' \in \mathcal{Q}$ are the source and the target locations respectively;*
   - *(b) $a \in \Sigma$ is the transition action;*
   - *(c) $g \in \mathcal{G}$ is the transition guard;*
   - *(d) $\mathcal{C}_{rst} \subseteq \mathcal{C}$ is the subset of clocks to be reset.*

A clock *valuation* $v(c)$ is a function $v : \mathcal{C} \to \mathbb{R}_{\geq 0}$. We denote by $\mathcal{V}$ the set of all clock valuations and by $\mathbf{d}$ the valuation which assigns the value d to every clock. Given a valuation v and $d \in \mathbb{R}_{\geq 0}$, we define $v + d$ to be the valuation $(v + d)(c) := v(c) + d$ for every $c \in \mathcal{C}$. The valuation $v[\mathcal{C}_{rst}]$, $\mathcal{C}_{rst} \subseteq \mathcal{C}$, is defined to be $v[\mathcal{C}_{rst}](c) = 0$ for $c \in \mathcal{C}_{rst}$ and $v[\mathcal{C}_{rst}](c) = v(c)$ for $c \notin \mathcal{C}_{rst}$.

The *semantics* of $A \in \text{NTA}$ is given by the *timed transition system* $[[A]] = (S, s_0, \mathbb{R}_{\geq 0}, \Sigma, T)$, where:

1. $S = \{(q, v) \in \mathcal{Q} \times \mathcal{V}\}$ is the set of states, with $s_0 = (q_0, \mathbf{0})$ the initial state;
2. $T \subseteq S \times (\Sigma \cup \mathbb{R}_{\geq 0}) \times S$ is the transition relation. The set T consists of
   - (a) *Timed transitions (delays):* $(q, v) \xrightarrow{d} (q, v + d)$, where $d \in \mathbb{R}_{\geq 0}$;

(b) *Discrete transitions (jumps):* $(q, v) \xrightarrow{a} (q', v')$, where $a \in \Sigma$ and there exists a transition $(q, a, g, \mathcal{C}_{rst}, q')$ in $\mathcal{T}$, such that the valuation v satisfies the guard g and $v' = v[\mathcal{C}_{rst}]$.

A (finite) *run* ϱ on $A \in$ eNTA is a sequence of alternating timed and discrete transitions of the form

$$(q_0, \mathbf{0}) \xrightarrow{d_1} (q_0, \mathbf{d_1}) \xrightarrow{a_1} (q_1, v_1) \xrightarrow{d_2} \cdots \xrightarrow{d_k} (q_{k-1}, v_{k-1} + d_k) \xrightarrow{a_k} (q_k, v_k).$$

The run ϱ on A induces the *timed trace* (*timed word*)

$$\tau = (t_1, a_1), (t_2, a_2), \ldots, (t_k, a_k),$$

with $a_i \in \Sigma$ and $t_i = \Sigma_{j=1}^{i} d_i$. The language $\mathfrak{L}(A)$ consists of the set of timed traces that are obtained from the runs that end in accepting locations. We remark that for simplification of presentation we did not include the location invariants in the definition of timed automata since they are more of a 'syntactic sugar': the invariants of location q are composed of upper bounds to the values of the clocks while being in q, but these constraints can be incorporated in the transition guards to q (for the clocks that are not reset at the transitions) and in those transitions that emerge from q, thus not affecting $\mathfrak{L}(A)$.

3   Augmented Region Automaton

Given a (finite) timed automaton A, the region automaton $\mathfrak{R}(A)$ [1] is a finite *discretized* version of A, such that time is abstracted and both automata define the same untimed language. Instead of looking at the clocks-space as a continuous space it is partitioned into regions. Suppose that the maximal integer appearing in the transition guards of A is M, then we denote by $\top$ a value of a clock which is greater than M. The regions partition the space of clock valuations into equivalent classes, where two valuations belong to the same equivalent class if and only if they agree on the clocks with $\top$ value and on the integral parts and the order among the fractional parts of the other clocks. The edges of $\mathfrak{R}(A)$ are labeled by the transition actions and they correspond to the actual transitions that occur in the runs on A.

The *augmented region automaton*, denoted $\mathfrak{R}^t(A)$, is defined as in [18]. First, we add to A a clock t that measures absolute time, is never reset to 0 and does not affect the runs and timed traced of A. Secondly, we want to construct $\mathfrak{R}^t(A)$ in a way that keeps track of absolute time and regain much of the information that is lost when passing from the timed automaton A to the regular region automaton $\mathfrak{R}(A)$. But since t does not appear in the transition guards of A, we need not know the exact value of the integral part of t but just how much time passes between two consecutive transitions. Thus, we assign t in $\mathfrak{R}^t(A)$ only two time-regions: $\{0\}$ and $(0, 1)$. However, in order to keep track of the absolute time that passes, each edge is assigned a 'weight', the time difference in the integral part of t between the target and the source regions. The ordering among the fractional part of the clocks does, however, take that of t into account. Overall, the number of regions of $\mathfrak{R}^t(A)$ is clearly finite (although potentially exponentially large).

Definition 2. *Given a non-deterministic timed automaton $A \in$ NTA with clocks $x_1, \ldots, x_s$ extended with absolute-time clock t, a corresponding (finite) augmented region automaton $\mathfrak{R}^t(A)$ is a tuple $(\mathcal{V}, v_0, \mathcal{E}, \Sigma, \mathcal{W}^*)$, where:*

1. *$\mathcal{V}$ is the set of vertices. Each vertex is a triple $(q, \mathbf{n}, \Delta)$, where q is a location of A and $r = (\mathbf{n}, \Delta)$ is a region, with $\mathbf{n} = (n_1, \ldots, n_s) \in \{0, 1, \ldots, M, \top\}^s$ consisting of the integral parts of the clocks $x_1, \ldots, x_s$ and Δ is the simplex (hyper-triangle) with vertices in the lattice $\mathbb{N}_0^{s+1}$ of all points that satisfy a fixed ordering of the fractional parts of the clocks $t = x_0, x_1, \ldots, x_s$:*

$$0 \preceq_0 \{x_{i_0}\} \preceq_1 \{x_{i_1}\} \preceq_2 \cdots \preceq_s \{x_{i_s}\} < 1, \tag{1}$$

   where $\preceq_i \in \{=, <\}$.
2. *$v_0 = (q_0, \mathbf{0}, \mathbf{0})$ is the initial vertex, where q_0 is the initial location of A and $(\mathbf{0}, \mathbf{0})$ indicates that all clocks have value 0.*
3. *$\mathcal{E}$ is the set of edges. There is an edge $(q, r) \xrightarrow{a} (q', r')$ if and only if there is a run on A containing $(q, v) \xrightarrow{d} (q, v + d) \xrightarrow{a} (q', v')$, such that, the clock valuation v is in the region r and v' is in r'.*
4. *Σ is the finite set of actions.*
5. *$\mathcal{W}^*$ is the set of weights m on the edges calculated as $m = \lfloor t_1 \rfloor - \lfloor t_0 \rfloor \in [0..M]$, where $\lfloor t_1 \rfloor$ ($\lfloor t_0 \rfloor$) is the integral part of t in the target (source) location in a corresponding run on A. There may be more than one edge between two vertices of $\mathfrak{R}^t(A)$, each one with a distinguished weight. A weight m may be marked as m^*, representing infinitely-many consecutive values $m, m+1, m+2, \ldots$ as weights between the same two vertices, for example when the regular clocks passed the maximal value M.*

An augmented region automaton can be seen in Fig. 1(b) (the example is taken from [1]).

4   Discretized Timed Automaton

After constructing the augmented region automaton $\mathfrak{R}^t(A)$, we turn it into a deterministic timed automaton A_d which discretizes (digitizes) A.

Definition 3. *A discretized timed automaton A_d is a timed automaton constructed from the augmented region automaton $\mathfrak{R}^t(A)$ in the following way.*

1. *The directed graph structure of locations and edges of A_d is the same as that of $\mathfrak{R}^t(A)$.*
2. *The transition labels (actions) are also as in $\mathfrak{R}^t(A)$.*
3. *There is a single clock in A_d, namely t, which is reset on each transition.*

4. *The transition guards of A_d are of the following form. Let $e = v_0 \to v_1$ be an edge of $\mathfrak{R}^t(A)$, let $w(e)$ be its weight and let $\{t_0\}, \{t_1\} \in [0, 1)$ be any fractional parts of t in the source and target regions. Let*

$$\delta = \frac{1}{2}(\lceil\{t_1\}\rceil - \lceil\{t_0\}\rceil) \in \{-\frac{1}{2}, 0, \frac{1}{2}\},$$

where $\lceil\{t_i\}\rceil \in \{0, 1\}$ is the ceiling function applied to t_i. Then, we set the transition guard of the corresponding edge of A_d to be

$$t = w(e) + \delta.$$

In case of a weight $w(e) = m^*$ then the transition guard is

$$t \geq m + \delta.$$

A discretized timed automaton can be seen in Fig. 1(c).

We remark that the fact that the transition guards of A_d are over $\frac{1}{2}\mathbb{N}_0$ and not over $\mathbb{N}_0$ need not bother us since the standard definition of timed automata holds also over the rational numbers. Indeed, by letting all clocks run twice as fast and multiplying by 2 all values in the constraints of the transition guards, we end up in an automaton over the integers.

5   The Conformance Distance

We want to define a metric on the set of timed traces in order to define (conformance) distance between timed languages.

Definition 4. *Given a set T of timed traces over the same alphabet Σ, we define the ∞-metric or max-metric d on T in the following way. Given two timed traces*

$$\tau_1 = (t_1^{T_1}, a_1^{T_1}), (t_2^{T_1}, a_2^{T_1}), \ldots, (t_m^{T_1}, a_m^{T_1}),$$
$$\tau_2 = (t_1^{T_2}, a_1^{T_2}), (t_2^{T_2}, a_2^{T_2}), \ldots, (t_n^{T_2}, a_n^{T_2}),$$

the distance between τ_1 and τ_2 is

$$d(\tau_1, \tau_2) = \begin{cases} \infty, & \text{if } m \neq n \text{ or } a_i^{T_1} \neq a_i^{T_2} \text{ for some } i, \\ \max_i |t_i^{T_1} - t_i^{T_2}|, & \text{otherwise.} \end{cases}$$

The above metric over the set of traces induces inclusion relation on timed languages (languages of timed automata).

Definition 5. *Given two timed languages $\mathfrak{L}_1$ and $\mathfrak{L}_2$, $\mathfrak{L}_1$ is ε-included in $\mathfrak{L}_2$, denoted $\mathfrak{L}_1 \subseteq_\varepsilon \mathfrak{L}_2$, if for every timed trace $\tau_1 \in \mathfrak{L}_1$ there exists a timed trace $\tau_2 \in \mathfrak{L}_2$ such that $d(\tau_1, \tau_2) \leq \varepsilon$.*
The conformance distance $c(\mathfrak{L}_1, \mathfrak{L}_2)$ *between $\mathfrak{L}_1$ and $\mathfrak{L}_2$ is*

$$c(\mathfrak{L}_1, \mathfrak{L}_2) = \inf\{\varepsilon : \mathfrak{L}_1 \subseteq_\varepsilon \mathfrak{L}_2\},$$

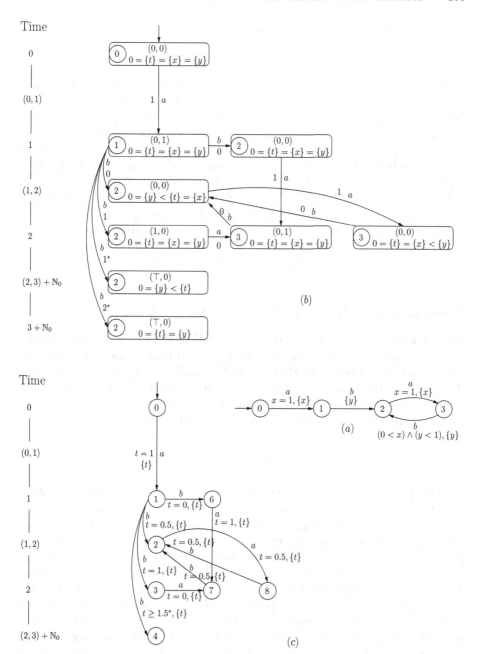

Fig. 1. (a) $A \in$ TA; (b) $\mathfrak{R}^t(A)$, the augmented region automaton of A; (c) A_d, the discretized timed automaton with $\Delta = 0.5$.

that is,

$$c(\mathfrak{L}_1, \mathfrak{L}_2) = \sup_{\tau_1 \in \mathfrak{L}_1} \inf_{\tau_2 \in \mathfrak{L}_2} d(\tau_1, \tau_2) = \sup_{\tau_1 \in \mathfrak{L}_1} d(\tau_1, \mathfrak{L}_2).$$

The distance $d(\mathcal{L}_1, \mathcal{L}_2)$ between $\mathcal{L}_1$ and $\mathcal{L}_2$ is

$$d(\mathcal{L}_1, \mathcal{L}_2) = \max\{c(\mathcal{L}_1, \mathcal{L}_2), c(\mathcal{L}_2, \mathcal{L}_1)\}. \tag{2}$$

In case of a finite conformance distance n that is reached as a limit of a sequence of distances, we can denote it as n^+ (for a limit from above) or as n^- (for a limit from below). Thus, $\mathcal{L}_1 \subseteq \mathcal{L}_2$ if and only if $c(\mathcal{L}_1, \mathcal{L}_2) = 0$. But when $c(\mathcal{L}_1, \mathcal{L}_2) = 0^+$ then $\mathcal{L}_1 \not\subseteq \mathcal{L}_2$ but $\mathcal{L}_1 \subseteq \overline{\mathcal{L}_2}$, where $\overline{\mathcal{L}_2}$ is the closure of $\mathcal{L}_2$ in the Euclidean topology, defined as follows. Fixing an untimed word $w \in \Sigma^*$ of length n, let $\mathcal{L}_2(w)$ be the timed traces in $\mathcal{L}_2$ whose untimed word is w and let $\mathbb{R}_w^n$ be a copy of $\mathbb{R}^n$ indexed by w. There is a natural embedding $\iota : \mathcal{L}_2(w) \to \mathbb{R}_w^n$. Then, $c(\mathcal{L}_1, \mathcal{L}_2) = 0^+$ implies that $\iota(\mathcal{L}_1) \subseteq \overline{\iota(\mathcal{L}_2)}$, where $\iota(\mathcal{L}_j) = \bigcup_{w \in \Sigma^*} \iota(\mathcal{L}_j(w))$, $j = 1, 2$, and $\overline{S}$ is the closure of S in the Euclidean topology.

Subadditivity (triangle inequality) holds for the conformance distance:

$$c(\mathcal{L}_1, \mathcal{L}_3) \leq c(\mathcal{L}_1, \mathcal{L}_2) + c(L_2, L_3).$$

Theorem 1. *Let $A, B \in$ NTA. Then $c(\mathfrak{L}(A), \mathfrak{L}(B)) \in \frac{1}{2}\mathbb{N}_0 \cup \{\infty\}$.*

Proof. Clearly, the conformance distance $c(\mathfrak{L}(A), \mathfrak{L}(B))$ can be ∞, for example, when the untimed language of A contains a word that is not in the untimed language of B. Suppose now that $\delta = c(\mathfrak{L}(A), \mathfrak{L}(B)) < \infty$. It suffices to show the following. Given a path γ^A in A and another path γ^B in B, where both define the same untimed trace (identical sequence of actions), let T^A (T^B) be the set of all timed traces along γ^A (γ^B). We need to show that

$$\sup_{\tau^A \in T^A} \inf_{\tau^B \in T^B} d(\tau^A, \tau^B) \in \frac{1}{2}\mathbb{N}_0. \tag{3}$$

By [18], the timestamp of each of the events along γ^A and γ^B is an interval of the form (m, n), $(m, n]$, $[m, n)$ or $[m, n]$, where $m \leq n$ and $m \in \mathbb{N}_0$, $n \in \mathbb{N}_0 \cup \{\infty\}$. This can be shown by writing equalities and inequalities over the integers and variables z_i, where z_i represents the time of the i-th event along the path. Then (3) becomes an optimization problem over the integers and variables for the events along γ^A as well as for those along γ^B. The solution lies in $\frac{1}{2}\mathbb{N}_0$ because it can be shown that for any other solution the timed traces can be shifted so that we are nearer $\frac{1}{2}\mathbb{N}_0$. In fact, it is quite clear that the solution should be looked for when considering the integral end-points of the event intervals. The solution is, in general, in $\frac{1}{2}\mathbb{N}_0$ and not in $\mathbb{N}_0$ as can be seen from the following example. Suppose that an event of τ^A occurs at time $0 < t < 1$ where the corresponding event in B can occur at time 0 or at time 1. Then, the maximal time difference, namely $\frac{1}{2}$, occurs when we choose the event of τ^A to be at time $t = \frac{1}{2}$. $\square$

By the way they are defined, the untimed runs on the augmented region automaton $\mathfrak{R}^t(A)$, as well as those on the discretized timed automaton A_d, are identical to the untimed runs on A. The runs differ in the exact time on which each event occurs. When the absolute time of occurrence of an event is $t_0 \in \mathbb{N}_0$ then A_d agrees with A. When $t_0 = n + \varepsilon$, $n \in \mathbb{N}_0$, $0 < \varepsilon < 1$ then the time of the event on A_d is set to be $n + \frac{1}{2}$, thus, the time difference is less than $\frac{1}{2}$ time units. The fact that the clock t of A_d is synchronized with the clock t that was added to A to measures absolute time guarantees that the cumulative error does not increase over time but remains bounded by $\frac{1}{2}$. That is, A_d is a $\frac{1}{2}$-time-unit approximation of A: there exits a surjective mapping

$$\pi : \mathcal{L}(A) \twoheadrightarrow \mathcal{L}(A_d), \tag{4}$$

such that if $\pi(\tau) = \tilde{\tau}$ then $d(\tau, \tilde{\tau}) < \frac{1}{2}$. We showed that the following holds.

Theorem 2. $d(\mathcal{L}(A), \mathcal{L}(A_d)) < \frac{1}{2}$.

Since t is reset only on values in $\frac{1}{2}\mathbb{N}_0$ then A_d is determinizable (see [5,19]). In fact, since t is reset at each transition, we can remove it altogether to obtain an action-labeled, weighted directed graph. The determinization algorithm is then straightforward by searching the graph in a breadth-first manner, unifying edges of the same source location that agree on their labels: (a, t), a - action, t -time, followed by unifying the target locations. The number of vertices, however, may grow exponentially.

6   Computing the Conformance Distance

Since A_d is determinizable, we can gain information about the relation between the languages of two timed automata by comparing their discretized languages.

Note that by the way the distance between languages is defined, it is clear that it refers to languages which are supposed to be (almost) identical or that one language is assumed to be (almost) included in the other, but this is normally the case in equivalence verification or when comparing the implication language with its specification. Note that even if the untimed languages of two TAs are identical, it is enough that there exists a cycle, in which the timed languages do not agree, then by repeatedly taking this cycle the distance between the timed traces of the two TAs may grow indefinitely, resulting in a distance of ∞, and it is of interest to be able to recognize when this phenomenon occurs. Thus, it seems that since the distance between A and its discretized timed automaton A_d is only $\frac{1}{2}$ time units, we may not lose much by comparing A_d instead of A with another TA. In fact, in order to be more precise in the computation of the distance between two languages we need to make the basic discretization interval, denoted Δ, shorter than $\frac{1}{2}$ time units. By setting $\Delta = \frac{1}{n}$ we get that $d(\mathcal{L}(A), \mathcal{L}(A_d)) < \frac{1}{n}$, thus we can make $\mathcal{L}(A)$ and $\mathcal{L}(A_d$ as close to one another as we like (of course, in the expense of complexity). However, it turns out that it suffices to choose $\Delta = \frac{1}{6}$ in order to get the maximal precision about $d(\mathcal{L}(A), \mathcal{L}(B))$.

For our convenience, since we prefer not to work with small fractions we accelerate the clocks to run at triple speed. That is, from now on, given the timed automata A and B under test, we first multiply by 3 all the numbers that appear in the transition guards, so they all belong to $3\mathbb{N}_0$. Then we proceed as before: we construct the region automata with respect to basic regions of size 1 time unit and the discretized automata with respect to $\Delta = \frac{1}{2}$. Now we have,

$$c(\mathcal{L}(A), \mathcal{L}(B)) \in \frac{3}{2}\mathbb{N}_0 \cup \{\infty\} \tag{5}$$

and

$$d(\mathcal{L}(A), \mathcal{L}(A_d)) < \frac{1}{2}, \quad d(\mathcal{L}(B), \mathcal{L}(B_d)) < \frac{1}{2}.$$

Theorem 3. *Let $A, B \in$ NTA with clocks running at triple speed and let A_d, B_d be their discretized timed automata with respect to $\Delta = \frac{1}{2}$. Then*

$$|c(\mathcal{L}(A), \mathcal{L}(B)) - c(\mathcal{L}(A_d), \mathcal{L}(B_d))| \leq \frac{1}{2}$$

and $c(\mathcal{L}(A), \mathcal{L}(B))$ is known in case $c(\mathcal{L}(A_d), \mathcal{L}(B_d))$ is known. In particular:

$$\mathcal{L}(A_d) \nsubseteq \mathcal{L}(B_d) \implies \mathcal{L}(A) \nsubseteq \mathcal{L}(B)$$

and

$$\mathcal{L}(A_d) \subseteq \mathcal{L}(B_d) \implies \mathcal{L}(A) \subseteq \overline{\mathcal{L}(B)},$$

so that the language inclusion problem between $\mathcal{L}(A)$ and the topological closure of $\mathcal{L}(B)$ is decidable.

Proof. A and A_d have the same untimed language. The timed languages $\mathcal{L}(A)$ (with clocks running at triple speed) and $\mathcal{L}(A_d)$ differ from one another in that every event of a run on A that occurs at time t, with $t = n + \varepsilon$ and $0 < \varepsilon < 1$, occurs at the 'rounded' time $n + \frac{1}{2}$ in the corresponding run on A_d. Similarly for B with respect to B_d. It follows that $\delta = c(\mathcal{L}(A), \mathcal{L}(B)) = \infty$ if and only if $\delta_d = c(\mathcal{L}(A_d), \mathcal{L}(B_d)) = \infty$.

Suppose now that $\delta < \infty$. We know (5) that $\delta \in \frac{3}{2}\mathbb{N}_0$. Since the timed traces of $\mathcal{L}(A_d)$ and $\mathcal{L}(B_d)$ are discretized to the set $\frac{1}{2}\mathbb{N}_0$ then, when computing δ_d instead of δ, we may have a difference of $\frac{1}{2}$ time units between the two. It follows that

$$\delta = \begin{cases} 3k, & \text{if } \delta_d \in \{3k - \frac{1}{2}, 3k, 3k + \frac{1}{2}\}, \\ 3k + \frac{3}{2}, & \text{if } \delta_d \in \{3k + 1, 3k + \frac{3}{2}, 3k + 2\}. \end{cases} \tag{6}$$

Let us elaborate on that. When δ is exactly k and not $3k^+$ or $3k^-$ then it means that it is achieved on specific timed traces and not as a limit. That is, it refers to an even occurring at time t^A on a run on A and event occurring at time t^B on a run on B, with $|t^A - t^B| = 3k$. Since the fractional parts of t^A and t^B are identical, the discretization in the corresponding runs on A_d and B_d are identical so that they occur at times t^{A_d} and t^{B_d} with $|t^{A_d} - t^{B_d}| = 3k$. The same applies when δ is exactly $3k + \frac{3}{2}$ since we are working with a resolution of $\frac{1}{2}$.

When $\delta = 3k^+$ or $\delta = 3k^-$ then it is achieved as a limit of timed traces. If $\delta = 3k^+$ then δ_d can be $3k + \frac{1}{2}$, for example, when $t^A = 3$ and $t^B = 3 + \varepsilon$, $\varepsilon > 0$. Then the discretized traces will occur at times $t^{A_d} = 3$ and $t^{B_d} = 3\frac{1}{2}$. Then by choosing a sequence of timed traces of $\mathfrak{L}(B)$ the time difference can tend to 0 while in the discretized automata it will remain $\frac{1}{2}$.

The other cases of an conformance distance δ that is a limit of converging distances are analogous, but we do not go here into detail.

Let us look at the last claims of the theorem. Suppose that $\mathfrak{L}(A) \subseteq \overline{\mathfrak{L}(B)}$. Then for each timed trace of $\mathfrak{L}(A)$ there is an identical timed trace of $\mathfrak{L}(B)$. The projection to the discretized timed trace will also be identical, thus,

$$\mathfrak{L}(A) \subseteq \mathfrak{L}(B) \;\Rightarrow\; \mathfrak{L}(A_d) \subseteq \mathfrak{L}(B_d).$$

If $\mathfrak{L}(A) \not\subseteq \overline{\mathfrak{L}(B)}$ then $\delta > 0$. By (6), we have that $\delta_d > 0$. It follows that

$$\mathfrak{L}(A) \not\subseteq \overline{\mathfrak{L}(B)} \;\Rightarrow\; \mathfrak{L}(A_d) \not\subseteq \mathfrak{L}(B_d).$$

$\square$

By (2), a similar result to Theorem 3 holds with respect to distances between languages.

By Theorem 3, in order to compute the conformance distance $c(\mathfrak{L}(A), \mathfrak{L}(B))$, we can compute $c(\mathfrak{L}(A_d), \mathfrak{L}(B_d))$, and know that we lie within an error of at most $\frac{1}{2}$ time unit. We may assume that A_d is deterministic, as this is feasible. It is not necessary to determinize B_d.

The general goal in computing $c(\mathfrak{L}(A_d), \mathfrak{L}(B_d))$ is to find the timed trace of $\mathfrak{L}(A_d)$ that is farthest from $\mathfrak{L}(B_d)$ (or a sequence of such timed traces if the distance is ∞). A heuristic approach is to play a timed game in which the player in white moves along A_d and tries to maximize her wins, while the player in black moves along B_d and tries to minimize his losses. The players start from the initial vertex of each graph. Then white makes a move by jumping to a vertex in A_d with transition label a, followed by a move of black on an edge in B_d with the same label a. Next, white moves on an edge with label a', followed by a move of black with the same label a' and so on. At each move we record the time difference between the absolute time duration of the paths along A_d and along B_d. The problem is that we may return to the same pair of locations $(q, q') \in Q^{A_d} \times Q^{B_d}$ but with a different time difference between the path along A_d and that along B_d. In addition, there are moves to locations where the time is not a single value but of the form $t \geq m$. Thus, the game may not be of finite type. One strategy to cope with the complexity of the game is a greedy max-min algorithm: each move of white is one that maximizes the new difference in times after the following move of black that tries to minimizes the time difference. A better, but more expensive, strategy on the part of white is to look-ahead more than one step.

So, let us then consider a seemingly easier question: is $c(\mathfrak{L}(A_d), \mathfrak{L}(B_d)) = \infty$? For this question we do not need to speed-up the clocks. An infinite conformal distance occurs in one of the following three situations.

S1. The untimed language of A_d is not included in that of B_d: there exists a path $q_0 \xrightarrow{a_1} q_1 \xrightarrow{a_2} \cdots \xrightarrow{a_n} q_n$ in A_d, with q_n an accepting location, which either cannot be realized in B_d with the same sequence of actions, or all such paths in B_d do not terminate in an accepting location.

S2. There exists a path in A_d of the form $q_0 \xrightarrow{a_1} q_1 \xrightarrow{a_2} \cdots \xrightarrow{a_n} q_n$, where the transition $q_{n-1} \xrightarrow{a_n} q_n$ has guard $t \geq m$, whereas for any path in B_d of the form $q_0' \xrightarrow{a_1} q_1' \xrightarrow{a_2} \cdots \xrightarrow{a_n} q_n'$ the guard of the last transition $q_{n-1}' \xrightarrow{a_n} q_n'$ bounds t from above.

S3. For each $N \in \mathbb{N}$ there exists a timed trace $\tau \in \mathfrak{L}(A_d)$, such that for each $\sigma \in \mathfrak{L}(B_d)$, $d(\tau, \sigma) > N$ and not because of S2.

In order to find out whether the conformance distance between $\mathfrak{L}(A_d)$ and $\mathfrak{L}(B_d)$ is infinite as a result of **S1** or **S2** we extend A_d and B_d as follows.

First, we add to the set Σ of actions a copy of it $\bar{\Sigma} = \{\bar{a} : a \in \Sigma\}$. Then, for each transition $q \xrightarrow{a} q'$ of A_d or of B_d with time constraint of type $t \geq m$, we add a transition $q \xrightarrow{\bar{a}} q'$ with guard $t = \infty$. Next, we complete B_d by adding a location s which is a 'sink': whenever there is no transition with action $b \in \Sigma \cup \bar{\Sigma}$ from location q of B_d, we add the transition $q \xrightarrow{b} s$. The sink location is supplemented by self-loops of all actions. We retain the names A_d and B_d for the resulting automata.

In the next step we form the untimed automaton $U(A_d)$ which is a determinization of A_d with respect to actions while ignoring the temporal part. Similarly, we construct $U(B_d)$.

Definition 6. *The automaton $U(A_d)$ is a tuple $(\mathcal{Q}, Q_0, \mathcal{F}, \Sigma \cup \bar{\Sigma}, \mathcal{E})$, where:*

1. *$\mathcal{Q} \subseteq \mathcal{P}(Q^{A_d})$ is a subset of the power set of the locations of A_d, where $Q_0 = \{q_0^{A_d}\}$ is the initial location;*
2. *$\mathcal{F} \subseteq \mathcal{Q}$ is the set of accepting locations, where $Q = \{q_1^{A_d}, \ldots, q_m^{A_d}\}$ is accepting if at least one of the $q_i^{A_d}$ is an accepting location of A_d;*
3. *$\Sigma \cup \bar{\Sigma}$ is the set of actions;*
4. *$\mathcal{E} \subseteq \mathcal{Q} \times (\Sigma \cup \bar{\Sigma}) \times \mathcal{Q}$ is a finite set of edges of the form (Q, a, Q'), where $Q' = \{q'^{A_d} : \exists q^{A_d} \in Q. (q^{A_d}, a, q'^{A_d}) \in T^{A_d}\}$.*

Finally, we construct a version of the untimed product automaton $U(A_d) \times U(B_d)$ in which the accepting locations are those pairs of locations (Q, Q') for which Q is an accepting location of $U(A_d)$ but Q' is not an accepting location of $U(B_d)$.

Definition 7. *The automaton $U(A_d) \times U(B_d)$ is a tuple $(\mathcal{Q}, Q_0, \mathcal{F}, \Sigma \cup \bar{\Sigma}, \mathcal{E})$, where:*

1. *$\mathcal{Q} \subseteq \mathcal{Q}^{U(A_d)} \times \mathcal{Q}^{U(B_d)}$, where $Q_0 = (q_0^{U(A_d)}, q_0^{U(B_d)})$ is the initial location;*
2. *$\mathcal{F} \subseteq \mathcal{Q}$ is the set of accepting locations (Q, Q'), where $Q \in \mathcal{F}^{U(A_d)}$ and $Q' \notin \mathcal{F}^{U(B_d)}$;*
3. *$\Sigma \cup \bar{\Sigma}$ is the set of actions;*
4. *$\mathcal{E} \subseteq \mathcal{Q} \times (\Sigma \cup \bar{\Sigma}) \times \mathcal{Q}$ is the set of edges, where for each $(Q_1, a, Q_1') \in \mathcal{E}^{U(A_d)}$ and $(Q_2, a, Q_2') \in \mathcal{E}^{U(B_d)}$ we have $((Q_1, Q_2), a, (Q_1', Q_2')) \in \mathcal{E}$,*

and $U(A_d) \times U(B_d)$ is the connected component of the initial location.

Theorem 4. $c(\mathfrak{L}(A_d), \mathfrak{L}(B_d)) = \infty$ *as a result of* **S1** *or* **S2** *if and only if the set of accepting locations of* $U(A_d) \times U(B_d)$ *is not empty.*

Proof. By completing B_d we made sure that the set of untimed traces of $U(B_d)$ consists of all possible traces. But if a path in $U(A_d) \times U(B_d)$ terminates in an accepting location, then there exists a path in A_d that ends in an accepting location, while all paths in B_d of the same sequence of actions either terminate in a non-sink location which is non-accepting, or enter the sink either on an edge with action $a \in \Sigma$ due to missing such an edge on the uncompleted B_d or on an edge labeled $\bar{a} \in \bar{\Sigma}$ due to reaching a transition that is bounded in time in (the uncompleted) B_d, but not bounded in A_d. □

Assume now that by constructing the automaton $U(A_d) \times U(B_d)$ it turns out that no possible infinite conformance distance exists when checking **S1** and **S2** and it remains to check **S3**. Hence, the goal is to find a sequence of traces in A_d which 'run-away' from B_d, and now we are interested in the exact delays between consecutive transitions. This problem may be of very high complexity and even it is not clear whether it is decidable. We will show that a (perhaps) restricted version is decidable.

First, we extend A_d and B_d with actions $\bar{\Sigma}$ as before, referring to transitions that are unbounded by time. Let M be the maximal integer that appears in a transition guard of A_d or B_d. Then, each transition $q \xrightarrow{a} q'$ of A_d or B_d with time constraint $t \geq m$, $m \leq M + \frac{1}{2}$, is replaced by the transitions $q \xrightarrow{a} q'$ with delays $t = m, t = m + \frac{1}{2}, ..., t = M + \frac{1}{2}$ and another transition $q \xrightarrow{\bar{a}} q'$ with delay $t = (M+1)^*$. The set of delays of A_d (B_d) is denoted by $\mathcal{D}$.

In the next step we determinize B_d into $D(B_d)$. The idea is to be able to compare each timed trace of A_d simultaneously with all equivalent (having the same untimed trace) time traces of B_d.

Definition 8. *The automaton $D(B_d)$ is a tuple $(\mathcal{Q}, Q_0, \mathcal{F}, \Sigma \cup \bar{\Sigma}, \mathcal{T})$, where:*

1. *$\mathcal{Q} \subseteq \mathcal{P}(\mathcal{Q}^{B_d})$ is a subset of the power set of the locations of B_d, where $Q_0 = \{q_0^{B_d}\}$ is the initial location;*
2. *$\mathcal{F} \subseteq \mathcal{Q}$ is the set of accepting locations, where $Q = \{q_1^{B_d}, \ldots, q_m^{B_d}\}$ is accepting if at least one of the $q_i^{B_d}$ is an accepting location of B_d;*
3. *$\Sigma \cup \bar{\Sigma}$ is the set of actions;*
4. *$\mathcal{T} \subseteq \mathcal{Q} \times (\Sigma \cup \bar{\Sigma}) \times \mathcal{E} \times \mathcal{Q}$ is a finite set of transitions of the form (Q, a, E, Q'), where*

$$E = \{(q^{B_d}, a, d, q'^{B_d}) \in \mathcal{T}^{B_d} : q^{B_d} \in Q, q'^{B_d} \in Q', a \in \Sigma \cup \bar{\Sigma}, d \in \mathcal{D}\}.$$

and Q' contains exactly the set of these target locations q'^{A_d}.

Note that the transitions of $D(B_d)$ retain the set of transitions of B_d including source and target locations.

In the next step we make the standard construction of the product automaton $A_d \times D(B_d)$. It has at most $L = |\mathcal{Q}^{A_d}| \cdot 2^{|\mathcal{Q}^{B_d}|}$ locations, where each location is of the form

$$Q^{A_d \times D(B_d)} = (q^{A_d}, \{q_1^{B_d}, \ldots, q_m^{B_d}\}).$$

Since the difference between a transition delay on A_d and a corresponding transition on B_d in parallel runs on A_d and B_d is at most M time units (actually, it is $M + \frac{1}{2}$, but it makes no difference for our argument), then a run on $A_d \times D(B_d)$ that does not visit the same location twice may result in a delay of at most LM time units between its projection to A_d and each of its projections to B_d.

At each transition of a run on $A_d \times D(B_d)$ we can subtract the delay of the edge of A_d from each of the delays of the corresponding edges of B_d and record at each location $q_i^{B_d}$ of $Q^{A_d \times D(B_d)}$ the set of *accumulated time differences* (ATDs), that is, the differences in absolute time between the runs on A_d and all possible runs on B_d of the same untimed trace when reaching $Q^{A_d \times D(B_d)}$. The ATD of the least absolute value gives the least difference in time at that location between the run on A_d and a corresponding run on B_d. When a delay is $(M + 1)^*$ (and then it is the same delay for both A_d and B_d) then we denote the difference 0^+, and this $+$ sign carries on to the next differences by defining $i^+ + j = (i + j)^+$, $i^+ + j^+ = (i + j)^{++}$, and so on. It means that i^+ is actually any value of $\frac{1}{2}\mathbb{N}_0$ which is greater than or equals i. The reason for that is that for a delay k in A_d we can choose any delay $l \geq k$ in B_d. In order to exclude the possibility of choosing also a delay in B_d which is smaller than k (and maybe reduce the distance between the corresponding paths in A_d and B_d), each transition of A_d that is unbounded in time is considered as a delay of $M + 1$ time units. Once a value of the form i^+ is realized as a concrete value $i + j$, for some $j \geq 0$, then in all the difference values that appear in the following locations the relevant $+$ sign is removed and the value j is added.

Every run ρ on $A_d \times D(B_d)$ can be uniquely written in the form

$$\rho = \rho_0 \sigma_1^{i_1} \rho_1 \sigma_2^{i_2} \rho_2 \cdots \sigma_r^{i_r} \rho_r,$$

for some $r \in \mathbb{N}_0$, $i_j \in \mathbb{N}$ and where each σ_j is a simple cycle of positive length and each ρ_j is without cycles and of length $0 \leq l < L$. We say that the number of *power cycles* of ρ is r, written $pc(\rho) = r$.

Theorem 5. *It is decidable whether there exists a fixed $K \in \mathbb{N}$, such that for every $N \in \mathbb{N}$ there exists a timed trace $\tau \in \mathcal{L}(A_d)$, such that $d(\tau, \mathcal{L}(B_d)) > N$ and the corresponding run ρ on $A_d \times D(B_d)$ satisfies $pc(\rho) \leq K$.*

Proof. The conformance distance $c(\mathcal{L}(A_d), \mathcal{L}(B_d))$ is ∞ if for every $N \in \mathbb{N}$ we can reach a location $Q^{A_d \times D(B_d)}$ with all ATDs of absolute value at least N. Since $pc(\rho) \leq K$, K fixed, it is clear that the unbounded increase in the ATDs can come only from the powers of simple cycles σ^{i_j}. Since the number of locations of $A_d \times D(B_d)$ is finite, all locations can be reached in a bounded number of steps. Then, for each location $Q^{A_d \times D(B_d)}$ and each simple cycle σ starting at $Q^{A_d \times D(B_d)}$, it can be checked for which locations $q_i^{B_d}$ of $Q^{A_d \times D(B_d)}$ the minimal (in absolute value) ATD increases indefinitely when repeating the cycle σ. Let P be the set of these locations $Q^{A_d \times D(B_d)}$ with at least one unbounded ATD.

Next we look at all the simple paths from each $Q^{A_d \times D(B_d)} \in P$ to the other locations of $A_d \times D(B_d)$ and update their sub-locations $q_i^{B_d}$ of having an unbounded ATD. Moreover, when reaching a location $Q'^{A_d \times D(B_d)} \in P$ from another location $Q^{A_d \times D(B_d)} \in P$ then it can be checked whether new sub-locations $q_i^{B_d}$ of $Q'^{A_d \times D(B_d)}$ become with unbounded ATD when repeating a cycle σ (even when its minimal ATD decreases by a bounded finite number at each round of σ, if we started with an unbounded value, we can end at an unbounded value). This process is repeated until no improvement in the maximum number of sub-locations of unbounded ATD can be achieved. Since the graph is finite, the whole algorithm is finite. Finally, $c(\mathfrak{L}(A_d), \mathfrak{L}(B_d)) = \infty$ when at some step of the algorithm a location $Q^{A_d \times D(B_d)}$ becomes with all its sub-locations $q_i^{B_d}$ of unbounded ATD. □

7   Conclusion and Suggested Future Research

In this paper we introduced a natural definition of the distance between the languages of non-deterministic timed automata in terms of the times at which events in one automaton occur compared to the times of corresponding events in the other automaton. We showed how one can effectively construct discretized deterministic timed automata and obtain the distance between the original timed automata from the distance between the discretized versions. Consequently, the problem of language inclusion for timed automata, which is undecidable in general, is decidable if we consider the closure of the languages with respect to the Euclidean topology.

Computing the distance between timed automata may not be an easy task. We even do not know whether the finiteness of the distance is a decidable problem. We showed, however, that under some restriction on the timed traces, this problem is decidable.

There is more than one reasonable way to define the distance between timed automata and the one we chose refers to the accumulated time difference that may occur between timed automata that are supposed to be (almost) the same or conformance distance between the language of an implementation and that of the specification. Other possible definitions of distances like a maximal time difference on a single transition or time difference mean on simple cycles are easier to compute on the discretized automata. For another notion of distance between implementation and specification we refer to [9]. Another interesting problem is to compute the distance between timed automata equipped with probabilities on transitions, where the distances are computed as expected values with respect to these probabilities.

Acknowledgements. This research was partly supported by the Austrian Science Fund (FWF) Project P29355-N35.

References

1. Alur, R., Dill, D.L.: A theory of timed automata. Theor. Comput. Sci. **126**(2), 183–235 (1994). https://doi.org/10.1016/0304-3975(94)90010-8
2. Alur, R., Fix, L., Henzinger, T.A.: Event-clock automata: a determinizable class of timed automata. Theor. Comput. Sci. **211**(1–2), 253–273 (1999). https://doi.org/10.1016/S0304-3975(97)00173-4
3. Alur, R., La Torre, S., Madhusudan, P.: Perturbed timed automata. In: Morari, M., Thiele, L. (eds.) HSCC 2005. LNCS, vol. 3414, pp. 70–85. Springer, Heidelberg (2005). https://doi.org/10.1007/978-3-540-31954-2_5
4. Alur, R., Madhusudan, P.: Decision problems for timed automata: a survey. In: Bernardo, M., Corradini, F. (eds.) SFM-RT 2004. LNCS, vol. 3185, pp. 1–24. Springer, Heidelberg (2004). https://doi.org/10.1007/978-3-540-30080-9_1
5. Baier, C., Bertrand, N., Bouyer, P., Brihaye, T.: When are timed automata determinizable? In: Albers, S., Marchetti-Spaccamela, A., Matias, Y., Nikoletseas, S., Thomas, W. (eds.) ICALP 2009. LNCS, vol. 5556, pp. 43–54. Springer, Heidelberg (2009). https://doi.org/10.1007/978-3-642-02930-1_4
6. Bérard, B., Petit, A., Diekert, V., Gastin, P.: Characterization of the expressive power of silent transitions in timed automata. Fundam. Inform. **36**(2–3), 145–182 (1998). https://doi.org/10.3233/FI-1998-36233
7. Bouyer, P., Dufourd, C., Fleury, E., Petit, A.: Updatable timed automata. Theor. Comput. Sci. **321**(2–3), 291–345 (2004). https://doi.org/10.1016/j.tcs.2004.04.003
8. Bouyer, P., Markey, N., Sankur, O.: Robust reachability in timed automata and games: a game-based approach. Theor. Comput. Sci. **563**, 43–74 (2015). https://doi.org/10.1016/j.tcs.2014.08.014
9. Cerný, P., Henzinger, T.A., Radhakrishna, A.: Simulation distances. Theor. Comput. Sci. **413**(1), 21–35 (2012). https://doi.org/10.1016/j.tcs.2011.08.002
10. Gupta, V., Henzinger, T.A., Jagadeesan, R.: Robust timed automata. In: Maler, O. (ed.) HART 1997. LNCS, vol. 1201, pp. 331–345. Springer, Heidelberg (1997). https://doi.org/10.1007/BFb0014736
11. Henzinger, T.A., Manna, Z., Pnueli, A.: What good are digital clocks? In: Kuich, W. (ed.) ICALP 1992. LNCS, vol. 623, pp. 545–558. Springer, Heidelberg (1992). https://doi.org/10.1007/3-540-55719-9_103
12. Lorber, F., Rosenmann, A., Ničković, D., Aichernig, B.K.: Boundeddeterminization of timed automata with silent transitions. R. Time Syst. **53**(3), 291–326 (2017). https://doi.org/10.1007/s11241-017-9271-x
13. Ouaknine, J.: Digitisation and full abstraction for dense-time model checking. In: Katoen, J.-P., Stevens, P. (eds.) TACAS 2002. LNCS, vol. 2280, pp. 37–51. Springer, Heidelberg (2002). https://doi.org/10.1007/3-540-46002-0_4
14. Ouaknine, J., Rabinovich, A., Worrell, J.: Time-bounded verification. In: Bravetti, M., Zavattaro, G. (eds.) CONCUR 2009. LNCS, vol. 5710, pp. 496–510. Springer, Heidelberg (2009). https://doi.org/10.1007/978-3-642-04081-8_33
15. Ouaknine, J., Worrell, J.: Revisiting digitization, robustness, and decidability for timed automata. In: Proceedings of the 18th IEEE Symposium on Logic in Computer Science (LICS 2003), Ottawa, Canada, 22–25 June 2003, pp. 198–207 (2003). https://doi.org/10.1109/LICS.2003.1210059
16. Ouaknine, J., Worrell, J.: On the language inclusion problem for timed automata: closing a decidability gap. In: LICS, pp. 54–63 (2004). https://doi.org/10.1109/LICS.2004.1319600

17. Ouaknine, J., Worrell, J.: Towards a theory of time-bounded verification. In: Abramsky, S., Gavoille, C., Kirchner, C., Meyer auf der Heide, F., Spirakis, P.G. (eds.) ICALP 2010. LNCS, vol. 6199, pp. 22–37. Springer, Heidelberg (2010). https://doi.org/10.1007/978-3-642-14162-1_3

18. Rosenmann, A.: The timestamp of timed automata. arXiv abs/1412.5669v4 (2019). http://arxiv.org/abs/1412.5669

19. Suman, P.V., Pandya, P.K., Krishna, S.N., Manasa, L.: Timed automata with integer resets: language inclusion and expressiveness. In: Cassez, F., Jard, C. (eds.) FORMATS 2008. LNCS, vol. 5215, pp. 78–92. Springer, Heidelberg (2008). https://doi.org/10.1007/978-3-540-85778-5_7

Time to Learn – Learning Timed Automata from Tests

Martin Tappler[1]([⊠]), Bernhard K. Aichernig[1], Kim Guldstrand Larsen[2], and Florian Lorber[2]

[1] Institute of Software Technology, Graz University of Technology, Graz, Austria
{martin.tappler,aichernig}@ist.tugraz.at
[2] Department of Computer Science, Aalborg University, Aalborg, Denmark
{kgl,florber}@cs.aau.dk

Abstract. Model learning has gained increasing interest in recent years. It derives behavioural models from test data of black-box systems. The main advantage offered by such techniques is that they enable model-based analysis without access to the internals of a system. Applications range from fully automated testing over model checking to system understanding. Current work focuses on learning variations of finite state machines. However, most techniques consider discrete time. In this paper, we present a novel method for learning timed automata, finite state machines extended with real-valued clocks. The learning method generates a model consistent with a set of timed traces collected via testing. This generation is based on genetic programming, a search-based technique for automatic program creation. We evaluate our approach on **44** timed systems, comprised of four systems from the literature (two industrial and two academic) and **40** randomly generated examples.

1 Introduction

Test-based model-learning techniques have gained increasing interest in recent years. Basically, these techniques derive formal system models from (test) observations. They therefore enable model-based reasoning about software systems while requiring only limited knowledge about the system at hand. Put differently, such techniques allow for model-based verification of black-box systems if they are amenable to testing.

Peled et al. [39] performed pioneering work in this area by introducing *Black Box Checking*, automata-based model checking for black-box systems. It involves interleaved model learning, model checking and conformance testing and built the basis for various follow-up works [11,17], including model checking of network protocols [12] and differential testing on the model level [7,43]. The framework we target is shown in Fig. 1. In the simplest case,

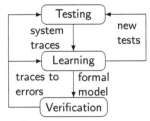

Fig. 1. General framework: test-based learning for verification.

É. André and M. Stoelinga (Eds.): FORMATS 2019, LNCS 11750, pp. 216–235, 2019.
https://doi.org/10.1007/978-3-030-29662-9_13

we interact with a system by testing, learn a model from system traces (logs) and then perform verification. Feedback loops are also possible: we can derive additional tests from the preliminary learned model, and we could use counterexample traces from model checking as tests.

Learning-based verification has great potential, but applications often use modelling formalisms with low expressiveness such as Mealy machines. This can be attributed to the availability of efficient implementations of learning algorithms for variations of finite automata, e.g. in LearnLib [22], and comparably low support for richer automata types; especially timed systems have received little attention. In addition, many of the proposed methods are not supported by implementations. Notable works include learning of deterministic real-time automata and a probabilistic variant thereof [46,47] by Verwer et al. and techniques for learning deterministic event-recording automata described by Grinchtein et al. [15,16]. The existing solutions on timed automata contain several limitations. Real-time automata are restricted to one clock, which is reset in every transition. Thus, they can only reason about delays in the current location, but not keep track of delays since earlier events. Event-recording automata are also less expressive than timed automata, and their learning has a high runtime complexity. To the best of our knowledge, the proposed solution is the first to implement a learning technique for general input-output timed automata, as used in the model-checker UPPAAL [8]. Such automata, usually do not have canonical forms [15] which complicates the development of learning techniques, therefore we follow a metaheuristic approach. The only restrictions required by our approach are that it considers the systems under learning to be output-urgent, deterministic and with isolated outputs (a special form of output determinism). While specifications are generally vague, especially on timing, and leave freedom to the actual implementation, implementations themselves are generally considered to reflect one specific choice satisfying the specification, and implement it deterministically [10]. Thus, since we learn from concrete implementations, we do not see these restrictions as too limiting. Notably, we consider input-enabled systems which makes our approach well-suited for a testing-based setting.

Scope and Contribution. Here, we focus on the *learning* part in Fig. 1. Generally, model learning may be performed either passively or actively [20]. Passive learning uses preexisting data, such as system logs or existing test data, as basis, while active learning actively queries the system, e.g. by testing, to gain relevant information. We use a form of genetic programming [25] to passively learn a deterministic timed automaton (TA) consistent with a given set of test cases. We evaluate this approach, a meta-heuristic search, on four manually created TA and several randomly generated TA. The evaluation demonstrates that the search reliably converges to a TA consistent with test cases given as training data. Furthermore, we simulate learned TA on independently produced test data to show that our identified solutions generalise well, thus do not overfit to training data. Our technique is passive, but active extensions are possible by testing based on intermediate versions of the learned model. Such an active approach is currently under development and first evaluations show promising results.

Our contribution is threefold: (1) We show that TA can be genetically programmed and present the corresponding parameters and techniques. (2) We implemented these techniques in a tool available for download [45]. (3) The evaluation results may serve as a benchmark for alternative TA learning methods.

Structure. Section 2.1 contains background information on TA and genetic programming. Section 3 describes our approach to learning TA. Applications of this approach are presented in Sect. 4. In Sect. 5, we provide a summary and discuss related work, as well as potential extensions.

2 Preliminaries

2.1 Timed Automata

TA are finite automata enriched with real-valued variables called clocks [6]. Clocks measure the progress of time which elapses while an automaton resides in some location. Transitions can be constrained based on clock values and clocks may be reset on transitions. We denote the set of clocks by $\mathcal{C}$ and the set of guards over $\mathcal{C}$ by $\mathcal{G}(\mathcal{C})$. Guards are conjunctions of constraints of the form $c \oplus k$, with $c \in \mathcal{C}, \oplus \in \{>, \geq, \leq, <\}, k \in \mathbb{N}$. Transitions are labelled by input and output actions, denoted by Σ_I and Σ_O respectively, with $\Sigma = \Sigma_I \cup \Sigma_O$. Input labels are suffixed by ? and output labels end with !. A TA over $(\mathcal{C}, \Sigma)$ is a triple $\langle L, l_0, E \rangle$, where L is a finite non-empty set of locations, $l_0 \in L$ is the initial location and E is the set of edges, with $E \subseteq L \times \Sigma \times \mathcal{G}(\mathcal{C}) \times 2^{\mathcal{C}} \times L$. We write $l \xrightarrow{g,a,r} l'$ for an edge $(l, g, a, r, l') \in E$ with guard g, label a, and clock resets r.

Example 1 (Train TA Model). Figure 2 shows a TA model of a train, for which we have $\Sigma_I = \{start?, stop?, go?\}$, $\Sigma_O = \{appr!, enter!, leave!\}$, $\mathcal{C} = \{c\}$, $L = \{l_0, \ldots, l_5\}$, and $E = \{l_0 \xrightarrow{\top, start?, \{c\}} l_1, \ldots\}$. From initial location l_0, the train accepts the input *start?*, resetting clock c. After that, it can produce the output *appr!* if $c \geq 5$, i.e the train may approach 5 time units after it is started.

The semantics of a TA is given by a timed transition system (TTS) $\langle Q, q_0, \Sigma, T \rangle$, with states $Q = L \times \mathbb{R}_{\geq 0}^{\mathcal{C}}$, initial state q_0, and transitions $T \subseteq Q \times (\Sigma \cup \mathbb{R}_{\geq 0}) \times Q$, for which we write $q \xrightarrow{e} q'$ for $(q, e, q') \in T$. A state $q = (l, \nu)$ is a pair consisting of a location l and a clock valuation ν. For $r \subseteq \mathcal{C}$, we denote resets of clocks in r by $\nu[r]$, i.e. $\forall c \in r : \nu[r](c) = 0$ and $\forall c \in \mathcal{C} \setminus r : \nu[r](c) = \nu(c)$. Let $(\nu+d)(c) = \nu(c)+d$ for $d \in \mathbb{R}_{\geq 0}, c \in \mathcal{C}$ denote the progress of time and $\nu \models \phi$ denote that valuation ν satisfies formula

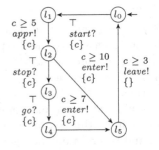

Fig. 2. Train TA.

ϕ. Finally, $\mathbf{0}$ is the valuation assigning zero to all clocks and the initial state q_0 is $(l_0, \mathbf{0})$. Transitions of TTSs are either delay transitions $(l, \nu) \xrightarrow{d} (l, \nu + d)$ for a delay $d \in \mathbb{R}_{\geq 0}$, or discrete transitions $(l, \nu) \xrightarrow{a} (l', \nu[r])$ for an edge $l \xrightarrow{g,a,r} l'$

such that $\nu \models g$. Delays are usually further constrained, e.g. by invariants [19] limiting the sojourn time in locations.

Timed Traces. We use the terms timed traces and test sequences similarly to [41]. The latter are sequences of inputs and corresponding execution times, while the former are sequences of inputs and outputs, together with their times of occurrence (produced in response to a test sequence). A test sequence ts is an alternating sequence of non-decreasing time stamps t_j and inputs i_j, i.e. $ts = t_1 \cdot i_1 \cdots t_n \cdot i_n \in (\mathbb{R}_{\geq 0} \times \Sigma_I)^*$ with $\forall j \in \{1, \ldots, n-1\} : t_j \leq t_{j+1}$. Informally, a test sequence prescribes that i_j should be executed at time t_j. A timed trace $tt \in (\mathbb{R}_{\geq 0} \times \Sigma)^*$ consists of inputs interleaved with outputs produced by a timed system. Analogously to test sequences, its timestamps are non-decreasing.

Assumptions on Timed Systems. Testing based on TA often places further assumptions on TA [19,41]. Since we learn models from tests we make similar assumptions (closely following [19]). We describe these assumptions on the level of semantics and use $q \xrightarrow{a}$ to denote $\exists q' : q \xrightarrow{a} q'$ and $q \xnrightarrow{a}$ for $\nexists q' : q \xrightarrow{a} q'$:

1. *Determinism.* A TA is deterministic iff for every state $s = (l, \nu)$ and every action $a \in \Sigma$, whenever $s \xrightarrow{a} s'$, and $s \xrightarrow{a} s''$ then $s' = s''$.
2. *Input Enabledness.* A TA is input enabled iff for every state $s = (l, \nu)$ and every input $i \in \Sigma_I$, we have $s \xrightarrow{i}$.
3. *Output Urgency.* A TA shows output-urgent behaviour if outputs occur immediately as soon as they are enabled, i.e. for $o \in \Sigma_O$, if $s \xrightarrow{o}$ then $s \xnrightarrow{d}$ for all $d \in \mathbb{R}_{\geq 0}$. Thus, outputs must not be delayed.
4. *Isolated Outputs.* A TA has isolated outputs iff whenever an output may be executed, then no other output is enabled, i.e. if $\forall o \in \Sigma_O, \forall o' \in \Sigma_O : q \xrightarrow{o}$ and $q \xrightarrow{o'}$ implies $o = o'$.

It is necessary to place restrictions on the sojourn time in locations to establish output urgency. Deadlines provide a simple way to model the assumption that systems are output urgent [9]. With deadlines it is possible to model eager actions. We use this concept and implicitly assume all learned output edges to be eager. This means that outputs must be produced as soon as their guards are satisfied. For that, we extend the semantics given above by adding the following restriction: delays $(l, \nu) \xrightarrow{d} (l', \nu + d)$ are only possible if $\forall d' \in \mathbb{R}_{\geq 0}, d' < d :$ $\nu + d' \models \neg \bigvee_{g \in G_O} g$, where $G_O = \{g | \exists l', a, r : l \xrightarrow{g, a, r} l', a \in \Sigma_O\}$ are the guards of outputs in location l. To avoid issues related to the exact time at which outputs should be produced, we further restrict the syntax of TA by disallowing strict lower bounds for output edges. UPPAAL [27] uses invariants rather than deadlines to limit sojourn time. In order to analyse TA using UPPAAL, we use the translation given in [14]. We implicitly add self-loops to all states $s = (l, \nu)$ for inputs i undefined in s, i.e. we add $(l, \nu) \xrightarrow{i} (l, \nu)$ if $\nu \not\models \bigvee_{\exists l', r : l \xrightarrow{g, i, r} l'} g$. This ensures input enabledness while avoiding TA cluttered with input self-loops. It also allows to ignore input enabledness during genetic programming, e.g. mutations may remove input edges.

The assumptions placed on systems under test (SUTs) ensure testability [19]. Assuming that SUTs can be modelled in some modelling formalism is usually referred to as *testing hypothesis*. Placing the same assumptions on learned models simplifies checking conformance between model and SUT. The execution of a test sequence on such a model uniquely determines a response [41], and due to input enabledness we may execute any test sequence. This allows us to use equivalence as conformance relation between learned models and SUT. What is more, we can approximate checking equivalence between the learned models and the SUT by executing test sequences on the models and check for equivalence between the SUT's responses and the response predicted by the models.

2.2   Genetic Programming

Genetic programming [25] is a search-based technique to automatically generate programs exhibiting some desired behaviour. Like *Genetic Algorithms* [35], it is inspired by nature. Programs, also called individuals, are iteratively refined by: (1) fitness-based selection followed by (2) operations altering program structure, like mutation and crossover. Fitness measures are problem-specific and may for instance be based on tests. In this case, one could assign a fitness value proportional to the number of tests passed by an individual. The following basic functioning principle underlies genetic programming.

1. Randomly create an initial population.
2. Evaluate the fitness of each individual in the population.
3. If an acceptable solution has been found or the maximum number of iterations has been performed: **stop** and output the best individual
4. Otherwise repeatedly select an individual based on fitness and apply one of:
   Mutation: change a part of the individual creating a new individual.
   Crossover: select another individual according to its fitness and combine both individuals to create offspring.
   Reproduction: copy the individual to create a new equivalent individual.
5. Form a new population from the new individuals and go to Step 2.

Due to their nature, genetic algorithms and genetic programming lend themselves to parallelisation. Several populations may, e.g., be evolved in parallel, which is particularly useful if speciation is applied [37]. In speciation, different subpopulations explore different parts of the search space. Information is commonly exchanged between subpopulations by migrating individuals.

3   Genetic Programming for Timed Automata

Figure 3a provides an overview of the steps we perform, while Fig. 3b shows the creation of a new population in more detail. We first test the SUT, by generating and executing n_{test} test sequences to collect n_{test} timed traces. Our goal is then to genetically program a TA consistent with the collected timed traces. Put differently, we want to generate a TA that produces the same outputs as the SUT in

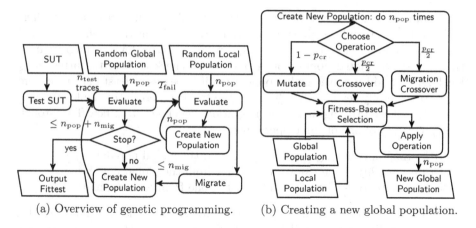

(a) Overview of genetic programming.   (b) Creating a new global population.

Fig. 3. Overview of the learning process.

response to the inputs of the test sequences. For the following discussion, we say that a TA passes a timed trace t if it produces the same outputs as the SUT when simulating the test sequence corresponding to t. Otherwise it fails t. In addition to passing all timed traces, the final TA shall be deterministic. This is achieved by assigning larger fitness values to deterministic solutions. Both mutation and crossover can create non-deterministic intermediate solutions, which might help the search in the short-term and will be resolved in future generations.

Generally, we evolve two populations of TA simultaneously, a global population, evaluated on all the traces, and a local population, evaluated only on the traces that fail on the fittest automaton of the global population. Both are initially created equally and contain n_{pop} TA. After initial creation, the global population is evaluated on all n_{test} traces. During that, we basically test the TA and check how many traces each TA passes and assign fitness values accordingly, i.e., the more passing traces the fitter. Additionally, we add a fitness penalty for model size. The local population is evaluated only on a subset $\mathcal{T}_{\mathrm{fail}}$ of the traces. This subset $\mathcal{T}_{\mathrm{fail}}$ contains all traces which the fittest TA fails, and which likely most of the other TA fail as well. With the local population, we are able to explore new parts of the search space more easily since we may ignore functionality already modelled by the global population. We integrate functionality found via this local search into the global population through migration and migration combined with crossover. To avoid overfitting to a low number of traces, we ensure that $\mathcal{T}_{\mathrm{fail}}$ contains at least $\frac{n_{\mathrm{test}}}{100}$ traces. If there are fewer actually failing traces, we add randomly chosen traces from all n_{test} traces to $\mathcal{T}_{\mathrm{fail}}$.

After evaluation, we stop if we either reached the maximum number of generations g_{max}, or the fittest TA passes all traces and has not changed in g_{change} generations. Note that two TA passing all traces may have different fitness values depending on model size, i.e. g_{change} controls how long we try to decrease the size of the fittest TA. The rationale behind this is that smaller TA are less complex and simpler to comprehend.

If not stopped, we create new populations of TA, which works slightly differently for the local and the global population. Figure 3b illustrates the creation of a new global population. Before creating new TA, existing TA may migrate from the local to the global population. For that, we check each of the fittest n_{mig} local TA and add it to the global population if it passes at least one trace from T_{fail}. We generally set n_{mig} to $\frac{5n_{pop}}{100}$, i.e. the top five percent of the local population are allowed to migrate. After migration, we create n_{pop} new TA through the application of one of three operations:

– *with probability* $1 - p_{cr}$: mutate a TA from the global population
– *with probability* $\frac{p_{cr}}{2}$: crossover of two TA from the global population
– *with probability* $\frac{p_{cr}}{2}$: crossover of two TA, one from each population

The rationale behind migration combined with crossover is that migrated TA may have low fitness from a global point of view and will therefore not survive selection. They may, however, have desirable features which can be transferred via crossover. For the local population, we perform the same steps, but without any migration, in order to keep the local search independent. Once we have new populations, we start a new generation by evaluating the new TA.

A detail not illustrated in Fig. 3a is our implementation of *elitism* [35]. We always keep track of the fittest TA found so far for both populations. In each generation, we add these fit TA to their respective populations after mutation.

Parameters. Our implementation could be controlled by a large number of parameters. To ease applicability and to avoid the need for meta-optimisation of parameter settings for a particular SUT, we fixed as many as possible to constant values. The actual values, like $\frac{5n_{pop}}{100}$ for n_{mig}, are motivated by experiments. The remaining parameters can usually be set to default values or chosen based on guidelines. For instance, n_{pop}, g_{max}, and n_{test} may be chosen as large as possible, given available memory and maximum computation time.

3.1 Creation of Initial Random Population

We initially create n_{pop} random TA, parameterised by: (1) the labels Σ_I and Σ_O, (2) the number of clocks n_{clock}, and (3) the appr. largest constant in clock constraints c_{max}. Note, c_{max} is an approximation, because mutations may increase constants. Each TA has initially only two locations, as we intend to increase size and thereby complexity only through mutation and crossover. Moreover, it is assigned the given action labels and has a set of n_{clock} clocks. During creation, we add random edges, such that at least one edge connects the initial location to the other location. We create edges entirely randomly, whereby the number of constraints in guards as well as the number of clock resets are geometrically distributed with fixed parameters. The edge label, the relational operators and constants in constraints are chosen uniformly at random from the respective sets Σ, $\{<, \leq, \geq, >\}$, and $[0..c_{max}]$ (operators for outputs exclude $>$). The source and target locations are also chosen uniformly at random from the set of locations, i.e. initially we choose from two locations. If the required number of clocks is not known a priori, we suggest setting $n_{clock} = 1$ and increasing it only if it is not possible to find a valid TA. A similar approach could be used for c_{max}.

3.2   Fitness Evaluation

Simulation. We simulate the TA to evaluate their fitness. Above, we discussed failing and passing traces, but evaluation is more fine grained. We execute the inputs of each timed trace and observe produced outputs until (1) the simulation is complete, (2) an expected output is not observed, or (3) output isolation is violated (output non-determinism).

In general, if $\mathcal{T}$ is a deterministic, input-enabled TA with isolated and urgent outputs and ts is a test sequence, then executing ts on $\mathcal{T}$ uniquely determines a timed trace tt [41]. By the testing hypothesis, the SUT fulfils these assumptions. However, TA generated through mutation and crossover are input-enabled, but may show non-deterministic behaviour. Hence, simulating a test sequence or a timed trace on a generated TA may follow multiple paths of states. Some of these paths may produce the expected outputs and some may not. Our goal is to find a TA that is both correct, i.e. produces the same outputs as the SUT, and is deterministic. Consequently, we reward these properties with positive fitness.

The simulation function $\text{SIM}(\mathcal{G}, tt)$ simulates a timed trace tt on a generated TA $\mathcal{G}$ and returns a set of timed traces. It uses the TTS semantics but does not treat outputs as urgent outputs. From the initial state $(l_0, \mathbf{0})$, where l_0 is the initial location of $\mathcal{G}$, it performs the following steps for each $t_i e_i \in tt$ with $t_0 = 0$:

1. From state $q = (l, \nu)$
2. Delay for $d = t_i - t_{i-1}$ to reach $q^d = (l, \nu + d)$
3. If $e_i \in \Sigma_I$, i.e. it is an input:
   3.1. If $\exists o \in \Sigma_O, d^o \leq d : (l, \nu + d^o) \xrightarrow{o}$, i.e. an output would have been possible while delaying or at time t_i
      $\rightsquigarrow$ then mark e_i
   3.2. If $\exists q^1, q^2, q^1 \neq q^2 : q^d \xrightarrow{e_i} q^1 \wedge q^d \xrightarrow{e_i} q^2$
      $\rightsquigarrow$ then mark e_i
   3.3. For all q' such that $q^d \xrightarrow{e_i} q'$
      $\rightsquigarrow$ carry on exploration with q'
4. If $e_i \in \Sigma_O$, i.e. it is an output:
   4.1. If $\exists o \in \Sigma_O, d^o < d : (l, \nu + d^o) \xrightarrow{o}$, i.e. an output would have been possible while delaying
      $\rightsquigarrow$ stop exploration
   4.2. If $\exists q^1, q^2, q^1 \neq q^2 : q^d \xrightarrow{e_i} q^1 \wedge q^d \xrightarrow{e_i} q^2$ or $\exists o, o \neq e_i : q^d \xrightarrow{o}$
      $\rightsquigarrow$ stop exploration
   4.3. If there is a q' such that $q^d \xrightarrow{e_i} q'$
      $\rightsquigarrow$ carry on exploration with q'

The procedure shown above allows for two types of non-determinism. During delays before executing an input, we may ignore outputs (3.1) and we may explore multiple paths with inputs (3.3). We mark these inputs to be non-deterministic, through (3.1 and 3.2). Since we explore multiple paths, a single input e_i may be marked along one path but not marked along another path. In contrast, we do not explore non-deterministic outputs, leading to lower fitness for respective traces. This avoids issues with trivial TA which produce each output all the time. Such TA would completely simulate all traces non-deterministically, but would not be useful.

During exploration, $\text{SIM}(\mathcal{G}, tt)$ collects and returns timed traces tts, which are prefixes of tt but with marked and unmarked inputs. For fitness computation, we defined four auxiliary functions. The first one assigns a simulation verdict:

$$\text{VERDICT}(tts) = \begin{cases} \text{PASS} & \text{if } |tts| = 1 \wedge tt \in tts \\ \text{NONDET} & \text{if } |tts| > 1 \wedge \exists tt' \in tts : |tt'| = |tt| \\ \text{FAIL} & \text{otherwise} \end{cases}$$

A TA, which produces a PASS verdict for all timed traces, behaves equivalently to the SUT for these traces. NONDET is returned in case of non-determinism with at least one correct execution path. Function $\text{STEPS}(tts)$ returns the maximum number of deterministic steps, and $\text{OUT}(tts)$ returns the number of outputs along the longest traces in tts. Finally, $\text{SIZE}(\mathcal{G})$ returns the number of edges.

Fitness Computation. In order to compute the fitness, we assign the weights w_{PASS}, w_{NONDET}, w_{FAIL}, w_{STEPS}, w_{OUT}, and w_{SIZE} to the gathered information of $\mathcal{G}$. Basically, we give some positive fitness for deterministic steps, correctly produced outputs, and verdicts, but penalise size. Let $\mathcal{TT}$ be the timed traces on which $\mathcal{G}$ is evaluated. The fitness $\text{FIT}(\mathcal{G})$ is then (note that $w_{\text{VERDICT}(tts)}$ evaluates to one of w_{PASS}, w_{NONDET}, or w_{FAIL}):

$$\text{FIT}(\mathcal{G}) = \sum_{tt \in \mathcal{TT}} \text{FIT}(\mathcal{G}, tt) - w_{\text{SIZE}} \, \text{SIZE}(\mathcal{G}) \quad \text{where}$$

$$\text{FIT}(\mathcal{G}, tt) = w_{\text{VERDICT}(tts)} + w_{\text{STEPS}} \, \text{STEPS}(tts) + w_{\text{OUT}} \, \text{OUT}(tts) \text{ and } tts = \text{SIM}(\mathcal{G}, tt)$$

Fitness evaluation adds further parameters. We identified guidelines for choosing them adequately. We generally set $w_{\text{FAIL}} = 0$ and use w_{OUT} as basis for other weights. Usually, we set $w_{\text{STEP}} = w_{\text{OUT}}/2$ and $w_{\text{PASS}} = k \cdot l \cdot w_{\text{OUT}}$, where l is the average length of test sequences and k is a small natural number, e.g. 4. More important than the exact value of k is setting $w_{\text{NONDET}} = w_{\text{PASS}}/2$ which gives positive fitness to correctly produced timed traces but with a bias towards deterministic solutions. The weight w_{SIZE} should be chosen low, such that it does not prevent adding of necessary edges. We usually set it to w_{STEP}. It needs to be non-zero, though. Otherwise an acceptable solution could be a tree-shaped automaton exactly representing $\mathcal{TT}$ without generalisation. As noted at the beginning of this section, we assign larger fitness to solutions that accept a larger portion of the traces deterministically, as our goal is to learn deterministic TA.

As noted above, a TA $\mathcal{T}$ producing only PASS verdicts behaves equivalently to the SUT with respect to $\mathcal{TT}$, i.e. $\mathcal{T}$ is "approximately trace equivalent" to the SUT. Due to the restriction to deterministic output-urgent systems, trace inclusion and trace equivalence coincide. As a result, a TA producing a FAIL verdict is neither an under- nor an over-approximation.

3.3   Creation of New Population

Table 1 lists all implemented mutation operators for TA. Whenever an operator selects an edge or a location, the selection is random, but favours locations and edges which are associated with faults and non-deterministic behaviour. We augment TA with such information during fitness evaluation. To create an edge, we create random guards and reset sets, and choose a random label, like for the initial creation of TA.

Table 1. Mutation operators

Name	Short description
Add constraint	Add a guard constraint to an edge
Change guard	Select edge and create a random guard if the edge does not have a guard, otherwise mutate a constraint of its guard
Change target	Change the target location of an edge
Remove guard	Remove either all or a single guard constraint from an edge
Change resets	Remove clocks from or add clocks to the clock resets of an edge
Remove edge	Remove a selected edge
Add edge	Add an edge connecting randomly chosen locations
Sink location	Add a new location
Merge location	Merge two locations
Split location	Split a location l by creating a new location l' and redirecting an edge reaching l to l'
Add location	Add a new location and two edges connecting the new location to existing locations
Split edge	Replace an edge e with either the sequence $e' \cdot e$ or $e \cdot e'$ where e' is a new random edge (adds a location to connect e and e')

The mutation operators form three groups separated by double horizontal lines. The first and largest group contains basic operators, which are sufficient to create all possible automata. The second group is motivated by the basic principle behind automata learning algorithms. Passive algorithms often start with a tree-shaped representation of traces and transform this representation into an automaton via iterated state-merging [20]. Active learning algorithms on the other hand usually start with a low number of locations and add new locations if necessary. This can be interpreted as splitting of existing locations, an intuition which also served as a basis for test-case generation in active automata learning [5]. The last two operators are motivated by observations during experiments: *add location* increases the automaton size but avoids creating deadlock states, unlike the operator *sink location*. *Split edge* addresses issues related to input enabledness, where an input i is implicitly accepted without changing state, although an edge labelled i should change the state. The operator aims to introduce such edges. For mutation, we generally select one of the operators uniformly at random.

In addition to mutation, we apply a simplification procedure. It changes the syntactic representation of TA without affecting semantics, by, e.g., removing unreachable locations. For further details regarding simplification, migration, selection and crossover we refer to our technical report [44].

3.4   Implementation

The presented algorithms have been implemented in a tool shown in Fig. 4 and can be found online [45]. The tool supports customisation of almost all relevant parameters. When selecting one of the presented experiments, the tool will propose the same values that were used in the evaluation presented in Sect. 4.

While the tool is general enough to learn from any set of timed traces given in the correct format, the prototype is currently only meant for evaluating the examples presented in this paper. A full release of the tool is planned soon.

The tool implements the presented automatic genetic-programming process, with the possibility to inspect the current status of the search, like the accepted traces by the current population. In case the search gets stuck, the tool also allows for manual changes to be performed, enabling semi-automatic modelling.

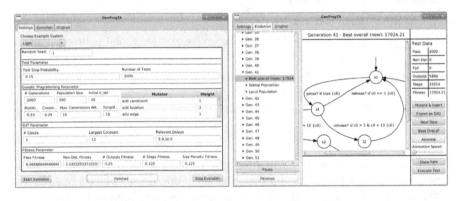

Fig. 4. Two screenshots of the genetic programming tool for time automata, illustrating the possible configurations (left) and the screen to view intermediate results (right).

4   Case Studies

Our evaluation is based on four manually created and 40 randomly generated TA, which serve as our SUTs. Using TA provides us with an easy way of checking whether we found the correct model. However, our approach and our tool are general enough to work on real black-box implementations. Our algorithms are implemented in Java. A demonstrator with a GUI is available in the supplementary material, which also includes Graphviz dot-files of the TA [45]. The demonstrator allows repeating all experiments presented in the following with freely configurable parameters. Moreover, the search progress can be inspected anytime. The user interface lists the fittest TA for each generation and visualises each of them along with the timed traces used for learning.

For the evaluation, we generated timed traces by simulating n_{test} random test sequences on the SUTs. The inputs in the test sequences were selected uniformly at random from the available inputs. The lengths of the test sequences are geometrically distributed with a parameter p_{test}, which is set to 0.15 unless otherwise noted. To avoid trivial timed traces, we ensure that all test sequences cause at least one output to be produced. The delays in test sequences were chosen probabilistically in accordance with the user-specified largest constant c_{max}. Additionally, one could specify important constants used in the SUTs, gathered from a requirements document if available. Specifying appropriate delays helps to ensure that the SUTs are covered sufficiently well by the test sequences.

Measurement Setup and Criteria. The measurements were done on a notebook with 16 GB RAM and an Intel Core i7-5600U CPU operating at 2.6 GHz. Our main goal is to show that we can learn models in a reasonable amount of time, but further improvements are possible, e.g., via parallelisation. We use a training set and a test set for evaluation, each containing n_{test} timed traces. First, we learn from the training set until we find a TA which produces a **PASS** verdict for all traces. Then, we simulate the traces from the test set and report all traces leading to a verdict other than **PASS** as erroneous. Note that since we generate the test set traces through testing, there are no negative traces. In other words, all traces are observable and can be considered positive. Consequently, notions like precision and recall do not apply to our setting.

Our four manually created TA, with number of locations and c_{max} in parentheses, are called car alarm system (CAS) $(14, 30)$, Train $(6, 10)$, Light $(5, 10)$, and particle counter (PC) $(26, 10)$. All of them use one clock. The CAS is an industrial case study, which served as a benchmark for test-case generation for timed systems [3]. Different versions of the Train and Light have been used as examples in real-time verification [8] and variants of them are distributed as demo examples with the real-time model-checker UPPAAL [27] and the real-time testing tool UPPAAL TRON [18]. The particle counter (PC) is the second industrial case study. Untimed versions of it were examined in model-based testing [2].

In addition to the manually created timed systems, we have four categories of random TA, each containing ten TA: C15/1, C20/1, C6/2, C10/2, where the first number gives the number of locations and the second the number of clocks. TA from the first two categories have alphabets containing 5 distinct inputs and 5 distinct outputs, while the TA from the other two categories have 4 inputs and 4 outputs. For all random TA, we have $c_{\text{max}} = 15$.

We used similar configurations for all experiments. Following the suggestions in Sect. 3, we set the fitness weights to $w_{\text{OUT}} = 0.25$, $w_{\text{STEPS}} = \frac{w_{\text{OUT}}}{2} = w_{\text{SIZE}}$, $w_{\text{PASS}} = \frac{4 w_{\text{OUT}}}{p_{\text{test}}}$, $w_{\text{NONDET}} = \frac{\text{PASS}}{2}$, and $w_{\text{FAIL}} = 0$, with the exception of CAS. Since the search frequently got trapped in minima with non-deterministic behaviour, we set $w_{\text{OUT}} = \frac{w_{\text{STEPS}}}{2}$, i.e. we valued deterministic steps more than outputs, and $w_{\text{NONDET}} = -0.5$, i.e. we added a small penalty for non-determinism. Other than

Table 2. Measurement results

TA	Test set errors	Generations	Time
CAS	0	147/246.0/305.8/595	27.3 min/57.2 min/1.2 h/2.7 h
Train	0	50/71.0/83.4/180	2.9 min/4.7 min/4.8 min/9.1 min
Light	0	42/77.5/84.5/240	3.2 min/7.4 min/8.7 min/31.1 min
PC	0	278/685.5/554.9/859	3.0 h/8.7 h/7.3 h/10.6 h
C15/1	0/2.0/1.8/6	201/404.5/401.3/746	1.4 h/3.1 h/3.2 h/6.6 h
C20/1	0/0.0/1.0/6	45/451.0/665.8/1798	23.4 min/6.7 h/7.4 h/18.3 h
C6/2	0/0.0/0.5/3	18/68.5/176.9/709	9.4 min/43.9 min/1.8 h/7.6 h
C10/2	0/2.5/2.6/8	73/239.0/344.9/984	35.8 min/3.1 h/3.4 h/9.3 h

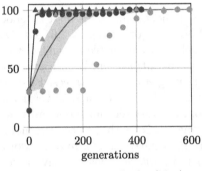 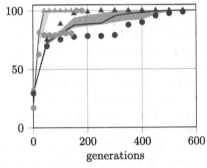

(a) Percentages for the Light (blue) and the CAS (red).

(b) Percentages for the PC (blue) and the Train (red).

Fig. 5. Percentages of accepted test steps of fittest individual. (Color figure online)

that, we set $g_{max} = 3000$, $n_{pop} = 2000$, the initial $n_{sel} = \frac{n_{pop}}{10}$, $n_{test} = 2000$, $p_{cr} = 0.25$, $g_{change} = 10$, $p_{mutinit} = 0.33$, and $g_{simp} = 10$, with the following exceptions. Train and Light require less effort, thus we set $n_{pop} = 500$. The categories C10/2, C15/1, and C20/1 require more thorough testing, so we configured $n_{test} = 4000$ for C10/2 and C15/1, and $n_{test} = 6000$ with $p_{test} = 0.1$ for C20/1. We determined the settings for n_{test} experimentally, by manually inspecting if the intermediate learned TA were approximately equivalent to the true models, so as to ensure that the training sets adequately cover the relevant behaviour.

All learning runs were successful by finding a TA without errors on the training set, except for two cases, one in C10/2 and one in C20/1. For the first, we repeated the experiment with a larger population $n_{pop} = 6000$, resulting in successful learning. For the random TA in C20/1, we observed a similar issue as for CAS, i.e. non-determinism was an issue, but used another solution. In some cases, crossover may introduce non-determinism, thus we decreased the probability for crossover p_{cr} to 0.05 and learned the correct model. Hence, we are able to learn TA that are consistent with given trace data via genetic programming.

Table 2 shows the learning results. The column *test set error* contains 0, if there were no errors on the test set. Otherwise, each cell in the table contains, from left to right, the minimum, the median and the mean, and the maximum computed over 10 runs for manually created TA and over 10 runs for each random category, i.e. one run per random TA.

Figure 5a and b illustrate the percentage of correct steps when simulating the test cases on the intermediate learned models. The solid line represents the median out of the 10 runs, the dots represent the minimum, the triangles the maximum and the coloured area is the area between first and third quartile. One can see a steep rise in the early generations, while later generations are mainly needed to minimise the learned models, which already correctly incorporate all test steps. The CAS is the model with the slowest initial learning, where, in the worst case, the first 200 generations did not improve the model.

The test set errors are generally low, so our approach generalises well and does not simply overfit to the training data. We also see that manually created systems produced no test set errors. While the more complex, random TA led to errors. However, for them the relative number of errors was at most two thousandths (8 errors out of 4000 tests). Such errors may, e.g., be caused by slightly too loose or too strict guards on inputs.

The computation time of at most 18.3 h seems acceptable, especially considering that fitness evaluation, as the most time-consuming part, is parallelisable. Finally, we want to emphasise that we identified parameters which almost consistently produced good results. In the exceptions where this was not the case, it was simple to adapt the configuration.

The size of our TA in terms of number of locations ranges between 5 and 26. To model real-world systems, it is therefore necessary to apply abstraction during the testing phase, which collects timed traces. Since model learning requires thorough testing, abstraction is commonly used in this area. Consequently, this requirement is not a strong limitation. Several applications of automata learning show that implementation flaws can be detected by analysing learned abstract models, e.g., in protocol implementations [12,40,43].

In conclusion, we have shown that we can learn models that are consistent with given training data and that these models generalise to test data that is produced equally, but which does not overlap with the training data. Since we learn from randomly generated data in our experiments, the learned models may not be equivalent to true underlying models. However, a manual inspection revealed that we generally learned correct models, with the exception of slight discrepancies in behaviour in some cases. We are currently working on extending our work to actively search for counterexamples to equivalence which could potentially provide stronger guarantees (see also our discussion on future work).

5   Conclusion

Summary. We presented an approach to learn deterministic TA with urgent outputs, an important subclass for testing timed systems [19]. The learned models may reveal flaws during manual inspection and enable verification of black-box systems via model-checking. Genetic programming serves as a basis. In our implementation of it, we parallelise search by evolving two populations simultaneously and developed techniques for mutation, crossover, and for a fine-grained fitness-evaluation. While, due to the heuristic nature of the proposed method, we cannot provide a convergence proof, we provide empirical evidence that the method performs well, can cope with big state spaces and generally converges to a solution consistent with given trace data. We evaluated the technique on non-trivial TA with up to 26 locations. We could learn all 44 TA models, only two random TA needed a small parameter adjustment.

Related Work. Verwer et al. [46,47] passively learned real-time automata via state-merging. These TA measure the time between two consecutive events and use guards in the form of intervals, i.e. they have a single clock which is reset on every transition. They do not distinguish between inputs and outputs. Improvements of [47] were presented in [34]. Similarly, Mao et al. applied state-merging to learn continuous time Markov chains [32]. A state-merging-based learning algorithm for more general stochastic timed systems has been proposed by de Matos Pedro et al. [33]. They target learning generalised semi-Markov processes, which are generated by stochastic timed automata. All these techniques have in common that they consider systems where the relation between events is fully described by a system's structure. Pastore et al. [38] learn specifications capturing the duration of (nested) operations in software systems. A timed trace therefore includes for each operation its start and end, i.e. the trace records two related events. Their algorithm is based on the passive learning technique *k-Tail.*

Grinchtein et al. [15,16] described active learning approaches for deterministic event-recording automata, a subclass of TA with one clock per action. The clock corresponding to an action is reset upon its execution essentially recording the time since the action has occurred. While the expressiveness of these automata suffices for many applications, the runtime complexity of the described techniques is high and may be prohibitive in practice. Currently, there is no implementation to actually measure runtime. Furthermore, this kind of TA cannot model certain timing patterns, e.g., in the case of input enabledness where always resetting a clock may not be appropriate. Lin et al. [29] also presented an active learning algorithm for event-recording automata and applied it to learn assumptions in compositional verification via assume-guarantee reasoning [30].

Meta-heuristic search as an alternative to classical automata learning has been proposed by Lai et al. for finite state machines [26]. They apply genetic algorithms and assume the number of states to be known. Lucas and Reynolds compared state-merging and evolutionary algorithms, but also fixed the number of states for runs of the latter [31].

Lefticaru et al. similarly assume the number of states to be known and generate state machine models via genetic algorithms [28]. Their goal, however, is to synthesise a model satisfying a specification given in temporal logics. Early work suggesting such an approach was performed by Johnson [23], which like our approach does not require the solution size to be known. In contrast, Johnson does not apply crossover. Further synthesis work from Katz and Peled [24] tries to infer a correct program or model on the source code level, while we aim at synthesising a model representing a black-box system. Nenzi et al. [36] presented an evolutionary algorithm for mining specifications in signal temporal logic (STL) distinguishing between regular and anomalous system behaviour. An important difference to our work is that they perform a classification task, while we learn models producing the same traces as the systems under consideration.

Evolutionary methods have been combined with testing in several areas: Abdessalem et al. [1] use evolutionary algorithms for the generation of test scenarios and learn decision trees to identify critical scenarios. Using the learned trees, they can steer the test generation towards critical scenarios. The tool Evosuite by Fraser and Arcuri [13] uses genetic operators for optimising whole test suites at once, increasing the overall coverage, while reducing the size of the test suite. Walkinshaw and Fraser presented Test by Committee, test-case generation using uncertainty sampling [49]. The approach is independent of the type of model that is inferred and an adaption of Query By Committee, a technique commonly used in active learning. In their implementation, they infer several hypotheses at each stage via genetic programming, generate random tests and select those tests which lead to the most disagreement between the hypotheses. In contrast to most other works considered, their implementation infers nonsequential programs. It infers functions mapping from numerical inputs to single outputs.

The work by Steffen et al. [21,42] is another good showcase for the strong possible relation between testing and model learning. They combine both areas, by performing black box tests and using the results to generate a model. Contrary to our work, they perform active learning, i.e., they use the intermediate versions of the learned models to guide the test generation. For a more comprehensive overview of combinations of learning and testing, we refer to [4].

Future Work. As indicated above, our technique is entirely passive, i.e. we learn from a set of timed traces (test observations), collected beforehand by random testing. There is no feedback from genetic programming to testing. In contrast to this, model-based testing could be applied to find discrepancies between the SUT and learned models [48]. These may then be used to iteratively improve the models. Active testing based on intermediate learned models may improve coverage of the SUT while requiring fewer tests, since we would benefit from additional knowledge about the system behaviour. This may therefore lead to improved accuracy of the model and increased performance through a reduction of tests and testing time. We are currently investigating this approach.

Assuming output urgency helps to approximate equivalence checks by "testing" candidate automata during learning. However, such models do not allow for uncertainty with respect to output timing. Relaxing this limitation represents an important next step. We are also currently working on this topic.

We demonstrated that TA can be genetically programmed, i.e. their structure is amenable to iterative refinement via mutation and crossover. Therefore, we could apply the same approach, but base the fitness evaluation on model checking by adapting the technique presented by Katz and Peled [24], to synthesise TA satisfying some properties. This would enable learning a black-box system, which may contain errors, and synthesising a controller ensuring that those errors do not lead to observable system failures.

Acknowledgment. The work of B. Aichernig and M. Tappler has been carried out as part of the TU Graz LEAD project "Dependable Internet of Things in Adverse Environments". The work of K. Larsen and F. Lorber has been conducted within the ENABLE-S3 project that has received funding from the ECSEL Joint Undertaking under grant agreement no. 692455. This joint undertaking receives support from the European Union's Horizon 2020 research and innovation programme and Austria, Denmark, Germany, Finland, Czech Republic, Italy, Spain, Portugal, Poland, Ireland, Belgium, France, Netherlands, United Kingdom, Slovakia, Norway. We would like to thank student Andrea Pferscher for her help in implementing the demonstrator. We also want to thank the anonymous reviewers for their insightful comments and suggestions.

References

1. Abdessalem, R.B., Nejati, S., Briand, L.C., Stifter, T.: Testing vision-based control systems using learnable evolutionary algorithms. In: ICSE 2018, pp. 1016–1026. ACM (2018). https://doi.org/10.1145/3180155.3180160
2. Aichernig, B.K., et al.: Model-based mutation testing of an industrial measurement device. In: Seidl, M., Tillmann, N. (eds.) TAP 2014. LNCS, vol. 8570, pp. 1–19. Springer, Cham (2014). https://doi.org/10.1007/978-3-319-09099-3_1
3. Aichernig, B.K., Lorber, F., Ničković, D.: Time for mutants — model-based mutation testing with timed automata. In: Veanes, M., Viganò, L. (eds.) TAP 2013. LNCS, vol. 7942, pp. 20–38. Springer, Heidelberg (2013). https://doi.org/10.1007/978-3-642-38916-0_2
4. Aichernig, B.K., Mostowski, W., Mousavi, M.R., Tappler, M., Taromirad, M.: Model learning and model-based testing. In: Bennaceur, A., Hähnle, R., Meinke, K. (eds.) Machine Learning for Dynamic Software Analysis: Potentials and Limits. LNCS, vol. 11026, pp. 74–100. Springer, Cham (2018). https://doi.org/10.1007/978-3-319-96562-8_3
5. Aichernig, B.K., Tappler, M.: Efficient active automata learning via mutation testing. J. Autom. Reason. (2018). https://doi.org/10.1007/s10817-018-9486-0
6. Alur, R., Dill, D.L.: A theory of timed automata. Theor. Comput. Sci. **126**(2), 183–235 (1994). https://doi.org/10.1016/0304-3975(94)90010-8
7. Argyros, G., Stais, I., Jana, S., Keromytis, A.D., Kiayias, A.: SFADiff: automated evasion attacks and fingerprinting using black-box differential automata learning. In: Proceedings of the 2016 ACM SIGSAC Conference on Computer and Communications Security, pp. 1690–1701. ACM (2016). https://doi.org/10.1145/2976749.2978383
8. Behrmann, G., David, A., Larsen, K.G.: A tutorial on UPPAAL. In: Bernardo, M., Corradini, F. (eds.) SFM-RT 2004. LNCS, vol. 3185, pp. 200–236. Springer, Heidelberg (2004). https://doi.org/10.1007/978-3-540-30080-9_7
9. Bornot, S., Sifakis, J., Tripakis, S.: Modeling urgency in timed systems. In: de Roever, W.-P., Langmaack, H., Pnueli, A. (eds.) COMPOS 1997. LNCS, vol. 1536, pp. 103–129. Springer, Heidelberg (1998). https://doi.org/10.1007/3-540-49213-5_5

10. David, A., Larsen, K.G., Legay, A., Nyman, U., Wasowski, A.: Timed I/O automata: a complete specification theory for real-time systems. In: Johansson, K.H., Yi, W. (eds.) HSCC 2010, pp. 91–100. ACM (2010). https://doi.org/10.1145/1755952.1755967

11. Elkind, E., Genest, B., Peled, D., Qu, H.: Grey-box checking. In: Najm, E., Pradat-Peyre, J.-F., Donzeau-Gouge, V.V. (eds.) FORTE 2006. LNCS, vol. 4229, pp. 420–435. Springer, Heidelberg (2006). https://doi.org/10.1007/11888116_30

12. Fiterău-Broştean, P., Janssen, R., Vaandrager, F.: Combining model learning and model checking to analyze TCP implementations. In: Chaudhuri, S., Farzan, A. (eds.) CAV 2016. LNCS, vol. 9780, pp. 454–471. Springer, Cham (2016). https://doi.org/10.1007/978-3-319-41540-6_25

13. Fraser, G., Arcuri, A.: EvoSuite: automatic test suite generation for object-oriented software. In: SIGSOFT/FSE 2011, pp. 416–419. ACM (2011). https://doi.org/10.1145/2025113.2025179

14. Gómez, R.: A compositional translation of timed automata with deadlines to UPPAAL timed automata. In: Ouaknine, J., Vaandrager, F.W. (eds.) FORMATS 2009. LNCS, vol. 5813, pp. 179–194. Springer, Heidelberg (2009). https://doi.org/10.1007/978-3-642-04368-0_15

15. Grinchtein, O., Jonsson, B., Leucker, M.: Learning of event-recording automata. Theor. Comput. Sci. **411**(47), 4029–4054 (2010). https://doi.org/10.1016/j.tcs.2010.07.008

16. Grinchtein, O., Jonsson, B., Pettersson, P.: Inference of event-recording automata using timed decision trees. In: Baier, C., Hermanns, H. (eds.) CONCUR 2006. LNCS, vol. 4137, pp. 435–449. Springer, Heidelberg (2006). https://doi.org/10.1007/11817949_29

17. Groce, A., Peled, D., Yannakakis, M.: Adaptive model checking. In: Katoen, J.-P., Stevens, P. (eds.) TACAS 2002. LNCS, vol. 2280, pp. 357–370. Springer, Heidelberg (2002). https://doi.org/10.1007/3-540-46002-0_25

18. Hessel, A., Larsen, K.G., Mikucionis, M., Nielsen, B., Pettersson, P., Skou, A.: Testing real-time systems using UPPAAL. In: Hierons, R.M., Bowen, J.P., Harman, M. (eds.) Formal Methods and Testing. LNCS, vol. 4949, pp. 77–117. Springer, Heidelberg (2008). https://doi.org/10.1007/978-3-540-78917-8_3

19. Hessel, A., Larsen, K.G., Nielsen, B., Pettersson, P., Skou, A.: Time-optimal real-time test case generation using UPPAAL. In: Petrenko, A., Ulrich, A. (eds.) FATES 2003. LNCS, vol. 2931, pp. 114–130. Springer, Heidelberg (2004). https://doi.org/10.1007/978-3-540-24617-6_9

20. de la Higuera, C.: Grammatical Inference: Learning Automata and Grammars. Cambridge University Press, New York (2010)

21. Hungar, H., Margaria, T., Steffen, B.: Test-based model generation for legacy systems. In: ITC 2003, pp. 971–980. IEEE (2003). https://doi.org/10.1109/TEST.2003.1271084

22. Isberner, M., Howar, F., Steffen, B.: The open-source LearnLib - a framework for active automata learning. In: Kroening, D., Păsăreanu, C.S. (eds.) CAV 2015. LNCS, vol. 9206, pp. 487–495. Springer, Cham (2015). https://doi.org/10.1007/978-3-319-21690-4_32

23. Johnson, C.G.: Genetic programming with fitness based on model checking. In: Ebner, M., O'Neill, M., Ekárt, A., Vanneschi, L., Esparcia-Alcázar, A.I. (eds.) EuroGP 2007. LNCS, vol. 4445, pp. 114–124. Springer, Heidelberg (2007). https://doi.org/10.1007/978-3-540-71605-1_11

24. Katz, G., Peled, D.: Synthesizing, correcting and improving code, using model checking-based genetic programming. STTT **19**(4), 449–464 (2017). https://doi.org/10.1007/s10009-016-0418-1

25. Koza, J.R.: Genetic Programming - On the Programming of Computers by Means of Natural Selection. Complex adaptive systems. MIT Press, Cambridge (1993)

26. Lai, Z., Cheung, S.C., Jiang, Y.: Dynamic model learning using genetic algorithm under adaptive model checking framework. In: QSIC 2006, pp. 410–417. IEEE (2006). https://doi.org/10.1109/QSIC.2006.25

27. Larsen, K.G., Pettersson, P., Yi, W.: UPPAAL in a nutshell. STTT **1**(1–2), 134–152 (1997). https://doi.org/10.1007/s100090050010

28. Lefticaru, R., Ipate, F., Tudose, C.: Automated model design using genetic algorithms and model checking. In: BCI 2009, pp. 79–84. IEEE (2009). https://doi.org/10.1109/BCI.2009.15

29. Lin, S.-W., André, É., Dong, J.S., Sun, J., Liu, Y.: An efficient algorithm for learning event-recording automata. In: Bultan, T., Hsiung, P.-A. (eds.) ATVA 2011. LNCS, vol. 6996, pp. 463–472. Springer, Heidelberg (2011). https://doi.org/10.1007/978-3-642-24372-1_35

30. Lin, S., André, É., Liu, Y., Sun, J., Dong, J.S.: Learning assumptions for compositional verification of timed systems. IEEE Trans. Softw. Eng. **40**(2), 137–153 (2014). https://doi.org/10.1109/TSE.2013.57

31. Lucas, S.M., Reynolds, T.J.: Learning DFA: evolution versus evidence driven state merging. In: CEC 2003, pp. 351–358. IEEE (2003). https://doi.org/10.1109/CEC.2003.1299597

32. Mao, H., Chen, Y., Jaeger, M., Nielsen, T.D., Larsen, K.G., Nielsen, B.: Learning deterministic probabilistic automata from a model checking perspective. Mach. Learn. **105**(2), 255–299 (2016). https://doi.org/10.1007/s10994-016-5565-9

33. de Matos Pedro, A., Crocker, P.A., de Sousa, S.M.: Learning stochastic timed automata from sample executions. In: Margaria, T., Steffen, B. (eds.) ISoLA 2012. LNCS, vol. 7609, pp. 508–523. Springer, Heidelberg (2012). https://doi.org/10.1007/978-3-642-34026-0_38

34. Mediouni, B.L., Nouri, A., Bozga, M., Bensalem, S.: Improved learning for stochastic timed models by state-merging algorithms. In: Barrett, C., Davies, M., Kahsai, T. (eds.) NFM 2017. LNCS, vol. 10227, pp. 178–193. Springer, Cham (2017). https://doi.org/10.1007/978-3-319-57288-8_13

35. Mitchell, M.: An Introduction to Genetic Algorithms. MIT Press, Cambridge (1998)

36. Nenzi, L., Silvetti, S., Bartocci, E., Bortolussi, L.: A robust genetic algorithm for learning temporal specifications from data. In: McIver, A., Horvath, A. (eds.) QEST 2018. LNCS, vol. 11024, pp. 323–338. Springer, Cham (2018). https://doi.org/10.1007/978-3-319-99154-2_20

37. Nowostawski, M., Poli, R.: Parallel genetic algorithm taxonomy. In: KES 1999, pp. 88–92. IEEE (1999). https://doi.org/10.1109/KES.1999.820127

38. Pastore, F., Micucci, D., Mariani, L.: Timed k-tail: automatic inference of timed automata. In: ICST 2017, pp. 401–411 (2017). https://doi.org/10.1109/ICST.2017.43

39. Peled, D.A., Vardi, M.Y., Yannakakis, M.: Black box checking. JALC **7**(2), 225–246 (2002)

40. de Ruiter, J., Poll, E.: Protocol state fuzzing of TLS implementations. In: USENIX Security 2015, pp. 193–206. USENIX Association (2015). https://www.usenix.org/conference/usenixsecurity15/technical-sessions/presentation/de-ruiter

41. Springintveld, J., Vaandrager, F.W., D'Argenio, P.R.: Testing timed automata. Theor. Comput. Sci. **254**(1–2), 225–257 (2001). https://doi.org/10.1016/S0304-3975(99)00134-6

42. Steffen, B., Howar, F., Merten, M.: Introduction to active automata learning from a practical perspective. In: Bernardo, M., Issarny, V. (eds.) SFM 2011. LNCS, vol. 6659, pp. 256–296. Springer, Heidelberg (2011). https://doi.org/10.1007/978-3-642-21455-4_8

43. Tappler, M., Aichernig, B.K., Bloem, R.: Model-based testing IoT communication via active automata learning. In: ICST 2017, pp. 276–287 (2017). https://doi.org/10.1109/ICST.2017.32

44. Tappler, M., Aichernig, B.K., Larsen, K.G., Lorber, F.: Learning timed automata via genetic programming. CoRR abs/1808.07744 (2018). http://arxiv.org/abs/1808.07744

45. Tappler, M., Pferscher, A.: Supplementary Material for "Learning Timed Automata via Genetic Programming" (2019). https://doi.org/10.6084/m9.figshare.5513575.v1. https://figshare.com/articles/Supplementary_Material_for_Learning_Timed_Automata_via_Genetic_Programming_/5513575

46. Verwer, S., De Weerdt, M., Witteveen, C.: An algorithm for learning real-time automata. In: Benelearn 2007 (2007)

47. Verwer, S., de Weerdt, M., Witteveen, C.: A likelihood-ratio test for identifying probabilistic deterministic real-time automata from positive data. In: Sempere, J.M., García, P. (eds.) ICGI 2010. LNCS (LNAI), vol. 6339, pp. 203–216. Springer, Heidelberg (2010). https://doi.org/10.1007/978-3-642-15488-1_17

48. Walkinshaw, N., Derrick, J., Guo, Q.: Iterative refinement of reverse-engineered models by model-based testing. In: Cavalcanti, A., Dams, D.R. (eds.) FM 2009. LNCS, vol. 5850, pp. 305–320. Springer, Heidelberg (2009). https://doi.org/10.1007/978-3-642-05089-3_20

49. Walkinshaw, N., Fraser, G.: Uncertainty-driven black-box test data generation. In: ICST 2017, pp. 253–263 (2017). https://doi.org/10.1109/ICST.2017.30

Munta: A Verified Model Checker
for Timed Automata

Simon Wimmer[✉]

Fakultät für Informatik, Technische Universität München, Munich, Germany
wimmers@in.tum.de

Abstract. Munta is a mechanically verified model checker for timed automata, a popular formalism for modeling real-time systems. Our goal is two-fold: first, we want to provide a reference implementation that is fast enough to test other model checkers against it on reasonably sized benchmarks; second, the tool should be practical enough so that it can easily be used for experimentation. Munta can be compiled to Standard ML or OCaml and additionally features a web-based GUI. Its modeling language has a simple semantics but provides the most commonly used timed automata modeling features.

1 Objective and Overview

Timed automata [1] are a widely used formalism for modeling real-time systems, which is employed in a class of successful model checkers such as UPPAAL [3]. These tools can be understood as trust-multipliers: we trust their correctness to deduce trust in the safety of systems checked by these tools. Consequently, we would like to ensure two things: first, the theory behind the tools should be sound and well-understood. Second, the implementations of the theory in real model checkers should be correct.

To address these concerns, we present Munta[1], a model checker for timed automata with a full correctness proof in the interactive theorem prover Isabelle/HOL [13]. Everything is in one place, in a formal and highly reliable format: the theory, from the basic formalism, over abstract formalizations of fundamental concepts such as regions and zones, down to concrete algorithms on Difference Bound Matrices (DBMs), is formalized and checked in Isabelle/HOL. Moreover, we can generate executable code from this formalization to obtain a trustworthy model checker.

Having a formally verified tool at hand gives rise to the possibility of testing other model checkers against it, in order to find errors in the other tools' implementations. Therefore, the verified checker needs to be fast enough to run it on reasonably sized benchmarks. To this end, we use refinement with the Imperative Refinement Framework (IRF) [11] to obtain efficient imperative implementations of the DBM algorithms that lie at the heart of state-of-the-art timed automata model checking.

---

[1] https://wimmers.github.io/munta/.

É. André and M. Stoelinga (Eds.): FORMATS 2019, LNCS 11750, pp. 236–243, 2019.
https://doi.org/10.1007/978-3-030-29662-9_14

Moreover, a formally verified tool can serve as a valuable basis for experimentation. First, it allows one to devise extensions and modifications of the theory, to prove them correct, and to experiment with them in a real tool—all in one place. Second, the tool can be used to gain definite insights into the formalism and the model checking process by evaluating results on small models or by examining the state space that was explored by the verified tool. To support these roles, Munta provides a clear-cut modeling language with a standard semantics. Additionally, typical useful features of real model checkers such as reporting the set of explored states and deadlock checking are supported.

This paper gives an overview of Munta's functionality and architecture from a user's perspective. A theoretical account of the main ideas for the construction of the verified checker can be found in previous work [16,17].

2   Functionality

2.1   Modeling Language

Munta's modeling language supports a typical set of features: networks of timed automata that can synchronize over channels and share a discrete finite state, which is characterized by a set of integer variables. Guards and updates on the discrete state can be expressed with a simple language of Boolean and arithmetic expressions. Additionally, Munta supports the popular features of broadcast channels, and urgent and committed locations. Currently, there still exist some restrictions compared to other commonly used modeling languages: automata need to be diagonal free (i.e. clock constraints cannot involve differences of clocks) and updates can only reset clocks to zero. These limitations could be removed, however, by elaborating the current formalization. Moreover, they are the most commonly found restrictions of the formalism in tools and literature.

The formalized semantics of this language is compact, i.e., only around 150 lines of Isabelle formalization (compare this to the informal description found in the UPPAAL reference manual, for instance). This is the main basis of trust: if one accepts that this semantics is sensible and one trusts the correctness of Isabelle/HOL, one can assert full trust in Munta.

2.2   Correctness Theorem

This section briefly describes the correctness theorem for Munta informally. For a formal account see our previous work [17] or the Isabelle/HOL formalization. The correctness theorem is formulated in a separation logic [11] for Imperative HOL [5], which extends HOL with imperative programming features.

The theorem shows that the model checker will terminate and either return a result (*sat* or *unsat*), or report an error. It is proved that, when a result is returned, that it correctly indicates whether the model satisfies the formula. Two kind of errors can be reported: they either signify that the input model is malformed, or that the correctness check for a certified part of Munta failed (c.f. Sect. 3.2). It is also proved that errors are only reported if they really arise.

Note that correctness is ensured only with respect to the semantics of the modeling language and the semantics of Imperative HOL. None of the individual proof steps nor our formalization of model checking algorithms need to be trusted as everything is checked by Isabelle/HOL's logical kernel.

2.3   Input Format

Input models to the checker are provided in a simple JSON format. On the one hand, this means that input files are rather easy to read and understand for a human. On the other hand, it facilitates data exchange with other tools as parsers and printers for this format are readily available in many programming languages. We refrain from using a templating mechanism (like, e.g. UPPAAL) to provide templates of models that can be instantiated to obtain a concrete network. This way, translating to and from our input format remains simple. Finally, arbitrary fields can be added to objects anywhere in the JSON files. This allows one to transport formally irrelevant meta-information, such as the coordinates of locations in a visual representation.

2.4   Modeling Checking Capabilities

Munta can check formulas from the subset of CTL that corresponds to the subset of TCTL that is supported by UPPAAL. Moreover, Munta provides a deadlock checker. This is essential for practical use of the tool, as usually one wants to ensure that models are deadlock free before verifying more complex properties. Additionally, Munta can compute the complete set of reachable states and provide this information to the user. This is vital for understanding and debugging models.

2.5   Graphical User Interface

We provide a web-based GUI for Munta, programmed in the OCaml derivative Reason[2] using the ReasonReact framework[3]. The GUI can interface with the model checker in two ways: first, we provide a server mode, where queries can be sent to a verification server running locally; second, we compile the OCaml version of our checker to JavaScript, running it directly in the browser. We use a *parse-print-parse* loop to ensure that the user's input is understood correctly by the model checker: the GUI can display a normalized version of the user's input that is guaranteed to parse to the same internal representation as the user's original input. Munta itself again uses another parse-print-parse loop to produce a JSON description of the model that is guaranteed to parse to the same object as the JSON description that was extracted from the internal representation in the GUI.

[2] https://reasonml.github.io/.
[3] https://reasonml.github.io/reason-react/.

In addition, the user can directly inspect this final JSON representation of the model, to ensure that no errors were introduced during the translation from the visual representation.

3   Architecture

Figure 1 gives an overview of the system architecture, which is described in more detail in this section.

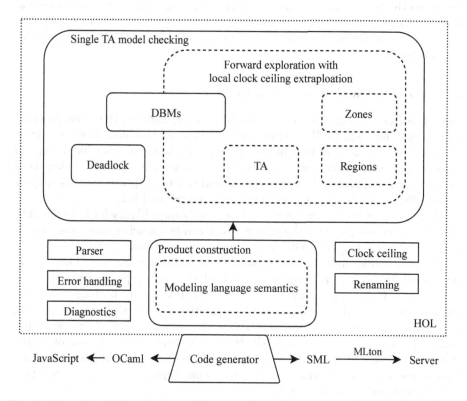

Fig. 1. Overview of the system architecture. Round boxes represent HOL formalizations. Boxes with sharp corners are pieces of unverified HOL code. Solid lines represent formalizations that include a refinement step to efficient (imperative) implementations.

3.1   Isabelle/HOL Formalization

The formalization consists of three main parts. The first part is an abstract formalization of the basic timed automata formalism (for a single automaton). This includes a formalization of the region construction, zones, and the local clock ceiling extrapolation operation for zones [2]. In the end, we can prove that forward analysis of timed automata with zones and extrapolation is correct [16].

The second part is an abstract formalization of DBMs and elementary model checking algorithms for CTL, which are refined to concrete, executable, and partly imperative implementations. Together with the first part, we obtain an executable model checker for single timed automata [17].

The third part is a formalization of the modeling language and of an on-the-fly product construction to obtain a single automaton. This construction yields descriptions of the single automaton's invariants and transitions as functional programs that can be plugged into the implementation obtained from the second part. To implement the product construction efficiently, a pre-processing step renames the labels in the model from human-readable strings to consecutive natural numbers.

3.2   Code Extraction and Glue Code

From the HOL specification of the model checker, Isabelle/HOL can generate code in Standard ML (SML) and OCaml [6]. However, this alone would not yield a usable tool. We need additional code for parsing the input, error handling, and retrieving diagnostic information. These functionalities are directly implemented as functional programs in HOL to keep the code portable, possibly to also export it to Isabelle/HOL's other target languages, Haskell and Scala.

To implement the parser, we use a parser combinator library for Isabelle/HOL [12]. A correctness proof for the parser is replaced by ensuring consistency of the parse-print-parse loop for each concrete input, as explained above.

Diagnostic information is obtained in a minimally intrusive way. This usually involves defining, e.g., a constant $PRINT$ of the HOL type $string \Rightarrow unit$ as $PRINT\ s = ()$. This constant can easily be stripped away by Isabelle's proof automation (by essentially unfolding its definition). To actually obtain output, we instruct the code generator to translate this specific constant in a way that some side-effect is performed, e.g., the string s is output to the console or logged in some background data structure. A similar technique can be used to obtain time measurements or to trace information about explored states by using other constants of some type $\alpha \Rightarrow unit$.

Two parts of the model checker, the pre-processing step to relabel the model, and the code to compute the local clock ceilings, are not verified but only certified: their computed results are checked for soundness by a verified part of the model checker.

The ability to target SML as well as OCaml holds some advantages. With SML, faster executables can be obtained by using the highly optimizing compiler MLton. In contrast, OCaml code compiles to less efficient executables but is very conveniently compatible with the implementation of our frontend: Reason hinges on the same backend as the one that we use to compile OCaml to JavaScript[4], making it easy to run our verified model checker directly in the browser.

---

[4] https://bucklescript.github.io/.

4   Discussion

4.1   Comparison to Other Tools

We have previously reported on an experimental evaluation of Munta, comparing it to the state-of-the-art timed automata model checker UPPAAL [17]. Generally, Munta's throughput (the number of explored states per time unit) is within an order of magnitude of UPPAAL's throughput. Munta is also fast enough to check medium-sized benchmarks within reasonable time.

Compared to UPPAAL, Munta is not only much slower, but also only provides a less sophisticated modeling language. UPPAAL supports such sophisticated features as a C-like language to describe guards and invariants on edges, channels with priorities, or a templating mechanism. However, our modeling language does not differ as significantly in its expressiveness from tools such as Prism (and its implementation of probabilistic timed automata) [9], TChecker [7], Rabbit [4] and RED [15]. Moreover, one can argue that for a tool which is mainly intended as a platform for experimentation, it is not crucial to provide an exhaustive array of modeling features. Instead, a simple modeling language with a clear semantics may even be advantageous.

4.2   Trusted Code Base

To trust the results of Munta, one needs to trust the following components:

(a) our formalization of the modeling language semantics as described above,
(b) the formalization of Imperative HOL and its corresponding separation logic,
(c) Isabelle/HOL's logical kernel,
(d) Isabelle/HOL's code generator,
(e) and the target language's compiler and runtime system.

Trust in (a) and (b) can only be obtained by manual inspection. Regarding (c), it is widely accepted within the community that Isabelle/HOL only admits valid theorems (at least on the user level). The trustworthiness of components (d) and (e) is more debatable, however. Recent (ongoing) work by Hupel and Nipkow [8] opens the prospect to improve on this situation in the future. It perfects (d) by generating code from Isabelle/HOL to CakeML [14] in a provably correct way (in the sense of mechanically checked proof). In turn, CakeML is a dialect of ML that comes with a verified compiler and runtime system, addressing the potential soundness issues of (e).

5   Conclusion and Future Work

We have presented Munta, a mechanically verified model checker for timed automata. As indicated in our discussion above, further efforts are conceivable to reduce the trusted code base. There are also several ways in which performance of the tool could be improved. One would be to verify the model checking algorithms with respect to a fully imperative target language such as LLVM [10] or C. As another approach, we are studying certification of reachability checking for timed automata in ongoing work.

Finally, the capabilities of Munta could be improved by either enriching the modeling formalism as discussed aboved, or by providing a more expressive specification language for model checking properties, such as full (T)CTL or LTL. To this end, we plan to extend our work on certification towards LTL model checking in the future.

References

1. Alur, R., Dill, D.L.: A theory of timed automata. Theor. Comput. Sci. **126**(2), 183–235 (1994). https://doi.org/10.1016/0304-3975(94)90010-8
2. Behrmann, G., Bouyer, P., Larsen, K.G., Pelánek, R.: Lower and upper bounds in zone based abstractions of timed automata. In: Jensen, K., Podelski, A. (eds.) TACAS 2004. LNCS, vol. 2988, pp. 312–326. Springer, Heidelberg (2004). https://doi.org/10.1007/978-3-540-24730-2_25
3. Bengtsson, J., Yi, W.: Timed automata: semantics, algorithms and tools. In: Desel, J., Reisig, W., Rozenberg, G. (eds.) ACPN 2003. LNCS, vol. 3098, pp. 87–124. Springer, Heidelberg (2004). https://doi.org/10.1007/978-3-540-27755-2_3
4. Beyer, D., Lewerentz, C., Noack, A.: Rabbit: a tool for BDD-based verification of real-time systems. In: Hunt, W.A., Somenzi, F. (eds.) CAV 2003. LNCS, vol. 2725, pp. 122–125. Springer, Heidelberg (2003). https://doi.org/10.1007/978-3-540-45069-6_13
5. Bulwahn, L., Krauss, A., Haftmann, F., Erkök, L., Matthews, J.: Imperative functional programming with Isabelle/HOL. In: Mohamed, O.A., Muñoz, C., Tahar, S. (eds.) TPHOLs 2008. LNCS, vol. 5170, pp. 134–149. Springer, Heidelberg (2008). https://doi.org/10.1007/978-3-540-71067-7_14
6. Haftmann, F., Nipkow, T.: Code generation via higher-order rewrite systems. In: Blume, M., Kobayashi, N., Vidal, G. (eds.) FLOPS 2010. LNCS, vol. 6009, pp. 103–117. Springer, Heidelberg (2010). https://doi.org/10.1007/978-3-642-12251-4_9
7. Herbreteau, F., Point, G.: TChecker (2019). https://github.com/fredher/tchecker
8. Hupel, L., Nipkow, T.: A verified compiler from Isabelle/HOL to CakeML. In: Ahmed, A. (ed.) ESOP 2018. LNCS, vol. 10801, pp. 999–1026. Springer, Cham (2018). https://doi.org/10.1007/978-3-319-89884-1_35
9. Kwiatkowska, M., Norman, G., Parker, D.: PRISM 4.0: verification of probabilistic real-time systems. In: Gopalakrishnan, G., Qadeer, S. (eds.) CAV 2011. LNCS, vol. 6806, pp. 585–591. Springer, Heidelberg (2011). https://doi.org/10.1007/978-3-642-22110-1_47
10. Lammich, P.: Generating verified LLVM from Isabelle/HOL. In: Proceedings of ITP 2019 (2019, to appear)
11. Lammich, P.: Refinement to Imperative/HOL. In: Urban, C., Zhang, X. (eds.) ITP 2015. LNCS, vol. 9236, pp. 253–269. Springer, Cham (2015). https://doi.org/10.1007/978-3-319-22102-1_17
12. Lammich, P.: Parser combinator library for Isabelle/HOL (2018). https://bitbucket.org/MohammadAbdulaziz/planning/src/master/isabelle/Parser_Combinator.thy

13. Nipkow, T., Wenzel, M., Paulson, L.C. (eds.): Isabelle/HOL - A Proof Assistant for Higher-Order Logic. LNCS, vol. 2283. Springer, Heidelberg (2002). https://doi.org/10.1007/3-540-45949-9

14. Tan, Y.K., Myreen, M.O., Kumar, R., Fox, A., Owens, S., Norrish, M.: A new verified compiler backend for CakeML. In: International Conference on Functional Programming (ICFP), pp. 60–73. ACM Press, September 2016. https://doi.org/10.1145/2951913.2951924, invited to special issue of Journal of Functional Programming

15. Wang, F.: Efficient verification of timed automata with BDD-like datastructures. Int. J. Softw. Tools Technol. Transf. **6**(1), 77–97 (2004). https://doi.org/10.1007/s10009-003-0135-4

16. Wimmer, S.: Formalized timed automata. In: Blanchette, J.C., Merz, S. (eds.) ITP 2016. LNCS, vol. 9807, pp. 425–440. Springer, Cham (2016). https://doi.org/10.1007/978-3-319-43144-4_26

17. Wimmer, S., Lammich, P.: Verified model checking of timed automata. In: Beyer, D., Huisman, M. (eds.) TACAS 2018. LNCS, vol. 10805, pp. 61–78. Springer, Cham (2018). https://doi.org/10.1007/978-3-319-89960-2_4

Special Session on Timed Systems and Probabilities

Sandboxing Controllers for Stochastic Cyber-Physical Systems

Bingzhuo Zhong[1]([✉]) [iD], Majid Zamani[2,3] [iD], and Marco Caccamo[1] [iD]

[1] Mechanical Engineering Department, Technical University of Munich, Munich, Germany
{bingzhuo.zhong,mcaccamo}@tum.de
[2] Computer Science Department, University of Colorado Boulder, Boulder, USA
majid.zamani@colorado.edu
[3] Computer Science Department, Ludwig Maximilian University of Munich, Munich, Germany

Abstract. Current cyber-physical systems (CPS) are expected to accomplish complex tasks. To achieve this goal, high performance, but unverified controllers (e.g. deep neural network, black-box controllers from third parties) are applied, which makes it very challenging to keep the overall CPS safe. By sandboxing these controllers, we are not only able to use them but also to enforce safety properties over the controlled physical systems at the same time. However, current available solutions for sandboxing controllers are just applicable to deterministic (a.k.a. non-stochastic) systems, possibly affected by bounded disturbances. In this paper, for the first time we propose a novel solution for sandboxing unverified complex controllers for CPS operating in noisy environments (a.k.a. stochastic CPS). Moreover, we also provide probabilistic guarantees on their safety. Here, the unverified control input is observed at each time instant and checked whether it violates the maximal tolerable probability of reaching the unsafe set. If this probability exceeds a given threshold, the unverified control input will be rejected, and the advisory input provided by the optimal safety controller will be used to maintain the probabilistic safety guarantee. The proposed approach is illustrated empirically and the results indicate that the expected safety probability is guaranteed.

Keywords: Stochastic cyber-physical systems · Fault-tolerance · Sandboxing controllers

This work was supported in part by the H2020 ERC Starting Grant AutoCPS (grant agreement No 804639) and German Research Foundation (DFG) through the grants ZA 873/1-1 and ZA 873/4-1. Marco Caccamo was supported by an Alexander von Humboldt Professorship endowed by the German Federal Ministry of Education and Research. Any opinions, findings, and conclusions or recommendations expressed in this publication are those of the authors and do not necessarily reflect the views of the Alexander von Humboldt Foundation.

E. André and M. Stoelinga (Eds.): FORMATS 2019, LNCS 11750, pp. 247–264, 2019.
https://doi.org/10.1007/978-3-030-29662-9_15

1   Introduction

Cyber-Physical Systems (CPS) are complex systems in which physical components are interacting tightly with cyber ones. These systems are widely used in various kinds of applications, such as automotive, aviation, manufacture plants and so on. Nowadays, these systems are expected to accomplish complex missions. As a result, complex, high performance but unverified controllers (e.g., deep neural network or black-box controllers from third parties) are applied to complete these complex missions, which makes it increasingly challenging to ensure the safety of CPS. To cope with this issue, we exploit the idea of *sandbox* from the community of computer security, which is a popular security mechanism for cyber systems [17]. In short, it provides a testing environment to isolate the untested and untrusted components from the critical part of a digital controller. The behaviour of the untrusted component is restricted and it can only access the critical part when it follows the rules given by the sandboxing mechanism. Hence, we designed a novel architecture that uses a **Safe**ty Advisor and a Super**visor** (Safe-visor in short). Instead of providing a testing environment and focusing on cyber security, Safe-visor architecture can be used to sandbox any types of unverified controllers in run time regarding the safety of the physical systems. The control inputs of the controller fed to the system are checked and can only be accepted when they are not disobeying the safety rule defined in the sandboxing mechanism. The architecture of safe-visor is illustrated in Fig. 1.

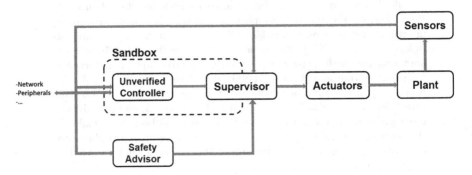

Fig. 1. **Safe**ty Advisor - Super**visor** (Safe-visor) Architecture for sandboxing unverified controller.

In this architecture, the safety of the physical system is characterized by the probability of fulfilling some safety specifications. In general, the Safe-visor specifies verifiable safety rules for the unverified controller to follow so that a specific level of safety probability of the physical system can be ensured. During the execution of the Safe-visor, the Safety Advisor is responsible for providing advisory input for the Supervisor based on the current state of the physical system, which seeks to maximize the safety probability. Meanwhile, the Supervisor checks the input given by the unverified controller according to the safety rule. Input from the unverified controller would only be accepted when it follows the rule; otherwise, the Supervisor would accept the advisory input from the Safety Advisor to maximize the safety probability of the physical system. In the rest of the paper, designing a Supervisor means designing its safety rule for checking the inputs from unverified controllers. It should be noted that inputs given by Safety Advisors only focus on the safety of the system, which should be treated as a fallback in case the unverified controllers are trying to perform some harmful actions. On the other hand, the unverified controller is designed for functionality. i.e. it is expected to realize some tasks which are much more complicated than purely keeping the system safe. By sandboxing the unverified controller, we are able to exploit its advantages for realizing complex tasks while preventing the system from being threatened by its harmful behaviour, if any.

In this paper, we deal with stochastic CPS modelled as controlled discrete-time Markov process (cdt-MP). We focus on the safety invariance specification, in which the system is expected to stay inside a pre-defined safety set. Here, we formulate the safety invariance specification as a reach-avoid problem in finite time horizon, and design the Safety Advisor based on a finite Markov Decision Process (MDP) constructed from the original cdt-MP. The inputs given by the unverified controller are checked by the Supervisor at every time instant based on an estimation of the probability of reaching the unsafe set (i.e., the complement of the pre-defined safety set).

Related Work

In [4, 7, 12], a shield is synthesized to correct erroneous output values from those unverified, complexed components in a system so that safety properties can be enforced at run time. This idea is mainly used for systems which can be modelled as automaton, e.g. reactive systems, while our method can be applied to systems with continuous state space and input space. The most relevant work to our proposed method is the one developed based on Simplex architecture [8,18], in which the unverified, high-performance controller is sandboxed by an elliptic recovery region associated with a verified, high-assurance controller. Inspired by the idea of sandboxing the unverifiable controllers by using Simplex architecture, many results have been proposed for different kinds of systems and invariance specifications. In the case that bounded uncertainty exists in the system dynamic, L1-Simplex [20] is applicable by using L1-adaptive controller [11] as the high-assurance controller with which the linear model uncertainty in the system dynamic is estimated and compensated. RSimplex [21] uses Robust Fault-Tolerant Controller (RFTC) with the similar idea of L1-Simplex, but it is capable of dealing with non-linear model uncertainty. Net-Simplex [22] is able to cope with bounded time delay introduced by the network connection in the system. It models the system as a linear parameter-varying system and accordingly designs time-delay-related recovery region. A recent result in [2] proposes a way to sandbox an unverified controller which may suffer from undetectable cyber attacks by dynamically planning and executing high-assurance controllers so that the physical system is not endangered. The common point of these results is that Lyapunov-function-based safety invariant sets are used as recovery regions.

The main difference between the Simplex architecture and our proposed result is that in our proposed solution, only the unverified controller is in charge of accomplishing the task, under the supervision of the Supervisor, rather than designing two parallel controllers (i.e. the high-assurance and high-performance controllers) for the given task and define a verified decision logic to decide which one to be used. The Safety Advisor is not expected to fully control the system and finish the complicated task, but it is only responsible for providing fallback to maximize the safety probability. Then, by properly designing the Supervisor, the unverified controller has more flexibility for functionality, and the safety probability can be guaranteed due to the existence of the fallback solution.

There are some other results which extend the concept of Simplex architecture using reachability analysis to cope with the aforementioned conservativeness. Results in [6] provide a backward reachability based method to generate a decision module between the mission controller and the safety one which mainly focuses on the safety of the system. Results in [5] propose a method in which real-time reachability is integrated into the Lyapunov invariance-based method. This largely increases the feasible region of the mission controller. Another idea to get rid of the conservativeness is to compute the safety invariant purely based on offline reachability analysis, as discussed in [3]. It should be noted that these methods are only designed for deterministic (non-stochastic) systems. To the best of our knowledge, our result is the first work with a solution for sandboxing unverified controllers in stochastic settings.

The rest of the paper is organized as follows: we provide preliminary discussion regarding the notations, models used in this work and formulation of the problem in Sect. 2. Then, a scheme to design the Safety Advisor and Supervisor is proposed in Sect. 3, which will be empirically tested by two case studies in Sect. 4. Finally, Sect. 5 concludes the paper.

2   Problem Formulation

2.1   Preliminaries

A topological space S is called a Borel space if it is homeomorphic to a Borel subset of a Polish space (i.e., a separable and completely metrizable space). One of the common examples of Borel space are the Euclidean spaces $\mathbb{R}^n$. Any Borel space S is assumed to be endowed with a Borel σ-algebra denoted by $\mathcal{B}(S)$. A map $f : X \to Y$ is measurable whenever it is Borel measurable. A map $f : X \to Y$ is universally measurable if the inverse image of every Borel set is measurable with respect to every complete probability measure on X that measures all Borel subsets of X.

For the stochastic kernel, we adopt the notation as in [19]. Given two Borel space X and Y, the stochastic kernel on X given Y is the map $P : Y \times \mathcal{B}(X) \to [0,1]$ such that $P(\cdot|y)$ is a probability measure on X for any point $y \in Y$ and $P(B|\cdot)$ is a measurable function on Y for any set $B \in \mathcal{B}(X)$.

2.2   Notations

We denote by $\mathbb{R}$ the set of real numbers and by $\mathbb{N}$ the set of natural numbers. We denote by $\overline{0,n} := \{0,1,\ldots,n\}$ an interval in $\mathbb{N}$ starting from 0 and ending at $n \in \mathbb{N}$. Set $\mathbb{R}^n$ represents the n-dimensional Euclidean space where $n \in \mathbb{N}$.

2.3   Model Description and Problem Formulation

In this paper, we focus on discrete-time stochastic control systems in the following form:

$$x(t+1) = f(x(t), u(t), w(t)), \tag{1}$$

in which $t, t+1 \in \overline{0,n}$ are two successive time instants in the time domain $\overline{0,n}$ of the system, where $n \in \mathbb{N}$. Here, $x(t) \in X$ is the state of the system at time t, where $X \subseteq \mathbb{R}^n$ is a Borel space as the state space of the system. We denote by $(X, \mathcal{B}(X))$ the measurable space with $\mathcal{B}(X)$ being the Borel sigma-algebra on the state space. We denote by $u(t) \in U$ the input to the system at time t, where $U \subseteq \mathbb{R}^m$ is a Borel space as the input space of the system. We denote by $w(t)$ the uncertainty at time instant t where $w : \mathbb{N} \to \mathbb{R}^d$ is a sequence of independent and identically distributed (i.i.d.) random variables. Map $f : X \times U \times \mathbb{R}^d \to X$ is a measurable function characterizing the state dynamic of the system. In this paper, we focus on stochastic systems, which can also be formulated as controlled discrete-time Markov Processes (cdt-MP).

Definition 1. *(cdt-MP)* [10] *A controlled discrete-time Markov process is a tuple*

$$\mathfrak{D} = (X, U, \{U(x)\}_{x \in X}, T_{\mathfrak{D}}),$$

where $X \subseteq \mathbb{R}^n$ is a Borel space representing the state space of the model and $U \subseteq \mathbb{R}^m$ is a Borel space referring to the input space. The set $\{U(x)\}_{x \in X}$ is a family of non-empty measurable subsets of U, and $U(x)$ is the set of feasible inputs when system is at state x. We denote by $T_{\mathfrak{D}}$ a Borel measurable stochastic kernel $T_{\mathfrak{D}} : \mathcal{B} \times X \times U \to [0,1]$, which assigns to any $x \in X$ and $u \in U(x)$ a probability measure on the Borel space $(X, \mathcal{B}(X))$ and characterizes the state transition of the Markov process.

In the rest of the paper, we focus on systems in which $U(x) = U$, i.e. all inputs are feasible at any state in the evolution of the system. The evolution of the system is described by paths as defined below.

Definition 2. *(Path) A path of a cdt-MP $\mathfrak{D}$ is*

$$\omega = (x(0), u(0), x(1), u(1), \ldots, x(t), u(t), \ldots),$$

where $x(t) \in X$ and $u(t) \in U$, $t \in \overline{0,n}$, $\overline{0,n} \subset \mathbb{N}$ is the time domain of the path. We denote by $\omega_x = \{x(i)\}_{i \in \overline{0,n}}$ and $\omega_u = \{u(i)\}_{i \in \overline{0,n}}$ the subsequences of states and inputs in ω.

Given a cdt-MP $\mathfrak{D}$, we are interested in Markov policies to control the system.

Definition 3. *(Markov policy) For a cdt-MP $\mathfrak{D} = (X, U, \{U(x)\}_{x \in X}, T_{\mathfrak{D}})$, a Markov policy μ is a sequence $\mu = (\mu_0, \mu_1, \mu_2, \ldots)$ of universally measurable map $\mu_t : X \to U$ at time $t \in \overline{0,n}$, where $\overline{0,n}$ is the time domain of $\mathfrak{D}$.*

With Markov policies, the input at time t is only determined by the state at the same time instant, i.e. $u(t) = \mu_t(x(t))$. In this paper, we are interested in the safety specification, where the state sequences are expected to stay (with a given probability threshold) inside a safe subset of the state set. We formulate this specification as a reach-avoid problem in finite time horizon.

Definition 4. *(Reach-avoid problem) Consider a safety set $\mathcal{A} \subset \mathcal{B}(S)$, a bounded Borel set as a safe set, and $\mathcal{A}^c = \mathcal{B}(S) \backslash \mathcal{A}$, as its complement, i.e. an unsafe set. We define the reach-avoid problem under Markov policy μ over time horizon $\overline{0,N}$ as the following:*

$$p_{s_0}^\mu(\mathcal{A}^c) = \mathbb{P}_{s_0}^\mu\{s(k) \in \mathcal{A}^c | \exists k \in \overline{0,N}, s(0) = s_0\},$$

where $s_0 \in \mathcal{A}$. The minimal probability of reaching the unsafe set is defined as:

$$p_{*,s_0}(\mathcal{A}^c) = \inf\{p_{s_0}^\mu(\mathcal{A}^c), \mu \in \Pi_M^N\},$$

where Π_M^N is the set of all Markov policies over time horizon $\overline{0,N}$. A Markov policy μ_* is optimal with respect to an initial state s_0 if $p_{s_0}^{\mu_*}(\mathcal{A}^c) = p_{*,s_0}(\mathcal{A}^c)$.

3   Design of Safe-Visor

As discussed in the introduction, designing the Safe-visor for sandboxing unverified controllers consists of designing a Safety Advisor and a Supervisor. The Safety Advisor is designed regarding the safety specification. The Supervisor, on the other hand, is designed for detecting (potential) harmful behaviours of the unverified controller and accordingly deciding the input fed to the system (either the one from the unverified controller or from the Safety Advisor).

Regarding the safety invariance specification, an optimal safety controller can be designed as discussed in [1,9], which provides optimal safety policy to guarantee a minimal probability of reaching the unsafe set in a finite time horizon. We use this controller as the Safety Advisor, which is introduced in details in Sect. 3.1.

Since the Safety Advisor only focuses on minimizing the probability of reaching the unsafe set, we need to turn to the unverified controller for functionality. Nevertheless, we still expect a high level of safety for the system. Therefore, we denote by ρ the **maximal tolerable probability of reaching the unsafe set** that we are able to accept, which quantifies the compromise between functionality and safety. Given ρ, the Supervisor can decide whether it should accept inputs from an unverified controller at some time instants by estimating the probability of reaching the unsafe set and compare it with ρ. Details for designing a

Supervisor working in this way is discussed in Sect. 3.2. It should be noted that the design of unverified controller is not the topic of this paper. The approach proposed here can be applied to any unverified controller as long as the set of all possible inputs provided by the unverified controller is a subset of the input set of the Supervisor. Moreover, we focus on those unverified controllers whose behaviour are unpredictable, i.e. we do not know the exact action of the unverified controller in a given state unless the system actually reaches that state, and the action of unverified controller at the same state may be time dependent. Otherwise, we may be able to verify this controller and sandboxing may not be needed anymore. In the rest of the paper, we denote by $u_{uc}(x,t)$ the input provided by the unverified controller at state x at time instant t.

3.1 Safety Advisor

As mentioned above, we use optimal safety controller with respect to safety invariance specification as the Safety Advisor. To synthesize the optimal safety controller, we define a value function [19]:

$$V_n^\pi(x) := P_x^\pi(\diamond^{\leq n}\mathcal{A}^c),\tag{2}$$

for $n \in \mathbb{N}$ to denote the probability of reaching the set $\mathcal{A}^c$ in the finite time horizon $\overline{0,n}$ from the initial state x, where $\pi \in \Pi_M$ is a Markov policy and $\diamond^{\leq n}\mathcal{A}^c := \{\omega \in \Omega : \omega_x(k) \in \mathcal{A}^c \text{ for some } 0 \leq k \leq n\}$, where Ω is the set of all possible paths within the time horizon $\overline{0,n}$. Since we formulate the safety invariance specification as reach-avoid problem in a finite time horizon, we should minimize the probability mentioned above and, hence, the optimal value function is given by

$$V_{*,n}(x) := \inf_{\pi\in\Pi} V_n^\pi(x),\tag{3}$$

initialized with $V_{*,0} = 1_{\mathcal{A}^c}(x)$, where $1_M(x) = 1$ when $x \in M$ and $1_M(x) = 0$ otherwise. In fact, this optimal value function can be recursively calculated in the following way ([19], Corollary 3):

$$V_{*,n+1}(x) = 1_{\mathcal{A}^c}(x) + 1_{\mathcal{A}}(x)\inf_{u\in U}\int_X V_{*,n}(y)T_{\mathfrak{D}}(dy|x,u),\tag{4}$$

and the optimal policy at time $t = k$ associated to $V_{*,n+1}(x)$ can be obtained as the following

$$\mu_{*,k} \in \arg\inf_{\mu_k}\int_X (1_{\mathcal{A}^c}(y) + 1_{\mathcal{A}}(y)V_{*,n}(y))T_{\mathfrak{D}}(dy|x,\mu_k(x)).\tag{5}$$

However, analytical solution of the value function as well as the optimal policy above is very difficult to be obtained in general. Alternatively, we abstract the original cdt-MP $\mathfrak{D}$ and construct a finite Markov Decision Process (MDP) as proposed in [19], and calculate the solutions based on this finite MDP. First, we use uniform grids to partition the safety region and input set of the cdt-MP.

Let $X_p = \bigcup_{i=1}^{N} \tilde{X}_i$ be a measurable partition of the safety set A and $U_p = \bigcup_{j=1}^{M} \tilde{U}_j$ a measurable partition of U. Let $\tilde{x}_i \in \tilde{X}_i$ for $1 \leq i \leq N$ be representative points of $\tilde{X}_i$ and let $\tilde{u}_j \in \tilde{U}_j$ for $1 \leq j \leq M$ be representative points of $\tilde{U}_j$. We define the discretization parameter $\delta_x = \max_{\tilde{x}_i, \tilde{x}_i' \in X_p} \mathbf{d}_X(\tilde{x}_i, \tilde{x}_i')$ for the state set and $\delta_u = \max_{\tilde{u}_j, \tilde{u}_j' \in U_p} \mathbf{d}_U(\tilde{u}_j, \tilde{u}_j')$ for the input set where $\mathbf{d}_X$ and $\mathbf{d}_U$ are the metrics (e.g. Euclidean ones) over sets X and U, respectively. Then, the constructed finite MDP is denoted by $\mathfrak{M} = \{\tilde{X}, \tilde{U}, \tilde{T}\}$, in which $\tilde{X} := \{\tilde{x}_i\}_{i=1}^{N} \cup \{\phi\}$, $\{\tilde{x}_i\}_{i=1}^{N}$ is the set of representative points of X_p, ϕ is a "sink" state representing the unsafe set $\mathcal{A}^c$ in the original cdt-MP, and $\tilde{U} := \{\tilde{u}_j\}_{j=1}^{M}$ is the set of representative points of U_p. The stochastic kernel $\tilde{T}$ is then a matrix, which can be computed as follows:

$$\tilde{T}(\tilde{x}_m|\tilde{x}_i, \tilde{u}_j) = \begin{cases} T_{\mathfrak{D}}(\tilde{X}_m|\tilde{x}_i, \tilde{u}_j) & \text{if } \tilde{x}_i, \tilde{x}_m \in \{\tilde{x}_i\}_{i=1}^{N}, \tilde{u}_j \in \tilde{U} \\ T_{\mathfrak{D}}(\mathcal{A}^c|\tilde{x}_i, \tilde{u}_j) & \text{if } \tilde{x}_i \in \{\tilde{x}_i\}_{i=1}^{N}, \tilde{x}_m \in \{\phi\}, \tilde{u}_j \in \tilde{U} \\ 1 & \text{if } \tilde{x}_i, \tilde{x}_m \in \{\phi\}, \tilde{u}_j \in \tilde{U} \\ 0 & \text{if } \tilde{x}_i \in \{\phi\}, \tilde{x}_m \in \{\tilde{x}_i\}_{i=1}^{N}, \tilde{u}_j \in \tilde{U} \end{cases}$$

For the finite MDP $\mathfrak{M}$, we denote by $\tilde{V}_{*,n}(\tilde{x})$ the n-horizon minimal value function for the reach-avoid problem. Similar to Eq. (4), we initialize it with $\tilde{V}_{*,0} = 1_{\{\phi\}}(\tilde{x})$ and it can be calculated recursively as follows:

$$\tilde{V}_{*,n+1}(\tilde{x}) = 1_{\{\phi\}}(\tilde{x}) + 1_{\{\phi\}^c}(\tilde{x}) \min_{\tilde{u} \in \tilde{U}} \sum_{\tilde{y} \in \tilde{X}} \tilde{V}_{*,n}(\tilde{y}) \tilde{T}(\tilde{y}|\tilde{x}, \tilde{u}), \tag{6}$$

and the optimal policy at time $t = k$ associated to $\tilde{V}_{*,n+1}(\tilde{x})$ is given by

$$\mu_{*,k}(\tilde{x}) \in \arg\min_{\tilde{\mu}_k} \sum_{\tilde{y} \in \tilde{X}} (1_{\{\phi\}^c}(\tilde{y}) + 1_{\{\phi\}}(\tilde{y})\tilde{V}_{*,n}(\tilde{y}))\tilde{T}(d\tilde{y}|\tilde{x}, \tilde{\mu}_k(\tilde{x})). \tag{7}$$

In principle, the optimal policy can be obtained for arbitrary long time horizon, but $\tilde{V}_{*,n}(\tilde{x})$ will keep decreasing, i.e. the probability of avoiding the unsafe set is decreasing, when n increases. Therefore, the time horizon of the optimal policy cannot be arbitrarily long, but it is tunable up to some degrees by setting the maximal tolerable value of the value function, i.e. the smaller (bigger) the maximal tolerable value of the value function is, the shorter (longer) the time horizon for the optimal safety policy is. This value should not be bigger than the maximal tolerable probability of reaching the unsafe set, i.e. ρ, as defined in the beginning of Sect. 3, so that ρ can be guaranteed at least by accepting advisory input from the Safety Advisor. Therefore, in our implementation, the time horizon $\overline{0, H}$ of the Safety Advisor is determined in a way such that $\forall \tilde{x} \in \tilde{X} \backslash \{\phi\}, \tilde{V}_{*,H}(\tilde{x}) \leq \rho$ and $\exists \tilde{x} \in \tilde{X} \backslash \{\phi\}, \tilde{V}_{*,H+1}(\tilde{x}) > \rho$.

3.2 Supervisor

As previously mentioned, the Supervisor is required to estimate the probability of reaching the unsafe set, in case it accepts inputs from the unverified controller.

Since the safety guarantee given by the Safety Advisor is calculated based on the abstraction of the original stochastic system, i.e. the finite MDP, for consistency of guarantee regarding safety probability, we use the same finite MDP to design the Supervisor.

As discussed in the previous section, the probability of reaching the unsafe set of the finite MDP is quantified by value function $\tilde{V}_H^\mu(s_0)$ according to Eq. (2). When the initial state s_0 and the time horizon $\overline{0, H}$ are fixed, the value function is varied by different μ. Meanwhile, compared with purely using the optimal safety policy μ_*, sandboxing the unverified controller and accepting it at some states at some time instants intrinsically result in a new Markov policy for controlling the system, according to the architecture of Safe-visor. Therefore, to ensure that the probability of reaching the unsafe set is lower than the predefined ρ in a given time horizon $\overline{0, H}$, the Supervisor should be designed in a way such that the following inequality holds:

$$\tilde{V}_H^{\mu'}(s_0) \le \rho, \tag{8}$$

where μ' is the Markov policy used to control the system, when the unverified controller is accepted at some states at some time instants by the Supervisor. In Sect. 3.1, the optimal safety policy is obtained by selecting a Markov policy minimizing the value function of each state at each time instant. In other way, when the Markov policy is fixed, we can calculate the value function in the way illustrated in the next theorem.

Theorem 1. *Given a Markov policy $\mu = (\mu_0, \mu_1, \ldots, \mu_{H-1})$ in a finite time horizon $\overline{0, H}$, the value function $\tilde{V}_n(\tilde{x})$ can be recursively calculated in the following way:*

$$\tilde{V}_{n+1}(\tilde{x}) = 1_{\{\phi\}}(\tilde{x}) + 1_{\{\phi\}^c}(\tilde{x}) \sum_{\tilde{y} \in \tilde{X}} \tilde{V}_n(\tilde{y})\tilde{T}(\tilde{y}|\tilde{x}, \mu_{H-n-1}(\tilde{x})), \tag{9}$$

where $\tilde{x} \in \tilde{X}$ and $\tilde{V}_0(x) = \tilde{V}_{*,0}(x)$.

Theorem 1 can be proved similar to the proof of Lemma 1 in [1], since Lemma 1 in [1] can be treated as a general case for Theorem 1. With having Theorem 1, the remaining question is how to determine μ' at run time. Let $\mu' = (\mu_0', \mu_2', \ldots, \mu_{H-1}')$. When the Supervisor is being executed, at every time instant $k \in \overline{0, H-2}$, μ_t' are unknown for all t where $k < t \le H - 1$ (i.e., the Markov policy used to control the system in the future time is unknown). To guarantee the safety threshold specified by ρ, at every time instant $k \in \overline{0, H-2}$, input from the unverified controller can only be accepted, when inequality (8) is at least fulfilled in the case that the Supervisor only accepts the advisory input from the safety advisor afterwards. This requirement is formally defined in Definition 5.

Definition 5. *Given current time instant k, where $0 \le k \le H-2$, ω is the path up to k and ρ is the maximal tolerable probability of reaching the unsafe set, the* input $u_{uc}(\omega_x(k), k)$ from the unverified controller can only be accepted, if there exists a Markov policy $\mu = \{\mu_0, \mu_1, \mu_2, \ldots, \mu_{H-1}\} \in M$ such that $\tilde{V}_H^\mu(\omega_x(0)) \le \rho$, where M denotes the set of all Markov policies, $\mu_k(\omega_x(k)) = u_{uc}(\omega_x(k), k)$, and for all t where $k < t \le H - 1$, $\mu_t = \mu_{*,t}$.

In general, it is difficult to calculate the exact value of $\tilde{V}_H^{\mu'}(s_0)$ at run time due to the lack of adequate information from the past. At each time instant k during the execution, where $k \in \overline{0, H-2}$, the only available information for the Supervisor is the path ω of the system up to k. In other words, the Supervisor does not have complete information about μ'_t for all $t \in \overline{0, k}$, since $\mu'_t(\tilde{x})$ is unknown when $\tilde{x} \in \tilde{X} \backslash \{\omega_x(t)\}$. To cope with this difficulty, we propose a novel Supervisor, namely *History-based Supervisor*, as defined in Definition 6, which is able to check the feasibility of the input provided by the unverified controller only based on the history information during the execution (i.e., path ω of the system up to the current time instant k during the execution).

Definition 6. *(History-based Supervisor) For all $k \in \overline{0, H-1}$ [1], given the history of path ω up to k, the input $u_{uc}(\omega_x(k), k)$ from the unverified controller can only be accepted, when quantity*

$$\prod_{t=1}^{k} \sum_{\tilde{x} \in \tilde{X} \backslash \{\phi\}} \tilde{T}(\tilde{x}|\omega_x(t-1), \omega_u(t-1)) \left(1 - \sum_{\tilde{x} \in \tilde{X}} \tilde{V}_{*,H-k-1}(\tilde{x})\tilde{T}(\tilde{x}|\omega_x(k), u_{uc}(\omega_x(k), k)) \right)$$

is not smaller than $1 - \rho$, where ρ is the maximal tolerable probability of reaching the unsafe set.

By using History-based Supervisor in Safe-visor architecture, it can be guaranteed that μ' fulfils inequality (8), as illustrated in the next theorem.

Theorem 2. *Given a finite MDP and the unsafe set A^c, by using History-based Supervisor at t for all $t \in \overline{0, H-1}$ in Safe-visor architecture, we have*

$$p_{s_0}^{\mu'}(\lozenge^{\le H} A^c) \le \rho,$$

where μ' is the Markov policy used to control the system when History-based Supervisor is applied.

Proof of Theorem 2 is provided in the appendix.

Note that $\tilde{V}_{*,n}$ and $\tilde{T}$ are calculated offline when synthesizing the Safety Advisor. Hence, the Supervisor defined in Definition 6 can be readily used in real-time, since the required computation can be efficiently performed. Concretely, at every time instant k during the execution:

---

[1] No input needed to be provided at $t = H$ since it is the end of the execution.

1. The number of operations required for computing $\prod_{t=1}^{k} \sum_{\tilde{x} \in \tilde{X} \setminus \{\phi\}} \tilde{T}(\tilde{x}|\omega_x(t-1), \omega_u(t-1))$ is constant, since

$$\prod_{t=1}^{k} \sum_{\tilde{x} \in \tilde{X} \setminus \{\phi\}} \tilde{T}(\tilde{x}|\omega_x(t-1), \omega_u(t-1))$$

$$= \sum_{\tilde{x} \in \tilde{X} \setminus \{\phi\}} \tilde{T}(\tilde{x}|\omega_x(k-1), \omega_u(k-1)) \times \prod_{t=1}^{k-1} \sum_{\tilde{x} \in \tilde{X} \setminus \{\phi\}} \tilde{T}(\tilde{x}|\omega_x(t-1), \omega_u(t-1))$$

$$= (1 - \tilde{T}(\phi|\omega_x(k-1), \omega_u(k-1)) \times \prod_{t=1}^{k-1} \sum_{\tilde{x} \in \tilde{X} \setminus \{\phi\}} \tilde{T}(\tilde{x}|\omega_x(t-1), \omega_u(t-1))$$

while $\prod_{t=1}^{k-1} \sum_{\tilde{x} \in \tilde{X} \setminus \{\phi\}} \tilde{T}(\tilde{x}|\omega_x(t-1), \omega_u(t-1))$ has already been computed at the previous time instant (i.e., $k-1$), and $\tilde{T}(\phi|\omega_x(k-1), \omega_u(k-1))$ can be directly obtained from $\tilde{T}$.

2. The number of operations required for computing

$$1 - \sum_{\tilde{x} \in \tilde{X}} \tilde{V}_{*,H-k-1}(\tilde{x}) \tilde{T}(\tilde{x}|\omega_x(k), u_{uc}(k))$$

is proportional to the number of states of the finite MDP, since $\tilde{V}_{*,H-k-1}(\tilde{x})$ and $\tilde{T}(\tilde{x}|\omega_x(k), u_{uc}(k))$ can directly be obtained in $\tilde{V}_{*,n}$ and $\tilde{T}$.

The real time applicability of the proposed Supervisor is shown in the experiments in Sect. 4.

4   Case Study

In this section, we apply our approach to two case studies. The first case study is a temperature control problem and the second one is a traffic control problem. We simulate each test case 1.0×10^6 times and analyze accordingly the percentage of paths staying in the safety set in the given time horizon. For comparison, we simulate these test cases by (1) only using the unverified controller and (2) only using the proposed safety advisor. Moreover, we compute the average execution time for our Supervisor in both cases to show feasibility of running it in real-time. The simulation in this section is performed in MATLAB 2018b, on a computer equipped with Intel(R) Xeon(R) E-2186G CPU (3.8 GHz) and 32 GB of RAM running Window 10.

4.1   Temperature Control Problem

In the temperature control problem, a room is equipped with a heater being controlled and the temperature of the room is required to be kept between 19 and 21 °C. The temperature of the room can be modelled as the following, which is adapted from [14]:

$$x(k+1) = (1 - \beta - \gamma u(k))x(k) + \gamma T_h u(k) + \beta T_e + \omega(k) \tag{10}$$

where $x(k)$ denotes the temperature at time $t = k$. Input $u(k)$ takes any real value between 0 to 0.6. Parameter β is conduction factor between the external environment and the room, γ is conduction factor between the heater and the room, T_e is the temperature of the external environment and T_h is the temperature of the heater. We denote by ω a Gaussian white noise. In this section, we set $\beta = 0.022$, $\gamma = 0.05$, $T_e = -1$, $T_h = 50$, the mean of ω is 0 and variance is 0.04. The sampling time interval in this example is 9 min.

Now, we synthesize the Safety Advisor as discussed in Sect. 3.1. We use the discretization parameter $\delta_x = 1.0 \times 10^{-3}$ and $\delta_u = 2.4 \times 10^{-2}$ to discretize the safety set (resulting in 2000 discrete states) and the input set (resulting in 25 discrete inputs) to construct a finite MDP. We set ρ as 1% and obtain a controller for time horizon $\overline{0, 40}$ (6 h). We set the initial state at 19.01 °C. The unverified controller tries to keep the heater idle at all time, i.e. $U_{uc}(t) \equiv 0$ for all $t \in \overline{0, 39}$. This is an unacceptable input which cools down the room to an unacceptable low level. For the given ρ, it is expected that at least 99% of the paths stay inside the safety set in the given time horizon. The result of the simulation is shown in Table 1 and Fig. 3. The temperature keeps decreasing and all paths go outside of the safety set, when the system is fully controlled by the unverified controller. Meanwhile, more than 99% of the paths stay within the safety set when our proposed method is applied.

4.2   Traffic Control Problem

In the traffic control problem, we focus on a road traffic control containing a cell with 2 entries and 1 exit, as illustrated in Fig. 2.

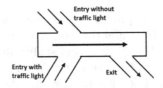

Fig. 2. Traffic control problem

One of the entry is controlled by a traffic light. The dynamic of the system can be modelled as the following, which is adapted from [15]:

$$x(k+1) = \left(1 - \frac{\tau v}{l} - q\right)x(k) + e_1 u(k) + \sigma(k) + e_2, \tag{11}$$

where $x(k)$ denotes the density of traffic at time k, $u(k) \in \{0, 1\}$ is the input to the system (1 means the green light is on while 0 means the red light is on).

Table 1. Result of simulation for both case studies.

	Temperature control	Traffic control
Percentage of paths in the safety set (with Safe-visor)	99.02%	99.958%
Average acceptance rate of the unverified controller	19.12%	8.5114%
Percentage of paths in the safety set (without Safe-visor)	0%	0%
Percentage of paths in the safety set (when system is fully controlled by the Safety Advisor)	99.18%	99.989%
Average execution time for the History-based Supervisor	33.42 μs	31.83 μs

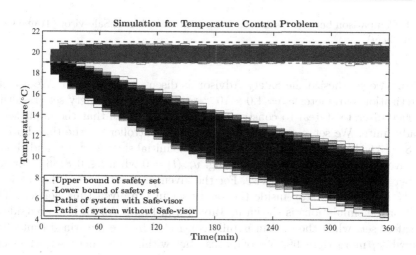

Fig. 3. Comparison between paths of system with and without Safe-visor (Temperature Control Problem).

Parameter v is the flow speed of the vehicle on the road, l is the length of the cell, σ is a white Gaussian noise, and τ denotes the sampling time interval of the system. In one sampling interval, e_1 is the number of cars that pass the entry controlled by the traffic light, e_2 refers to the number of cars that pass the entry without traffic light, and q is the percentage of cars which leave the cell through the exit. In the simulation, we set $l = 500[\mathrm{m}]$, $v = 25[\mathrm{m/s}]$, $\tau = 6\,\mathrm{s}$, $e_1 = 3$, $e_2 = 6$, $q = 10\%$, the mean of σ is 0 and variance is 2. In this case study, it is desired that the density of traffic is lower than 20.

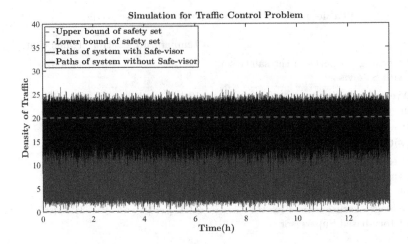

Fig. 4. Comparison between paths of system with and without Safe-visor (Traffic Control Problem)

Now, we synthesize the Safety Advisor as discussed in Sect. 3.1. We use the discretization parameter $\delta_x = 1.0 \times 10^{-3}$ to discretize the safety set (resulting in 20000 discrete states) to construct a finite MDP. Note that the input set is already finite. We set ρ as 0.05% and obtain a controller for the time horizon $\overline{0, 8186}$ (13.64 h). For the simulation, we set the initial state at $x = 9$, and choose the unverified controller as the following: $u_{uc}(t) = 0$ when $t \in \overline{0, 8186}$ is an odd number and $u_{uc}(t) = 1$ otherwise. For the given ρ, it is expected that at least 99.95% of the paths stay inside the safety set in the given time horizon. The result of the simulations is shown in Table 1 and Fig. 4. All paths go outside of the safety set, when the system is fully controlled by the unverified controller. Meanwhile, more than 99.95% of paths stay within the safety set when our proposed method is applied.

According to the empirical result, by sandboxing the unverified controller with Safe-visor architecture, the probabilistic guarantees are respected while some of the inputs from the unverified controller are still accepted for functionality. The average execution time for the History-based Supervisor shows its good real-time applicability, which makes it practical to be applied in real time.

5 Conclusion and Future Work

In this paper, we developed a new framework for sandboxing unverified controllers for stochastic cyber-physical systems regarding safety invariance specification. In comparison with the Simplex architecture, our framework is applicable to stochastic systems, and provides more flexibility for the unverified controllers to accomplish complex tasks. According to the empirical results for two case studies, the pre-proposed safety probability is guaranteed by using our method.

In the future, we would like to extend this method to (1) systems modelled by Partially Observable Markov Decision Processes [16] (2) more general safety specifications, e.g. those expressed as co-safe linear temporal logic formulae [13].

Acknowledgements. The authors would like to thank Abolfazl Lavaei for the discussions on synthesizing optimal safety controllers for stochastic systems.

Appendix: Proof of Theorem 2

The Proof of Theorem 2 is done with the help of the following lemma.

Lemma 1. *Given a finite MDP $\mathfrak{M} = \{\tilde{X}, \tilde{U}, \tilde{T}\}$ and a Markov policy $\mu = (\mu_0, \mu_1, \ldots, \mu_{H-1})$ in a finite time horizon $\overline{0, H}$, we have*

$$1 - \tilde{V}_{n+1}(\tilde{x}) = \sum_{\tilde{y} \in \tilde{X} \setminus \{\phi\}} (1 - \tilde{V}_n(\tilde{y})) \tilde{T}(\tilde{y} | \tilde{x}, \mu_{H-n-1}(\tilde{x}))$$

where $\tilde{V}_n(\tilde{x})$ is the value function for the reach-avoid problem and $\tilde{x} \in \tilde{X}$.

The proof can be readily derived based on Theorem 1 and the definition of $\tilde{T}$. Let μ' be the Markov policy used to control the system when the unverified controller is accepted at some states at some time instants. Here, we use $\tilde{X}_s$ to represent $\tilde{X} \setminus \{\phi\}$. Let's define:

$$f(\tilde{x}(k), \mu'_k(\tilde{x}(k))) = 1 - \sum_{\tilde{x}(k+1) \in \tilde{X}_s} \tilde{V}_{*,H-k-1}(\tilde{x}(k+1)) \tilde{T}(\tilde{x}(k+1) | \tilde{x}(k), \mu'_k(\tilde{x}(k))),$$

and

$$g(\tilde{x}(k-1), \mu'_{k-1}(\tilde{x}(k-1))) = \tilde{T}(\tilde{x}(k) | \tilde{x}(k-1), \mu'_{k-1}(\tilde{x}(k-1))).$$

Given initial state $s_0 \in \tilde{X}_s$, at each time instant $t = k$ where $k \in \overline{0, H-1}$, we have

$$1 - \tilde{V}_H^{\mu'}(s_0)$$

$$= \sum_{\tilde{x}(1) \in \tilde{X}_s} \left(\sum_{\tilde{x}(2) \in \tilde{X}_s} \left(\cdots \left(\sum_{\tilde{x}(k) \in \tilde{X}_s} f(\tilde{x}(k), \mu'_k(\tilde{x}(k))) g(\tilde{x}(k-1), \mu'_{k-1}(\tilde{x}(k-1))) \right. \right. \right.$$

$$\left. \left. \left. \cdots \right) g(\tilde{x}(1), \mu'_1(\tilde{x}(1))) \right) g(s_0, \mu'_0(s_0)) \right.$$

$$\geq \sum_{\tilde{x}(1)\in \tilde{X}_s} \left(\sum_{\tilde{x}(2)\in \tilde{X}_s} \left(\cdots \left(f(\underline{\tilde{x}(k), \mu_k'(\tilde{x}(k))}) \sum_{\tilde{x}(k)\in \tilde{X}_s} g(\tilde{x}(k-1), \mu_{k-1}'(\tilde{x}(k-1))) \right) \right. \right.$$

$$\cdots \left. \left. \right) g(\tilde{x}(1), \mu_1'(\tilde{x}(1))) \right) g(s_0, \mu_0'(s_0))$$

$$\geq \sum_{\tilde{x}(1)\in \tilde{X}_s} \left(\sum_{\tilde{x}(2)\in \tilde{X}_s} \left(\cdots \left(\left(\sum_{\tilde{x}(k)\in \tilde{X}_s} g(\underline{\tilde{x}(k-1), \mu_{k-1}'(\tilde{x}(k-1))}) \right) f(\underline{\tilde{x}(k), \mu_k'(\tilde{x}(k))}) \right. \right. \right.$$

$$\left. \left. \left. \sum_{\tilde{x}(k-1)\in \tilde{X}_s} g(\tilde{x}(k-2), \mu_{k-2}'(\tilde{x}(k-2))) \right) \cdots \right) g(\tilde{x}(1), \mu_1'(\tilde{x}(1))) \right) g(s_0, \mu_0'(s_0))$$

$$\geq \sum_{\tilde{x}(1)\in \tilde{X}_s} \left(\sum_{\tilde{x}(2)\in \tilde{X}_s} \left(\cdots \left(\left(\sum_{\tilde{x}(k-1)\in \tilde{X}_s} g(\underline{\tilde{x}(k-2), \mu_{k-2}'(\tilde{x}(k-2))}) \right) \right. \right. \right.$$

$$\left(\sum_{\tilde{x}(k)\in \tilde{X}_s} g(\underline{\tilde{x}(k-1), \mu_{k-1}'(\tilde{x}(k-1))}) \right) f(\underline{\tilde{x}(k), \mu_k'(\tilde{x}(k))})$$

$$\left. \left. \left. \sum_{\tilde{x}(k-2)\in \tilde{X}_s} g(\tilde{x}(k-3), \mu_{k-3}'(\tilde{x}(k-3))) \right) \cdots \right) g(\tilde{x}(1), \mu_1'(\tilde{x}(1))) \right) g(s_0, \mu_0'(s_0))$$

$$\cdots$$

$$\geq \prod_{t=1}^{k} \sum_{\tilde{x}(t)\in \tilde{X}_s} g(\underline{\tilde{x}(t-1), \mu_{t-1}(\tilde{x}(t-1))})(f(\underline{\tilde{x}(k), \mu_k'(\tilde{x}(k))}))$$

where

$$(\underline{\tilde{x}(t-1), \mu_{t-1}(\tilde{x}(t-1))}) = \underset{\substack{\tilde{x}(t-1)\in \tilde{X}_s \\ \mu_{t-1}(\tilde{x}(t-1))}}{\arg\min} \sum_{\tilde{x}(t)\in \tilde{X}_s} g(\tilde{x}(t-1), \mu_{t-1}(\tilde{x}(t-1)))$$

for all $t \in \overline{0, k}$, and

$$(\underline{\tilde{x}(k), \mu_k(\tilde{x}(k))}) = \underset{\substack{\tilde{x}(k)\in \tilde{X}_s \\ \mu_k(\tilde{x}(k))}}{\arg\min} f(\tilde{x}(k), \mu_k'(\tilde{x}(k))).$$

Noted that $\omega = (\tilde{x}(0), \mu_0(\tilde{x}(0)), \tilde{x}(1), \mu_1(\tilde{x}(1)) \cdots \tilde{x}(k))$ is one of the paths up to time instant k which can be generated by the system controlled by the Markov policy μ', and the History-based Supervisor ensures that for all paths ω up to arbitrary time instant $k \in \overline{0, H}$,

$$\prod_{t=1}^{k} \sum_{\tilde{x}\in \tilde{X}_s} g(\omega_x(t-1), \omega_u(t-1)) (f(\omega_x(k), u_{uc}(\omega_x(k), k))) \geq 1 - \rho.$$

Note that we have $1 - \tilde{V}_H^{\mu'}(s_0) \geq 1 - \rho$, i.e. $p_{s_0}^{\mu'}(\diamond^{\leq H}\mathcal{A}^c) = \tilde{V}_H^{\mu'}(s_0) \leq \rho.$

References

1. Abate, A., Prandini, M., Lygeros, J., Sastry, S.: Probabilistic reachability and safety for controlled discrete time stochastic hybrid systems. Automatica **44**(11), 2724–2734 (2008). https://doi.org/10.1016/j.automatica.2008.03.027
2. Abdi, F., Chen, C.Y., Hasan, M., Liu, S., Mohan, S., Caccamo, M.: Preserving physical safety under cyber attacks. IEEE Internet Things J. (2018). https://doi.org/10.1109/JIOT.2018.2889866
3. Abdi, F., Tabish, R., Rungger, M., Zamani, M., Caccamo, M.: Application and system-level software fault tolerance through full system restarts. In: 2017 ACM/IEEE 8th International Conference on Cyber-Physical Systems (ICCPS), pp. 197–206. IEEE (2017). https://doi.org/10.1145/3055004.3055012
4. Alshiekh, M., Bloem, R., Ehlers, R., Könighofer, B., Niekum, S., Topcu, U.: Safe reinforcement learning via shielding. In: Thirty-Second AAAI Conference on Artificial Intelligence (2018)
5. Bak, S., Johnson, T.T., Caccamo, M., Sha, L.: Real-time reachability for verified simplex design. In: 2014 IEEE Real-Time Systems Symposium, pp. 138–148. IEEE (2014). https://doi.org/10.1109/RTSS.2014.21
6. Bak, S., Manamcheri, K., Mitra, S., Caccamo, M.: Sandboxing controllers for cyber-physical systems. In: 2011 IEEE/ACM Second International Conference on Cyber-Physical Systems, pp. 3–12. IEEE (2011). https://doi.org/10.1109/ICCPS.2011.25
7. Bloem, R., Könighofer, B., Könighofer, R., Wang, C.: Shield synthesis: runtime enforcement for reactive systems. In: International Conference on Tools and Algorithms for the Construction and Analysis of Systems, pp. 533–548. Springer (2015). https://doi.org/10.1007/978-3-662-46681-0_51
8. Crenshaw, T.L., Gunter, E., Robinson, C.L., Sha, L., Kumar, P.: The simplex reference model: limiting fault-propagation due to unreliable components in cyber-physical system architectures. In: 28th IEEE International Real-Time Systems Symposium, RTSS 2007, pp. 400–412. IEEE (2007). https://doi.org/10.1109/RTSS.2007.34
9. Esmaeil Zadeh Soudjani, S.: Formal abstractions for automated verification and synthesis of stochastic systems. Ph.D. thesis, Technical University of Delft (2014). https://doi.org/10.4233/uuid:201d5145-0717-4dea-b0d0-c018e510fdaa
10. Hernández-Lerma, O., Lasserre, J.B.: Discrete-Time Markov Control Processes: Basic Optimality Criteria. Springer, New York (1996). https://doi.org/10.1007/978-1-4612-0729-0
11. Hovakimyan, N., Cao, C., Kharisov, E., Xargay, E., Gregory, I.M.: L 1 adaptive control for safety-critical systems. IEEE Control Syst. Mag. **31**(5), 54–104 (2011). https://doi.org/10.1109/MCS.2011.941961
12. Humphrey, L., Könighofer, B., Könighofer, R., Topcu, U.: Synthesis of admissible shields. In: Bloem, R., Arbel, E. (eds.) HVC 2016. LNCS, vol. 10028, pp. 134–151. Springer, Cham (2016). https://doi.org/10.1007/978-3-319-49052-6_9
13. Kupferman, O., Vardi, M.Y.: Model checking of safety properties. Form. Methods Syst. Des. **19**(3), 291–314 (2001). https://doi.org/10.1023/A:1011254632723
14. Lavaei, A., Soudjani, S., Zamani, M.: From dissipativity theory to compositional construction of finite Markov decision processes. In: Proceedings of the 21st International Conference on Hybrid Systems: Computation and Control (part of CPS Week), pp. 21–30. ACM (2018). https://doi.org/10.1145/3178126.3178135
15. Lavaei, A., Soudjani, S., Zamani, M.: Compositional synthesis of large-scale stochastic systems: a relaxed dissipativity approach. arXiv preprint arXiv:1902.01223 (2019)

16. Monahan, G.E.: State of the art–a survey of partially observable markov decision processes: theory, models, and algorithms. Manag. Sci. **28**(1), 1–16 (1982). https://doi.org/10.1287/mnsc.28.1.1

17. Reis, C., Barth, A., Pizano, C.: Browser security: lessons from google chrome. Commun. ACM **52**(8), 45–49 (2009). https://doi.org/10.1145/1536616.1536634

18. Sha, L.: Using simplicity to control complexity. IEEE Softw. 20–28 (2001). https://doi.org/10.1109/MS.2001.936213

19. Tkachev, I., Mereacre, A., Katoen, J.P., Abate, A.: Quantitative automata-based controller synthesis for non-autonomous stochastic hybrid systems. In: Proceedings of the 16th International Conference on Hybrid Systems: Computation and Control, pp. 293–302. ACM (2013). https://doi.org/10.1145/2461328.2461373

20. Wang, X., Hovakimyan, N., Sha, L.: L1simplex: fault-tolerant control of cyber-physical systems. In: 2013 ACM/IEEE International Conference on Cyber-Physical Systems (ICCPS), pp. 41–50. IEEE (2013). https://doi.org/10.1145/2502524.2502531

21. Wang, X., Hovakimyan, N., Sha, L.: RSimplex: a robust control architecture for cyber and physical failures. ACM Trans. Cyber Phys. Syst. **2**(4), 27 (2018). https://doi.org/10.1145/3121428

22. Yao, J., Liu, X., Zhu, G., Sha, L.: Netsimplex: controller fault tolerance architecture in networked control systems. IEEE Trans. Ind. Inform. **9**(1), 346–356 (2013). https://doi.org/10.1109/TII.2012.2219060

Proportional Lumpability

Andrea Marin[1] , Carla Piazza[2] , and Sabina Rossi[1(✉)]

[1] Università Ca' Foscari Venezia, Venice, Italy
{marin,sabina.rossi}@unive.it
[2] Università di Udine, Udine, Italy
carla.piazza@uniud.it

Abstract. We deal with the lumpability approach to cope with the state space explosion problem inherent to the computation of the performance indices of large stochastic models using a state aggregation technique. The lumpability method applies to Markov chains exhibiting some structural regularity and allows one to efficiently compute the exact values of the performance indices when the model is actually lumpable. The notion of quasi-lumpability is based on the idea that a Markov chain can be altered by relatively small perturbations of the transition rates in such a way that the new resulting Markov chain is lumpable. In this case only upper and lower bounds on the performance indices can be derived. In this paper we introduce a novel notion of quasi lumpability, named *proportional lumpability*, which extends the original definition of lumpability but, differently than the general definition of quasi lumpability, it allows one to derive exact performance indices for the original process.

1 Introduction

In the context of performance evaluation of computer systems, continuous time Markov chains (CTMCs) constitute the underlying semantics model of a plethora of modelling formalisms such as Stochastic Petri nets [21], Stochastic Automata Networks (SAN) [22], queueing networks [6] and a class of Markovian process algebras (MPAs), e.g., [14,15]. Usually, one is interested in computing the stationary performance indices of the model such as throughput, expected response time, resource utilization and so on. This requires the preliminary computation of the stationary probability distribution of the CTMC underlying the model.

Although the use of high-level modelling formalisms highly simplifies the specification of quantitative models by exploiting the compositional properties and the hierarchical approach, the stochastic process underlying even a very compact model may have a number of states that makes its analysis a difficult, even computationally impossible, task. In order to study models with a large state space without using approximations or resorting to simulation we can attempt to reduce the state space of the underlying Markov chain by aggregating states with equivalent behaviours (according to a notion of equivalence that may vary).

In this paper, we deal with the lumpability approach to cope with the state space explosion problem inherent to the computation of the performance indices

© Springer Nature Switzerland AG 2019
E. André and M. Stoelinga (Eds.): FORMATS 2019, LNCS 11750, pp. 265–281, 2019.
https://doi.org/10.1007/978-3-030-29662-9_16

of large stochastic models using a state aggregation technique. The lumpability method applies to Markov chains exhibiting some structural regularity and allows one to efficiently compute the exact values of the performance indices when the model is actually lumpable. In the literature, several notions of lumping have been introduced. Interestingly, it has been shown that for Markovian process algebras there is a strong connection between the idea of *bisimulation* and that of *strong lumping* (see, e.g., [15]). However, it is well known that not all Markov chains are lumpable. In fact, only a small percentage of Markov chains arising in real-life applications is expected to be lumpable. The notion of *quasi-lumpability* is based on the idea that a Markov chain can be altered by relatively small perturbations of the transition rates in such a way that the new resulting Markov chain is lumpable. In this case only upper and lower bounds on the performance indices can be derived [12,13]. Here, we face the problem of relaxing the conditions of strong lumpability while allowing one to derive the exact performance indices for the original process.

Related Work. At the stochastic process level of abstraction, several approaches, both exact and approximate, have been proposed to cope with the state space explosion problem. Hereafter we focus on lumping methods. In [17, Ch. 6] the authors introduce the notion of strong lumping of states in a discrete time Markov chain (DTMC) but the concept can be straightforwardly extended to CTMCs. In *strong lumping* the states of the Markov chain are clustered according to some structural properties of the transition rate matrix so that a CTMC with a smaller number of states can be defined. Since the complexity of the analysis of this latter chain is lower than that required by the original one, lumping can be an effective way for studying the properties of large Markov chains. A structural-based approach to lumping for SPNs is studied in [2,4], where structural symmetries of the net are exploited to derive a lumped underlying CTMC in an efficient way. In the context of Markovian process algebras, structural process properties are studied in [5,7–9,15,18] for state space reduction purposes by means of equivalence relations inspired by bisimulation. In [5,9] Markovian bisimulations are deeply studied for Interactive Markov Chains. In [7,8,15] equivalence relations in the style of bisimulation (coinductive definition) are introduced. If two components are equivalent it is possible to replace one of them (that with more states) with the other without affecting the behaviour of the remaining parts of the system. Specifically, in [7,8] the author proposes different weak Markovian bisimulation equivalences in the context of a Markovian process calculus. In all cases he shows that the CTMC-level aggregation induced by the bisimulation is a lumping only for specific classes of processes. Conversely, the notion of *strong equivalence* introduced in [15] for processes expressed as terms of the Performance Evaluation Process Algebra (PEPA) always induces a lumping of the CTMC underlying a PEPA process, although in general the opposite is not true. In [12] the notion of quasi-lumpable Markov chain is introduced. The idea is that a quasi lumpable Markov Chain is one which can be made lumpable by a relatively small perturbation of the transition rates. In [12,13] a technique for the computation of bounds based on the Courtois and

Semal's method is presented. The notion of quasi lumpability in the context of a Markovian process algebra has been studied in [20] where the authors introduce the concept of approximate strong equivalence for PEPA components and propose a partitioning strategy which involves the use of a clustering algorithm that minimizes an upper bound for approximate strong equivalence.

Contribution. In this paper we introduce a novel notion of quasi lumpability, named *proportional lumpability*, which extends the original definition of lumpability but, differently than the general definition of quasi lumpability, it allows one to derive exact performance indices for the original process. Then we study this notion in the context of a Markovian process algebra. We consider the Performance Evaluation Process Algebra (PEPA) [15] and introduce the concept of *proportional bisimilarity* over PEPA components. Proportional bisimilarity induces a proportional lumpability on the underlying Markov Chains.

Structure of the Paper. The paper is structured as follows: In Sect. 2 we review the theoretical background on continuous-time Markov chains and recall the concept of lumpability. The notions of quasi lumpability and proportional lumpability are introduced and illustrated through an example. In Sect. 3 we recall the Performance Evaluation Process Algebra (PEPA) [15] that is an algebraic calculus enhanced with stochastic timing information which may be used to calculate performance measures as well as prove functional system properties. The notions of quasi bisimulation and proportional bisimilarity are defined. Section 4 concludes the paper.

2   CTMCs and Proportional Lumpability

In this section we review the theoretical background on continuous-time Markov chains and the concept of lumpability.

Continuous-Time Markov Chains. A Continuous-Time Markov Chain (CTMC) is a stochastic process $X(t)$ for $t \in \mathbb{R}^+$ taking values into a discrete state space S such that (1) $X(t)$ is *stationary*, i.e., $(X(t_1), X(t_2), \ldots, X(t_n))$ has the same distribution as $(X(t_1 + \tau), X(t_2 + \tau), \ldots, X(t_n + \tau))$ for all $t_1, t_2, \ldots, t_n, \tau \in \mathbb{R}^+$; (2) $X(t)$ has the *Markov property*, i.e., the conditional (on both past and present states) probability distribution of its future behaviour is independent of its past evolution until the present state:

$$Prob(X(t_{n+1}) = s_{n+1} \mid X(t_1) = s_1, X(t_2) = s_2, \ldots, X(t_n) = s_n)$$
$$= Prob(X(t_{n+1}) = s_{n+1} \mid X(t_n) = s_n).$$

A CTMC $X(t)$ is said to be *time-homogeneous* if the conditional probability $Prob(X(t + \tau) = s \mid X(t) = s')$ does not depend upon t, and is *irreducible* if every state in S can be reached from every other state. A state in a Markov process is called *recurrent* if the probability that the process will eventually return to the same state is one. A recurrent state is called *positive-recurrent* if the expected number of steps until the process returns to it is finite. A CTMC is *ergodic* if it is irreducible and all its states are positive-recurrent. In the case of finite Markov chains, irreducibility is sufficient for ergodicity. Henceforth, we assume the ergodicity of the CTMCs that we study.

An ergodic CTMC possesses an *equilibrium* (or *steady-state*) *distribution*, that is the *unique* collection of positive real numbers $\pi(s)$ with $s \in S$ such that

$$\lim_{t \to \infty} Prob(X(t) = s \mid X(0) = s') = \pi(s).$$

Notice that the above equation for $\pi(s)$ is independent of s'. We denote by $q(s, s')$ the transition rate between two states s and s', with $s \neq s'$. The infinitesimal generator matrix $\mathbf{Q}$ of a CTMC $X(t)$ with state space S is the $|S| \times |S|$ matrix whose off-diagonal elements are the $q(s, s')$'s and whose diagonal elements are the negative sum of the extra diagonal elements of each row, i.e., $q(s, s) = -\sum_{s' \in S, \, s' \neq s} q(s, s')$. Any non-trivial vector of positive real numbers $\boldsymbol{\mu}$ satisfying the system of global balance equations (GBEs)

$$\boldsymbol{\mu}\mathbf{Q} = \mathbf{0} \tag{1}$$

is called *invariant measure* of the CTMC. For an irreducible CTMC $X(t)$, if $\boldsymbol{\mu}_1$ and $\boldsymbol{\mu}_2$ are two invariant measures of $X(t)$, then there exists a constant $k > 0$ such that $\boldsymbol{\mu}_1 = k\boldsymbol{\mu}_2$. If the CTMC is ergodic, then there exists a unique invariant measure $\boldsymbol{\pi}$ whose components sum to unity, i.e., $\sum_{s \in S} \pi(s) = 1$. In this case $\boldsymbol{\pi}$ is the *equilibrium* or *steady-state distribution* of the CTMC.

Lumpability. In the context of performance and reliability analysis, the notion of *lumpability* provides a model simplification technique which can be used for generating an aggregated Markov process that is smaller than the original one but allows one to determine exact results for the original process.

The concept of lumpability can be formalized in terms of equivalence relations over the state space of the Markov chain. Any such equivalence induces a *partition* on the state space of the Markov chain and aggregation is achieved by clustering equivalent states into macro-states, thus reducing the overall state space. If the partition can be shown to satisfy the so-called *strong* lumpability condition [3,17], then the equilibrium solution of the aggregated process may be used to derive an exact solution of the original one.

Strong lumpability has been introduced in [17] and further studied in [1,10, 19,24].

Definition 1 (Strong lumpability). *Let $X(t)$ be a CTMC with state space S and $\sim$ be an equivalence relation over S. We say that $X(t)$ is strongly lumpable with respect to $\sim$ (resp., $\sim$ is a strong lumpability for $X(t)$) if $\sim$ induces a partition on the state space of $X(t)$ such that for any equivalence class $S_i, S_j \in S/\sim$ with $i \neq j$ and $s, s' \in S_i$,*

$$\sum_{s'' \in S_j} q(s, s'') = \sum_{s'' \in S_j} q(s', s'').$$

Thus, an equivalence relation over the state space of a Markov process is a strong lumpability if it induces a partition into equivalence classes such that for any two states within an equivalence class their aggregated transition rates to any other class are the same. Notice that every Markov process is strongly lumpable with respect to the identity relation, and also with respect to the trivial relation having only one equivalence class.

In [17] the authors prove that for an equivalence relation $\sim$ over the state space of a Markov process $X(t)$, the aggregated process is a Markov process for every initial distribution if, and only if, $\sim$ is a strong lumpability for $X(t)$. Moreover, the transition rate between two aggregated states $S_i, S_j \in \mathcal{S}/\sim$ with $i \neq j$ is equal to $\sum_{s' \in S_j} q(s, s')$ for any $s \in S_i$.

Proposition 1 *(Aggregated process for strong lumpability). Let $X(t)$ be a CTMC with state space $\mathcal{S}$, infinitesimal generator $\mathbf{Q}$ and equilibrium distribution π. Let $\sim$ be a strong lumpability for $X(t)$ and $\widetilde{X}(t)$ be the aggregated process with state space $\mathcal{S}/\sim$ and infinitesimal generator $\widetilde{\mathbf{Q}}$ defined by: for any equivalence class $S_i, S_j \in \mathcal{S}/\sim$ with $i \neq j$*

$$\widetilde{q}(S_i, S_j) = \sum_{s' \in S_j} q(s, s')$$

for any $s \in S_i$. Then the equilibrium distribution $\widetilde{\pi}$ of $\widetilde{X}(t)$ satisfies: for any equivalence class $S \in \mathcal{S}/\sim$,

$$\widetilde{\pi}(S) = \sum_{s \in S} \pi(s).$$

In general, a non-trivial lumpable partition might not exist. The notion of *quasi lumpability* has been introduced in [12] to characterize those Markov chains which can be made lumpable by a relatively small perturbation to the transition rates.

Definition 2 (Quasi lumpability). *Let $X(t)$ be a CTMC with state space $\mathcal{S}$ and $\sim$ be an equivalence relation over $\mathcal{S}$. We say that $X(t)$ is quasi lumpable with respect to $\sim$ (resp., $\sim$ is a quasi lumpability for $X(t)$) if $\sim$ induces a partition on the state space of $X(t)$ such that for any equivalence class $S_i, S_j \in \mathcal{S}/\sim$ with $i \neq j$ and $s, s' \in S_i$,*

$$|\sum_{s'' \in S_j} q(s, s'') - \sum_{s'' \in S_j} q(s', s'')| \leq \epsilon, \ \epsilon \geq 0.$$

The notion of quasi-lumpability coincides with the concept of *near-lumpability* presented in [10]. Techniques for computing bounds to the steady state probabilities of quasi-lumpable Markov chains have been studied in [11–13,23].

In this paper we introduce a novel notion of lumpability, named *proportional lumpability* which, as the notion of quasi lumpability extends the original definition of strong lumpability but differently from the general definition of quasi lumpability it allows us to derive an exact solution of the original process.

Definition 3 (Proportional lumpability). *Let $X(t)$ be a CTMC with state space $\mathcal{S}$ and $\sim$ be an equivalence relation over $\mathcal{S}$. We say that $X(t)$ is proportionally lumpable with respect to $\sim$ (resp., $\sim$ is a proportonal lumpability for $X(t)$) if there exists a function κ from $\mathcal{S}$ to $\mathbb{R}^+$ such that $\sim$ induces a partition on the state space of $X(t)$ satisfying the property that for any equivalence class $S_i, S_j \in \mathcal{S}/\sim$ with $i \neq j$ and $s, s' \in S_i$,*

$$\frac{\sum_{s'' \in S_j} q(s, s'')}{\kappa(s)} = \frac{\sum_{s'' \in S_j} q(s', s'')}{\kappa(s')}.$$

We say that $X(t)$ is κ-proportionally lumpable with respect to $\sim$ (resp., $\sim$ is a κ-proportonal lumpability for $X(t)$) if $X(t)$ is proportionally lumpable with respect to $\sim$ and function κ.

The following proposition proves that proportional lumpability allows one to compute an exact solution for the original model.

Proposition 2 *(Aggregated process for proportional lumpability). Let $X(t)$ be a CTMC with state space $\mathcal{S}$, infinitesimal generator $\mathbf{Q}$ and equilibrium distribution $\boldsymbol{\pi}$. Let κ be a function from $\mathcal{S}$ to $\mathbb{R}^+$, $\sim$ be a κ-proportional lumpability for $X(t)$ and $\widetilde{X}(t)$ be the aggregated process with state space $\mathcal{S}/\sim$ and infinitesimal generator $\widetilde{\mathbf{Q}}$ defined by: for any equivalence class $S_i, S_j \in \mathcal{S}/\sim$ with $i \neq j$*

$$\widetilde{q}(S_i, S_j) = \frac{\sum_{s' \in S_j} q(s, s')}{\kappa(s)}$$

for any $s \in S_i$. Then the invariant measure $\widetilde{\boldsymbol{\mu}}$ of $\widetilde{X}(t)$ satisfies: for any equivalence class $S \in \mathcal{S}/\sim$,

$$\widetilde{\mu}(S) = \sum_{s \in S} \pi(s)\kappa(s).$$

Proof. Let $\widetilde{X}(t)$ be the aggregated process defined as above. For all $S \in \mathcal{S}/\sim$, the corresponding global balance equation is

$$\widetilde{\mu}(S) \sum_{\substack{S' \in \mathcal{S}/\sim \\ S' \neq S}} \widetilde{q}(S, S') = \sum_{\substack{S' \in \mathcal{S}/\sim \\ S' \neq S}} \widetilde{\mu}(S')\widetilde{q}(S', S). \tag{2}$$

The proof follows by substituting the definitions of $\widetilde{q}$ and $\widetilde{\mu}$ given above. Indeed, the left-hand side of Eq. (2) can be written as follows, where s is an arbitrary state in S:

$$\left(\sum_{s \in S} \pi(s)\kappa(s)\right) \sum_{\substack{S' \in \mathcal{S}/\sim \\ S' \neq S}} \frac{\sum_{s' \in S'} q(s, s')}{\kappa(s)}$$

$$= \sum_{s \in S} \pi(s) \sum_{\substack{S' \in \mathcal{S}/\sim \\ S' \neq S}} \sum_{s' \in S'} q(s, s').$$

The right-hand side of Eq. (2) can be written as:

$$\sum_{\substack{S' \in \mathcal{S}/\sim \\ S' \neq S}} \left(\sum_{s' \in S'} \pi(s')\kappa(s') \right) \frac{\sum_{s \in S} q(s', s)}{\kappa(s')}$$

$$= \sum_{\substack{S' \in \mathcal{S}/\sim \\ S' \neq S}} \sum_{s' \in S'} \pi(s') \sum_{s \in S} q(s', s)$$

$$= \sum_{s \in S} \sum_{\substack{S' \in \mathcal{S}/\sim \\ S' \neq S}} \sum_{s' \in S'} \pi(s')q(s', s).$$

From the general conservation law we have that for any closed boundary, the effective flow inward must equal the effective flow outward, i.e., for any $S \subseteq \mathcal{S}$

$$\sum_{s \in S} \pi(s) \sum_{s' \in \mathcal{S}, s' \notin S} q(s, s') = \sum_{s \in S} \sum_{s' \in \mathcal{S}, s' \notin S} \pi(s')q(s', s)$$

and this concludes the proof.   □

We now show how to compute the equilibrium distribution of a proportionally lumpable CTMC $X(t)$ from the equilibrium distribution of a class of perturbations $X'(t)$ defined as follows.

Definition 4 *(Perturbation w.r.t. κ and $\sim$). Let $X(t)$ be a CTMC with state space $\mathcal{S}$, and infinitesimal generator $\mathbf{Q}$. Let κ be a function from $\mathcal{S}$ to $\mathbb{R}^+$ and $\sim$ be a κ-proportional lumpability for $X(t)$. We say that a CTMC $X'(t)$ with infinitesimal generator $\mathbf{Q}'$ is a perturbation of $X(t)$ with respect to κ and $\sim$ if $X'(t)$ is obtained from $X(t)$ by perturbing its rates such that for all $s \in \mathcal{S}$, $S \in \mathcal{S}/\sim$,*

$$\sum_{\substack{s' \in S \\ s' \neq s}} q'(s, s') = \frac{\sum_{s' \in S, s' \neq s} q(s, s')}{\kappa(s)}.$$

Proposition 3 *(Equilibrium distribution for proportionally lumpable CTMCs). Let $X(t)$ be a CTMC with state space $\mathcal{S}$, infinitesimal generator $\mathbf{Q}$ and equilibrium distribution $\boldsymbol{\pi}$. Let κ be a function from $\mathcal{S}$ to $\mathbb{R}^+$, $\sim$ be a κ-proportional lumpability for $X(t)$ and $\tilde{X}(t)$ be the aggregated process with state space $\mathcal{S}/\sim$ and infinitesimal generator $\tilde{\mathbf{Q}}$ as defined in Proposition 2. Then, for any perturbation $X'(t)$ of the original chain $X(t)$ with respect to κ and $\sim$ according to Definition 4, the equilibrium distribution $\boldsymbol{\pi}'$ of $X'(t)$ satisfies the following property: let $K = \sum_{s \in \mathcal{S}} \pi'(s)/\kappa(s)$ then*

$$\pi(s) = \frac{\pi'(s)}{K \, \kappa(s)}.$$

Proof. For all $s \in \mathcal{S}$, the corresponding global balance equation is

$$\pi(s) \sum_{\substack{s' \in \mathcal{S} \\ s' \neq s}} q(s, s') = \sum_{\substack{s' \in \mathcal{S} \\ s' \neq s}} \pi(s')q(s', s). \tag{3}$$

From the fact that $\sim$ induces a partition on the state space of $X(t)$, the above equation can be re-written as:

$$\pi(s) \left(\sum_{\substack{S \in \mathcal{S}/\sim \\ s \notin S}} \sum_{s' \in S} q(s, s') + \sum_{\substack{S \in \mathcal{S}/\sim \\ s \in S}} \sum_{\substack{s' \in S \\ s' \neq s}} q(s, s') \right)$$

$$= \sum_{\substack{S \in \mathcal{S}/\sim \\ s \notin S}} \sum_{s' \in S} \pi(s')q(s', s) + \sum_{\substack{S \in \mathcal{S}/\sim \\ s \in S}} \sum_{\substack{s' \in S \\ s' \neq s}} \pi(s')q(s', s). \tag{4}$$

We now replace the definition of $\pi(s)$ given above. Indeed, the left-hand side of Eq. (4) can be written as follows:

$$\frac{\pi'(s)}{K \, \kappa(s)} \left(\sum_{\substack{S \in \mathcal{S}/\sim \\ s \notin S}} \sum_{s' \in S} q(s, s') + \sum_{\substack{S \in \mathcal{S}/\sim \\ s \in S}} \sum_{\substack{s' \in S \\ s' \neq s}} q(s, s') \right)$$

$$= \frac{\pi'(s)}{K} \left(\sum_{\substack{S \in \mathcal{S}/\sim \\ s \notin S}} \sum_{s' \in S} \frac{q(s, s')}{\kappa(s)} + \sum_{\substack{S \in \mathcal{S}/\sim \\ s \in S}} \sum_{\substack{s' \in S \\ s' \neq s}} \frac{q(s, s')}{\kappa(s)} \right)$$

$$= \frac{\pi'(s)}{K} \sum_{\substack{s' \in \mathcal{S} \\ s' \neq s}} q'(s, s').$$

The right-hand side of Eq. (4) can be written as follows:

$$\sum_{\substack{S \in \mathcal{S}/\sim \\ s \notin S}} \sum_{s' \in S} \frac{\pi'(s')}{K \, \kappa(s')} q(s', s) + \sum_{\substack{S \in \mathcal{S}/\sim \\ s \in S}} \sum_{\substack{s' \in S \\ s' \neq s}} \frac{\pi'(s')}{K \, \kappa(s')} q(s', s)$$

$$= \frac{1}{K} \sum_{\substack{S \in \mathcal{S}/\sim \\ s \notin S}} \sum_{s' \in S} \pi'(s') \frac{q(s', s)}{\kappa(s')} + \frac{1}{K} \sum_{\substack{S \in \mathcal{S}/\sim \\ s \in S}} \sum_{\substack{s' \in S \\ s' \neq s}} \pi'(s') \frac{q(s', s)}{\kappa(s')}$$

$$= \frac{1}{K} \sum_{\substack{s' \in \mathcal{S} \\ s' \neq s}} \pi'(s')q'(s', s).$$

Hence, for all $s \in \mathcal{S}$ the global balance equation of $X'(t)$ is satisfied, i.e.,

$$\pi'(s) \sum_{\substack{s' \in \mathcal{S} \\ s' \neq s}} q'(s, s') = \sum_{\substack{s' \in \mathcal{S} \\ s' \neq s}} \pi'(s')q'(s', s).$$

We now prove that the normalizing condition also holds: i.e., $\sum_{s\in\mathcal{S}}\pi(s)=1$. The proof follows trivially from the fact that $K=\sum_{s\in\mathcal{S}}\pi'(s)/\kappa(s)$, in fact:

$$\sum_{s\in\mathcal{S}}\pi(s)=\sum_{s\in\mathcal{S}}\frac{\pi'(s)}{K\,\kappa(s)}=\frac{1}{K}\sum_{s\in\mathcal{S}}\frac{\pi'(s)}{\kappa(s)}=\frac{1}{K}\,K=1.$$

□

Example 1. Consider a system with multiple CPUs, each with its own private memory and one common memory which can be accessed only by one processor at a time. The CPUs execute in private memory for a random time before issuing a common memory access request. Assume that this random time is exponentially distributed with parameter λ_P for processor P. The common memory access duration is also assumed to be exponentially distributed with parameter μ_P for processor P (i.e., the average duration of a common memory access is $1/\mu_P$).

Let us analyze a two-processor version with processors A and B. Assume that the processors have different timing characteristics: the private and common memory accesses of A are governed by two exponential distributions with parameters λ_A and μ_A, respectively, while the private and common memory accesses of B are governed by two exponential distributions with parameters λ_B and μ_B, respectively. The CTMC describing the behaviour of this two-processor system is depicted in Fig. 1, it has five states as follows:

- State 1: A and B both executing in their private memories;
- State 2: B executing in private memory, and A accessing common memory;
- State 3: A executing in private memory, and B accessing common memory;
- State 4: A accessing common memory, B waiting for common memory;
- State 5: B accessing common memory, A waiting for common memory.

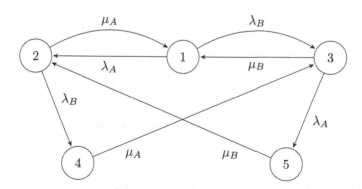

Fig. 1. Two processor system

Suppose that the rates are related as follows:

$$\lambda_A=k_1\lambda \quad \lambda_B=k_2\lambda \quad \mu_A=k_2\mu \quad \mu_B=k_1\mu$$

for $\lambda, \mu, k_1, k_2 \in \mathbb{R}^+$. In this case the CTMC appears as represented in Fig. 2. We can observe that it is proportionally lumpable with respect to the equivalence classes $S_1 = \{1\}$, $S_{2,3,} = \{2,3\}$ and $S_{4,5} = \{4,5\}$ and the function κ defined by: $\kappa(1) = 1$, $\kappa(2) = k_2$, $\kappa(3) = k_1$, $\kappa(4) = k_2$, $\kappa(5) = k_1$. We can then analyze the reduced chain represented in Fig. 3 and, by Propositions 2 and 3, we can compute the exact solution of the original model.

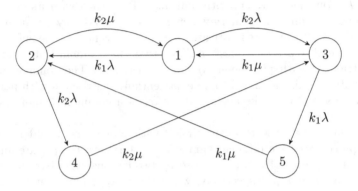

Fig. 2. Two processor system with proportional factors

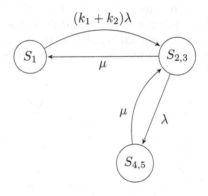

Fig. 3. Two processor reduced system

3   PEPA and Proportional Lumpability

In this section we recall the Performance Evaluation Process Algebra (PEPA) [15] that is an algebraic calculus enhanced with stochastic timing information which may be used to calculate performance measures as well as prove functional system properties.

The basic elements of PEPA are *components* and *activities*. Each activity is represented by a pair (α, r) where α is a label, or *action type*, and r is its *activity rate*, that is the parameter of a negative exponential distribution determining its duration. We assume that there is a countable set, $\mathcal{A}$, of possible action types, including a distinguished type, τ, which can be regarded as the *unknown* type. Activity rates may be any positive real number, or the distinguished symbol $\top$ which should be read as *unspecified*.

The syntax for PEPA terms is defined by the grammar:

$$P ::= P \underset{L}{\bowtie} P \mid P/L \mid S$$
$$S ::= (\alpha, r).S \mid S + S \mid A$$

where S denotes a *sequential component*, while P denotes a *model component* which executes in parallel. We assume that there is a countable set of *constants*, A. We write $\mathcal{C}$ for the set of all possible components.

Structural Operational Semantics. The structural operational semantics of PEPA is described below. Component $(\alpha, r).P$ carries out the activity (α, r) of type α at rate r and subsequently behaves as P. When $a = (\alpha, r)$, component $(\alpha, r).P$ may be written as $a.P$. Component $P + Q$ represents a system which may behave either as P or as Q. $P + Q$ enables all the current activities of both P and Q. The first activity to complete distinguishes one of the components, P or Q. The other component of the choice is discarded. Component P/L behaves as P except that any activity of type within the set L are *hidden*, i.e., they are relabeled with the unobservable type τ. The meaning of a constant A is given by a defining equation such as $A \stackrel{def}{=} P$ which gives the constant A the behaviour of the component P. The cooperation combinator $\underset{L}{\bowtie}$ is in fact an indexed family of combinators, one for each possible set of action types, $L \subseteq \mathcal{A} \setminus \{\tau\}$. The *cooperation set* L defines the action types on which the components must synchronize or *cooperate* (the unknown action type, τ, may not appear in any cooperation set). It is assumed that each component proceeds independently with any activity whose type does not occur in the cooperation set L (*individual activities*). However, activities with action types in the set L require the simultaneous involvement of both components (*shared activities*). These shared activities will only be enabled in $P \underset{L}{\bowtie} Q$ when they are enabled in both P and Q. The shared activity will have the same action type as the two contributing activities and a rate reflecting the rate of the slower participant [15]. If an activity has an unspecified rate in a component then the component is passive with respect to that action type. In this case, the rate of the shared activity will be completely determined by the other component. For a given process P and action type α, the *apparent rate* of α in P, denoted $r_\alpha(P)$, is the sum of the rates of the α activities enabled in P.

The semantics of each term in PEPA is given via a labeled *multi-transition system* where the multiplicities of arcs are significant. In the transition system, a state or *derivative* corresponds to each syntactic term of the language and an arc represents the activity which causes one derivative to evolve into another.

The set of reachable states of a model P is termed the *derivative set* of P, denoted by $ds(P)$, and constitutes the set of nodes of the *derivation graph* of P ($\mathcal{D}(P)$) obtained by applying the semantic rules exhaustively. We denote by $\mathcal{A}(P)$ the set of all the *current action types* of P, i.e., the set of action types which the component P may next engage in. We denote by $Act(P)$ the multiset of all the *current activities* of P. Finally, we denote by $\boldsymbol{\mathcal{A}}(P)$ the union of all $\mathcal{A}(P')$ with $P' \in ds(P)$, i.e., the set of all action types syntactically occurring in P. For any component P, the *exit rate* from P will be the sum of the activity rates of all the activities enabled in P, i.e., $q(P) = \sum_{a \in Act(P)} r_a$, with r_a being the rate of activity a. If P enables more than one activity, $|Act(P)| > 1$, then the dynamic behaviour of the model is determined by a race condition. This has the effect of replacing the nondeterministic branching of the pure process algebra with probabilistic branching. The probability that a particular activity completes is given by the ratio of the activity rate to the exit rate from P.

Underlying Stochastic Process. In [15] it is proved that for any finite PEPA model $P \stackrel{def}{=} P_0$ with $ds(P) = \{P_0, \ldots, P_n\}$, if we define the stochastic process $X(t)$, such that $X(t) = P_i$ indicates that the system behaves as component P_i at time t, then $X(t)$ is a continuous time Markov chain.

The *transition rate* between two components P_i and P_j, denoted $q(P_i, P_j)$, is the rate at which the system changes from behaving as component P_i to behaving as P_j. It is the sum of the activity rates labeling arcs which connect the node corresponding to P_i to the node corresponding to P_j in $\mathcal{D}(P)$, i.e.,

$$q(P_i, P_j) = \sum_{a \in Act(P_i | P_j)} r_a$$

where $P_i \neq P_j$ and $Act(P_i | P_j) = \{\!| a \in Act(P_i)| \; P_i \stackrel{a}{\to} P_j |\!\}$. Clearly, if P_j is not a one-step derivative of P_i, $q(P_i, P_j) = 0$. The $q(P_i, P_j)$ (also denoted q_{ij}), are the off-diagonal elements of the infinitesimal generator matrix of the Markov process, $\mathbf{Q}$. Diagonal elements are formed as the negative sum of the non-diagonal elements of each row. We use the following notation: $q(P_i) = \sum_{j \neq i} q(P_i, P_j)$ and $q_{ii} = -q(P_i)$. For any finite and irreducible PEPA model P, the steady-state distribution $\Pi(\cdot)$ exists and it may be found by solving the normalization equation and the global balance equations:

$$\sum_{P_i \in ds(P)} \Pi(P_i) = 1 \quad \wedge \quad \Pi\mathbf{Q} = \mathbf{0}.$$

The *conditional transition rate* from P_i to P_j via an action type α is denoted $q(P_i, P_j, \alpha)$. This is the sum of the activity rates labeling arcs connecting the corresponding nodes in the derivation graph with label α. It is the rate at which a system behaving as component P_i evolves to behaving as component P_j as the result of completing a type α activity. The *total conditional transition rate* from P to $S \subseteq ds(P)$, denoted $q[P, S, \alpha]$, is defined as

$$q[P, S, \alpha] = \sum_{P' \in S} q(P, P', \alpha),$$

where $q(P, P', \alpha) = \sum_{P \xrightarrow{(\alpha, r_\alpha)} P'} r_\alpha$.

Quasi-Lumpable and Proportional Bisimilarity. In a process algebra, actions, rather than states, play the role of capturing the observable behaviour of a system model. This leads to a formally defined notion of equivalence in which components are regarded as equal if, under observation, they appear to perform exactly the same actions.

In this section we introduce a bisimulation-like relation, named *quasi-lumpable bisimilarity* that extends the notion of *lumpable bisimilarity* for PEPA models defined [16] and induces a quasi-lumpability on the underlying Markov chain.

Two PEPA components are *quasi-lumpably bisimilar with respect to* ϵ with $\epsilon \geq 0$ if there is an equivalence relation between them such that, for any action type α different from τ, the total conditional transition rates from those components to any equivalence class, via activities of this type, are equal after small a perturbation of the system.

Definition 5 (Quasi-lumpable bisimulation). *An equivalence relation over PEPA components,* $\mathcal{R} \subseteq \mathcal{C} \times \mathcal{C}$, *is a* quasi-lumpable bisimulation *with respect to* ϵ *with* $\epsilon \geq 0$ *if whenever* $(P, Q) \in \mathcal{R}$ *then for all* $\alpha \in \mathcal{A}$ *and for all* $S \in \mathcal{C}/\mathcal{R}$ *such that*

- *either* $\alpha \neq \tau$,
- *or* $\alpha = \tau$ *and* $P, Q \notin S$,

it holds

$$|q[P, S, \alpha] - q[Q, S, \alpha]| \leq \epsilon, \ \epsilon \geq 0.$$

It is easy to prove that a quasi-lumpable bisimulation over the state space of a PEPA component P induces a quasi-lumpability on the state space of the Markov chain underlying P.

Notice that our definition is similar to the notion of *approximate strong equivalence* introduced by Milos and Gilmore in [20]. However our definition is stricter than that of approximate strong equivalence because the latter allows arbitrary activities with type τ among components belonging to the same equivalence class. Moreover, it holds that, in general, a quasi-lumpable bisimulation induces a coarser aggregation than the approximate strong equivalence of [20].

Unfortunately, the notion of quasi-lumpable bisimulation with respect to a specific bound $\epsilon \geq 0$ is not preserved under union in the sense that the union of two quasi-lumpable bisimulations with respect to ϵ is a quasi-lumpable bisimulation but, in general, not with respect to the same bound ϵ. In [20] a partitioning strategy for PEPA components which involves the use of a clustering algorithm that minimizes an upper bound for approximate strong equivalence is proposed. Here we introduce the notion of proportional bisimulation with respect to a function κ that associates a real value κ_P to each PEPA component P.

Definition 6 (Proportional bisimulation). *Let κ be a function from PEPA components to $\mathbb{R}^+$. An equivalence relation over PEPA components, $\mathcal{R} \subseteq \mathcal{C} \times \mathcal{C}$, is a proportional bisimulation with respect to κ if whenever $(P, Q) \in \mathcal{R}$ then for all $\alpha \in \mathcal{A}$ and for all $S \in \mathcal{C}/\mathcal{R}$ such that*

- *either $\alpha \neq \tau$,*
- *or $\alpha = \tau$ and $P, Q \notin S$,*

it holds

$$\frac{q[P, S, \alpha]}{\kappa_P} = \frac{q[Q, S, \alpha]}{\kappa_Q}.$$

It is clear that the identity relation is a proportional bisimulation for any function κ. We are interested in the relation which is the largest κ-proportional bisimulation, formed by the union of all κ-proportional bisimulations. However, it is not straightforward to see that this will indeed be a lumpable bisimulation.

The following proposition states that any union of κ-proportional bisimulations generates a κ-proportional bisimulation.

Proposition 4. *Let I be a set of indices and $\mathcal{R}_i$ be a κ-proportional bisimulation for all $i \in I$. Then the transitive closure of their union, $\mathcal{R} = (\cup_{i \in I} \mathcal{R}_i)^*$, is also a κ-proportional bisimulation.*

Proof. The proof follows by induction on i and is in the line of that of Proposition 8.2.1 in [15]. □

Based on the above result we can define the maximal κ-proportional bisimulation as the union of all κ-proportional bisimulations.

Definition 7 (Proportional bisimilarity). *Let κ be a function from PEPA components to $\mathbb{R}^+$. Two PEPA components P and Q are κ-proportionally bisimilar, written $P \approx_l^\kappa Q$, if $(P, Q) \in \mathcal{R}$ for some κ-proportional bisimulation $\mathcal{R}$, i.e.,*

$$\approx_l^\kappa = \bigcup \{\mathcal{R} \mid \mathcal{R} \text{ is a } \kappa\text{-proportional bisimulation}\}.$$

$\approx_l^\kappa$ is called κ-proportional bisimilarity and it is the largest symmetric κ-proportional bisimulation over PEPA components.

The relation $\approx_l^\kappa$ partitions the set of components $\mathcal{C}$, and it is easy to see that if restricted to the derivative set of any component P, the relation partitions this set. Let $ds(P)/ \approx_l^\kappa$ denote the set of equivalence classes generated in this way. It is easy to prove the following result.

Proposition 5. *For any PEPA component P, $ds(P)/ \approx_l^\kappa$ induces a proportional lumpability on the state space of the Markov process corresponding to P.*

Proof. The proof is analogous to that of Proposition 8.5.1 in [15]. □

Example 2. We consider a simple buffer in which messages are added according to a Poisson process with rate λ and which is cleared at exponentially spaced instants. The mean time between successive clearances is $n\mu^{-1}$ where n denotes the number of items in the buffer. The buffer has capacity M and, when full, arrivals are lost. This buffer clearly follows a Markov process and can be specified in PEPA as:

$$B_n = (\tau, \lambda).B_{n+1} \quad 0 \le n \le M - 1$$
$$B_n = (cl, \mu n^{-1}).B_0 \quad 0 \le n \le M$$

The derivation graph for this system is shown in Fig. 4.

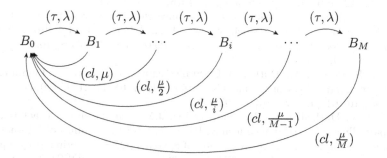

Fig. 4. Original buffer system

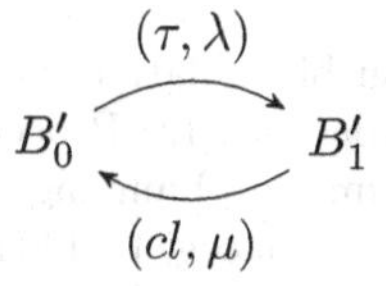

Fig. 5. The buffer reduced system

If we consider the function κ from PEPA components to $\mathbb{R}^+$ such that $\kappa_{B_0} = 1$ and $\kappa_{B_n} = 1/n$ for all n with $0 < n \le M$ then it is easy to prove that $B_0 \approx^\kappa B_0'$ where B_0' is depicted in Fig. 5. From the equilibrium distribution of the reduced system we can then compute the equilibrium distribution of the original system by applying Proposition 3.

4   Conclusion

In this paper we have introduced a novel notion of quasi lumpability, named *proportional lumpability*, which extends the original definition of lumpability but, differently than the general definition of quasi lumpability, it allows one to derive exact performance indices for the original process. Moreover we illustrate the concept of proportional bisimilarity for PEPA components which induces a proportional bisimulation on the underlying Markov chain. We plan to investigate the compositionality and contextual properties of proportional bisimulation for our future work. Moreover, the notion of proportional lumpability in the discrete time setting should be explored.

References

1. Alzetta, G., Marin, A., Piazza, C., Rossi, S.: Lumping-based equivalences in markovian automata: algorithms and applications to product-form analyses. Inf. Comput. **260**, 99–125 (2018). https://doi.org/10.1016/j.ic.2018.04.002
2. Baarir, S., Beccuti, M., Dutheillet, C., Franceschinis, G.: From partially to fully lumped Markov chains in stochastic well formed Petri nets. In: Proceedings of Valuetools 2009 Conference, p. 44. ACM (2009). https://doi.org/10.4108/ICST.VALUETOOLS2009.7733
3. Baarir, S., Beccuti, M., Dutheillet, C., Franceschinis, G., Haddad, S.: Lumping partially symmetrical stochastic models. Perform. Eval. **68**(1), 21–44 (2011). https://doi.org/10.1016/j.peva.2010.09.002
4. Baarir, S., Dutheillet, C., Haddad, S., Iliè, J.M.: On the use of exact lumping in partially symmetrical Well-formed Petri Nets. In: Proceedings of International Conference on Quantitative Evaluation of Systems (QEST), Torino, Italy, pp. 23–32. IEEE Computer Society (2005). https://doi.org/10.1109/QEST.2005.26
5. Baier, C., Katoen, J.P., Hermanns, H., Wolf, V.: Comparative branching-time semantics for Markov chains. Inf. Comput. **200**(2), 149–214 (2005). https://doi.org/10.1016/j.ic.2005.03.001
6. Balsamo, S., Marin, A.: Queueing networks. In: Bernardo, M., Hillston, J. (eds.) SFM 2007. LNCS, vol. 4486, pp. 34–82. Springer, Heidelberg (2007). https://doi.org/10.1007/978-3-540-72522-0_2
7. Bernardo, M.: Weak Markovian bisimulation congruences and exact CTMC-level aggregations for concurrent processes. In: Proceedings of the 10th Workshop on Quantitative Aspects of Programming Languages and Systems (QALP 2012), pp. 122–136. EPTCS (2012). https://doi.org/10.4204/EPTCS.85.9
8. Bernardo, M.: Weak Markovian bisimulation congruences and exact CTMC-level aggregations for sequential processes. In: Bruni, R., Sassone, V. (eds.) TGC 2011. LNCS, vol. 7173, pp. 89–103. Springer, Heidelberg (2012). https://doi.org/10.1007/978-3-642-30065-3_6
9. Bravetti, M.: Revisiting interactive Markov chains. Electr. Notes Theor. Comput. Sci. **68**(5), 65–84 (2003). https://doi.org/10.1016/S1571-0661(04)80520-6
10. Buchholz, P.: Exact and ordinary lumpability in finite Markov chains. J. Appl. Probab. **31**, 59–75 (1994). https://doi.org/10.1017/S0021900200107338
11. Daly, D., Buchholz, P., Sanders, W.: Bound-preserving composition for Markov reward models. In: Third International Conference on the Quantitative Evaluation of Systems (QEST 2006), pp. 243–252 (2006). https://doi.org/10.1109/QEST.2006.8
12. Franceschinis, G., Muntz, R.R.: Bounds for quasi-lumpable Markov chains. Perform. Eval. **20**(1–3), 223–243 (1994). https://doi.org/10.1016/0166-5316(94)90015-9
13. Franceschinis, G., Muntz, R.R.: Computing bounds for the performance indices of quasi-lumpable stochastic well-formed nets. IEEE Trans. Softw. Eng. **20**(7), 516–525 (1994). https://doi.org/10.1109/32.297940

14. Hermanns, H.: Interactive Markov Chains. Springer, Heidelberg (2002). https://doi.org/10.1007/3-540-45804-2
15. Hillston, J.: A Compositional Approach to Performance Modelling. Cambridge Press, Cambridge (1996)
16. Hillston, J., Marin, A., Piazza, C., Rossi, S.: Contextual lumpability. In: Proceedings of Valuetools 2013 Conference, pp. 194–203. ACM Press (2013). https://doi.org/10.4108/icst.valuetools.2013.254408
17. Kemeny, J.G., Snell, J.L.: Finite Markov Chains. Springer, New York (1976)
18. Marin, A., Rossi, S.: Autoreversibility: exploiting symmetries in Markov chains. In: Proceedings of IEEE MASCOTS, San Francisco, CA, USA, pp. 151–160 (2013). https://doi.org/10.1109/MASCOTS.2013.23
19. Marin, A., Rossi, S.: On the relations between Markov chain lumpability andreversibility. Acta Informatica **54**(5), 447–485 (2017). https://doi.org/10.1007/s00236-016-0266-1
20. Milios, D., Gilmore, S.: Component aggregation for PEPA models: an approach based on approximate strong equivalence. Perform. Eval. **94**, 43–71 (2015). https://doi.org/10.1016/j.peva.2015.09.004
21. Molloy, M.K.: Performance analysis using stochastic Petri nets. IEEE Trans. Comput. **31**(9), 913–917 (1982). https://doi.org/10.1109/TC.1982.1676110
22. Plateau, B.: On the stochastic structure of parallelism and synchronization models for distributed algorithms. SIGMETRICS Perform. Eval. Rev. **13**(2), 147–154 (1985). https://doi.org/10.1145/317795.317819
23. Smith, M.: Compositional abstractions for long-run properties of stochastic systems. In: Eighth International Conference on Quantitative Evaluation of Systems, QEST 2011, pp. 223–232 (2011). https://doi.org/10.1109/QEST.2011.37
24. Sumita, U., Reiders, M.: Lumpability and time-reversibility in the aggregation-disaggregation method for large Markov chains. Commun. Stat. Stoch. Model. **5**, 63–81 (1989). https://doi.org/10.1080/15326348908807099

Expected Reachability-Price Games

Shibashis Guha[1][(✉)] and Ashutosh Trivedi[2]

[1] Université libre de Bruxelles, Brussels, Belgium
shibashis.guha@ulb.ac.be
[2] University of Colorado Boulder, Boulder, USA
ashutosh.trivedi@colorado.edu

Abstract. Probabilistic timed automata(PTA) model real-time systems with non-deterministic and stochastic behavior. They extend Alur-Dill timed automata by allowing probabilistic transitions and a price structure on the locations and transitions. Thus, a PTA can be considered as a Markov decision process (MDP) with uncountably many states and transitions. Expected reachability-price games are turn-based games where two players, player Min and player Max, move a token along the infinite configuration space of PTA. The objective of player Min is to minimize the expected price to reach a target location, while the goal of the Max player is the opposite. The undecidability of computing the value in the expected reachability-price games follows from the undecidability of the corresponding problem on timed automata. A key contribution of this work is a characterization of sufficient conditions under which an expected reachability-price game can be reduced to a stochastic game on a stochastic generalization of corner-point abstraction (a well-known finitary abstraction of timed automata). Exploiting this result, we show that expected reachability-price games for PTA with single clock and price-rates restricted to $\{0, 1\}$ are decidable.

1 Introduction

Two-player zero-sum games on finite automata were introduced by Ramadge and Wonham [27] as a mechanism for supervisory controller synthesis of discrete event systems. In this setting the two players—called Min and Max—represent the *controller* and the *environment*, and controller synthesis corresponds to finding a winning (or optimal) strategy of the controller for some given performance objective. Timed automata [2](TA) extend finite automata by providing a mechanism to model real-time behaviour, while priced timed automata are timed automata with (time-dependent) prices attached to the locations of the automata. If the game structure or objectives are dependent on time or price, e.g. when the objective corresponds to completing a given set of tasks within some deadline or within some cost, then games on timed automata are a well-established approach for controller synthesis, see e.g. [1,3,6,11,15].

We study an extension of the above approach to a setting that is quantitative in terms of both timed and probabilistic behavior. For this purpose, we consider an extension of probabilistic timed automata (PTA) [5,19,24]—a model for

© Springer Nature Switzerland AG 2019
É. André and M. Stoelinga (Eds.): FORMATS 2019, LNCS 11750, pp. 282–300, 2019.
https://doi.org/10.1007/978-3-030-29662-9_17

real-time systems exhibiting nondeterministic and probabilistic behavior—with a partition of locations between two players. In our model, priced probabilistic timed game arena (PTGA), a token is placed on a configuration of a PTA and a play of the game corresponds to a player selecting a timed move (i.e. a time delay and an enabled action) and the token is moved according to the probabilistic transition function of the PTA. Players Min and Max choose their moves in order to minimize and maximize, respectively, the objective function. The *upper value* of a game is the minimum expected value that Min can ensure, while the *lower value* of a game is the maximum expected value that Max can ensure. A game is *determined* if the lower and upper values are equal, and in this case the *optimal value* of the game exists and equals the upper and lower values.

We are interested in *reachability-price* objectives, which express the *expected price* to reach a given target set. It is well known that two-player reachability-price games on timed arenas often lead to undecidability [1,11,12], even in non-probabilistic setting [9,14]. We study restrictions of PTGA in order to recover decidability. Our approach makes use of *boundary region abstraction* (BRA) for probabilistic timed automata [17]. Boundary region abstraction is similar to PTGA except that it restricts time delays to region boundaries. Boundary region abstraction has the property that starting from any state, only a finitely many other states can be reached. In particular, the reachable sub-graph of the boundary region abstraction from the initial state is same as the corner-point abstraction [8,10].

We characterize sufficient conditions under which the expected reachability-price games on PTA can be reduced to expected reachability-price games on the corresponding boundary region abstraction. This in particular characterizes conditions under which, for starting states with integral clock valuations, the expected reachability-price games can be reduced to corresponding corner-point abstractions. Using this result, we show the decidability of expected reachability-price problem for one-clock binary-priced PTGAs by reducing it to solving stochastic games on corresponding corner-point abstractions. To our best knowledge, this is the first decidability result for games on PTGA.

To understand the importance of our decidability result, let us review the challenges in solving games on timed automata on various related sub-classes. Brihaye et al. [12] showed the undecidability of deciding the existence of winning strategy for reachability-price games (on non-stochastic timed game arenas) with both positive and negative price-rates and two or more clocks. The next two examples highlight that permitting negative prices, or permitting non-binary prices may require non-positional or non-boundary strategies even in non-stochastic one-clock setting. The first example demonstrates that if negative prices are allowed, positional strategies may not be sufficient even for one-clock PTGA. The second example shows that even when positive prices are allowed, region boundary strategies may not be optimal even for one-clock PTGA.

Example 1 (Negative prices may require non-positional strategies). The Min player locations are represented using circles while the Max player locations are represented using squares. The number in each location is the cost that is incurred

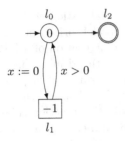

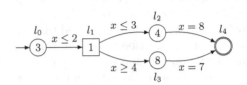

Fig. 1. Timed game arena with negative prices: no player has positional strategies.

Fig. 2. Timed game arena with non-negative prices other than 0 and 1: boundary strategies may not be optimal; for Min player, the optimal transition from l_0 to l_1 takes place at a time $\frac{4}{3}$.

when the token stays in that location for one time unit. The example in Fig. 1 appears in [12] where location l_1 of player Max has a negative cost that is -1. It has been shown in [12] that player Max needs an infinite memory strategy by staying for a duration $\varepsilon/2^n$ for the n-th visit to location l_1 to ensure a payoff of $-\varepsilon$. Since this is true for every ε, it leads to a value 0 of the game. Besides, player Min also needs a finite memory in order to achieve an arbitrarily small payoff.

Example 2. Consider the timed game arena in Fig. 2. A similar example with two clocks appears in [11]. However, in this example there is only one clock x that is never reset. We show that for the timed automaton in this example, the reachability price problem *cannot* be reduced to the same problem in the corresponding corner-point abstractions/boundary region abstraction. The cost function at location l_1 to reach the goal location l_4 when the token reaches l_4 with a clock value of $x \leq 2$ is $\max(28 - x, 32 - 4x)$. This leads to the optimal reachability price strategy for player Min to reach the goal location l_4 to have an associated cost of $30\frac{2}{3}$ when the transition from location l_0 to location l_1 is taken at time $\frac{4}{3}$.

Related Work. Hoffman and Wong-Toi [18] were the first to define and solve the optimal controller synthesis problem for timed automata. For a detailed introduction to the topic of qualitative games on timed automata, see e.g. [4]. Asarin and Maler [3] initiated the study of quantitative games on timed automata by providing a symbolic algorithm to solve reachability-time objectives. The works of [13] and [22] show that the decision problem for such games over timed automata with at least two clocks is EXPTIME-complete. The tool UPPAAL Tiga [6] is capable of solving reachability and safety objectives for games on timed automata. Jurdziński and Trivedi [23] show the EXPTIME-completeness for average-time games on automata with two or more clocks.

A natural extension of games with reachability-time objectives are games on priced timed automata where the objective concerns the cumulated price of reaching a target. Both [1] and [11] present semi-algorithms for computing the value of such games for linear prices, while the semi-algorithms always terminate under strongly Non-Zeno assumption on prices. In [12], it has been shown that the problem is decidable for a class of one-clock bivalued timed automata where the location prices can be any two from the set $\{-1, 0, 1\}$. In [14] the problem of checking the existence of optimal strategies is shown to be undecidable, with [9] showing undecidability holds even for three clocks and stopwatch prices.

Regarding one-player games on PTAs, [20] uses simple functions to devise a symbolic algorithm for computing minimum reachability-time. In [7] the problem of deciding whether a target can be reached within a given price and probability bound is shown to be undecidable for PTAs with three clocks and binary prices. Jurdziński et al. [21] show that the optimal expected cost problem is decidable for concavely-priced probabilistic timed automata.

Organization. The structure of the paper is the following. In the next section we recall required definitions to introduce turn-based priced probabilistic timed game arena and boundary region abstraction. We introduce expected reachability-price games in Sect. 3. In Sect. 4 we characterize conditions on the value of expected reachability-price game on the boundary region abstraction such that this value is equal to the value of the expected reachability-price game on the corresponding PTGA. Finally, in Sect. 5 we use these conditions to prove decidability of the expected reachability-price games on one-clock binary-priced PTGA.

2 Preliminaries

A *discrete probability distribution* over a countable set Q is a function $d : Q \to [0, 1]$ such that $\sum_{q \in Q} d(q) = 1$. For a possible uncountable set Q', we define $\mathcal{D}(Q')$ to be the set of functions $d : Q' \to [0, 1]$ such that the support set $supp(d) = \{q \in Q \mid d(q) > 0\}$ is countable and d is a distribution over $supp(d)$. We say that $d \in \mathcal{D}(Q)$ is a *point* if $d(q) = 1$ for some $q \in Q$.

2.1 Markov Decision Processes (MDPs)

We next introduce MDPs as modeling formalism for systems exhibiting nondeterministic and probabilistic behavior.

Definition 1 (Markov Decision Processe (MDP)). *An MDP is a tuple* $\mathsf{M} = (S, F, A, p, \pi)$ *where:*

- S *is the set of* states *including the set* F *of final states;*
- A *is the set of* actions;
- $p : S \times A \to \mathcal{D}(S)$ *is the* probabilistic transition function;
- $\pi : S \times A \to \mathbb{R}_{\geqslant 0}$ *is the* cost function.

We write $A(s)$ for the set of actions available at s, i.e., the set of actions a for which $p(s, a)$ is defined. For technical convenience we assume that $A(s)$ is nonempty for all $s \in S$. In an MDP $\mathcal{M}$, if the current state is s, then there is a non-deterministic choice between the actions in $A(s)$ and if action a is chosen the probability of reaching the state $s' \in S$ is denoted by $p(s'|s, a) \stackrel{\text{def}}{=} p(s, a)(s')$.

2.2 Probabilistic Timed Automata

We fix a constant $k \in \mathbb{N}$ and finite set of *clocks* $\mathcal{Y}$. Let $[\![k]\!]_{\mathbb{R}}$ denote the set of reals in $[0, k]$, while $[\![k]\!]_{\mathbb{N}}$ denotes the set of naturals $\{0, 1, \ldots, k\}$. A (k-bounded) *clock valuation* is a function $\nu : \mathcal{Y} \to [\![k]\!]_{\mathbb{R}}$ and we write V for the set of clock valuations. Although clocks are usually allowed to take arbitrary non-negative values, for technical convenience [8,17], we have restricted their values to be bounded by the constant k.

If $\nu \in V$ and $t \in \mathbb{R}_{\geqslant 0}$ then we write $\nu + t$ for the clock valuation defined by $(\nu + t)(c) = \nu(c) + t$, for all $c \in \mathcal{Y}$. For $C \subseteq \mathcal{Y}$, we write $\nu[C := 0]$ for the clock valuation where $\nu[C := 0](c) = 0$ if $c \in C$, and $\nu[C := 0](c) = \nu(c)$ otherwise. For $X \subseteq V$, we write $\overline{X}$ for the smallest closed (topological) set in V containing X. Let $X \subseteq V$ be a convex subset of clock valuations and let $F : X \to \mathbb{R}$ be a continuous function. We write $\overline{F}$ for the unique continuous function $F' : \overline{X} \to \mathbb{R}$, such that $F'(\nu) = F(\nu)$ for all $\nu \in X$.

The set of *clock constraints* over $\mathcal{Y}$ is the set of conjunctions of *simple constraints*, which are constraints of the form $c \bowtie i$ or $c - c' \bowtie i$, where $c, c' \in \mathcal{Y}, i \in [\![k]\!]_{\mathbb{N}}$, and $\bowtie \in \{<, >, =, \leqslant, \geqslant\}$. For every $\nu \in V$, let $\mathrm{CC}(\nu)$ be the set of simple constraints that hold in ν. A *clock region* is a maximal set $\zeta \subseteq V$, such that $\mathrm{CC}(\nu) = \mathrm{CC}(\nu')$ for all $\nu, \nu' \in \zeta$. Every clock region is an equivalence class of the indistinguishability-by-clock-constraints relation, and vice versa. Note that ν and ν' are in the same clock region if and only if the integer parts of the clocks and the partial orders of the clocks, determined by their fractional parts, are the same in ν and ν', and if the fractional part of a clock c be 0 in ν, then it should be 0 in ν', and if it is positive in ν, then so it should be in ν'. We write $[\nu]$ for the clock region of ν and, if $\zeta = [\nu]$, write $\zeta[C := 0]$ for the clock region $[\nu[C := 0]]$.

A *clock zone* is a convex set of clock valuations, that is a union of a set of clock regions. We write $\mathcal{Z}$ for the set of clock zones. For any clock zone W and clock valuation ν, we use the notation $\nu \in W$ to denote that $[\nu] \subseteq W$. A set of clock valuations is a clock zone if and only if it is definable by a clock constraint. Observe that, for every clock zone W, the set $\overline{W}$ is also a clock zone.

Definition 2 (Syntax). *A priced probabilistic timed automaton (PPTA) is a tuple* $\mathsf{T} = (L, L_F, \mathcal{Y}, Inv, Act, E, \delta, r)$ *where:*

- *L is the finite set of* locations *including the set L_F of final locations;*
- *$\mathcal{Y}$ is the finite set of clocks;*
- *$Inv : L \to \mathcal{Z}$ is the invariant condition;*
- *Act is the finite set of actions;*
- *$E : L \times Act \to \mathcal{Z}$ is the action enabledness function;*
- *$\delta : (L \times Act) \to \mathcal{D}(2^{\mathcal{Y}} \times L)$ is the transition probability function;*
- *$r : L \cup L \times Act \to \mathbb{R}_{\geqslant 0}$ is the price information function. A PPTA is binary-priced when $r(\ell) \in \{0, 1\}$ for all $\ell \in L$.*

A *probabilistic timed automaton* (PTA) is a PPTA in which the cost on every edge is 0, while the cost on the locations are all 1, i.e., $r((\ell, \ell')) = 0$ for all $(\ell, \ell') \in L \times L$ and $r(\ell) = 1$ for all $\ell \in L$. A *timed automaton* is a PTA with the property that $\delta(\ell, a)$ is a point distribution for all $\ell \in L$ and $a \in Act$.

A *configuration* of a PPTA T is a pair (ℓ, ν), where $\ell \in L$ is a location and $\nu \in V$ is a clock valuation over $\mathcal{Y}$ such that $\nu \in Inv(\ell)$. For any $t \in \mathbb{R}_{\geq 0}$, we let $(\ell, \nu) + t$ equal the configuration $(\ell, \nu + t)$. Informally, the behaviour of a PPTA is as follows: In configuration (ℓ, ν) time passes before an available action from Act is triggered, after which a discrete probabilistic transition occurs. Time passage is available only if the invariant condition $Inv(\ell)$ is satisfied while time elapses, and an action a can be chosen after time t elapses only if it is enabled after time elapse, i.e., if $\nu + t \in E(\ell, a)$. Both the time and the action chosen are nondeterministic. If an action a is chosen, then the probability of moving to a location ℓ' and resetting all of the clocks in $C \subseteq \mathcal{Y}$ to 0 is given by $\delta[\ell, a](C, \ell')$.

Formally, the semantics of a PPTA is given by an MDP which has both an uncountable number of states and an uncountable number of transitions.

Definition 3 (Semantics). *Let* $\mathsf{T} = (L, L_F, \mathcal{Y}, Inv, Act, E, \delta, r)$ *be a PPTA. The semantics of* T *is the MDP* $[\![\mathsf{T}]\!] = (S, F, A, p, \pi)$ *where*

- $S \subseteq L \times V$, *the set of* states, *is such that* $(\ell, \nu) \in S$ *if and only if* $\nu \in Inv(\ell)$;
- $F = S \cap (L_F \times V)$ *is the set of* final states;
- $A = \mathbb{R}_{\geq 0} \times Act$ *is the set of* timed actions;
- $p : S \times A \to \mathcal{D}(S)$ *is the* probabilistic transition function *such that for* $(\ell, \nu) \in S$ *and* $(t, a) \in A$, *we have* $p((\ell, \nu), (t, a)) = d$ *if and only if*
  - $\nu + t' \in Inv(\ell)$ *for all* $t' \in [0, t]$;
  - $\nu + t \in E(\ell, a)$;
  - $d((\ell', \nu')) = \sum_{C \subseteq \mathcal{Y} \wedge (\nu + t)[C := 0] = \nu'} \delta[\ell, a](C, \ell')$ *for all* $(\ell', \nu') \in S$.
- $\pi : S \times A \to \mathbb{R}$ *is the* price function *where* $\pi(s, (t, a)) = r(\ell) \cdot t + r(\ell, a)$ *for* $s = (\ell, \nu) \in S$ *and* $(t, a) \in A$.

For the sake of notational convenience, we often write $d(\ell, \nu)$ for $d((\ell, \nu))$.

2.3 Priced Probabilistic Timed Game Arena

Definition 4. *A* priced probabilistic timed game arena *(PTGA)* $\mathcal{T}$ *is a triplet* $(\mathsf{T}, L_{Min}, L_{Max})$ *where* $\mathsf{T} = (L, L_F, \mathcal{Y}, Inv, Act, E, \delta, r)$ *is a priced probabilistic timed automaton and* (L_{Min}, L_{Max}) *is a partition of* L.

The semantics of a PTGA $\mathcal{T}$ is the stochastic game arena $[\![\mathcal{T}]\!] = ([\![\mathsf{T}]\!], S_{\mathrm{Min}}, S_{\mathrm{Max}})$ where $[\![\mathsf{T}]\!] = (S, F, A, p, \pi)$ is the semantics of T, and $S_{\mathrm{Min}} = S \cap (L_{\mathrm{Min}} \times V)$ and $S_{\mathrm{Max}} = S \setminus S_{\mathrm{Min}}$. Intuitively S_{Min} is the set of states controlled by player Min, and S_{Max} is the set of states controlled by player Max.

In a turn-based game on $\mathcal{T}$, players Min and Max move a token along the states of the PPTA in the following manner. If the current state is s, then the player controlling the state chooses an action $(t, a) \in A(s)$ after which state $s' \in S$ is reached with probability $p(s'|s, a)$. In the next turn, the player controlling the state s' chooses an action in $A(s')$ and a probabilistic transition is made accordingly. We say that $(s, (t, a), s')$ is a transition in $\mathcal{T}$ if $p(s'|s, (t, a)) > 0$ and a *play* of $\mathcal{T}$ is a sequence $\langle s_0, (t_1, a_1), s_1, \ldots \rangle \in S \times (A \times S)^*$ such that $(s_i, (t_{i+1}, a_{i+1}), s_{i+1})$ is a transition for all $i \geq 0$. We write Runs (FRuns) for the

set of infinite (finite) plays and Runs$_s$ (FRuns$_s$) for the sets of infinite (finite)
plays starting from state s. For a finite play η let Last(η) denote the last state of
the play. Let X_i and Y_i denote the random variables corresponding to i^{th} state
and action of a play.

A *strategy* of player Min in $\mathcal{T}$ is a partial function $\mu : \text{FRuns} \to \mathcal{D}(A)$, defined
for $\eta \in \text{FRuns}$ if and only if Last(η) $\in S_{\text{Min}}$, such that $supp(\mu(\eta)) \subseteq A(\text{Last}(\eta))$.
Strategies of player Max are defined analogously. We write Σ_{Min} and Σ_{Max} for
the set of strategies of players Min and Max, respectively. Let $\text{Runs}_s^{\mu,\chi}$ denote the
subset of Runs$_s$ which corresponds to the set of plays in which the players play
according to $\mu \in \Sigma_{\text{Min}}$ and $\chi \in \Sigma_{\text{Max}}$, respectively. A strategy σ is *pure* if $\sigma(\eta)$ is
a Dirac distribution for all $\eta \in \text{FRuns}$ for which it is defined, while it is *positional*
if Last(η)=Last(η') implies $\sigma(\eta)=\sigma(\eta')$ for all $\eta, \eta' \in \text{FRuns}$. We write Π_{Min} and
Π_{Max} for the set of positional strategies of player Min and player Max.

To analyse a stochastic game on $\mathcal{T}$ under a strategy pair (μ, χ), for every
state s of $\mathcal{T}$, we define a probability space $(\text{Runs}_s^{\mu,\chi}, \mathcal{F}_{\text{Runs}_s^{\mu,\chi}}, Prob_s^{\mu,\chi})$ over the
set of infinite plays under strategies μ and χ with s as the initial state. Given a
real-valued random variable $f : \text{Runs} \to \mathbb{R}$, we can then define the expectation of
this variable $\mathbb{E}_s^{\mu,\chi}\{f\}$ with respect to strategy pair (μ, χ) when starting in s. For
technical reasons we make the following assumption [26] (a similar assumption
is required for finite MDP [16]):

Assumption 1 (Stopping Game assumption): *For every strategy pair* $(\mu, \chi) \in$
$\Sigma_{Min} \times \Sigma_{Max}$, *and state* $s \in S$ *we have that* $\lim_{i \to \infty} Prob_s^{\mu,\chi}(X_i \in F) = 1$.

Given any PPTA without Assumption 1, a PPTA can be constructed for which
Assumption 1 holds using standard attractor computation in a two-player game.
This can be done by constructing the region graph of the PPTA.

2.4   Boundary Region Abstraction

A *region* is a pair (ℓ, ζ), where ℓ is a location and ζ is a clock region such that
$\zeta \subseteq Inv(\ell)$. For every $s=(\ell, \nu)$, we write $[s]$ for the region $(\ell, [\nu])$ and, we denote
by $\mathcal{R}$ the set of regions. A set $Z \subseteq L \times V$ is a *zone* if, for every $\ell \in L$, there is
a clock zone W_ℓ (possibly empty), such that $Z = \{(\ell, \nu) \mid \ell \in L \wedge \nu \in W_\ell\}$. For
a region $R=(\ell, \zeta) \in \mathcal{R}$, we write $\overline{R}$ for the zone $\{(\ell, \nu) \mid \nu \in \overline{\zeta}\}$, recall $\overline{\zeta}$ is the
smallest closed set in V containing ζ.

For $R, R' \in \mathcal{R}$, we say that R' is in the future of R, or that R is in the past
of R', if there is $s \in R$, $s' \in R'$ and $t \in \mathbb{R}_{\geq 0}$ such that $s' = s+t$; we then write
$R \to_* R'$. We say that R' is the *time successor* of R if $R \to_* R'$, $R \neq R'$, and
$R \to_* R'' \to_* R'$ implies $R''=R$ or $R''=R'$ and denote it by both $R \to_{+1} R'$ and
$R' \leftarrow_{+1} R$. We say that a region $R \in \mathcal{R}$ is *thin* if $[s] \neq [s+\varepsilon]$ for every $s \in R$
and $\varepsilon > 0$; other regions are called *thick*. We write $\mathcal{R}_{\text{Thin}}$ and $\mathcal{R}_{\text{Thick}}$ for the sets
of thin and thick regions, respectively. Note that if $R \in \mathcal{R}_{\text{Thick}}$ then, for every
$s \in R$, there is an $\varepsilon > 0$, such that $[s] = [s+\varepsilon]$. Observe that the time successor
of a thin region is thick, and vice versa.

We say $(\ell, \nu) \in L \times V$ is in the *closure of the region* (ℓ, ζ), and we write
$(\ell, \nu) \in \overline{(\ell, \zeta)}$, if $\nu \in \overline{\zeta}$. For any $\nu \in V$, $b \in [\![k]\!]_{\mathbb{N}}$ and $c \in \mathcal{Y}$ such that $\nu(c) \leq b$,

we let $time(\nu, (b,c)) \stackrel{\text{def}}{=} b - \nu(c)$. Intuitively, $time(\nu, (b,c))$ returns the amount of time that must elapse from ν before clock c reaches the integer value b. Note that, for any $(\ell, \nu) \in L \times V$ and $a \in Act$, if $t = time(\nu, (b,c))$ is defined, then $(\ell, [\nu+t]) \in \mathcal{R}_{\text{Thin}}$ and $supp(p(\cdot \mid (\ell, \nu), (t,a))) \subseteq \mathcal{R}_{\text{Thin}}$. Observe that, for every $R' \in \mathcal{R}_{\text{Thin}}$, there is a number $b \in [\![k]\!]_{\mathbb{N}}$ and a clock $c \in \mathcal{Y}$, such that, for every $R \in \mathcal{R}$ in the past of R', we have $s \in R$ implies $s + (b - s(c)) \in R'$; and we write $R \rightarrow_{b,c} R'$.

Intuition. The boundary region abstraction is motivated by the following. Consider an $a \in Act$, $s = (\ell, \nu)$ and $R = (\ell, \zeta) \rightarrow_* R' = (\ell, \zeta')$ such that $s \in R$ and $R' \in E(\ell, a)$.

- If $R' \in \mathcal{R}_{\text{Thick}}$, then there are infinitely many $t \in \mathbb{R}_{\geqslant 0}$ such that $s + t \in R'$. However, amongst all such t's, for one of the boundaries of ζ', the closer $\nu + t$ is to this boundary, the 'better' the timed action (t, a) becomes for a player's objective. However, since R' is a thick region, the set $\{t \in \mathbb{R}_{\geqslant 0} \mid s + t \in R'\}$ is an open interval, and hence does not contain its boundary values. Observe that the infimum equals $b_- - \nu(c_-)$ where $R \rightarrow_{b_-, c_-} R_- \rightarrow_{+1} R'$ and the supremum equals $b_+ - \nu(c_+)$ where $R \rightarrow_{b_+, c_+} R_+ \leftarrow_{+1} R'$. In our abstraction we include these 'best' timed actions through the actions $((b_-, c_-, a), R')$ and $((b_+, c_+, a), R')$. Stated otherwise, b_- and b_+ respectively denote the lower and the upper boundary of the thick region R' and the clocks c_- and c_+ correspond to the best timed actions.
- If $R' \in \mathcal{R}_{\text{Thin}}$, then there exists a unique $t \in \mathbb{R}_{\geqslant 0}$ such that $(\ell, \nu + t) \in R'$. Moreover since R' is a thin region, there exists a clock $c \in C$ and a number $b \in \mathbb{N}$ such that $R \rightarrow_{b,c} R'$ and $t = b - \nu(c)$. In the boundary region abstraction we summarise this 'best' timed action from region R to region R' through the action $((b, c, a), R')$.

Based on this intuition the abstraction is formalized below.

Definition 5. *Let* $\mathsf{T} = (L, L_F, \mathcal{Y}, Inv, Act, E, \delta)$ *be a PPTA. The* boundary region abstraction *of* T *is defined as the MDP* $\widehat{\mathsf{T}} = (\widehat{S}, \widehat{F}, \widehat{A}, \widehat{p}, \widehat{\pi})$ *where*

- $\widehat{S} = \{((\ell, \nu), (\ell, \zeta)) \mid (\ell, \zeta) \in \mathcal{R} \wedge \nu \in \overline{\zeta}\}$ *and* $\widehat{F} = \{((\ell, \nu), (\ell, \zeta)) \in \widehat{S} \mid \ell \in L_F\}$;
- $\widehat{A} \subseteq ([\![k]\!]_{\mathbb{N}} \times \mathcal{Y} \times Act) \times \mathcal{R}$ *is the finite set of boundary actions and for* $R \in \mathcal{R}$ *we let* $\widehat{A}(R) = \{\alpha \in \widehat{A}((\ell, \nu), R) \mid ((\ell, \nu), R) \in \widehat{S}\}$;
- *for* $((\ell, \nu), (\ell, \zeta)) \in \widehat{S}$ *and boundary action* $((b, c, a), (\ell, \zeta_a)) \in \widehat{A}$ *we have* $\widehat{p}((\ell, \nu), (\ell, \zeta), ((b, c, a), (\ell, \zeta_a))) = d$ *if and only if*

$$d((\ell', \nu'), (\ell, \zeta')) = \sum_{\substack{C \subseteq \mathcal{Y} \wedge \nu_a[C:=0] = \nu' \\ \wedge \zeta_a[C:=0] = \zeta'}} \delta[\ell, a](C, \ell')$$

for all $((\ell', \nu'), (\ell, \zeta')) \in \widehat{S}$ *where* $\nu_a = \nu + time(\nu, (b, c))$ *and one of the following conditions holds:*

- $(\ell, \zeta) \rightarrow_{b,c} (\ell, \zeta_a)$ *and* $\zeta_a \in E(\ell, a)$;

- $(\ell, \zeta) \to_{b,c} (\ell, \zeta_-) \to_{+1} (\ell, \zeta_a)$ for some (ℓ, ζ_-) and $\zeta_a \in E(\ell, a)$; and
- $(\ell, \zeta) \to_{b,c} (\ell, \zeta_+) \leftarrow_{+1} (\ell, \zeta_a)$ for some (ℓ, ζ_+) and $\zeta_a \in E(\ell, a)$.

- $\widehat{\pi} : \widehat{S} \times \widehat{A} \to \mathbb{R}$ is such that for $((\ell, \nu), (\ell, \zeta)) \in \widehat{S}$ and $((b, c, a), R) \in \widehat{A}(((\ell, \nu), (\ell, \zeta)))$ we have

$$\widehat{\pi}(((\ell, \nu), (\ell, \zeta)), ((b, c, a), R)) = r(\ell, a) + r(\ell) \cdot (b - \nu(c)).$$

Although the boundary region abstraction is uncountably infinite, for a fixed initial state we can restrict attention to a finite state subgraph, thanks to the following observation [17].

Lemma 1. *For every state of a boundary region abstraction, its reachable sub-graph is finite. Moreover, the reachable sub-graph from the initial valuation corresponds to the standard corner-point abstraction [8].*

3   Expected Reachability-Price Games

In an expected reachability-price game (ERPG) on $\mathcal{T} = (\mathsf{T}, L_{\mathrm{Min}}, L_{\mathrm{Max}})$ player Min attempts to reach the final states with cost as low as possible, while the objective of player Max is the opposite. In fact, the cost is infinity if player Max has a strategy such that a configuration in $F \times V$, that is one corresponding to a goal location is never reached. More precisely, Min is interested in minimising her losses, while player Max is interested in maximising his winnings where, if player Min uses the strategy $\mu \in \Sigma_{\mathrm{Min}}$ and player Max uses the strategy $\chi \in \Sigma_{\mathrm{Max}}$, player Min loses the following to player Max:

$$\mathrm{EReach}(s, \mu, \chi) \stackrel{\mathrm{def}}{=} \mathbb{E}_s^{\mu, \chi} \left\{ \sum_{i=1}^{\min\{i \,|\, X_i \in F\}} \pi(X_{i-1}, Y_i) \right\}.$$

Observe that player Max can choose his actions to win at least an amount arbitrarily close to $\sup_{\chi \in \Sigma_{\mathrm{Max}}} \inf_{\mu \in \Sigma_{\mathrm{Min}}} \mathrm{EReach}(s, \mu, \chi)$. This is called the *lower value* $\underline{\mathrm{Val}}(s)$ of the expected reachability-price game starting at s:

$$\underline{\mathrm{Val}}(s) \stackrel{\mathrm{def}}{=} \sup_{\chi \in \Sigma_{\mathrm{Max}}} \inf_{\mu \in \Sigma_{\mathrm{Min}}} \mathrm{EReach}(s, \mu, \chi).$$

Similarly, player Min can choose to lose at most an amount arbitrarily close to $\inf_{\mu \in \Sigma_{\mathrm{Min}}} \sup_{\chi \in \Sigma_{\mathrm{Max}}} \mathrm{EReach}(s, \mu, \chi)$. This is the *upper value* $\overline{\mathrm{Val}}(s)$ of the game:

$$\overline{\mathrm{Val}}(s) \stackrel{\mathrm{def}}{=} \inf_{\mu \in \Sigma_{\mathrm{Min}}} \sup_{\chi \in \Sigma_{\mathrm{Max}}} \mathrm{EReach}(s, \mu, \chi).$$

It is easy to verify that $\underline{\mathrm{Val}}(s) \leqslant \overline{\mathrm{Val}}(s)$ for all $s \in S$. We say that the expected reachability-price game is determined if $\underline{\mathrm{Val}}(s) = \overline{\mathrm{Val}}(s)$ for all $s \in S$. In this case we also say that the value of the game exists and denote it by $\mathrm{Val}(s) = \underline{\mathrm{Val}}(s) = \overline{\mathrm{Val}}(s)$ for all $s \in S$. The determinacy of expected reachability-price games follow from Martin's determinacy theorem [25].

Proposition 1. *Every Expected reachability-price game is determined.*

For $\mu \in \Sigma_{\text{Min}}$ and $\chi \in \Sigma_{\text{Max}}$ we define $\text{Val}^{\mu}(s) = \sup_{\chi \in \Sigma_{\text{Max}}} \text{EReach}(s, \mu, \chi)$ and $\text{Val}_{\chi}(s) = \inf_{\mu \in \Sigma_{\text{Min}}} \text{EReach}(s, \mu, \chi)$. For an $\varepsilon > 0$, we say that $\mu \in \Sigma_{\text{Min}}$ or $\chi \in \Sigma_{\text{Max}}$ is ε-*optimal* if $\text{Val}^{\mu}(s) \leqslant \text{Val}(s) + \varepsilon$ or $\text{Val}_{\chi}(s) \geqslant \text{Val}(s) - \varepsilon$, respectively, for all $s \in S$. Since an expected reachability-price game is determined, for every $\varepsilon > 0$, both players have ε-optimal strategies. We say that a game is *positionally-determined* if for every $\varepsilon > 0$ we have strategies $\mu_{\varepsilon} \in \Pi_{\text{Min}}$ and $\chi_{\varepsilon} \in \Pi_{\text{Max}}$ such that for every initial state $s \in S$, we have that

$$\underline{\text{Val}}(s) - \varepsilon \leqslant \text{Val}_{\chi_{\varepsilon}}(s) \text{ and } \overline{\text{Val}}(s) + \varepsilon \geqslant \text{Val}^{\mu_{\varepsilon}}(s).$$

Given an expected reachability-price game $\mathcal{T}$, and initial state $s \in S$, and a bound $B \in \mathbb{R}$, the *expected reachability-price game problem* is to decide whether $\text{Val}(s) \leqslant B$.

Optimality Equations. We now review optimality equations for characterising the value in an expected reachability-price game. Let $\mathcal{T}$ be a priced probabilistic timed game arena and let $P : S \to \mathbb{R}_{\geqslant 0}$. We say that P is a solution of optimality equations $\text{Opt}(\mathcal{T})$, and we write $P \models \text{Opt}(\mathcal{T})$ if, for all $s \in S$:

$$P(s) = \begin{cases} 0 & \text{if } s \in F \\ \inf_{\tau \in A(s)} \{\pi(s, \tau) + \sum_{s' \in S} p(s'|s, \tau) \cdot P(s')\} & \text{if } s \in S_{\text{Min}} \backslash F \\ \sup_{\tau \in A(s)} \{\pi(s, \tau) + \sum_{s' \in S} p(s'|s, \tau) \cdot P(s')\} & \text{if } s \in S_{\text{Max}} \backslash F. \end{cases}$$

Under Assumption 1, we have the following proposition.

Proposition 2. *If $P \models \text{Opt}(\mathcal{T})$, then $\text{Val}(s) = P(s)$ for all $s \in S$ and, for every $\varepsilon > 0$, both players have* pure *ε-optimal strategies.*

Proof. We show that for every $\varepsilon > 0$, there exists a pure strategy $\mu_{\varepsilon} : \text{FRuns} \to A$ for player Min, such that for every strategy χ for player Max, we have $\text{EReach}(s, \mu_{\varepsilon}, \chi) \leqslant P(s) + \varepsilon$. The proof, that for every $\varepsilon > 0$, there exists a pure strategy $\chi_{\varepsilon} : \text{FRuns} \to A$ for player Max, such that for every strategy μ for player Min, we have $\text{EReach}(s, \mu, \chi_{\varepsilon}) \geqslant P(s) - \varepsilon$, follows similarly. Together, these claims imply that P is equal to the value function of the expected reachability-time game, and the pure strategies μ_{ε} and χ_{ε}, defined in the proof below for all $\varepsilon > 0$, are ε-optimal.

Let us fix $\varepsilon > 0$ and μ_{ε} be a pure strategy where for every $n \in \mathbb{N}$ and finite play $r \in \text{FRuns}$ of length n, we have $\mu_{\varepsilon}(r) = (t, a)$ such that

$$\pi(t, a) + \sum_{s' \in S} p(s'|\text{Last}(r), (t, a)) \cdot P(s') \leqslant P(\text{Last}(r)) + \frac{\varepsilon}{2^{n+1}}.$$

Observe that for every state $s \in S_{\text{Min}}$ and for every $\varepsilon' > 0$, there is a ε'-optimal timed action because $P \models \text{Opt}(\mathcal{T})$.

Again using the fact that $P \models \mathrm{Opt}(\mathcal{T})$, it follows that, that for every $s \in S_{\mathrm{Max}} \setminus F$ and $(t, a) \in A(s)$, we have

$$P(s) \geqslant \pi(t, a) + \sum_{s' \in S} p(s'|s, a) \cdot P(s'). \tag{1}$$

Now for an arbitrary strategy χ for player Max, it follows by induction that for every $n \geqslant 1$:

$$P(s) \geqslant \mathbb{E}_s^{\mu_\varepsilon, \chi} \left\{ \sum_{i=1}^{\min\{i\,|\,X_i \in F\}} \pi(X_{i-1}, Y_i) \right\} \tag{2}$$
$$+ \sum_{s' \in S \setminus F} Prob_s^{\mu_\varepsilon, \chi}(X_n = s') \cdot P(s') - (1 - \tfrac{1}{2^n}) \cdot \varepsilon.$$

Using Assumption 1, we have $\lim_{n \to \infty} \sum_{s' \in S \setminus F} Prob_s^{\mu_\varepsilon, \chi}(X_n = s') = 0$, and therefore taking the limit in (2) we get the inequality:

$$P(s) \geqslant \mathbb{E}_s^{\mu, \chi} \{ \sum_{i=1}^{\min\{i\,|\,X_i \in F\}} \pi(X_{i-1}, Y_i) \} - \varepsilon = \mathrm{EReach}(s, \mu_\varepsilon, \chi) - \varepsilon,$$

which completes the proof. □

Using Proposition 2, it follows that the problem of solving an expected reachability-price game on $\mathcal{T}$ can be reduced to solving the optimality equations $\mathrm{Opt}(\mathcal{T})$. Forejt et al. [17] showed that solving optimality equations for a reachability-time game on a probabilistic timed automata $\mathcal{T}$ can be reduced to solving a reachability-time game on an abstraction, called the boundary region abstraction. In the following section we study expected reachability-price games on boundary region abstraction.

4   ERPG on Boundary Region Abstractions

For the rest of the paper, we assume that $\mathcal{T}$ is a binary-priced PTGA. The partition of the locations of a PTGA $\mathcal{T} = (\mathsf{T}, L_{\mathrm{Min}}, L_{\mathrm{Max}})$ gives rise to a partition $(\widehat{S}_{\mathrm{Min}}, \widehat{S}_{\mathrm{Max}})$ of the set of states $\widehat{S}$ of its boundary region graph and let $\widehat{\mathcal{T}} = (\widehat{\mathsf{T}}, \widehat{S}_{\mathrm{Min}}, \widehat{S}_{\mathrm{Max}})$. Before we present our main theorem, we study the properties of non-expansive and monotone value functions. For brevity, we call such functions *nice functions*.

4.1   Nice Functions over Clock Valuations

Let $X \subseteq V$ be a subset of valuations. A function $F : X \to \mathbb{R}$ is *non-expansive* if $|F(\nu) - F(\nu')| \leqslant \|\nu - \nu'\|$ for all $\nu, \nu' \in X$.

Lemma 2 (Properties of Nice Functions). *A function $F : X \to \mathbb{R}$ is nice if it is non-expansive and monotonically decreasing. We say a function $F : \widehat{S} \to \mathbb{R}_{\geqslant 0}$ is regionally nice if for every region $(\ell, \zeta) \in \mathcal{R}$ the function $F((\ell, \cdot), (\ell, \zeta))$ is nice. The nice functions satisfy the following properties.*

1. **Continuous Closure.** *If $F : X \to \mathbb{R}$ is nice, then its unique continuous closure $\overline{F} : \overline{X} \to \mathbb{R}$ is also a nice function.*
2. **Minimum and Maximum.** *If the functions $F, F' : \widehat{S} \to \mathbb{R}$ are regionally nice functions, then $\max(F, F')$ and $\min(F, F')$ are also regionally nice.*
3. **Convex Combination.** *The $\langle f_i \rangle_{i=1}^n$ are nice functions then for $\langle p_i \in [0, 1] \rangle_{i=1}^n$ with $\sum_{i=1}^n p_i = 1$, the function $\sum_{i=1}^n p_i \cdot f_i$ is nice.*
4. **Limit.** *The limit of a sequence of nice functions is nice.*

The following property of nice functions is useful in proving the correctness of the reduction to the boundary region abstraction.

Lemma 3. *Consider a binary-priced PTGA $\mathcal{T}$. Let $s = (\ell, \nu) \in S$ and $(\ell, \varsigma) \in \mathcal{R}$ such that $(\ell, [\nu]) \to_* (\ell, \varsigma)$. If $F : \widehat{S} \to \mathbb{R}$ is regionally nice, then the function $F_{s,\varsigma,a}^{\oplus} : I \to \mathbb{R}$ defined as*

$$t \mapsto \pi(s, (t, a)) + \sum_{(C, \ell') \in 2^{\mathcal{Y}} \times L} \delta[\ell, a](C, \ell') \cdot F((\ell', \nu_C^t), (\ell', \varsigma^C))$$

is continuous and monotone, where $I = \{t \in \mathbb{R}_{\geqslant 0} \mid \nu + t \in \varsigma\}$, $\nu_C^t = \nu + t[C := 0]$ and $\varsigma^C = \varsigma[C := 0]$.

Proof. To prove this lemma we consider a $t_1 \in I$, and for all $t_2 \in I$ and $t_2 \geq t_1$, we show that $F_{s,\varsigma,a}^{\oplus}(t_2) - F_{s,\varsigma,a}^{\oplus}(t_1)$ is either greater than or equal to 0, or less than or equal to 0. Since $\mathcal{T}$ is binary-priced, there are two cases: (i) $r(\ell) = 1$ and (ii) $r(\ell) = 0$.

For $r(\ell) = 1$, by definition we have $F_{s,\varsigma,a}^{\oplus}(t_2) - F_{s,\varsigma,a}^{\oplus}(t_1)$ equals:

$$t_2 - t_1 + \sum_{(C, \ell') \in 2^{\mathcal{Y}} \times L} \delta[\ell, a](C, \ell') \cdot \big(F((\ell', \nu_C^{t_2}), (\ell', \varsigma^C)) - F((\ell', \nu_C^{t_1}), (\ell', \varsigma^C)) \big)$$

$$= t_2 - t_1 - \sum_{(C, \ell') \in 2^{\mathcal{Y}} \times L} \delta[\ell, a](C, \ell') \cdot \big(F((\ell', \nu_C^{t_1}), (\ell', \varsigma^C)) - F((\ell', \nu_C^{t_2}), (\ell', \varsigma^C)) \big)$$

$$\geqslant t_2 - t_1 - \sum_{(C, \ell') \in 2^{\mathcal{Y}} \times L} \delta[\ell, a](C, \ell') \cdot (t_2 - t_1) \geqslant 0$$

where the inequality is due to the fact the F is nice.

For the case $r(\ell) = 0$, we have that

$$F_{s,\varsigma,a}^{\oplus}(t_2) - F_{s,\varsigma,a}^{\oplus}(t_1) \geqslant - \sum_{(C, \ell') \in 2^{\mathcal{Y}} \times L} \delta[\ell, a](C, \ell') \cdot (t_2 - t_1)$$

Hence for the case for the case when $r(\ell) = 0$, given a $t_1 \in I$, for all $t_2 \geqslant t_1$, we have that $F_{s,\varsigma,a}^{\oplus}(t_2) - F_{s,\varsigma,a}^{\oplus}(t_1) \leqslant 0$, and we are done. $\square$

4.2 Optimality Equations

Consider the optimality equations for an expected reachability-price game on a boundary region graph $\widehat{\mathcal{T}}$. Let $P : \widehat{S} \to \mathbb{R}_{\geq 0}$. We say that P is a solution of optimality equations $\mathrm{Opt}(\widehat{\mathcal{T}})$, and we write $P \models \mathrm{Opt}(\widehat{\mathcal{T}})$, if for every $s \in \widehat{S}$:

$$
P(s) = \begin{cases}
0 & \text{if } s \in \widehat{F} \\
\min\limits_{\alpha \in \widehat{A}(s)} \{\pi(s,\alpha) + \sum\limits_{s' \in S} p(s'|s,\alpha) \cdot P(s')\} & \text{if } s \in \widehat{S}_{\mathrm{Min}} \backslash \widehat{F} \\
\max\limits_{\alpha \in \widehat{A}(s)} \{\pi(s,\alpha) + \sum\limits_{s' \in S} p(s'|s,\alpha) \cdot P(s')\} & \text{if } s \in \widehat{S}_{\mathrm{Max}} \backslash \widehat{F}.
\end{cases}
$$

For a given function $f : \widehat{S} \to \mathbb{R}$ over boundary region abstraction, we define a transfer function $\widetilde{f} : S \to \mathbb{R}$ over PTGA by $\widetilde{f}(\ell, \nu) = f((\ell, \nu), (\ell, [\nu]))$. The following theorem characterizes the conditions under which expected reachability-price games on PTGAs can be reduced to expected reachability-price games over the boundary region abstraction.

Theorem 1. *Let $\mathcal{T}$ be a binary-priced priced probabilistic timed game. If $P \models \mathrm{Opt}(\widehat{\mathcal{T}})$ and P is regionally nice then $\widetilde{P} \models \mathrm{Opt}(\mathcal{T})$.*

Proof. Suppose $P \models \mathrm{Opt}(\widehat{\mathcal{T}})$. To prove this theorem it is sufficient to show that for every $s = (\ell, \nu) \in S_{\mathrm{Min}}$ we have:

$$
\widetilde{P}(s) = \inf_{(t,a) \in A(s)} \left\{ \pi(s, (t,a)) + \sum_{(C,\ell') \in 2^{\mathcal{Y}} \times L} \delta[\ell, a](C, \ell') \cdot \widetilde{P}(\ell', (\nu+t)[C := 0]) \right\}
\tag{3}
$$

and for every $s = (\ell, \nu) \in S_{\mathrm{Max}}$ we have:

$$
\widetilde{P}(s) = \sup_{(t,a) \in A(s)} \left\{ \pi(s, (t,a)) + \sum_{(C,\ell') \in 2^{\mathcal{Y}} \times L} \delta[\ell, a](C, \ell') \cdot \widetilde{P}(\ell', (\nu+t)[C := 0]) \right\}.
\tag{4}
$$

In the remainder of the proof we restrict attention to Min states as the case for Max states follows similarly. Therefore we fix $s = (\ell, \nu) \in S_{\mathrm{Min}}$ for the remainder of the proof. For $a \in Act$, let $\mathcal{R}^a_{\mathrm{Thin}}$ and $\mathcal{R}^a_{\mathrm{Thick}}$ denote the set of thin and thick regions respectively that are successors of $[\nu]$ and are subsets of $E(\ell, a)$. Considering the right hand side (RHS) of (3) we have:

$$
\text{RHS of (3)} = \min_{a \in Act} \{R_{\mathrm{Thin}}(s, a), R_{\mathrm{Thick}}(s, a)\},
\tag{5}
$$

where $R_{\mathrm{Thin}}(s, a)$ ($R_{\mathrm{Thick}}(s, a)$) is the RHS of (3) over all actions (t, a) such that $[\nu+t] \in \mathcal{R}^a_{\mathrm{Thin}}$ ($[\nu+t] \in \mathcal{R}^a_{\mathrm{Thick}}$). For the first term of (5) we have that $R_{\mathrm{Thin}}(s,a)$ equals:

$$\min_{\substack{(\ell,\zeta)\in\mathcal{R}^a_{\text{Thin}}}} \inf_{\substack{t\in\mathbb{R}\wedge\\\nu+t\in\zeta}} \left\{\pi(s,(t,a)) + \sum_{(C,\ell')\in2^{\mathcal{Y}}\times L} \delta[\ell,a](C,\ell')\cdot\widetilde{P}(\ell',\nu^t_C)\right\}$$

$$= \min_{\substack{(\ell,\zeta)\in\mathcal{R}^a_{\text{Thin}}}} \inf_{\substack{t\in\mathbb{R}\wedge\\\nu+t\in\zeta}} \left\{\pi(s,(t,a)) + \sum_{(C,\ell')\in2^{\mathcal{Y}}\times L} \delta[\ell,a](C,\ell')\cdot P((\ell',\nu^t_C),(\ell',\zeta_C))\right\}$$

$$= \min_{\substack{(\ell,\zeta)\in\mathcal{R}^a_{\text{Thin}}}} \left\{\pi(s,(t^{(\ell,\zeta)},a)) + \sum_{(C,\ell')\in2^{\mathcal{Y}}\times L} \delta[\ell,a](C,\ell')\cdot P((\ell',\nu^{t^{(\ell,\zeta)}}_C),(\ell',\zeta^C))\right\}$$

where ν^t_C denotes the clock valuation $(\nu+t)[C:=0]$, $t^{(\ell,\zeta)}$ the time to reach the region R from s and ζ^C the region $\zeta[C:=0]$. Considering the second term of (5) we have that $R_{\text{Thick}}(s,a)$ equals

$$\min_{\substack{(\ell,\zeta)\in\mathcal{R}^a_{\text{Thick}}}} \inf_{\substack{t\in\mathbb{R}\wedge\\\nu+t\in\zeta}} \left\{\pi(s,(t,a)) + \sum_{(C,\ell')\in2^{\mathcal{Y}}\times L} \delta[\ell,a](C,\ell')\cdot\widetilde{P}(\ell',\nu^t_C)\right\}$$

$$= \min_{\substack{(\ell,\zeta)\in\mathcal{R}^a_{\text{Thick}}}} \inf_{\substack{t\in\mathbb{R}\wedge\\\nu+t\in\zeta}} \left\{\pi(s,(t,a)) + \sum_{(C,\ell')\in2^{\mathcal{Y}}\times L} \delta[\ell,a](C,\ell')\cdot P((\ell',\nu^t_C),(\ell',\zeta^C))\right\}$$

$$= \min_{\substack{(\ell,\zeta)\in\mathcal{R}^a_{\text{Thick}}}} \inf_{\substack{t^s_{R_-}<t<t^s_{R_+}\\R\leftarrow_{+1}R_-\\R\rightarrow_{+1}R_+}} \left\{\pi(s,(t,a)) + \sum_{(C,\ell')\in2^{\mathcal{Y}}\times L} \delta[\ell,a](C,\ell')\cdot P((\ell',\nu^t_C),(\ell',\zeta^C))\right\}$$

Now P is regionally nice and, from Lemma 3 it follows that

$$\pi(s,(t,a)) + \sum_{(C,\ell')\in2^{\mathcal{Y}}\times L} \delta[\ell,a](C,\ell')\cdot P((\ell',\nu^t_C),(\ell',\zeta^C))$$

is continuous and monotone over $\{t\mid\nu+t\in\zeta\}$, and hence minimized at one of the boundaries, that is, either at $t^s_{R_-}$ or at $t^s_{R_+}$. Therefore it follows that $R_{\text{Thick}}(s,a)$ equals

$$\min_{\substack{(\ell,\zeta)\in\mathcal{R}^a_{\text{Thick}}}} \min_{\substack{t=t^s_{R_-},t^s_{R_+}\\(\ell,\zeta)\leftarrow_{+1}R_-\\(\ell,\zeta)\rightarrow_{+1}R_+}} \left\{\pi(s,(t,a)) + \sum_{(C,\ell')\in2^{\mathcal{Y}}\times L} \delta[\ell,a](C,\ell')\cdot P((\ell',\nu^t_C),(\ell',\zeta^C))\right\}$$

Substituting the values of $R_{\text{Thin}}(s,a)$ and $R_{\text{Thick}}(s,a)$ into (5) and observing that, for every thin region $(\ell,\zeta)\in\mathcal{R}^a_{\text{Thin}}$, there exist $b\in\mathbb{Z}$ and $c\in C$ such that $\nu+(b-\nu(c))\in\zeta$, it follows from Definition 5 that RHS of (3) equals:

$$\min_{\alpha\in\widehat{A}(s,[s])} \left\{\widehat{\pi}((s,[s]),\alpha) + \sum_{(s',R')\in\widehat{S}} \widehat{p}((s',R')\mid(s,[s]),\alpha)\cdot P(s',R')\right\}$$

which by definition equals $\widetilde{P}(s)$ as required. $\square$

5   One-Clock Binary-Priced PTGA

Theorem 1 characterizes conditions on the solution of optimality equations of the boundary region abstraction for binary-priced PTGA under which its solution also gives the solution for the corresponding PTGA. In this section we study binary-priced one-clock PTGA and show that the solution of optimality equations for such games remain regionally nice. This result together with Theorem 1 proves the correctness of reduction of the expected reachability-price games for 1-clock binary-priced PTGA to the similar problem on the corresponding boundary region abstraction. Let $\mathcal{T}$ be a one-clock binary-priced PTGA (1BPTA) and we denote by x the only clock of the 1BPTA.

We prove the following property of nice functions in the context of one-clock binary-priced PTGAs.

Lemma 4. *Let $\mathcal{T}$ be a one-clock binary-priced PTGA and $\widehat{\mathcal{T}}$ be its boundary region abstraction. If F is regionally nice, then, for every $R = (\ell, \zeta)$ and $\alpha \in \widehat{A}(R)$, the function $F^{\boxplus}_{(\ell,R,\alpha)} : V \to \mathbb{R}$ defined as*

$$\nu \mapsto \pi(((\ell, \nu), R), \alpha) + \sum_{s' \in S} p(s' | ((\ell, \nu), R), \alpha) \cdot F(s')$$

is nice.

Proof. Let us rewrite the function $F^{\boxplus}_{(\ell,R,\alpha)} : V \to \mathbb{R}$ as

$$\nu \mapsto \sum_{s' \in S} p(s' | ((\ell, \nu), R), \alpha) \cdot (\pi(((\ell, \nu), R), \alpha) + F(s')).$$

From Lemma 2 (3), it suffices to show that $(\pi(((\ell, \nu), R), \alpha) + F(s'))$ is a nice function. Let $\nu(x) - \nu'(x) = d$. There are several cases to consider.

1. Price-rate of ℓ is 0. There are two cases to consider.
    (a) The action α resets the clock. In this case, the function $(\pi(((\ell, \nu), R), \alpha) + F(s'))$ is constant, and hence nice.
    (b) The action α does not reset the clock. There are two cases to consider. The first case is when α suggests 0 time delay. In this case, $(\pi(((\ell, \nu), R), \alpha) + F(s')) = F(\ell', \nu)$ and that is a nice function in ν as F is a regionally nice function. The second case is when α suggests $d - \nu(x)$ time delay. In this case, $(\pi(((\ell, \nu), R), \alpha) + F(s')) = 0 * (d - \nu(x)) + F(\ell', d)$ is constant, and hence a nice function.
2. Price-rate of ℓ is 1. In this case there are two cases to consider.
    (a) The action α resets the clock. In this case, the function $(\pi(((\ell, \nu), R), \alpha) + F(s'))$ is a simple function, and hence nice.
    (b) The action α does not reset the clock. There are two cases to consider. The first case is when α suggests 0 time delay. In this case, $(\pi(((\ell, \nu), R), \alpha) + F(s')) = F(\ell', \nu)$ and that is a nice function in ν as F is a regionally nice function. The second case is when α suggests $d - \nu(x)$ time delay.

In this case, $(\pi(((\ell, \nu), R), \alpha) + F(s')) = d - \nu(x) + F(\ell', d) = c' - \nu(x)$. It is easy to see that this function is also non-expansive and monotonically decreasing.

The proof is now complete.   □

We are now ready to state the key result of this section.

Proposition 3. *Let $\mathcal{T}$ be a one-clock binary-priced PTGA. If $P \models Opt(\widehat{\mathcal{T}})$, then P is regionally nice.*

Proof. Based on the optimality equations, we define the value improvement function $\Psi : [\widehat{S} \to \mathbb{R}_{\geqslant 0}] \to [\widehat{S} \to \mathbb{R}_{\geqslant 0}]$ such that for any $f : \widehat{S} \to \mathbb{R}_{\geqslant 0}$ and $s \in \widehat{S}$:

$$\Psi(f)(s) = \begin{cases} 0 & \text{if } s \in \widehat{F} \\ \min_{\alpha \in \widehat{A}(s)} \left\{ \pi(s, \alpha) + \sum_{s' \in S} p(s'|s, \alpha) \cdot f(s') \right\} & \text{if } s \in \widehat{S}_{\text{Min}} \setminus \widehat{F} \\ \max_{\alpha \in \widehat{A}(s)} \left\{ \pi(s, \alpha) + \sum_{s' \in S} p(s'|s, \alpha) \cdot f(s') \right\} & \text{if } s \in \widehat{S}_{\text{Max}} \setminus \widehat{F}. \end{cases} \tag{6}$$

Since we consider stopping assumption on PTGA, (Assumption 1) and in $\widehat{\mathcal{T}}$ every state can only reach a finite sub-graph (Lemma 1), it follows that Ψ^N is a p-contractive mapping where p is the smallest probability appearing on the transitions of the PTGA and N is a finite upper bound (Lemma 1) on the number of states reachable from any state in the corresponding BRA. Therefore, from Banach's fixed point theorem Ψ can be used in an iterative scheme to converge to the solution of optimality equations $Opt(\widehat{\mathcal{T}})$.

Starting the iterative scheme with a regionally nice function, from Lemma 4, along with Lemmas 2(1–3), it follows that the intermediate iterates of Ψ in (6) remain regionally nice. Now Lemma 2 (4) implies that the limit of these sequences in also regionally nice, it follows that the fixpoint is also regionally nice. Hence, for every one-clock binary-priced PTGA, the value of the optimality equations $Opt(\widehat{\mathcal{T}})$ is regionally nice.   □

The following theorem follows from Theorem 1 and Proposition 3.

Theorem 2. *The value of the expected reachability-price game on a one-clock binary-priced PTGA $\mathcal{T}$ is equal to the value of the game on the corresponding corner-point abstraction.*

Corollary 1. *The expected reachability-price game problem is decidable for one-clock binary-priced PTGA.*

6   Conclusion

In this work, we consider two-player games with expected reachability-price objective over probabilistic timed automata. We show the decidability for one-clock binary-priced PTGA where the expected reachability-price problem can be reduced to the same problem over a boundary region graph abstraction. For this purpose, we use the notion of *nice functions* that is a generalization of simple functions introduced by Asarin and Maler in [3].

One clock timed automata have been widely studied for two-player games. They can be used to model the time difference between two actions or time needed to finish an action and so on. For two-player games, reachability time objectives have been studied in [3] and [17]. Having both 0 and 1 costs is certainly more expressive than having only cost 1 and the latter is well studied. On the other hand, in [13] it has been shown that the reachability-price problem becomes undecidable even for timed automata with more than two costs. This along with the different examples shown in the paper indicate that the decidability result is strong enough and may lead to undecidability by generalizing the class of one-clock binary-priced PTGAs.

We note that the definition of boundary region abstraction has been developed for general PTGA and decidability can be recovered for cases where solutions of $Opt(\widehat{\mathcal{T}})$ is regionally nice and the cost functions are minimized or maximized at some boundary of a region. In particular, this has been shown to be the case for one-clock binary-priced PTGA using Lemma 4 and Lemma 3. However, it may be possible to extend the technique to broader classes of PTGA.

References

1. Alur, R., Bernadsky, M., Madhusudan, P.: Optimal reachability for weighted timed games. In: Díaz, J., Karhumäki, J., Lepistö, A., Sannella, D. (eds.) ICALP 2004. LNCS, vol. 3142, pp. 122–133. Springer, Heidelberg (2004). https://doi.org/10.1007/978-3-540-27836-8_13

2. Alur, R., Dill, D.: A theory of timed automata. Theor. Comput. Sci. **126**(2), 183–235 (1994). https://doi.org/10.1016/0304-3975(94)90010-8

3. Asarin, E., Maler, O.: As soon as possible: time optimal control for timed automata. In: Vaandrager, F.W., van Schuppen, J.H. (eds.) Proceedings of HSCC, pp. 19–30 (1999). https://doi.org/10.1007/3-540-48983-5_6

4. Asarin, E., Maler, O., Pnueli, A.: Symbolic controller synthesis for discrete and timed systems. In: Antsaklis, P., Kohn, W., Nerode, A., Sastry, S. (eds.) HS 1994. LNCS, vol. 999, pp. 1–20. Springer, Heidelberg (1995). https://doi.org/10.1007/3-540-60472-3_1

5. Beauquier, D.: On probabilistic timed automata. Theor. Comput. Sci. **292**(1), 65–84 (2003). https://doi.org/10.1016/S0304-3975(01)00215-8

6. Behrmann, G., Cougnard, A., David, A., Fleury, E., Larsen, K.G., Lime, D.: UPPAAL-tiga: time for playing games!. In: Damm, W., Hermanns, H. (eds.) CAV 2007. LNCS, vol. 4590, pp. 121–125. Springer, Heidelberg (2007). https://doi.org/10.1007/978-3-540-73368-3_14

7. Berendsen, J., Chen, T., Jansen, D.N.: Undecidability of cost-bounded reachability in priced probabilistic timed automata. In: Chen, J., Cooper, S.B. (eds.) TAMC 2009. LNCS, vol. 5532, pp. 128–137. Springer, Heidelberg (2009). https://doi.org/10.1007/978-3-642-02017-9_16

8. Bouyer, P., Brihaye, T., Bruyère, V., Raskin, J.F.: On the optimal reachability problem on weighted timed automata. Formal Meth. Syst. Des. **31**(2), 135–175 (2007). https://doi.org/10.1007/s10703-007-0035-4

9. Bouyer, P., Brihaye, T., Markey, N.: Improved undecidability results on weighted timed automata. Inf. Process. Lett. **98**, 188–194 (2006). https://doi.org/10.1016/j.ipl.2006.01.012

10. Bouyer, P., Brinksma, E., Larsen, K.G.: Staying alive as cheaply as possible. In: Alur, R., Pappas, G.J. (eds.) HSCC 2004. LNCS, vol. 2993, pp. 203–218. Springer, Heidelberg (2004). https://doi.org/10.1007/978-3-540-24743-2_14

11. Bouyer, P., Cassez, F., Fleury, E., Larsen, K.G.: Optimal strategies in priced timed game automata. In: Lodaya, K., Mahajan, M. (eds.) FSTTCS 2004. LNCS, vol. 3328, pp. 148–160. Springer, Heidelberg (2004). https://doi.org/10.1007/978-3-540-30538-5_13

12. Brihaye, T., Geeraerts, G., Krishna, S.N., Manasa, L., Monmege, B., Trivedi, A.: Adding negative prices to priced timed games. In: Proceedings of CONCUR, pp. 560–575 (2014). https://doi.org/10.1007/978-3-662-44584-6_38

13. Brihaye, T., Henzinger, T.A., Prabhu, V.S., Raskin, J.-F.: Minimum-time reachability in timed games. In: Arge, L., Cachin, C., Jurdziński, T., Tarlecki, A. (eds.) ICALP 2007. LNCS, vol. 4596, pp. 825–837. Springer, Heidelberg (2007). https://doi.org/10.1007/978-3-540-73420-8_71

14. Brihaye, T., Bruyère, V., Raskin, J.-F.: On optimal timed strategies. In: Pettersson, P., Yi, W. (eds.) FORMATS 2005. LNCS, vol. 3829, pp. 49–64. Springer, Heidelberg (2005). https://doi.org/10.1007/11603009_5

15. Cassez, F., Jessen, J.J., Larsen, K.G., Raskin, J.-F., Reynier, P.-A.: Automatic synthesis of robust and optimal controllers – an industrial case study. In: Majumdar, R., Tabuada, P. (eds.) HSCC 2009. LNCS, vol. 5469, pp. 90–104. Springer, Heidelberg (2009). https://doi.org/10.1007/978-3-642-00602-9_7

16. Alfaro, L.: Computing minimum and maximum reachability times in probabilistic systems. In: Baeten, J.C.M., Mauw, S. (eds.) CONCUR 1999. LNCS, vol. 1664, pp. 66–81. Springer, Heidelberg (1999). https://doi.org/10.1007/3-540-48320-9_7

17. Forejt, V., Kwiatkowska, M., Norman, G., Trivedi, A.: Expected reachability-time games. Theor. Comput. Sci. **631**, 139–160 (2016). https://doi.org/10.1016/j.tcs.2016.04.021

18. Hoffmann, G., Wong-Toi, H.: The input-output control of real-time discrete event systems. In: IEEE Real-Time Systems Symposium (RTSS). pp. 256–265 (1992). https://doi.org/10.1109/REAL.1992.242655

19. Jensen, H.: Model checking probabilistic real time systems. In: Bjerner, B., Larsson, M., Nordström, B. (eds.) Proceedings 7th Nordic Workshop Programming Theory, pp. 247–261. Report 86:247–261, Chalmers University of Technology (1996). https://doi.org/10.1.1.23.2754

20. Jovanović, A., Kwiatkowska, M., Norman, G.: Symbolic minimum expected time controller synthesis for probabilistic timed automata. In: Sankaranarayanan, S., Vicario, E. (eds.) FORMATS 2015. LNCS, vol. 9268, pp. 140–155. Springer, Cham (2015). https://doi.org/10.1007/978-3-319-22975-1_10

21. Jurdziński, M., Kwiatkowska, M., Norman, G., Trivedi, A.: Concavely-priced probabilistic timed automata. In: Bravetti, M., Zavattaro, G. (eds.) CONCUR 2009. LNCS, vol. 5710, pp. 415–430. Springer, Heidelberg (2009). https://doi.org/10.1007/978-3-642-04081-8_28

22. Jurdziński, M., Trivedi, A.: Reachability-time games on timed automata. In: Arge, L., Cachin, C., Jurdziński, T., Tarlecki, A. (eds.) ICALP 2007. LNCS, vol. 4596, pp. 838–849. Springer, Heidelberg (2007). https://doi.org/10.1007/978-3-540-73420-8_72

23. Jurdziński, M., Trivedi, A.: Average-time games. In: Hariharan, R., Mukund, M., Vinay, V. (eds.) Proceedings of FSTTCS. Dagstuhl Seminar Proceedings (2008). https://doi.org/10.4230/LIPIcs.FSTTCS.2008.1765

24. Kwiatkowska, M., Norman, G., Segala, R., Sproston, J.: Automatic verification of real-time systems with discrete probability distributions. Theor. Comput. Sci. **282**, 101–150 (2002). https://doi.org/10.1016/S0304-3975(01)00046-9

25. Martos, B.: The direct power of adjacent vertex programming methods. Manage. Sci. **12**(3), 241–252 (1965). https://doi.org/10.1287/mnsc.12.3.241. http://www.jstor.org/stable/2627581

26. Neyman, A., Sorin, S. (eds.): Stochastic Games and Applications. NATO Science Series C, vol. 570. Kluwer Academic Publishers, Dordrecht (2004). https://doi.org/10.1007/978-94-010-0189-2

27. Ramadge, P.J., Wonham, W.M.: The control of discrete event systems. IEEE **77**, 81–98 (1989). https://doi.org/10.1109/5.21072

Author Index

Printed in the United States
By Bookmasters